The Best American
Travel Writing 2019

D0019362

GUEST EDITORS OF
THE BEST AMERICAN TRAVEL WRITING

2000 BILL BRYSON
2001 PAUL THEROUX
2002 FRANCES MAYES
2003 IAN FRAZIER
2004 PICO IYER
2005 JAMAICA KINCAID
2006 TIM CAHILL
2007 SUSAN ORLEAN
2008 ANTHONY BOURDAIN
2009 SIMON WINCHESTER
2010 BILL BUFORD
2011 SLOANE CROSLEY
2012 WILLIAM T. VOLLMANN
2013 ELIZABETH GILBERT
2014 ANDREW MCCARTHY
2015 PAUL THEROUX
2016 BILL BRYSON
2017 LAUREN COLLINS
2018 CHERYL STRAYED
2019 ALEXANDRA FULLER

The Best American Travel Writing™ 2019

Edited with an Introduction
by **Alexandra Fuller**

Jason Wilson, Series Editor

Mariner Books

HOUGHTON MIFFLIN HARCOURT

BOSTON • NEW YORK 2019

www.hmhbooks.com

ISSN 1530-1516 (print)   ISSN 2537-4830 (e book)
ISBN 978-0-358-09423-4 (print)   ISBN 978-0-358-09426-5 (e-book)

Printed in the United States of America
DOC 10 9 8 7 6 5 4 3 2 1

Contents

Contents

Foreword

THIS IS THE 20th YEAR of *The Best American Travel Writing*, and in those two decades of sifting through the thousands of articles, essays, dispatches, and reports, I figured I'd seen just about everything in the realm of travel storytelling. Then I received my September 23, 2018, copy of the *New York Times Magazine*. This was the magazine's fall Voyages Issue, its special twice-a-year travel-themed edition, which more than once in the past has featured a piece that has ended up in this anthology.

In this particular Voyages Issue, not a single sentence of travel narrative appeared. Nearly all the pages in the print edition were given over to large photographs from various locations around the world, each with a number. Those numbers corresponded to a soundtrack, available online, and each marked a recording of unique sounds in the particular place shown in the photo. In the issue's opening explanatory essay, Kim Tingley writes, "Paradoxically, the photographs on the following pages, accompanied by the recordings, are fixed. They are defined by the page, whereas sound has no similar boundary. We see them in the present tense, but we listen (always, but doubly so with recordings) to the past."

Readers, like me, listened to audio of hot lava pouring from an active volcano in Hawaii; the piercing cries of male and female indris, the largest living lemurs in Madagascar; the high-pitched "conversations" of New York City sewer rats; the cracking of the earth in the Atacama Desert of Chile; the bustle of a bus station in Lagos, Nigeria; the buzz of a coral reef in the US Virgin Islands. Some of the sounds were startling: Who knew that hot lava sounded like breaking glass? Who knew that coral reefs sounded like bacon sizzling in a pan? Who knew what rat laughter sounded like? The whole experience was entirely engrossing.

Yet for a travel writer, the exercise itself was likely more disturbing than even the rat laughter. The photographs may have been "fixed" in the present tense and the audio in the past, but the words were absent from both present and past. It didn't take a pessimist to understand the suggestion of what the future of travel publishing may look like, too.

There's been a lot of "reimagining" of travel writing over the past few years. In fact, I would argue that no other literary genre gets as much "reimagining." And I can understand why. There's a lot of bad travel writing. And bad travel writing can be self-indulgent, ill-informed, overwrought with purple prose, and lacking context. Worse, it can be full of prejudice and stereotypes, and historically was an instrument of colonialism and propaganda. But the best travel writing is none of these.

About a month and a half after the no-text, audio Voyages Issue, the same newspaper's Travel section changed editors. The new editor, Amy Virshup, posted a piece titled "We're Reimagining Our Travel Journalism. Tell Us What You'd Like to See." There were a number of wrongheaded assertions about travel writing that Virshup put forth. She insisted, for instance, that travel journalism would be best accomplished by "using more writers who actually live in the places readers want to visit." The idea driving this seemed to be that the editors hear complaints from locals who live in places they cover, "and often they want to tell us what we missed."

The cynical view of this, of course, is to believe that the *Times* is actually "reimagining" its travel budget and wants to save money by using people who already live in a particular locale. But if it truly does represent a sincere, philosophical reimagining, it's still misguided. The genre is called *travel* writing for a reason: it involves a traveler. Mostly, the traveler in good travel writing is not a local and doesn't pretend to be.

Good travel writing brings fresh eyes, and an outsider's view, to a place—even if it's a traveler returning to somewhere they were born, or their parents were born, or somewhere they lived for a long time but not anymore. To be clear, being an outsider is what makes travel writing incredibly difficult. An outsider describing and telling stories about a foreign place is challenging, and the potential to offend or go awry is always there. But that challenge is what also creates dynamic, tense, thrilling, and important stories. An honest, engaging traveler inspires us to make our own journeys and helps us to see and understand new (to us) places. Good travel writing is about human connection.

In fact, one of the most misguided principles espoused by the *Times'* new travel editor is to move away from first-person narratives. She writes, "In general I want to take the word 'I' out of our coverage." This probably sounded great in a conference room. But a true first-person "I" actually gives the reader some point of view to work with or against—agree or disagree—and some basis and context for the human experience. Removing the "I" altogether and doing some faux-objective third-person, or even crowdsourced, travel coverage feels like a fool's errand, the Yelp of travel. Can there be true insight if the reader doesn't know what filter that insight is coming through?

Virshup contends that the first person "made more sense when travel was harder, when most people were never going to take that trip to Patagonia or the Australian outback, so the writer really was the reader's window into a different world." That's a pretty privileged posture for a travel editor to take. Plenty of people who read and love travel writing haven't traveled widely at all. And even if they have, they've likely visited a place only once in their life, and will have done so as a traveler. I travel a lot, professionally, and I've never been to Patagonia or Australia. If I do get an opportunity to go, I'd like to read a first-person account by an engaging travel writer. Just like the ones we're publishing in this year's anthology.

The stories included here are, as always, selected from among dozens of pieces in dozens of diverse publications—from mainstream glossies to cutting-edge websites to Sunday newspaper travel sections to literary journals to niche magazines. I did my best to be fair and representative, and in my opinion I forwarded the best travel stories from 2018 to guest editor Alexandra Fuller, who made the final selections. I can't think of a better writer than Fuller to have edited our 20th-anniversary edition. I'm grateful to Rosemary McGuinness at Houghton Mifflin Harcourt for her help in producing this year's wonderful collection.

I now begin anew by reading the travel stories published in

2019. As I have for years, I am asking editors and writers to submit the best of whatever it is they define as travel writing—the wider the better. These submissions must be nonfiction and published in the United States during the 2019 calendar year. They must not be reprints or excerpts from published books. They must include the author's name, the date of publication, and the publication name, and must be tear sheets, the complete publication, or a clear photocopy of the piece as it originally appeared. I must receive all submissions by January 1, 2020, in order to ensure full consideration for the next collection.

Further, publications that want to make certain their contributions will be considered for the next edition should make sure to include this anthology on their subscription list. Submissions or subscriptions should be sent to: Jason Wilson, Best American Travel Writing, 230 Kings Highway East, Suite 192, Haddonfield, NJ 08033.

JASON WILSON

Introduction:
Travel in the Time of Awakening

There's a saying in Haiti: A rich man travels, a poor man leaves."
—Alex MacGregor, from *Is This the Most Crowded Island in the World? (And Why That Question Matters)*

THIS MUCH IS OBVIOUS: travel is not a means of escaping the self; travel is a means of revealing the self. Or, in the process of journeying the road less traveled, the self is unraveled and thereby revealed. But, as the essays in this collection reveal, the road less traveled need not be uncrowded—see Ben Mauk's startling "The Floating World" and Anne Helen Petersen's refreshing "How Nashville Became One Big Bachelorette Party"—merely approached differently, without an editorial agenda, for example, or without the traditional defensive stance of the heartless third person. And the selves that are revealed are just as likely to be our collective selves, the common human condition, rendered up close and recognizably personal. In any case, when writers put themselves—ourselves I should say—in play, in plight, we can see that there is always room for less of us, and that, as Charles Wright says in his long-form poem *Littlefoot*, "The voyage into the interior is all that matters, / Whatever your ride."

In other words, properly done, travel shows us who we really are without everything *not* needed on that necessarily lonely voyage. And, ultimately, there is a joy in the casting off, however bleak the circumstances that force reduction, however unwilling our emptying, however much must be lost en route. I think of Wes Anderson's 2007 fictional comedy-drama, *The Darjeeling Limited*,

Anderson's 2007 fictional comedy-drama, *The Darjeeling Limited*, about three brothers who finally fling away their late father's expensive luggage, literally and figuratively, on their journey across India to find their mother/themselves. We cheer their eventual disburdenment the same way we cheer great travel writing because the brutal mental slog of that casting off, of that exposure, has been done for us and it is, we know, much harder to do than it looks. In the case of travel writing, it often requires a simultaneous and reflexive look inward, outward, backward, forward: driving on the soul's busy highway of ideas, weaving lanes (see Alice Gregory's "Finished," David Fettling's "Uncomfortable Silences: A Walk in Myanmar," and Peter Hessler's mordant "Morsi the Cat").

Vacation, on the other hand, is not travel. It is precisely the opposite of travel, a kind of absenting of responsibility, a means of denying the limits of what we can carry in our expensive luggage. On vacation, a shinier, glossier world than really exists is promised and, depending on one's ability to pay, delivered. We are supposed to emerge from this vacating place shinier, glossier people. But there is, as the word suggests, a vacuous, vacant aspect to the consolations of the ego, a suffocation by pampering, a regret for the glutted appetite. How much luxury can one body absorb before the soul is itching for something substantial?

That said, essays on vacations, or vacation destinations, are two of the more satisfying, and telling, pieces in this collection. Jianying Zha's dystopian "Tourist Trap" had me in tears by the end; forced luxury vacations are one of the new and surprising ways China is attempting to control outspoken government critics. And "'The Greatest,'" Jason Wilson's slightly unhinged and unhinging romp around five Trump-branded properties (yes, *that* Trump) in four countries, is a reminder that there is no need to numb people who are more than willing to numb themselves. (Wilson is the series editor of Best American Travel Writing.)

But the promise of ease is not as common as the promise of disease in our near-apocalyptic times, an oft-evoked idea in this year's selection of essays (see Maddy Crowell's "The Great Divide," Lauren Markham's "If These Walls Could Talk," Nick Paumgarten's "Water and the Wall," and Noah Sneider's "Cursed Fields"). And yet, surely, these from-the-ground (or melting-tundra, or desiccating-river) pieces are precisely the smelling salts we need to awaken us. Our world from the view of these daring writers is crowded, climate-changed, and increasingly nationalistic. But the experience of reading these well-crafted, necessarily astringent stories, while unsettling, isn't all unpleasant. Great travel writing doesn't only awaken us, but it also emboldens, inspires, and shakes us, precisely because it refuses platitudes and numbness and could care less about feel-good. These stories bring our shared world up to our noses and remind us that we, too, live here, one person among more than 7.5 billion on a tiny, lonely, imperiled planet.

The year of these stories, 2018, was troubling for many. For myself, I lost my 21-year old son—inexplicably seized in his sleep—and the suffering of that loss has anchored me, temporarily or permanently it is too soon to tell, to the piece of ground in which he is now buried, in Wyoming where he was also born. My home country, Zimbabwe, or the country that raised me—how I longed for it, and for the people of my youth, in the days after my son's sudden arrival as my ancestor—is, like the home of a few of the writers in this piece, no longer the place I knew as a child (see Devon O'Neil's "Irmageddon," Jessica Yen's "Tributary," and Lucas Loredo's commendable "Mother Tongue"). As I write this, Zimbabwe is suffering from the double devastation of Cyclone Idai on top of decades of corruption and war and oppression.

And yet, I took strange comfort in these essays not only for my own heart, but for the hearts of all humanity, precisely because they reminded me that clear minds and generous hearts are scouring the world for the fragments that might connect and heal us through this moment, through our terrible broken present. The essays found here demanded my scattered, grief-stricken attention and reminded me that mine is a puny suffering, a suffering among many greater sufferings, bravely born. Or, as my Zimbabwean friend consoled me (using my old nickname) when I told her of my son's death, "Nematambudziko, Bobo: the first one is hardest."

The United States—although many of these pieces are written about other places, all of the writers are based here or have some connection to this soil—hasn't yet faced its wounds squarely, let alone begun to dress and heal them. But the time for denial and deferment does appear to be up. Of course, such times also bring with them, as with all cycles of grief, denial and anger and bargaining before we can reach the blessed relief of acceptance, and from there, the ability to work repair into the fabric of ourselves. Cameron Hewitt's "A Visit to Chernobyl: Travel in the Postapocalypse" is oddly uplifting and an example of can-do courage and repair in the USA's now defunct mirror image, the USSR. Closer to home in every way, Jeff MacGregor's "Taming the Lionfish" suggests the US may yet eat itself out of some of its problems with the help of a few seriously determined women. And finally, Rahawa Haile's important, timely "I Walked from Selma to Montgomery" reminds us the way may be hot, and violent, and baffling, but that doesn't remove from us the shared responsibility of strapping on our boots, or reinforcing our crutches and wheelchairs, and going where Martin Luther King Jr. pointed, all those years ago, together.

ALEXANDRA FULLER

The Best American
Travel Writing 2019

STEPHEN BENZ

Overlooking Guantánamo

FROM *New England Review*

> One day, our dispatch-boat found the shores of Guantánamo Bay flowing past on either side. It was at nightfall, and on the eastward point a small village was burning, and it happened that a fiery light was thrown upon some palm-trees so that it made them into enormous crimson feathers. The water was the colour of blue steel; the Cuban woods were sombre; high shivered the gory feathers. The last boatloads of the marine battalion were pulling for the beach.
>
> —Stephen Crane, "War Memories"

TWENTY YEARS AGO, I went to Santiago de Cuba to gather material for a magazine article on the centennial of the Spanish-American War. Over the course of several days, I visited Daiquirí, Siboney, Las Guásimas, El Caney, and of course San Juan Hill—all the main sites associated with that war. All, that is, except one: Guantánamo Bay. But visiting Guantánamo was practically impossible, even then, five years before it became a detention camp for prisoners of the "War on Terror." The sites related to the Spanish-American War were located inside the perimeter of the US naval base—"Gitmo," to use the military's shorthand designation—and there was no access to the base from Cuba proper. The only way to enter Gitmo was to fly in on a Navy transport airplane from Virginia Beach, Virginia. And to do that, I would have to obtain permission—rarely granted—from naval authorities. So, much as I would have liked to visit the scene of the war's first clash between Spanish and American troops, I had to accept the impracticality of such a visit.

Forgoing Guantánamo was especially disappointing because of Stephen Crane's connection to the place. Crane's writing about the war and his various adventures in Cuba had long intrigued me. He was one of the few reporters to witness both the landing of the Marines at Guantánamo and their subsequent skirmish with Spanish troops. He wrote several accounts of the event, a couple of which are counted among his best work. In fact, a significant portion of Crane's writing concerns Cuba, including a book of short stories (*Wounds in the Rain*), a long semiautobiographical essay ("War Memories"), and some of his best journalism. The time he spent on the island—a little over five months all told—holds outsized significance in his biography and his oeuvre. It was in Cuba that Crane—already famous for writing a war novel—finally witnessed warfare firsthand and up close. Shortly after hostilities ended, Crane came down with a severe bout of either yellow fever or malaria and had to be evacuated in a state of delirium. The "Cuban fever," as he called it, certainly exacerbated his latent tuberculosis; nevertheless, while he was still recovering Crane mysteriously returned to Cuba—well after the other correspondents had left—and spent the better part of four months living a kind of underground existence in Havana. Though he filed an occasional report for Hearst's *Journal,* he was for the most part incommunicado; even his closest companions and his common-law wife had no idea where he was or what he was doing. The Havana sojourn remains something of an enigma in Crane's biography.

As it turned out, though I had all but given up on the possibility of visiting Gitmo, while I was in Santiago I fortuitously learned of an opportunity to see the base—or at least to see *into* it. I was told that a Cuban travel agency, Gaviota, offered tours to a Cuban military facility, an observation post called Mirador de Malones, located on a hillside just outside the American-occupied site. From there, one could look through a telescope and spy on the naval base. It sounded too bizarre to be true—as so many things in Cuba do; but when I inquired at the Gaviota office in Santiago, the bizarre turned out to be true—as it so often does in Cuba. The agent told me that a German tour group was going to the military lookout the next day. I could join the group if I wished. Moreover, the Germans were going to pass the night in Caimanera, the small town closest to the naval base, a town normally off-limits to visitors. This, too, I could do if interested. I booked the tour.

The following day I joined the Germans on a sleek tour bus that raced along a highway all but devoid of motorized traffic. There were plenty of bicycles, horses, and pedestrians, but few buses or trucks and even fewer private cars. After a couple of hours, we passed through Guantánamo City, once a favorite destination of American sailors on liberty call but now a sleepy provincial town "with little to recommend it," as guidebooks like to say. Beyond Guantánamo City, the road passed through sugarcane fields until, after 25 kilometers or so, it arrived at the northern edge of Guantánamo Bay. The bus left the main highway and came to a checkpoint, the entrance to Cuba's military zone. From there, the road led into the hills overlooking the wide southern portion of the bay where the US base was located. At the foot of one hill, we exited the bus, passed through a concrete bunker, and climbed steps to the lookout—which proved to be not much more than a ramada draped with camouflage netting.

A thousand feet below and several miles distant, the bay and the naval base rippled in the tropical haze. It looked unreal, like some mythic realm. But once I got my turn at the military telescope, what I saw through the viewfinder was not mythic in the least. It was, in fact, all too familiar and mundane: cars on a boulevard, a shopping center, a church, a golf course, the American flag flapping. What made it strange, of course, was that this all-American scenery was on Cuban soil, situated behind concertina-wire fencing and bordered by a minefield.

The guide, speaking in German, drew attention to various features of the base, first on a detailed map and then in reality, pointing to one hazy sector or another while the German tourists craned necks, snapped photos, and tried to clarify for one another what the guide was pointing to. Unable to follow the German conversation, I moved a little way off and tried to correlate the panorama before me with what I knew from reading Stephen Crane's account of the Guantánamo episode that began the Spanish-American War.

*

On June 6, 1898, Crane arrived at Guantánamo Bay just after the Marines had landed and secured the location. With night falling, Cuba appeared "sombre" to Crane. Come daylight, he would note that it was a craggy country cut with ravines. Sandy paths disappeared into thickets of tropical vegetation. Along the coastline, chalky cliffs and cactus-covered ridges overlooked the sea. "The droning of insects" competed with the sound of waves lapping the shore. Crane watched as the Marines—a force of over 600—set up camp and dug trenches. Encamped on the beach beneath ridges, they were in a vulnerable position. But the Marines had met no resistance upon landing, and for a day and a half all was tranquil: "There was no firing," Crane reported. "We thought it rather comic."

The tranquility did not last. The next night, Spanish snipers opened fire and the Americans scrambled for cover. "We lay on our bellies," Crane wrote. "It was no longer comic." Crane, who had written his famous war novel, *The Red Badge of Courage*, without any personal knowledge of warfare, was finally experiencing what he had only guessed at beforehand. For the first time, he felt "the hot hiss of bullets trying to cut [his] hair."

But whatever satisfaction or thrill he felt in finally experiencing battle conditions was soon undercut: On the third night, the sniper fire intensified. The company's surgeon, struck by a Spanish bullet, lay suffering a few yards from Crane. "I heard someone dying near me," Crane wrote.

> He was dying hard. Hard. It took him a long time to die. He breathed as all noble machinery breathes when it is making its gallant strife against breaking, breaking. But he was going to break. He was going to break. It seemed to me, this breathing, the noise of a heroic pump which strives to subdue a mud which comes upon it in tons. The darkness was impenetrable. The man was lying in some depression within seven feet of me. Every wave, vibration, of his anguish beat upon my senses. He was long past groaning. There was only the bitter strife for air which pulsed out into the night in a clear penetrating whistle with intervals of terrible silence in which I held my own breath in the common unconscious aspiration to help. I thought this man would never die. I wanted him to die. Ultimately he died.

Crane did not know the man's identity until a voice in the darkness announced that the doctor had died. He then realized that the dead man was John Gibbs, whom Crane had befriended during the previous two days. War was suddenly very real to the previously inexperienced war correspondent: "I was no longer a cynic," he wrote. These first nights under fire proved to be trying in the extreme: "With a thousand rifles rattling; with the field-guns booming in your ears; with the diabolical Colt automatics clacking; with the roar of the *Marblehead* coming from the bay, and, last, with Mauser bullets sneering always in the air a few inches over one's head, and with this enduring from dusk to dawn, it is extremely doubtful if any one who was there will be able to forget it easily."

The next day, there were services for Gibbs even as the Spanish resumed their sniping. Crane retreated to the beach and sat on a rickety pier with a bottle of whisky that he had procured from a fellow journalist. He stared into "the shallow water where crabs were meandering among the weeds, and little fishes moved slowly in the shoals."

Though he confessed to feeling somewhat unnerved from "the weariness of the body, and the more terrible weariness of the mind" that came with being under fire, Crane accepted an invitation to tag along with a detachment of Marines on an expedition to flush Spanish guerrillas from the surrounding hills. Some 200 Marines left camp at dawn, guided by a contingent of 50 Cuban insurgents. American correspondents covering the war generally expressed a negative view of Cuban soldiers such as these. Crane's impression of them was more ambivalent: "They were a hard-bitten, under-sized lot," he wrote in a dispatch for Pulitzer's *World*, "most of them negroes, and with the stoop and curious gait of men who had at one time labored at the soil. They were, in short, peasants— hardy, tireless, uncomplaining peasants—and they viewed in utter calm these early morning preparations for battle." In Crane's view, they demonstrated a similar stolidity and nonchalance in response to their officers' orders.

Crane thought he detected greater determination in the American soldiers: "Contrary to the Cubans, the bronze faces of the Americans were not stolid at all. One could note the prevalence of a curious expression—something dreamy, the symbol of minds striving to tear aside the screen of the future and perhaps expose the ambush of death. It was not fear in the least. It was simply a moment in the lives of men who have staked themselves and come to wonder who wins—red or black?"

The Cuban terrain impressed Crane as he followed the American soldiers. A narrow path wound around the bases of some high, bare spurs then ascended a chalky cliff and passed through dense thickets. Insects hummed all around. Reaching a clearing, Crane and the soldiers could look down the chaparral-covered ridges to the sea. Next came a steep climb through cactus patches and then a hike along a ridge to where the troops—exhausted and thirsty but also, according to Crane, "contented, almost happy"—encountered the Spanish guerrillas who were hidden in a thicket, waiting to open fire on the Americans and Cubans.

"The fight banged away with a roar like a forest fire," Crane observed. During the ensuing combat, this intense noise proved overwhelming. "The whole thing was an infernal din. One wanted to clap one's hands to one's ears and cry out in God's name for the noise to cease; it was past bearing." Amidst this din, Crane detected a variety of sounds, the nuanced noise of war: "And still crashed the Lees and the Mausers, punctuated by the roar of the [USS] Dolphin's guns. Along our line the rifle locks were clicking incessantly, as if some giant loom was running wildly, and on the ground among the stones and weeds came dropping, dropping a rain of rolling brass shells."

Crane's propensity for eliciting such precise details from a scene amazed—and exasperated—his fellow correspondents. They readily perceived his obvious disdain for the grind of daily journalism; Crane often said his real aim was not to produce dispatches but to collect material for a new novel. According to his colleague Ernest McCready, Crane was "contemptuous of mere news getting or news reporting." In composing his dispatches, Crane was, according to another colleague, "an artist, deliberating over this phrase or that, finicky about a word, insisting upon frequent changes and erasures." Reportedly, he went through many cigarettes as he wrote (despite being tubercular). McCready, a journalist with long experience, urged Crane "to forget scenery and the 'effects'" and stick to the fundamentals: "This has to be news," the veteran correspondent told him, "sent at cable rates. You can save your flubdub and shoot it to New York by mail. What I want is the straight story of the fight."

But Crane could not easily settle for the straight story, even if months had to pass before his personal impressions yielded up the deeper story that he sought. In the case of Guantánamo, half a year went by before Crane turned those impressions into what his colleague and rival Richard Harding Davis called "one of the finest examples of descriptive writing of the war." The story, published in *McClure's Magazine* (February 1899) and later in Crane's collection *Wounds in the Rain,* was "Marines Signalling Under Fire at Guantánamo." The narrative concerns "four Guantánamo marines, officially known for the time as signalmen, [whose duty it was] to lie in the trenches of Camp McCall, that faced the water, and, by day, signal the *Marblehead* with a flag and, by night, signal the *Marblehead* with lanterns." No other journalist mentions these signalmen; Crane, however, devoted an entire story to them, closely observing them and detailing their extraordinary courage —a trait that always fascinated Crane—as they were called upon "to coolly take and send messages." Crane described how, without hesitation, a signalman would stand on a cracker box to send messages to the ships offshore, exposing himself to sniper fire. "Then the bullets began to snap, snap, snap at his head, while all the woods began to crackle like burning straw." Watching the signalman's face "illumed as it was by the yellow shine of lantern light," Crane noted "the absence of excitement, fright, or any emotion at all in his countenance" as the signalman performed his duty. In contrast, watching from the relative safety of the trench, Crane felt "utterly torn to rags," his nerves "standing on end like so many bristles."

Later, during the hilltop skirmish with Spanish guerrillas, another signalman stood exposed on a ridge to send the requisite message. "I watched his face," Crane wrote, "and it was as grave and serene as that of a man writing in his own library. He was the very embodiment of tranquility in occupation . . . There was not a single trace of nervousness or haste." Crane's admiring account of this "very great feat" emphasizes the stoic, masculine qualities that he saw in the regulars, the foot soldiers who did the arduous fighting. Elsewhere, he would criticize the press corps for ignoring these paragons of courage in favor of heaping praise on volunteers such as Teddy Roosevelt and the Rough Riders. Crane refused to overlook the regulars, making them the focus of his dispatches and stories, lauding their stoicism and grace under pressure, and holding them up as exemplars of what Crane perceived as American ideals.

Crane tried to live up to those ideals himself, according to those who observed his activities during the fight. A letter from a Marine commander recalled Crane's bravery at Guantánamo. An official Navy report recognized Crane's "material aid during the action" in delivering messages between platoons. The report does not say whether Crane did more than carry messages, but a biographer (Paul Sorrentino) says that "he quietly carried supplies, built entrenchments, dragged artillery up hills, and helped to fire guns." In "War Memories," which is taken to be semiautobiographical, Crane's stand-in narrator (named Vernall) is asked by a Marine captain to undertake a brief scouting mission. Crane/Vernall does so: "All the time my heart was in my boots," he says, contrasting his fear with the stoic regulars "who did not seem to be afraid at all, men with quiet composed faces who went about this business as if they proceeded from a sense of habit."

Shortly after the hilltop battle, an exhausted and somewhat unnerved Crane left Guantánamo on the dispatch boat with his fellow journalists. Ahead of him were the events at Daiquirí, Siboney, Las Guásimas, and San Juan Hill, followed by a breakdown (perhaps malaria or yellow fever), which further eroded his already precarious health. Just shy of two years after the events at Guantánamo, Stephen Crane was dead at 28.

Standing at the Malones Lookout, gazing across the hills at the approximate location of these events, I recalled Crane's description of this same landscape. He wrote two versions—one version in a news dispatch and a second version in "War Memories." Both passages involve a panoramic survey from atop the mountain where the skirmish took place. In the dispatch, Crane noticed the view in the heat of combat: "The sky was speckless, the sun blazed out of it as if it would melt the earth. Far away on one side were the waters of Guantánamo Bay; on the other a vast expanse of blue sea was rippling in millions of wee waves. The surrounding country was nothing but miles upon miles of gaunt, brown ridges. It would have been a fine view if one had had time."

In the second version, Crane (through his fictional narrator Vernall) takes in the view during the relative calm after the fight is over: "I discovered to my amazement that we were on the summit of a hill so high that our released eyes seemed to sweep over half the world. The vast stretch of sea, shimmering like fragile blue silk in the breeze, lost itself ultimately in an indefinite pink haze, while in the other direction, ridge after ridge, ridge after ridge, rolled brown and arid into the north."

This was essentially the same panoramic view that I now had at the Malones Lookout, although my view—if I had the geography right—was a little farther inland and a little higher up. And, of course, later in time by a century. Because of the time that had passed, I could see what Crane could not: the upshot, the end result of the Marine action at Guantánamo in June 1898—namely, the naval base spread out before me. As Crane sailed out of view, off to report on the coming battles of the war, I turned my attention to Gitmo, one of the principal prizes of that war.

What a convoluted history had gone into the making of the base and the odd little township that had developed along with the naval facility. Following Spain's surrender in the Spanish-American War, Cuba became a protectorate of the United States. Overt American administrative control of the country lasted a little over three years while US officials and Cuban representatives negotiated the conditions of Cuba's independence. That any terms at all should be imposed was outrageous to Cubans; even worse, the United States insisted on particularly onerous terms. These were outlined in the notorious Platt Amendment of 1901, which the United States insisted on inserting into the new Cuban constitution. The Platt Amendment (so called because, as introduced by Senator Orville Platt, it had amended an Army appropriations bill in the US Congress) gave the United States the right to intervene in Cuban affairs whenever American interests were threatened. It also stipulated that Cuba would lease territory to the United States for the purpose of establishing a coaling station and port facilities. The territory in question was Guantánamo Bay.

The war had demonstrated to the Navy the bay's strategic value: a protected body of water from which the Navy could monitor approaches to New Orleans and the Panama Canal (then in the planning stages). Although Cubans were loath to accept the base of a foreign power within Cuban territory, the United States insisted: no base, no independence. By 1903, it was a done deal; the United States had secured the right to operate, essentially in perpetuity, a naval base of 45 square miles on Guantánamo Bay. Remuneration was to be around $2,000 a year. "Naval Station Guantánamo Bay" became one of America's first overseas naval bases, and it remains the oldest overseas American base still in operation.

Despite the Navy's insistence on Guantánamo's importance, development of the facilities occurred fitfully. Congress did not provide sufficient funding for many years. Early photos show that the naval station was not much more than a camp with rows of tents for Marines and sailors. Early on, however, the base proved useful as a staging area for American interventions in Cuba and the Caribbean region, and eventually the facilities were improved. By 1920, the base could accommodate visits from the naval fleet; periodically, training exercises involving 20,000 sailors were conducted there. A *National Geographic* correspondent accompanied the fleet in 1921 and reported that Guantánamo, a "plant of extraordinary value," featured rifle ranges, a landing strip, a balloon school (at the time, hot-air balloons were considered to have military utility), hospitals, clubhouses, canteens, and a sports complex with baseball fields and tennis courts. There was also a pigpen, which the *National Geographic* writer called a "principal attraction" for sailors from the Midwest "with fond recollections of the old farm."

The correspondent marveled at the base's natural setting: "Now and then the sharp fin of a shark is seen. Pelicans drift overhead with their air of aldermanic dignity. Fish hawks are forever circling against a sky of almost incandescent blue." Summarizing the near-pristine quality of the place, the writer called it a "sanctuary" for "the wild animals of the hills."

In years to come, the base continued to expand with more permanent facilities and housing for military personnel. A community developed, a small American town in the tropics, as families of officers arrived. By 1927, according to a visiting journalist, there were "low green bungalows" nestled "in a tangle of palms and trumpet vines, a flowery oasis in a desert of scrub and thorn." The wives of naval officers rode "lazy ponies over the hill to call on the ladies of the Marine Corps at Deer Point." It was, when the fleet was not in port, a place of "vast, placid stillness"—a languid and somewhat dull outpost of the expanding American Empire. "Old Civil Service clerks thankfully close their desks as the shadows start to lengthen," the journalist observed, "and scramble into motor boats to go home and loll on their breezy porches on the bare yellow crest of Hospital Key. A shout or a loud, hearty laugh would be as noteworthy in Guantánamo as it would be in a church. There was just enough tennis to keep in condition, just enough swimming to keep moderately cool, just enough bridge of an evening to exhaust the conversation of your neighbors."

Such were the appearances. Beneath the placid surface, Gitmo could be stultifying and dismal. This was the impression conveyed in an anonymously written "tell-all" magazine article published in 1930. Under the byline of "Navy Wife," the writer described what she called the "Guantánamo Blues." The article's subtitle coyly promised "A Taste of Tropical Fruits of Prohibition." For the most part, the writer agreed with previous observers that life on the base was merely dull: "no daily papers, no real news except a few items that sifted in by radio." During the Prohibition years, not even alcohol was available on the base—at least not officially. According to the Navy Wife, American women living on the base spent the bulk of their time playing bridge, holding teas and dinner parties, and gossiping, sometimes ruthlessly, about one another ("the usual post-mortems," she called such gossip). It was a life of "coffee cups, long ribald conversations about nothing." One lived with "an inescapable smell of stale paint . . . the buzz and thud of tropical insects against the screens."

But when the fleet returned, so did the excitement—sometimes more than was welcome. With men outnumbering women 40 to 1, every woman, even those who were married, received plenty of unwanted attention, especially at fleet dances. These were "a nightmare," the Navy Wife recalled. She was sweet-talked, pulled onto the dance floor, propositioned, and groped. She was "protected only by the thin shred of circumstance which lies in the proximity of others." Her "woman's instinct" told her she "must not dare get outside the circle of light and moving white figures," lest she become subject to "a violent seizure as if I were to be the victim of a rape."

This undercurrent of lust, potential violence, and vicious gossip hidden below the superficial boredom made Guantánamo seem like a tropical Peyton Place. Over the decades, other residents and visitors noticed this undercurrent as well, even as the base was growing and taking on the appearance of a typical all-American town with outdoor movie theaters, hamburger joints (including, eventually, a McDonald's), Little Leagues, Scout troops, bowling alleys, golf courses, skating rinks, playgrounds, and skateboard parks. But this surface placidity concealed (barely) drug and alcohol addiction, racism, classism, and sexism. Crime was minimal, but visiting journalists noted that violence did occur now and then, particularly alcohol- and jealousy-fueled spousal abuse.

In the publications it provided to newly arrived families, however, the Navy continued to project the image of Guantánamo as an idyllic community. "One of the nice luxuries of Guantánamo Bay," one such publication noted, was "the fact that domestic help is available." Besides the cheap labor of Cuban maids, residents on the base could enjoy a variety of recreational activities, hobby shops, libraries, and theater, along with "dances, special parties, bingo and the like." There were religious services, Bible studies, choirs, and Sunday school. Residents could join any number of clubs, from the PTA to Toastmasters. Touting these perks, the Navy publications presented life on the base as pleasant, even blissful. And indeed, former residents typically have fond memories of their time at Gitmo.

After 1960 and the success of Fidel Castro's revolution, however, life on the base became even more insular. As tensions between the United States and the new Cuban government mounted, the gates to Guantánamo closed. US personnel were no longer allowed to venture beyond the perimeter to explore and enjoy Cuba proper. Both sides mined the area around the perimeter—making it the largest minefield in the Western Hemisphere—and cacti were planted to make the barrier even more difficult to penetrate. This so-called "cactus curtain" featured sandbagged outposts, watchtowers, and perimeter patrols. The base was turned into a sealed-off garrison. Guantánamo became what a *National Geographic* reporter in 1961 called "an idyllic prison camp." One military wife told the reporter that life at Gitmo could be described as "comfortable claustrophobia." The base had everything families needed, she said, "but in fifteen minutes you can drive from one end of it to the other . . . It's the same old thing day after day."

In such circumstances, the "Guantánamo Blues" that the anonymous writer struggled with in the 1930s became all the more acute. Visiting journalists in the 1960s and 1970s reported on racial tensions, drug and alcohol problems, and occasional violence. According to a 1973 article in *Esquire*, "Guantánamo is a good place to become an alcoholic. During the last twelve months gin has been the leading seller at the base Mini-Mart, with vodka a close second."

A strange place to begin with, Gitmo became even stranger

during the Cold War period, given that it was a US military facility on the sovereign territory of a country aligned with the Soviet bloc. By the time I stood at the Malones Lookout in 1998, with the Cold War supposedly a thing of the past, Gitmo seemed like a weird anachronism of both neocolonialism and the Cold War. My opinion at the time was that Guantánamo was outdated and unnecessary; keeping it seemed counterproductive, and returning it to Cuba seemed like the right thing to do. I had said as much in some of my conversations with Cubans. In fact, I had told many of my interlocutors that I had a gut feeling President Clinton was going to normalize relations with Cuba and begin the process of returning Guantánamo before he left office in two years' time. What I didn't understand then—even though I lived in Miami—was that both political parties were already anticipating that Florida would be the decisive state in the 2000 presidential election, so Clinton could not possibly consider jeopardizing the Florida electoral vote by making amends with Cuba.

As I studied Gitmo from the overlook, I thought the base was an absurdity, a ludicrous embodiment of America's imperial ambitions (past and present); but I did not regard the base as particularly invidious or inimical or evil—a characterization of the place that shortly would become more accurate. Moreover, on that day in 1998, I had forgotten that just a few years before my visit Guantánamo had already been deployed as a prison camp of sorts. In the early 1990s, Haitian refugees captured on the open seas had been diverted to Guantánamo and held there in what were reported to be deplorable conditions; the practice, which included isolating HIV-positive people, ended in 1995 after the camp was declared illegal by a US district court judge. At the time, US government officials were already claiming that Gitmo was not subject to laws of the mainland because Guantánamo was not technically US territory. In retrospect, dealing with the Haitian refugees turned out to be a logistical trial run for what was to come later, after 9/11.

The tour guide had finished with his overview of Guantánamo's topography. The German tourists had taken their photographs and wandered away from the lookout platform to the outpost's other attraction—a diner that served up chicken and drinks. In fact, the price of the tour included a complimentary drink from the bar, your choice of rum mixed with fruit juice or cola. The Germans were jovially imbibing. I went over to the bar for my drink. It was very strong, more rum than juice, and I said as much in Spanish to the bartender. He beamed. This was the highest-quality rum, he asserted, the best in Cuba. In the world. Of course, it was strong. Cuban rum was the strongest and the best. He asked me how to say "best" in German.

Not German, I told him. American.

His response was typical of what I had encountered in Cuba—surprise and keen interest.

"A Yanqui!" He called over to the waiter to tell him the news: a Yanqui in their midst. The waiter came over to have a look. "A Yanqui, eh? Don't you know you're supposed to be down there" —he waved toward the base—"not up here? Did you get lost? Or maybe you are a defector!" He smiled broadly. He was getting a kick out of teasing me.

No, just a tourist, I said.

"So you want to see what your imperialist government is up to, eh?"

Yes, I agreed, that pretty much summarized it.

He nodded. "Tell me, amigo, are you a baseball fanatic? Yes? Then tell me—I need inside information—who is strong this year? Who will win the championship of American baseball? I have bets with my *compañeros*."

"Hard to say," I said, "but definitely not Miami."

"No? But they are last year's champions, the defenders."

"Yes, but they sold their best players."

"Sold?"

"Yes, or traded them."

"Sold. Traded. I see, like slaves."

"Something like that."

"This," he asserted, "is why Cuban baseball is better than American baseball. In America, the players must perform as slaves for the owners. No matter how much money the players get, they are still property. In Cuba, they play for love of the sport. They play with their hearts. Now, then, tell me, who will win this year's championship?"

"Good question," I said. "Probably the Yankees. The Yankees always win."

"Always? Well, we will see. We will see. Perhaps one day the

Yankees will prove not so powerful as they think." He smiled and
shook my hand.

Having basked in the warm sun and indulged in the strong drinks,
we tourists tipsily boarded the bus for the short ride down to Caimanera, a fishing village situated just outside the perimeter of the
naval base. There were more checkpoints, then a causeway lined
with salt dehydration ponds. On the other side of the causeway,
Caimanera was perched on an extension of Guantánamo Bay. The
hotel occupied a small hill looking onto the waterfront. The hotel
grounds included a pool and a watchtower, the latter built to give
hotel guests a better view of the perimeter of the base.

After getting settled in my room, I went out to ascend the tower.
Meanwhile, the Germans, lolling around the pool, were drinking
again—mojitos and daiquiris. Music played over the loudspeakers,
including, inevitably, the popular song "Guantanamera."

The observation tower offered a partial view of the inner bay
and the base, but nothing like the view from the overlook where
I had just been. So I turned my attention to the little town. It appeared to be as sleepy and slow as you would imagine a waterfront town in the tropics to be. A few people strolled the streets,
kids played in the dirt, dogs sniffed puddles and trash cans. Here
and there people stood in clusters or sat on doorsteps engaged
in casual and sometimes spirited chatter. As usual in Cuba, the
conversations were not hushed; voices carried, and I could almost
eavesdrop on the gossip, the friendly arguments, the earnest conversations taking place several blocks away. Three men peered into
the open hood of a car, deep in deliberation over the vehicle's
malfunction and possible solutions. Two women laughed heartily
at a joke. A boy whistled as he rode a bicycle.

During Gitmo's heyday, in the years before Castro came to
power, Caimanera was quite a lively town, with several bars and
brothels attending to the desires of American servicemen. During Prohibition, when drinking was not allowed on the base, Caimanera was especially active—and atmospheric. According to
National Geographic's reporter in 1921, "One thousand associated
smells assail the nostrils when one climbs on [Caimanera's] rickety
boat wharf" to visit the town with its "sordid streets of one-story
shanties." Dogs and "naked gourd-shaped babies" predominated

while a two-goat cart hauled water to the plaza for domestic use. There were "dark-skinned women dressed in flowing white, languidly fanning themselves as the ship's barge puts in." The bars were Sis's Place, The Two Sisters, and The American Bar. These were open-air saloons, and the action was frenetic. The bartenders would "rain perspiration from their dark brows" as they prepared "the seductive daiquiri." On Sundays, the town featured daylong cockfights. Beyond the bars, "down the dingy, dusty, sometimes flagrantly muddy street, with its weird multitude of vicious odors," the *National Geographic* writer detected the symbolic aura of another continent: "All the way up the Guantánamo River the atmosphere has suggested Joseph Conrad's African backgrounds. The dark currents, the violent green of the contorted mangroves that curtain the banks, the 'Red Mill' at which a sugar schooner bakes lazily in the sun and near which a solitary saloon is thrust invitingly forward over water—all have a remote and exotic air." In such a setting, American soldiers could well imagine that they had truly taken up "the white man's burden," as Kipling had exhorted them to do in his well-known poem written on the occasion of America's defeat of Spain in 1898—the victory that had delivered Guantánamo to the United States. In the poem, Kipling spoke of America's "new-caught, sullen peoples / Half-devil and half-child."

The pre-1959 literature on Guantánamo Naval Base—primarily magazine and newspaper articles—usually gave Caimanera a lot of attention. For example, a 1927 article published in H. L. Mencken's *American Mercury* described Caimanera as a "queer little village" where American officers drank daiquiris in "a rickety wooden building like a squat barn built on piles over whispering, greenish water." At "a long, battered mahogany bar," the sailors sang songs about life on the base with lines like "We're sitting here so free swallowing Bacardi" and "Put your troubles on the bum, here we come full of rum." Dogs scavenged the floor and a character named Peanut Mary stood in the doorway hawking peanuts and lottery tickets. (In *American Mercury*'s rendition, Peanut Mary is made to speak with some sort of southern black or perhaps Jamaican dialect.) Meanwhile, the residents of Caimanera were on the outside looking in: "A hundred grinning black faces at the wide glassless windows on the street side." The Navy Wife, too, in her 1930 article "Guantánamo Blues," ventured into Caimanera to describe Pepe's Bar, "a small picturesque but smelly shed which might have been put together in a movie studio for a Mexican melodrama."

In 1958, when civic unrest during Castro's rebellion put Americans in danger, Caimanera and the rest of Cuba became off-limits for Gitmo's personnel. But in the years leading up to the closing of the gates, Caimanera was a riotous—and repugnant—place. Sailors who had been stationed at the base later recalled Caimanera's muddy streets and wretched poverty. Shacks wobbled on stilts over the bay. Garbage and human waste drifted in putrid water. Atrocious smells predominated, venereal diseases were prevalent, typhoid a constant concern. Caimanera was "a large-scale brothel," according to one sailor who visited in the 1940s, with girls available for the going rate of $2.50. The Navy operated an off-base first-aid station right in Caimanera, dispensing condoms and penicillin.

Cuban discontent over the US presence at Guantánamo began the moment the treaty granting occupancy to the United States was signed. It continued through the decades and fed the ire of revolutionaries. Cuba had been prostituted to the United States both metaphorically—billions in profits from sugar production, casinos, and tourism left the country for the United States—and literally in places like Caimanera. The United States was always quick to point out that American investment had brought major improvements to Cuba, especially in terms of infrastructure. The base at Guantánamo, the argument went, was the economic engine for the region (a similar argument was made about the US naval base at Subic Bay in the Philippines). Many locals had jobs on the base—good jobs—and without those jobs the region would be mired in economic depression. Such arguments did not account for the huge social costs that Caimanera and nearby Guantánamo City were forced to pay. The sailors' and journalists' descriptions of the towns at the time suggest that seediness prevailed, that the wealth supposedly generated by the American presence never really trickled down.

Certainly the vast majority of Cubans have seen little to no good in the US occupation of Guantánamo. Like the Filipinos who objected to the US naval base at Subic Bay, Cubans have longed desperately for an end to the imperial occupation. Fidel Castro called the base "a dagger in the heart of Cuba," and there is every reason to believe that he spoke from the deep anguish of a patriot and not as a posturing propagandist (as many American officials were keen to characterize him).

The wounds have been very real. Consider "Guantanamera," the irresistible song that celebrates the charms of a young woman from Guantánamo province. It is probably the most famous, the most world-renowned piece of music to come out of Cuba (and that is saying something given how musically prolific the island has been), a universally recognized manifestation of Cuban culture. Americans never think of this, but many Cubans do: during the years when the song was gaining in popularity and earning international renown, there was a very good chance that any given Guantanamera was a prostitute entertaining American servicemen for two dollars and fifty cents.

My view of Caimanera from the observation tower suggested that the little town was much better off now that it had no traffic with the base. It was relatively clean and sanitation was adequate. People were not rich but they were able to get by with dignity. Prostitution was a thing of the past. Life was tranquil and, by all appearances, pleasant enough. I doubted that anyone wanted to go back to prior arrangements.

The sun was now setting and the people ambling the streets of Caimanera were receding into shadows. The bay waters flashed with silver. At that moment, I felt fortunate to have had the chance to visit this part of Cuba, fortunate to have had a glimpse of the base, fortunate to have seen this once notorious little town now so much changed from what it had been when the sailors and Marines hooted and howled and puked on its streets. Most of all, I felt fortunate to have had the chance to see, however distantly, a place of importance to Stephen Crane's personal history and to the ongoing story of Cuban-American relations.

In retrospect, my casual and pleasant visit with its complimentary rum drink has taken on a more sobering quality. The tropical haze hovering over the place has become thicker, darker. Imagine someone in 1950 recalling a 1925 visit to the once tranquil German village of Dachau: that is how I now feel about my brief glimpse of Guantánamo. Years after that glimpse, Gitmo, having been repurposed as a Kafkaesque penal colony, can no longer be dismissed as the odd neocolonial outpost that I thought I saw from the Malones

Lookout. What had seemed merely ludicrous and anachronistic in 1998 has become, in hindsight, something much more insidious.

By 2004, nearly 800 prisoners in the War on Terror had been brought to Guantánamo and incarcerated in an isolated sector of the base known as Camp Delta. Over the years, reports of mistreatment and torture have surfaced, leading to international condemnation. Though the number of prisoners has steadily been reduced, to this day the prison camp remains operational and, by presidential executive order in 2017, will remain operational indefinitely. Meanwhile, the United States has no plans to turn the naval base over to Cuba.

By coincidence, the place where Stephen Crane and the Marines landed in 1898 is located just four miles from Camp Delta. As Crane reported, he and the Marines came ashore at nightfall. Nearby, a small village was burning—the result of American bombardment. From this first beachhead, the Cuban interior appeared "sombre," a place of "mysterious hills" covered with "a thick, tangled mass." The Marines did not know what awaited them in that interior, but they were, as Crane described them, confident that they could subdue whatever force they encountered.

In 1898, with one of the nation's major writers as witness, some of the defining attributes of American hubris were on display from San Juan Hill to the shores of Guantánamo Bay. They still are.

The Great Divide

FROM *Harper's Magazine*

LIKE MOST THINGS in Kashmir, the Baramulla railway station is surrounded by barbed wire, Indian Army bunkers, and frost-tipped mountains that, at sunset, look bloodstained and haunted. When I walked into the station in July 2016, I was stopped by a group of Indian soldiers armed with AK-47s who demanded to know what I was doing in Baramulla, a town just 30 miles from the Line of Control that has divided the disputed region between India and Pakistan since 1972. I told them I was a journalist, working on a story about the construction of India's first rail line into Kashmir. They waved me through. "The train is a very good project," one of the soldiers told me as I walked onto the platform.

At half past noon, the 10:50 southbound to Srinagar announced itself with a long baritone whistle. Hundreds of passengers rushed off the cars as the soldiers prodded them with wooden batons. I found a spot by the door. As the train began to pick up speed, a group of young boys jumped aboard, blasting Punjabi music from their phones.

A lanky 20-year-old named Sayeed Ahmad crouched beneath a window. Ahmad, who was from the village of Budgam, had spent the day picnicking with his friends. Like many young men and women in Kashmir, he regarded the Indian Army as an occupying force. He described how, every Friday after prayers, he would pelt the soldiers with stones. "They beat us," he said. He took off his light-green polo to show me a scar on his shoulder. It looked like a purple worm. "We are forced to take up the gun."

"We want liberation from India," said his friend, 22-year-old Sameer Ahmad. The train shook and the windows began to rattle. "Pakistan is the best. They are our Muslim brothers."

Many of the younger Kashmiris on the train were born in the '90s, as thousands of Pakistanis were slipping across the border to join militant groups such as the Jammu Kashmir Liberation Front and Hizbul Mujahideen. At one time, there were more than 60 such organizations, some fighting for an independent Kashmir, others insisting that the region, where some 90 percent of residents are Muslim, become part of Pakistan. Unlike their parents, who grew up in a time when the leaders of Kashmir's separatist movement were proponents of nonviolence, this generation has been inspired by young fighters who share posts and videos calling for armed resistance to Indian rule. "Students here, they will take up a gun instead of a pen now," said my translator, a 25-year-old photographer named Khurshid Ahanger. They've grown up seeing India "through the barrel of a gun."

As our train crawled toward Srinagar, I huddled near an open window to catch a breeze, watching the emerald fields swirl in the distance. A young boy dressed in white leaned out the window. "I feel like a king here," he told me with a shy smile. He'd moved to Kashmir with his family from Uttar Pradesh, a Hindu-majority state. (Since Prime Minister Narendra Modi and his Hindu-nationalist Bharatiya Janata Party came into power in 2014, there has been a marked rise in the number of attacks against Muslims in India. According to Amnesty International, at least 10 Muslim men were publicly killed over a three-month period last year.)

We pulled into the Srinagar station. Mothers on the platform were fanning flushed babies. Young boys attempted to climb on top of the already full train as the conductor blew the whistle. Army officers beat them back with batons.

"Every time it's like this," a soldier said to me as I got off the train.

Trains have long been intertwined with colonial ambitions in India. The British opened the subcontinent's first railroad in 1853, a line from Bombay to Thane that hastened the export of goods to Europe. Though the railways were a commercial boon, they also provided, as the governor-general, Lord Dalhousie, wrote to London that year, "immeasurable . . . political advantages." They "would enable the government to bring the main bulk of its military strength to bear upon any given point in as many days as it would now require months." By 1900, the system had grown to become Asia's largest.

Indians, whose taxes had funded the creation of the railroads, soon began to see them as a symbol of British power. Mahatma Gandhi blamed trains for destroying local, self-sufficient economies. "Good travels at a snail's pace," he wrote in *Hind Swaraj.* "It can, therefore, have little to do with the railways." But Gandhi's concerns went unheard. By the time India became independent, in 1947, more than 30,000 miles of rail crisscrossed the country.

Half a century later, Kashmir would confront the same threat that Gandhi had articulated, this time from the Indian government. During the fourth war between the two countries, in 1999, Pakistani generals authorized a secret infiltration of Kargil, a mountainous city on India's side of the Line of Control. With few roads and no rail line in the region, India struggled to send supplies and reinforcements. In just six weeks of fighting, the country lost more than 500 soldiers.

Kashmir's inaccessibility was a wake-up call for India's then prime minister, Atal Behari Vajpayee. When he returned to New Delhi after visiting Kargil, he remarked, "We have not attacked any country in our fifty years of independence, but we have been attacked several times and lost our land . . . We are determined not to lose our land in the future." Preparations for a rail link in the Kashmir Valley began immediately.

In 2002, the Indian government broke ground on the railway, which it hopes will one day connect Baramulla, Kashmir's northernmost city, to New Delhi. But despite being prioritized by Vajpayee as a "project of national importance," construction has been plagued by a number of setbacks. For example, in 2009, a protracted dispute over gradients broke out between two private companies that had been commissioned to work on separate sections of the line. But the biggest delay by far has been due to the plan's most ambitious feature, the Chenab Bridge: a mile-long crossing made of blast-proof steel designed to withstand both earthquakes and explosives. When completed, it will be the loftiest railway span in the world, stretching across the Chenab River at a height greater than that of the Eiffel Tower. Scheduled to be completed in 2009, the bridge is the only section of the railway still unfinished. The latest target date is summer of next year.

Undeterred by delays, Modi paid a one-day visit to Jammu and Kashmir in July 2014. Dressed in a creaseless light-blue kurta and surrounded by reporters, he stood before a steel train car strung with marigolds and inaugurated the railway's latest link, connecting Katra to Udhampur. "Our aim is to win over the hearts and minds of the people of Jammu and Kashmir through development," he said. The train whistled and the crowd clapped. "Soon Kashmir will be prosperous and peaceful."

When our train pulled into the Srinagar station, two years after Modi's speech, Kashmir did appear prosperous: crowds of people were arriving for the Amarnath Yatra, a Hindu ritual in which worshippers climb to the mountainous shrine of Lord Shiva. My hotel was just around the corner from Dal Lake, which is home to hundreds of Victorian boats, some with their own floating gardens. Shikara rowers sat by the shore, waiting to pick up tourists. When I reached the hotel, the owner offered me Kashmiri tea. "It's all peaceful," he said, before picking up the phone to inform another potential customer that the hotel was fully booked.

Around sunset, I met with a journalist in his 50s who has covered Kashmir for three decades. We sat barefoot in his office, sipping Mountain Dew.

I asked him what he thought about the new train. He was quick to draw a parallel to China's rail into Tibet, which Beijing built in 2004 to gain control over its volatile region. "When the rail line is finished, Indians will feel they've vanquished their territory," he said, leaning back in his chair. "Kashmiris will feel they're still in India's golden chains."

I returned to the hotel to find the owner sitting in front of a small television, chewing on his thumbnail. "Burhan Wani has been shot," he told me. Wani was a 22-year-old Hizbul Mujahideen commander and a local hero. He had been radicalized as a teenager after being beaten by soldiers, and started making videos to inspire young men to turn against India. The TV flickered with a photo that would go on to become the iconic image of that summer: Wani in a tan polo shirt, eyelids half-shut, face white, a thin stream of blood dripping from his forehead.

The next morning, soldiers were stationed at every corner, blocking the streets. There was no cell service, no internet. Schools and businesses shut down.

An hour southeast of Srinagar, in Tral, Wani's funeral began at dawn. More than 200,000 men and women flocked to the town on foot, a sea of turquoise, pink, and black hijabs. *"Azadi! Azadi!"* they shouted: "Freedom!" Cloaked in an orange blanket, Wani's body was passed through the crowd. Thousands of hands reached out to touch it.

Wani was one of the youngest leaders of Hizbul Mujahideen. The group had become a bewildering menace to the Indian Army, which issued a million-rupee ($15,000) bounty for Wani in 2015. That same year, the Army was suspected of murdering his older brother, a 25-year-old economics student and lab technician named Khalid. The government claimed he'd gone to visit Burhan in the forests and was killed by gunfire, but according to the boys' father, Muzaffar, when Khalid's body was returned to the family, there were no bullet wounds. "His skull was crushed and all thirty-two of his teeth were broken," Muzaffar told me. "He was tortured to death by police." In December 2016, the state government offered four lakh rupees ($6,000) to the Wani family in compensation for Khalid's death.

The clashes between protesters and police began in Tral, but soon spread throughout Kashmir. By nightfall, thousands more had turned out. *"Indian dogs go back!"* they shouted. In Anantnag, police began shooting live bullets. Aijaz Ahmad Thakur, a 29-year-old father of two, was one of the first to be hit. His cousin found his body later that evening, the stomach torn open.

A dozen people died in a few hours that night, and the protests continued into the next day. The government imposed a curfew and sent in more troops, but the protesters didn't let up. Photographs of people maimed by shotgun pellets appeared in the local papers; the one to go viral was of Insha Malik, a 14-year-old who was hit while looking out the window of her home. Her face was so riddled with shot that it looked as though she had a bloody case of chicken pox.

In Srinagar, I met a 31-year-old ophthalmologist named Raashid Maqbool Wani, who said he worked 24-hour shifts for four straight days after Burhan Wani died. He told me that his hospital normally receives about 5 patients a week. In the wake of Wani's death, 60 to 80 people came through the doors each day. Gurneys were converted into operating tables, waiting rooms into emergency wards.

One patient was a boy who had been shot in the face in the district of Kupwara. His eyes were wide open, the retinas detached. Clots of blood clouded his pupils. "He said something I'll never forget," Raashid told me later. "He said, 'It's okay, doctor, I don't need my eyes to see what's happening.'"

That night, when I returned home, the hotel owner told me to leave Srinagar. "What is there left to see?" he asked when I passed him in the lobby. I told him I was waiting for the train to start running again. He rolled his eyes. The government had suspended service indefinitely.

The train still wasn't running two weeks later. I decided to take a car 150 miles south to Katra, in Jammu. It was the closest station still operating. Around midnight, a car came to pick me up. "Be safe," the hotel owner said, shaking my hand. He instructed me to call him when I arrived—and to give him a good rating on Trip-Advisor.

My driver, a 20-year-old named Sajad Farooq, said he'd been protesting by day and driving tourists by night; he hadn't slept in three days. He threw his first rock at the Indian Army when he was 16 years old, after seeing a soldier shoot and kill his cousin. "I would die protesting," he said. "I'd die for Kashmir."

We drove through the night, past charred vehicles and tanks. Everywhere, shop windows were smashed. Stones and barbed wire were strewn across the ground. Wani's name was written across walls on the outskirts of Srinagar. BURHAN OUR HERO. BURHAN STILL ALIVE. Farooq told me a slogan was being spoken at funerals that hadn't been heard since the '90s: *Tere khoon se inqilab aayega*—"Your blood will bring forth the revolution!"

We drove along Highway 44, speeding past signs for Pampore, Awantipora, Bijbehara, Anantnag—stops that would remain closed for the next five months. A few hours later, we approached a sea of glowing red brake lights. We'd reached the Chenani–Nashri tunnel, a barrel of concrete cutting through six miles of mountain, connecting the Kashmir Valley to Jammu, the southwestern region of the state. It is the longest tunnel in India. Farooq sped up as the traffic subsided, and his music seemed to get louder. Orange tunnel lights streaked by overhead. A few minutes later, a massive Indian flag greeted us from the other side. Cars gently swerved off the highway, stopping at a nighttime market with glowing stalls that sold magnolia flowers, perfumed incense sticks, jewelry, and tea. Children walked around barefoot, tapping on car windows to sell scarves and nuts.

The mountains that divide Jammu from the Kashmir Valley are partly responsible for the contrast in their identities. "Jammu and Kashmir was not part of British India and was ruled by the maharaja. Hence, it was not part of the political mobilization that took place in the rest of India during the nationalist movement," Partha Chatterjee, an anthropologist at Columbia University, later told me. "After the maharaja joined the Indian Union in 1947, the Kashmir Valley, separated by the mountains, was for a long time very poorly connected with the rest of India, unlike Jammu."

The discrepancy became apparent as dawn broke, revealing pastel-colored temples and well-manicured parks. There were large Indian flags on every corner and the words *"Jai Hind"*—"Long live India!"—painted across fading hotel signs. As we drove past a mile-long Army base in Udhampur, the propaganda signs read WE DON'T STOP WHEN WE'RE TIRED, WE STOP WHEN WE'RE DONE! EVEN IN REST, PLANNING FOR THE NEXT, the text juxtaposed with a photo of a leaping cheetah.

Deep in Jammu's remote Reasi district is the future home of the Chenab Bridge. When work on the crossing began in 2004, Indian engineers blasted a road into the side of the mountains, only to discover a tiny village, called Sarmega, directly in their path. The residents were suddenly living side by side with cement trucks and 50 of India's top engineers.

During a tour of the site, I met a geological engineer named Santosh Maharaj. I asked him when he thought the project would be completed. "When? *If*," he said, laughing. "Don't write that down."

Around us, steel beams poked out of the soft ground. It was unclear whether they'd been there for 12 years or 2 months; everything looked half-started. From above, I watched a group of construction workers share a cigarette as they dangled their legs off a girder protruding from the mountain. In the canteen, a concrete bunker, an engineer pulled out his phone to show me a video of the project. The camera panned over a rendering of the finished bridge, moving through the fog as a voice declared: "The Chenab Bridge will be as strong as its foundations." We attempted to drive down to those foundations, but when it began to rain, Maharaj ordered the driver to turn around. It wasn't safe, he said as the ground melted into a red stream beneath us.

Back in his office, Maharaj showed me samples taken from the site. The mountains here are made up of more than 20 different types of rock, including limestone, slate, dolomite, sandstone, and shale. "The whole train will pass through these," he said. The composition of the mountains, along with the steep slopes and the threat of rockslides, presents a daunting challenge.

Maharaj's friend Naresh Sharma, another engineer, cut in. "Some people said the geology is not suitable to make that bridge. Concerning this point, this is actually the most suitable location for building the bridge." He added that the government had delayed the project because of safety concerns. "But now we have a green signal."

A horn blasted, and a truck arrived to pick up a handful of construction workers in the rain. I'd spoken to several earlier that morning as they walked to work from Sarmega, swinging tin lunch pails. One had told me that a few years ago, four people died when a crane broke, dropping them a thousand feet to the floor of the gorge below. Despite the danger, most workers were paid between $100 and $200 per month to work 12-hour shifts.

The head of the project, Surajit Choudhury, came by. He'd been working on the bridge since construction began. "This bridge is a *very* good project," he said as we sat in his windowless office. He assured me that they'd finish in five years or so. "This rail line will bring the Kashmiris into the mainstream of this Indian culture."

By car, the Katra railway station is about an hour and a half south of the Chenab crossing. Completed in 2014, it is the newest station on the line. Inside, I found thousands of Indian pilgrims stranded en route to Kashmir. Down here, Wani was not a martyr but a terrorist, and *azadi* was a Pakistani myth. I stood in line to buy a ticket to Jammu Tawi, the last stop on the southbound rail. A young man named Mukul, who sold clothes in New Delhi, told me that Kashmir was beautiful. He hoped to visit the valley "as soon as they kill all the terrorists."

On the train, I mentioned Wani's death to an older man named Vikas Singh. He grew agitated. "Kashmir is an integral part of India," he said.

I pointed out that most Kashmiris with whom I had spoken said they didn't feel that they were an integral part of India. Many wanted Kashmir to become a separate country.

"There are only two to three people who want to get separated from India," he replied. "Ninety percent of people are against getting separated."

The maroon late-afternoon light faded as our train crawled toward the city of Jammu. Outside, cracked red soil marked the paths of what once had been marshy streams. When we arrived, the temperature had yet to fall much below a hundred degrees. I set out from the station for Nagrota, a town that is home to many Kashmiri Pandits—Hindus who fled the valley in the '90s after they became targets of a new wave of Muslim insurgency. Over the course of a decade, thousands of Pandits were killed, threatened, or forced to flee their homes, many of which remain abandoned on the outskirts of Srinagar.

I met Kanwal Pandita, a government worker, in his home. We sat cross-legged while his wife brought out plates of honey-coated sweets. Pandita had been working in Kashmir when a mob attacked the camp he lived in with other Pandits. According to him, the crowd pelted stones at their windows for hours, until Army officers showed up. He and 80 other Pandits fled by car that night.

"Treatment is not good there," he said. "Pandits are like bonded laborers and slaves. We have no freedom of expression, no freedom of state, no freedom to pursue our religion. They want to convert us to Islam, which is not possible." He added that the Army was doing a "great job" in Kashmir.

Like Pandita, many Pandits still regard the Kashmir Valley as their homeland. Hanging on his bedroom wall was a photo of his family smiling from a houseboat on Dal Lake, the sunlight glistening on the water. After touring their house, my hands sticky from the sweets, I paused by the door. "We would never support an independent state," Pandita said. "Kashmiris have no claim on Kashmir. We're all Indians. We will die as Indians."

The next morning, I boarded the train to New Delhi and headed for home. Twelve hours later, the familiar scent of pollution, car fumes, and dust entered the train. I leaned out the window and watched the lights glitter over the City of Dreams, as it is called.

It was past midnight, but the station was bustling with people:

families from northern villages, Sikhs, businessmen, South Indians —but not a single Kashmiri.

I stepped out of the station and pushed my way through the crowd fighting to flag down three-wheeled rickshaws.

"Where you coming from?" my driver asked as we sped away from the station.

"Kashmir," I said.

"Terrorists."

DAVID FETTLING

Uncomfortable Silences: A Walk in Myanmar

FROM *Longreads*

NOW WHAT I REMEMBER most about him is what he said about the Rohingya: that they were troublemakers, not really citizens of his country, undeserving of sympathy, that he hated them. He had said it standing under a banyan tree, and I had noticed, again, his dress: he was wearing a *longyi*, a Burmese sarong, and with it, new-looking, Western hiking boots. His *longyi*'s knot was tied impeccably. His boots appeared to me to not quite fit him.

But I spent three days and walked 50 kilometers with him before he said this. Through a trekking agency I'd arranged to meet him in Kalaw, in hill country in central Myanmar, and took an overnight bus there from Yangon. The bus was ultramodern, air-conditioned, and near-empty. Arriving at dawn, I disembarked into cold air and a fog that obscured the tops of pine trees. I found the café where we were to meet, ordered a tea. Every few minutes a man sidled up to me and asked if I needed a guide. When I said I had one already they looked not merely disappointed but resentful; slinking away, I saw them lingering on the café's margins.

This was a year ago, so Myanmar was still in vogue: after decades of oppressive military government and isolation internationally, it had begun to "open" and appeared to be moving toward democratization. A perception of the country as a dramatic "good-news story"—a newly liberated populace, pursuing long-denied opportunities—was drawing increasing international interest. I badly wanted to see Myanmar and Kalaw through this lens; but those sullen, hands-in-pockets would-be guides kept straying into my field of vision.

He arrived 15 minutes late. He looked extremely young: early 20s, I guessed. He introduced himself as Thomas—I blinked, asked him to repeat it. Thomas was at once exuberantly friendly and palpably nervous: as he met me he profusely apologized. "I'm sorry, sir"—I never got him to stop calling me sir—"I am running late. I still have to get some things from the supermarket. I am *running late*, I am sorry. I think maybe you will write this on TripAdvisor." I told him it was no problem, and we walked two streets over, not to a supermarket but to a small, dowdy grocery store. Thomas disappeared; I waited outside. Next door was an internet café. Young men played computer games, their faces near-expressionless. The fog was clearing to a powder-blue sky, yet I felt a sense of anticlimax: this, apparently, was Myanmar's transformation in actuality. Thomas reappeared; walking quickly, he continued to apologize. "I am sorry about this," he said, into the chilly blue morning. "I am sorry about this."

We walked toward the hills. Rapidly the streets became less busy. Small houses sat amid ferns. Then, the trekker's worst nightmare: I felt something awry in my bowels.

The crisis was immediate. I told Thomas, who spoke Burmese to an elderly couple sitting on their porch. I was led to a wooden shed behind their house: there, the apocalypse duly took place. Back outside, I found a bowl of water and bottle of soap. I soaped my hands, washed them in the bowl; then, gazing at the soapsuds unmoving in the water, I knew I'd done the wrong thing. There was no drainage mechanism: clearly you were supposed to wash your hands some other way. I had defiled the water. Thomas had accepted a tea, and the three of them were sitting without speaking, the couple calm in this disruption to what looked like a familiar, well-honed daily routine. I said nothing about the suds. We walked on.

My mood had changed. That gleaming, empty bus, those furtive, loitering would-be guides, the expressionless cybercafé teens, my guide's inexplicable anxiety, my own failing bowels, the floating soapsuds—everything seemed to go together, somehow; there was something not quite right about the entire morning, something fundamentally off-kilter. Thomas and I resumed walking. "I'm sorry," Thomas said, again. "I'm sorry."

Thomas turned onto a dirt track. We walked through a glade of pine trees, then into a more open country of tawny-yellow grass.

Soon we were climbing, following a ridgeline; green valleys appeared below us.

Thomas talked compulsively. He probably had instructions—making conversation was a way of making happy guests. Yet I had a sense he also genuinely wanted to make a connection with me. There was something in his tone when he questioned me that suggested he acutely wanted to hear the answers, and something in the way he told me things that suggested he wanted me to hear what he had to say. I wanted to chat, too, but my bowels had made me less talkative than normal.

"This is your first trip to Myanmar?"

"It is."

"Oh: *great.*" That turned out to be a recurring expression of his, at permanent odds with his nervousness.

Thomas had a smartphone, a Samsung, and he often flicked and swiped on it as he spoke. I looked again at his *longyi*-and-hiking-boot combination. I noticed that, young as Thomas appeared, he had several white hairs.

"I've been a guide for one year."

"It must be exciting living in Myanmar now," I said, trying to return to my preferred way of thinking about the country. "Democracy, reform—many new opportunities for people, right?" Thomas nodded, but I saw him frowning just slightly. I asked, "What did you do before you were a guide?"

"I worked in Mandalay, in a factory that mixed cement bricks."

"And you want to be a guide for a while, or move on to something else?"

"Actually, I am studying law. But I haven't been able to pass yet." He didn't elaborate. I knew entire universities had been shut down for long periods under military rule. I told him to keep studying, then wondered if that was helpful or even applicable advice.

"I want to get married," Thomas said—he had a girlfriend—"but, she told me, 'not enough money.'" So he was trying to get as much guiding work, as many treks, as possible. I wondered if this explained his anxiety: a fretful determination to ace every trip, the success of which he was measuring constantly. I asked how he and his girlfriend met. "In our village," he replied, with a tone that suggested this was rather a dumb question, that it was self-evident people would meet in their own village. Below in the valley, an old man slowly walked across a rice field. "Not enough money," Thomas repeated, *"not enough money."* I said everything would work out, then pondered again whether that was a useful thing to say.

"Yes," Thomas said. "But so much time will have passed. We will be old. We will not be young. I think it's better to be married when you're young." Tall clumps of bamboo lined our path; on one leaf, a butterfly opened and closed its yellow-and-red wings. I told him that in the West, people typically got married when they were much older than he was. But he only nodded, as if that fact, while interesting, had no relevance to him.

For perhaps 40 seconds, we didn't speak. "It's so quiet," Thomas said, and laughed nervously. I saw him searching for a topic. "Do you have brothers and sisters?" Before answering I looked at him, tried to read his expression. "Three?" he said. "Oh: *great*"—and he did look like he thought it was great. "I have two. But I never see them. They are still in my village. I have not been back." Now he was the one who let the silence resume. I wondered if this meant he hadn't seen his girlfriend in that time.

The silence extended; again, he looked mortified. Then he said, in what appeared to be an analysis of causation, "I think my English is not good." I assured him it was. He looked at the ground: unthinkingly following his gaze, I saw the precision of his footwork on the rock-strewn path. He said, "My father died when I was small. He spoke very good English. So after that, for many years, I couldn't practice my English." Sadness suddenly emanated from him like a heat.

All morning we walked along the ridge. We stopped for lunch at a restaurant that advertised itself as Nepalese. I said I would eat only a little because of my bowels and Thomas looked startled, as if I had discarded some carefully prepared script, and he feared for the consequences. He reached for his phone. I glanced at his screen, saw him playing a Tetris-like game: by stabbing at the screen he was smashing colored blocks, attempting to clear a straight path for himself. He collapsed that game, then I saw squiggles of Burmese text on the familiar blue and white of Facebook.com. "Are all these messages from friends of yours?" I asked. He pursed his lips, as if thinking about the question. He scrolled and scrolled, as if searching for some piece of information that was eluding him. He talked of TripAdvisor and Booking.com, about travelers posting critical comments; he mentioned, with an embarrassed grin, the benefits of me leaving a five-star review. His expression, staring into the phone, was tight-lipped, pensive.

As the Nepalese staff served curries and breads, I noticed that Thomas's features looked more than slightly Indian. Certainly he was physically distinct from the typical Bamar, Myanmar's dominant ethnic group. Interested in the presence of South Asians in the country, I asked about his ethnic background. Thomas looked at me with surprise. "I am Burmese," he said. So much else was fluid, undergoing transformation: but this assertion landed in our conversation solid as a rock.

Now we walked downhill, into the valley. We began following a train line. Thick, dry undergrowth was on one side of the tracks, rice fields on the other. Inevitably I thought about the laying of the rail lines by the British Empire, about that well-worn trope of trains as symbols of modernity. "What if a train comes?" I asked. But Thomas knew the times: he said the next one was not due for five hours. The track gauge was strikingly narrow. The wooden planks were beginning to rot. A small train station, with a village wrapped around it, appeared on our left. A man sat on a bench on the platform. I wondered if he could be waiting for the distant evening train. Perhaps he was waiting for something else. Perhaps he was not waiting for anything.

Fog was now back around the treetops. I saw two bulbuls in a tree. We arrived at the outskirts of the village where we would spend the night. The houses, basic two-story constructions, all had electric paint jobs. One had purple doors and green walls, another green doors and blue walls. The colors stood out in the foggy dusk. Thomas turned left, into our homestay. A Burmese family greeted me with the wordless wide grins by which people with no common language communicate. I sat exhausted on the front step.

There, abruptly, I remembered other news and analysis I'd read about Myanmar, things I had chosen to ignore since my arrival, preferring airbrushed accounts. That still-unmet expectations were causing rising frustration. That people's predominant feelings were not merely or even mostly of dramatically opened possibilities, but of a scramble for resources and opportunities which they saw as palpably finite. That change, displacing traditions and disrupting communities, was causing anxiety and disorientation

—and prompting searches for reassuringly simple racial-religious-nationalist ideas of identity.

I found myself watching Thomas as he unlaced his hiking boots and put on flip-flops. I saw his feet. They were wrinkled, calloused feet, the feet of someone who'd grown up walking without shoes. He'd been tied into village life enough to want to marry from there. But the old rural patterns had been disrupted—not only had Thomas himself moved, to Mandalay for factory work, then Kalaw, but back in his village, his prospective wife was demanding more money. Thomas was attempting, through the tourist industry, to plug into a nascent Myanmar of greater economic opportunity. Yet his constant talking to me, tending me like an overwatered plant, suggested an entrenched notion that foreign travelers were a scarce and precious resource. On his phone Thomas always had anxiety on his face, as if he believed Mark Zuckerberg's "connected world" could bring as many disasters as windfalls, as if one bad TripAdvisor review could sink all his dreams, as if all that he'd built for himself remained fundamentally insecure. His hiking boots now sat on the balcony, socks scrunched into them, juxtaposed against the rural dusk. I remembered his words inside the Nepalese restaurant: *I am Burmese.* The only truly confident declaration he'd made.

Night came. In the house three low-wattage light bulbs flickered on. Each illuminated perhaps four feet. In the kitchen, Thomas and the homestay family chopped vegetables I didn't recognize. He spoke to the family familiarly in Burmese. I offered to help; he switched back to English to tell me it wasn't necessary, resumed talking Burmese. His face looked washed of the concern I'd seen earlier. I heard water trickling in an irrigation channel of a neighboring rice paddy: I wondered how many generations had tended it. A puttering sound: a motorbike came up the driveway. Its sole headlight glowed, far stronger than any light in the house. The driver parked; chatted briefly in the kitchen; left again. I watched the headlight's glow become smaller, then disappear.

Through the small porthole of a window beyond my bed's mosquito netting, I could see only fog. I stepped outside. Although fog enveloped the multicolored houses, in the rice field I could make out the long green stalks, heavy rice grains at their tops. Next door

a young girl was on a swing made from rope and a hessian bag.
I felt better this morning, in this house, amid this countryside.
The girl swung with an unchanging, entirely predictable rhythm.
Thomas put away his flip-flops, wrenched on and laced up his hik-
ing boots. We started walking.

Bright yellow squares appeared on the hillsides. Thomas said
they were sesame fields. Old women were spreading chiles on
blankets on the road, to dry in the sun. Thomas told me about
that, and other crops, and harvesting methods. In his pocket his
phone beeped. "Over there they are growing potatoes." His phone
beeped again. "And that is corn." His phone beeped again.

Then, a pivot: after speaking about Myanmar's countryside, he
wanted, amid the sesame-checkered hillsides, to know about my
country.

"Is there rice in Australia?"

"Only a little."

"Is the weather warm in Australia?"

"It depends. In the south it gets cold in winter."

"I like wintertime the best," said Thomas. In Kalaw, he told me,
it became quite chilly in December. I told him that in the Australian city where I used to live there was often frost on the ground in
the early mornings, and it looked almost like snow.

"Oh: *great,*" Thomas said. Then he said, "I like this about my
job. I meet people from everywhere. France, the Netherlands,
America. And they tell me things." He paused. "I have not seen
snow." A plane was flying overhead, and he said, "Actually, I have
not been on a plane." He laughed, put his hands in his pockets,
took them out again. Another rice field. Thomas told me that in
this area, farmers got two harvests per year. Then he said he had
a cousin working in Malaysia, in construction, and maybe one day
he would visit him. I watched his hiking boots scuff the ground,
left, right, left, right, as our conversation shifted between inward-
ness and outwardness, between old and new worlds.

We began climbing again, into another set of hills. Blue-black
clouds appeared on the horizon.

"Are there earthquakes in Australia?" Thomas asked.

"Not many."

"Oh: *great,*" Thomas said. "Here in Myanmar we just had an
earthquake in Bagan"—the ancient city, comparable to Angkor,

filled with archaeological monuments. "*Two hundred* buildings were damaged," he said. "It is *terrible*. It is terrible, because it is like our heritage is disappearing. We are *in mourning*." He said the word "mourning" very carefully.

I said, "We're certainly getting more extreme weather in Australia. Fires, floods, rain at strange times of the year, things like that."

"Same in Myanmar!" said Thomas, and I noticed his excitement at finding a point of commonality. "Like now. There shouldn't be rain like this, in November. *This is not normal*."

As if on cue, we saw, below us, a rice field that had been flattened, the rice stalks horizontal against the ground—it was like a movie scene of a UFO landing. "This is from heavy rain last week," Thomas said. "It is damaging because it is coming at a different time in the rice cycle. It has destroyed a lot of crops." He paused. "I think the world is changing very fast."

I said, "In Australia farmers can buy insurance against poor crops or bad weather. Sometimes they get help from the government, as well. Is there any talk of that, yet, in Myanmar?"

Thomas asked me for clarification. Then, he said, "No."

"It started in Australia in the Great Depression," I said. "After the economy collapsed, a lot of farms had big difficulties, a lot of people had it very tough." Then, listening to myself, I stopped speaking.

The clouds were closer to us. We put on raincoats. It began to bucket. Brown water poured down our path; the earth turned to sludge. Thomas calmly found footfalls in the muck; I stepped where he stepped. A large monastery appeared. Thomas gestured for us to enter. We walked into the courtyard, then stood under a sloping red roof at the main entrance. Rain poured off the roof. Monks in yellow robes walked slowly up the steps.

Thomas said, "Are you religious?"

"I'm not, no."

"You have no religion at all," he said, declaratively. "A lot of my clients from the West are like that." I had a feeling he'd been about to instinctively say "Oh: *great*," but had pulled back just in time. I noticed his use of "client." He looked at the rain, adjusted his jacket. Then he said, "But you know, in Myanmar, that would be very difficult—to have no religion at all.

"Villages around here are all losing the old religion," Thomas continued. "Here people practice a Buddhism, but an old-fashioned Buddhism, with animism and other traditions mixed in. Now the old still believe that, but the young don't."

"Why do you think the young don't follow the old style?"

"It takes a lot of time," Thomas said. "Young people now, they don't have time." Back on the path, two locals were attempting to walk in the rain. They squinted, held up their hands to shield their faces, disoriented.

"So you're more of a conventional Buddhist, Thomas?"

"Yes," he said. "Yes, I am a Buddhist." A second confident assertion from him, and it seemed to me again, given all his other freely expressed doubts, jarringly so.

The rain lightened; we left the monastery. Our boots squelched in the earth. Visibility was still poor, so it took a while for me to see a large poster stuck on a house. I opened my jacket, wiped my glasses on my shirt, then saw pictures of a man I didn't recognize, and Aung San Suu Kyi.

"Who's the guy on the left?"

"That's the new president."

"What do you think of the new government, then?"

"For a long time things were terrible. Now everything is better. We are very happy." From his tone, he made it sound like the well-worn verse of a school song—he sang it dully, as if by rote. Whether he did so for my benefit or his own, I didn't know.

The rain stopped, and the valley and next range of hills became visible again. Now I could see a startlingly conical-shaped hill among the range, and Thomas said, "A hermit lives there."

"Really?"

"He went there and became a monk. He lives up there and works on his religion."

I looked. On the hill's summit was a small hut, surrounded by maybe a half dozen pine trees. For a second I thought I could make out a figure, but of course I couldn't.

"He gave up everything," Thomas repeated, "and became a monk."

On some impulse I said, "You ever feel like doing that?"

He said, "Do you?"

"Sure, some days." But I said it with a dumb grin on my face. When he replied, "Yes, sometimes," he looked contemplative, and grave.

We arrived in the village where we would stay the night. One shop on its outskirts had several outside tables and was selling beer to tourists. At one of the tables was a group of newly bronzed northern Europeans, and one of them said, "Hey, Thomas!"

He had escorted them to Inle Lake several days ago. They had stayed there, and were now heading back to Kalaw by another route. There was a shouted recollection of some mid-trail embarrassment which left ambiguous who was being mocked; they invited Thomas to have a beer with them. We walked quickly to the homestay so he could drop off his things before heading back. He asked if I wanted to come; I declined.

At the homestay I went to the outside shower, poured cold water from a bucket over myself, put on my last clean clothes, went to the house's second floor, and opened my book. Night came. I had a sudden appreciation for simplicity. *Old routines in an old house,* I thought to myself. Thomas still wasn't back. On my arrival the old man at this homestay had nodded to me only slightly. As I read he sat on the floor on the opposite side of the room, underneath framed pictures of presumably deceased relatives. But my presence in this house likely complicated any practice of household routines for him. At around nine o'clock, a confused rooster began to crow.

When I woke up and went outside, I found Thomas already on the veranda packing his bag. We walked on, in more fog. He hadn't shaved: it made him look older. On the village's outskirts was a field of corn, dead. After two hours of walking Thomas realized he had left behind his rain jacket.

Now we were passing through different country again, an open grassy valley with scattered banyan trees and rocky limestone cliffs to our left and right. Inle Lake, gray, calm, was visible ahead. A thin trail of Western tourists was moving through this valley from various tributary paths in the hills. I saw once again the country's potential—this could indeed be a major tourist attraction.

Then, I felt again the dreaded sensation in my bowels. Why now? I told Thomas through a self-deprecating joke, then went broodingly quiet. Yet Thomas still insisted on speaking, asking one question after another. Preoccupied with Richter scale rumblings in my intestines, my responses became terser until I was answering in monosyllables. I looked at him, saw his now familiar anxiety.

Eventually he said, simply, "We are silent." I looked at him. He was desperately unhappy.

In an attempt to reset the situation, I said, "But people can be silent, sometimes, Thomas. There's such a thing as a comfortable silence."

It had no effect at all: his face was the same. I thought: *But he isn't "comfortable." He is in no position to be comfortable.* And I found myself asking again—what was it, precisely, about silence which Thomas couldn't tolerate? Was it the importance he ascribed to each trekking trip, elevated by an idea of the scarcity of trekkers in Kalaw? For the tourists around us in this valley were still few in number, given this was peak tourist season. I thought again of those would-be guides loitering by the café, desperate for business. Or was he genuinely searching for a human connection? He had moved only recently to Kalaw, I reasoned; he would be spending a lot of his life on trekking trips with strangers. Amid his disrupted, dislocated life, far from family and other anchors, did he, quite simply, want to talk?

"Do you have pets?" Thomas asked. I told him a dog and a cat. "Oh: *great.* In Myanmar, we keep mostly dogs," he said. "I had a dog—here, in Kalaw. I had him for a while. Then, he got sick, and he died. I guess in Myanmar there is a lot of death. When I went trekking he would sit outside my house and wait for me when I came home."

I asked to sit. We entered a banyan tree's shade, rested our backs against its roots. I shut my eyes. Thomas sat pensively. I could feel his concern that I'd stopped speaking, knew he was interpreting it, again, as a setback. A cool breeze came from the lake. I could see he was thinking of a new topic. But it seemed to me that all his anxieties conditioned the one he now chose.

"Today in Myanmar," he said, "we have a problem with the Rohingya."

I looked around: at gray rock, yellow grass, the banyan tree's fat trunk and leaves, the distant lake. I felt another quake in my bowels.

"Burmese people don't like them because they are so violent," Thomas said. "They carry out many terrorist attacks. They live inside Myanmar but they are not *from* Myanmar. They are from Bangladesh."

The banyan tree's enormous roots, knee-high, curled in all directions; to me, now, they resembled a tentacled monster rising from the earth. He asked—and I recognized the same sentence structure from our conversation yesterday—"Is it like that with Muslims in Australia?" Searching for a new point of connection between us, he'd settled on this. So many differences separated us. But he knew—from previous trekkers?—that our societies had this tension in common. He was looking at me expectantly, hopeful this would solve the problem of the silence between us.

I did no calibrating, no soft-pedaling; I did the opposite of what people do who want to make a connection with someone else: lobbed my own differing perspectives and values straight at him, unvarnished. "In my country," I said, "it's similar in that too many people believe ugly things about Muslims." A butterfly floated past. "It's unfair, because of course, all but a handful are as peaceful as you or me. But people like to have somebody to blame." As I said it, I watched hurt spread across his face. He had suggested a commonality between us; I had pointedly denied it.

He clenched his lip. He said, "They have too many children. They will take everything. This country should be for real Myanmar people."

I looked again at his Western-style hiking boots; I looked at his face, his South Asian–looking face. Three foreign backpackers, small in the distance, walked through the valley. Like the rest of Myanmar, he had been waiting a long time, with increasing impatience, and had sacrificed much—moving to Mandalay to mix bricks, leaving family and girlfriend behind. Now, guiding tourists to Inle Lake, he presumably felt himself achingly close to his goals. But could he already see, I wondered, that his goals were not quite being realized—and likely would not be? All this dislocation—and for what? I remembered his comment yesterday: *I think the world is changing very fast.* Alone in the hills with a tourist who'd gone mysteriously quiet, an event boding ill for his professional success, he had reached for another assertion that, like *I am Burmese,* like *I am a Buddhist,* had a solidity to it. *We have a problem with the Rohingya.* In his pocket, his phone bipped. Perhaps a TripAdvisor notification. An ancient-looking farmer walked past us, carrying a full basket on her back. His phone bipped again. "It's about defending the Myanmar culture," he said. At this, I was entirely silent. One more uncomfortable silence. I could almost hear him say it: *We are silent.* But he didn't say anything. His face was stony.

We walked toward a rocky hillside—the last ridge. Now Thomas did something drastic. He took out his phone and put on music. It was, of all things, the pop song "I'm Yours" by Jason Mraz. In this moment of stress, it was American pop he had turned toward. Thomas clearly knew the lyrics, the ridiculously Californian lyrics. They rang out in central Myanmar. *"I fell right through the cracks."*

We were approaching an enormous construction site. A luxury resort was being built. I saw my chance to use a bathroom. We entered a world of wooden scaffolding, pouring concrete, gaping muddy holes in the earth. The scaffolding looked precarious. I found a beautiful modern toilet—which was not yet working. A sign warned against use. Another wooden shed it was. Sitting there, I had an impulse to take my own advice: I attempted a silence. I found myself listening to small birds, tiny rustlings, a wind. Then, those sounds were extinguished by a cement mixer's guttural chug. Then I heard, faintly, Jason Mraz.

The final ridge. Another blue-black cloud. Another rainstorm approaching. I zipped up my jacket, but Thomas's was still hanging at the silent old man's homestay: he had nothing to protect himself. I looked at him. His face was now without anxiety; it was the face of a stoic, settling in for protracted discomfort, protracted disappointment. He got out a plastic bag, carefully wrapped his phone up in it. The last thing we heard before he turned off his pop song was: *"well open up your mind and see like me."*

ALICE GREGORY

Finished

FROM *The New Yorker*

THIS PAST SUMMER, as Austrian glaciers melted and Swedish forests burned, the Swiss Air Force, which exists to protect a nation that hasn't fought a war in 500 years, was tasked with supplying tens of thousands of gallons of water to herds of parched cows stranded in Alpine pastures. Meanwhile, in Glion, a tiny village roosting high above the city of Montreux and accessible by funicular, it was already above 70°F by 8:30 a.m., which is when classes begin at the Institut Villa Pierrefeu.

To Viviane Neri, the school's headmistress, the heat wave engulfing Europe came as a pleasant surprise. "We haven't had a summer like this in a hundred years," she told me. "It's quite lucky." She smiled and gestured graciously toward Lake Geneva, which, like the sky above it, was an oversaturated blue, as though photographed on expired film. Several women, some as young as 18, others in late middle age, could be seen scrambling, chamois-like, up the terraced hillside. An email, sent by the school a few weeks prior to their arrival, advised the women to "dress in good taste," and they had interpreted the cryptic guidance with remarkable consistency. Their appearance—blow-dried hair, dry-clean-only dresses—suggested an abundance of wealth and time, both of which are de facto prerequisites of admission at the Institut Villa Pierrefeu, where the summer course lasts six weeks and costs an average of $30,000.

Housed in a traditional chalet, built in 1911 for a Dutch baroness, the institute bills itself as the last finishing school in Switzerland. The prosperous canton of Vaud, where IVP is located, was at

various times home to Charlie Chaplin, Zelda Fitzgerald, Graham
Greene, and Vladimir Nabokov; it was also a sort of capital for
establishments where, as Muriel Spark wrote in her final novel,
The Finishing School, "parents dump their teenage children after
their schooldays and before their universities or their marriages or
careers." In the 1920s, Lausanne alone boasted 45 such schools.
Their advertisements in the *Swiss Monthly,* a long-vanished periodi-
cal dedicated to horoscopes and the autobiographies of amateur
alpinists, ran amid ones for "dietetic specialties" and "colonial
goods." Some promised pastoral luxury ("large gardens on lake
shore"), others a pedagogical focus on domestic science and modern languages. Unaccredited, expensive, and, typically, family run,
Swiss finishing schools took the place of men's university education for many wealthy Western European women with matrimonial
ambitions. "It's the same as the watch industry," Neri's son, who
tends to the school's business matters, has said. "If you want the
highest quality, you stick with Swiss."

Institut Alpin Videmanette, whose alumnae include Princess
Diana as well as her sons' nanny, Tiggy Legge-Bourke, closed in
1991, and Château Mont-Choisi, attended by France's former First
Lady Carla Bruni-Sarkozy and, reportedly, by Princess Elena of Romania, shut in 1995. Le Manoir, the alma mater of the British spy
Vera Atkins, is now the world headquarters of the multinational
food-packaging company Tetra Pak. The real estate these schools
sat on was valuable, and the feminist movement all but obliterated
demand for their offerings, as the domestic talents once suggestive
of elegance and good breeding began to look more like instru-
ments of oppression. Why learn how to run one's home like a corporation if suddenly it was possible to run the corporation itself?

This change was perhaps responsible for the discretion that is
a hallmark of IVP, where one student told me that she was hiding
from her friends the fact that she had come. Students spoke to me
on the condition that I use only their first names, in keeping with
the policy at IVP, which forgoes last names entirely. Like Switzerland's military and banking strategies, IVP's devotion to privacy
borders on the neurotic. Though invited to spend a week attending classes, I was scolded on more than one occasion for photo-
graphing the chalet's interior, for recording lectures, and for attempting to ascertain basic biographical facts about the school's

students, a group that Neri claims has included the daughters of presidents and prime ministers. For the most elite, true discretion is achievable. Neri will sometimes coach the daughters of sheikhs within their own palace walls.

Toward the end of the 1970s, Neri said, IVP's primarily European students were largely replaced by women from Latin America, India, the Middle East, Japan, China, and Russia. (A few years ago, one alumna, the art-collecting daughter of a Moscow oligarch, penned a widely mocked etiquette column for the Russian edition of *Tatler*, in which she advised her readers against hiring Filipina staff.) Of the 29 students present when I visited, one was a Canadian CEO and another an American mother of five; there were six young Chinese women, a few lawyers from India and Australia, a Nigerian chemical engineer, a marketing manager from Dubai, a Harvard Business School graduate from Honduras, and a handful of university students from countries that included Kuwait, Saudi Arabia, and Mexico. The only three Europeans were an 18-year-old aspiring fashion designer from Portugal, a former Emirates flight attendant from Romania, and a Ukrainian cryptocurrency investor currently living in Singapore.

The women, many of whom had attended MBA programs, were there not to learn how to make money but to acquire the gestures of having inherited it. The pursuit of such a goal might strike us as anachronistic, but the archetype of woman as family ambassador is as relevant as ever. During my time at IVP, Ivanka Trump's name was never mentioned, but, in the students' preemptive smiles and refusal to talk politics, it was impossible not to feel her presence.

When I arrived at the Institut Villa Pierrefeu, a recent thunderstorm had stranded the receptionist in Paris and also disabled the area's internet, which enhanced the school's atmosphere of secluded obsolescence. Neri apologized for the mayhem as she led me into the house, which had parquet floors and a marble staircase. "See?" she said, pointing to a formal dining room, where the table was already set for lunch. "Everywhere is a classroom."

Neri, who has run IVP for nearly half a century, accessorizes with silk scarves, pearl earrings, and navy pumps. She speaks as fastidiously as she dresses. Averse to extemporaneous talk, she often apologized, more to herself than to me, it seemed, for going "off track." My entreaties for her to continue along whatever conversational rail she had found herself on were always met with refusal. "No, no," Neri would say. "I'm off track."

"Ah!" she cried, as we made our way into the sitting room, which was outfitted with gilded mirrors and Oriental carpets. "I told the girls not to put them this way!" She approached a celadon sofa and rearranged a series of neatly aligned pillows into a more spontaneous configuration. "We're not in the army, after all." She proceeded to lead me upstairs, tsk-tsking at a descending student, who, apparently, should have given me the banister.

The idea of IVP's curriculum is not, necessarily, to train women from developing countries in the mores of Western Europe but to expose students to the oddities and taboos of one another's nations. In addition to learning how to clean marble, address a dowager duchess, and serve a luncheon, the students attend lectures devoted to the customs of 20 countries. In a 90-minute class on Nigeria taught by a Cordon Bleu–trained Canadian chef turned etiquette coach, I learned that, at a formal dinner in Lagos, appropriate topics of conversation include Benin bronzes and the local film industry. The Biafran War, it was emphasized, is best avoided. In a class on Mexico, we were warned that marigolds, red roses, and silver all make for inappropriate gifts (marigolds are morbid; red roses are lusty; silver, mined locally in Mexico, would fail to impress). As Neri says, "It's better to learn from us than from your mother-in-law."

IVP offers classes throughout the year, but the summer faculty who were there when I visited included an Austrian florist, a Guatemalan etiquette consultant, and a former Nestlé communications director with a self-proclaimed passion for the work of the controversial social psychologist Stanley Milgram, known for his experiments in obedience. A man named Siegfried, who used to supervise mining conglomerates in Burkina Faso but whose business card now bears the name of a Zug-based private-equity company, was also hanging around. Neri casually explained his presence by saying that she was thinking of adding a class the following summer on the manners of Francophone West Africa, and Siegfried, a friend of her son's, might, she thought, be capable of teaching it.

One afternoon, John Robertson, a butler formerly employed by the Duke and Duchess of Northumberland, who had just arrived in Europe after a seven-day transatlantic crossing on the *Queen*

Mary 2, gave a lesson on how to hire and manage staff. He wore monk-strap shoes, creased trousers, a blue-and-white-checked shirt with French cuffs, and a hat, which he removed upon entering the classroom and placed upon a coffee-table book about Alnwick Castle. The wall behind him glinted with small reflections cast by the many crystal-faced watches present in the room. Robertson began by outlining the "ten functions of a household," which include security and groundskeeping. "Believe me," he said, referring to household administration, which he recommends leaving to the butler, "this is nothing you want to be involved with."

Robertson's raised eyebrows and perpetual half smile gave him an ironic appearance. He stressed the importance of having clearly defined domestic preferences that together would add up to something like self-knowledge. "How do you like your bed made up?" he asked. It sounded like a rhetorical question, and nobody answered. "Well, if you don't know, then your housekeeper is going to do it however she learned how," he said. Robertson provided the students with sample questions to ask a potential butler ("Where do you place the oyster fork?" "Can you make me a Martini straight up?"). A gardener should be able to tell you his favorite seed catalog, a housekeeper her preference among vacuum-cleaner brands. It would be wise, he said, to quiz a potential housekeeper on how she might clean, for example, a hardwood floor without stripping it of varnish. "Because it's not just the cost," he said with a sigh. "It's the inconvenience."

Neri herself teaches a handful of classes. In one, on international titles and forms of address, she expressed outrage that once, at a press conference, President Obama had called the German chancellor, Angela Merkel, by her first name. Students learned that, when in Asia, one should never write on another person's business card, and that, rather than provide one's own at the beginning of the meeting, they should offer it at the end. Italy, Libya, and Afghanistan are all examples of countries with pretenders— individual aspirants to a long-toppled monarchy who must be addressed accordingly. Neri then walked the class through the 25 levels of peerage in the United Kingdom. "This is the type of thing you need to keep updated on," she said.

It was difficult to imagine such knowledge being remembered when the time came, if it ever did. But the women scribbled notes furiously, their Cartier bangles clinking. Later, by the pool, Toki, a

23-year-old from Nigeria living in London, insisted, gently, on the
curriculum's utility. "People notice," she said. "I think most likely
they wouldn't say anything to you, but they'll leave thinking, *Wow,
she's really refined.*" The Canadian CEO, with whom I spoke the following day, expressed a similar sentiment, though more anxiously.
"There are unspoken rules in business and in life," she said. "Our
success is based at least a little bit on how much we violate them."
She paused and then added, "This is a very safe place for me to
practice."

Her attitude was echoed by the instructors at IVP, who tended
to present the outside world as a place of unrelenting menace,
of career-ruining faux pas and ego-bruising mistakes. To believe
them is to see life, like the surrounding high-altitude landscape, as
precipitous. Pastry is "deadly" for carpets. Lilies, with their impo-
litely strong fragrance and orange pollen ("worse than saffron"),
are to be avoided, as are, at cocktail parties, candles, which Neri
described with a pained reverie suggesting personal experience
with dozens of Savonnerie carpets disfigured by hot wax. "Unless,"
she added, "you're at the Hall of Mirrors at Versailles." Her students dutifully recorded the comment, failing to recognize it as
a joke and interpreting it instead as useful advice for the type of
person who might plausibly host drinks at a UNESCO World Heritage Site.

Neri, who believes orange juice to be an "unimaginative" mixer
(she prefers kiwi), explained that cocktail parties are "an efficient
and economical way of simultaneously returning multiple favors,"
and asked if anyone in the class had ever organized one. Vidhi,
a 25-year-old lawyer from Nashik, India, had thrown one for the
opening of an art exhibition curated by her sister; so had Chris-
tine, the mother of five, for the teachers at her children's school
in Minneapolis. Neri nodded approvingly. Daniella, the Hondu-
ran Harvard graduate, said, "Yes, I have. For my birthday!" Neri,
aghast, raised her eyebrows. "Wow," she said, appearing stricken.
"I've never heard of that."

For the next hour, aided by diagrams and charts projected onto
a screen, Neri proceeded to offer a litany of forcefully worded warnings. The table for the buffet should never be near the bar; the two
are to be kept "as far away from each other as possible" to facilitate
mingling. Hired help might be illiterate, so one should be certain
to instruct staff verbally rather than with a printed schedule. A

cocktail party for a hundred, hosted at the chalet, in Neri's estimation would require two coatroom attendants (who, upon receiving a fur coat, should affix the ticket number inside the garment rather than on the fur), at least two valets, an elevator attendant, two people working the kitchen, two for washing up, one maître d'hôtel, and six—"absolute minimum!"—waiters. The host ought also to notify the local police a few days in advance as to the potential for traffic jams, and hire two security-staff members. "Why do we need security here, anyway?" Neri asked, correctly divining the question that had been running through my head. "Isn't this supposed to be a safe country?" She paused for what seemed like 10 full seconds. *"Gate-crashers."* Tight security, she added, is especially necessary in the summer—"because people will come through the French windows, as you can imagine."

Neri added that one should plan to provide, among other things, two "surprise breads" and approximately 600 hors d'oeuvres. As for drinks, 30 bottles of champagne should suffice, but, along with some nonalcoholic options, one must also have on hand 4 bottles each of whisky, gin, and vodka "for the men who don't like champagne." Neri then accelerated the slide show, presenting a procession of structurally unsound canapés and encouraging a discussion about whether each appeared too large to be eaten in a single bite, as a canapé should be. Most of the tightly cropped photographs did not include forks or wineglasses, so it required some imagination to assess their scale. Before class let out, Neri invited the students to come to the front of the classroom and practice holding, in one hand, a cocktail napkin, an appetizer plate, and a champagne flute. "Come, come," she beckoned. Mila, a 30-year-old who grew up in Guinea-Bissau, bravely volunteered. Neri showed her how to pinch the stem, palm up, between her ring finger and pinkie, slide the plate between her thumb, index finger, and middle finger, and then tuck the napkin under the plate and over her middle finger. All this was to be done with the left hand, leaving the right available for introductions. Mila absorbed the demonstration attentively and glanced up at Neri for a nod of encouragement before attempting the feat on her own. She aced it on the first try. "It looks more complicated than it is," she said.

The question of how we ought to comport ourselves in the public sphere has preoccupied philosophers for millennia. Confucius's teachings address etiquette, as, arguably, do Plato's, in *The Laws,* when he catalogs how various types of guests from abroad should be treated. And if Jesus walks through our world in disguise, rudeness is un-Christian. "Be not forgetful to entertain strangers: for thereby some have entertained angels unawares," the New Testament warns. Various theories of etiquette's purpose have been posited over the centuries. Erasmus had a magnanimous conception when he wrote, in 1530, of the rustic's duty to "compensate for the malignity of fate with the elegance of good manners," whereas the Victorians saw the role of etiquette as something closer to a behavioral amulet capable of protecting one from the polluting forces of vulgarity and vice. The social anthropologist, classicist, and etiquette historian Margaret Visser wrote, in her canonical 1991 book, *The Rituals of Dinner,* that manners "do not constitute virtue, but they do set out to imitate virtue's outward appearance."

Etiquette can be understood as a codified but unspoken system of culturally specific rules, used across time and continents to contend with our most primal aversions: violence and disease and confusion. That Switzerland, a nation famous for a dearth of all three, would be a place where etiquette is taught makes a certain amount of symbolic sense. "What makes Switzerland special is that we are fairly neutral," Neri has said. "Other countries would try to push culture down their throats, such as France. Here we don't have that kind of cultural imperialism."

One afternoon in an upstairs classroom, Neri told me, "My mother never liked the term 'finishing school.' It just means so many things to so many different people. The British, for example, think it's a place for women too stupid to go to university." Neri's mother, Dorette Faillettaz, who never attended a finishing school, founded what became IVP in 1954 with a loan from her parents, as no Swiss bank at the time would lend to a woman. A translator of the Brothers Grimm and, according to Neri, "one of the first women to dare to ask for a divorce in Zurich," Faillettaz established a school that was, for its time, a kind of protofeminist alternative to the tea-party training occurring elsewhere around the canton. Vegetarian cooking was taught, as was family planning, psychology, and car maintenance. Faillettaz devised her pedagogy in response to her own profound hatred of housework. Domestic efficiency, she believed, created more time for higher-order pursuits: reading, playing music, learning languages. Her school's aim, according to a 1965 brochure, was to teach its charges how to "have a lively and well-run home where there exists a real interest in all that is going on in the world."

In the early years, the school's students were mostly from West Germany and the Netherlands. "The French did not come to Switzerland," Neri said. "They would maybe go to England, because it's a kingdom, but not to a peasant country." Every so often, the school received what Neri referred to as "an exotic student"— once, she said, the school hosted a cousin of the emperor of Japan. "My mother wanted her students to be knowledgeable about other countries and other cultures, which was rather revolutionary at that time. She felt we were too ethnocentric in Europe." Neri continued, "Everyone looked up to France and Britain, but there are other cultures that are far older, and they also have refinement and beautiful art, and we should not look down on them."

Neri grew up in Zurich, attended school in England, moved to Montreux after her mother's divorce, and then to California, where she majored in Latin American studies at UCLA. She returned to Switzerland after graduation and married the director of a textile-machine company. "I always said that I would never take over a school and I would never marry a Swiss German, but that's exactly what I did," she said, laughing. In 1971, women in Switzerland gained the right to vote, and the following year Neri's mother retired and Neri assumed leadership of IVP. "It was 1972!" she exclaimed. "We really got the brunt of the student revolution. Class size plummeted. Those who did attend didn't tell their friends. They just said they were going to a language school." In America, too, many finishing schools closed, and the few that remained open, such as Miss Porter's, in Connecticut, and the now defunct Finch College, in Manhattan, elected to emphasize rigorous academics.

IVP's increasingly international clientele makes it tempting to think of the school as a vehicle for cultural assimilation or class mobility, but in practice the school's exorbitant tuition renders it inaccessible to most. Now, of course, those people have YouTube, with its instructional videos on table setting and the pronunciation of the word "Gstaad." With the exception of a peculiar lecture on the importance of protecting one's metadata, IVP's curriculum does not include online etiquette, arguably the most preoccupying sort, on which a well-researched class might actually be useful.

Over the week, I observed many multiple-course lunches, each one set, hosted, served, and attended by students, all of whom were assigned various parts, as in a play, and graded on their performance. The "servants" wore white gloves and frilly aprons and, when they were not pouring water, stood near a sideboard with their hands folded neatly. The "guests" cocked their heads solicitously and inquired after one another's make-believe families. Occasionally, the charade would grow too burdensome, and the women would slip up, becoming, for a moment, themselves. Once, between salad and fish, a college-aged girl pretending to be a guest employed as an attorney tired of discussing her invented career and began talking instead about *The Handmaid's Tale,* which she was watching and enjoying immensely. Toward the end of my stay, the students' general chatter, previously about final exams, turned to weekend plans. A few were going to Geneva; others thought they might like to dine at a nearby restaurant known for a dish called "carrier pigeon," in which the bird is cooked sous vide and served in an airmail envelope. Soon they would be alone in a world of gala events attended, if the IVP's instructors were to be believed, not by friends but by suspicious acquaintances, fault-finding diplomats, and Nigerians eager to talk Benin bronzes.

One afternoon, Andreea, a 30-year-old Romanian woman, arranged a perfectly symmetrical bouquet under the tutelage of the Austrian florist, and then went out onto the chalet's flagstone terrace. Unlike most of the other women at IVP, many of whom have never made a bed, Andreea, who has amber eyes and a doll-like mouth, does not come from family money. Originally from Târgoviște—"the town where Ceaușescu was killed"—she now lives in Dubai. She moved there not knowing anyone, five weeks after winning a bet with a co-worker that she could get a job as an Emirates flight attendant. She has worked in private aviation—often for royal families in the Middle East—for almost seven years.

The daughter of an Orthodox priest and a nurse, Andreea paid her IVP tuition with the earnings she made working on private jets during Ramadan. She appreciates etiquette the way a hostess does a successful Saturday-night dinner service—as a choreography worthy of both aesthetic and moral attention. For this, she credits her royal employers, who looked her in the eye and thanked her genuinely for the smallest services. In her years working in aviation, Andreea said, she had tried to learn, in advance of each flight, at least a few words—hello, please, thank you—in the languages of her passengers. "You cannot believe how people's faces light up when you greet them as they're accustomed to at home," she said. When she first moved to Dubai, Andreea realized that she suddenly represented not only herself, but also Romania. "You're not just you," she told me. "We're all so cosmopolitan now, but we're separated by ignorance, not diversity." Andreea recounted the apocryphal story of Queen Victoria, who, upon noticing her foreign guests drinking from their finger bowls, drank from hers as well. "It's a question of empathy," Andreea said. "You can't have etiquette if you can't open your heart and mind and listen to other people—and truly listen, truly want to know who they are and who they come from, and want to make them feel comfortable."

As we spoke, a blue butterfly fluttered between us and landed on Andreea's arm. She admired it quietly and explained that she would like to start her own finishing school, perhaps in Ethiopia. Andreea maintains an Instagram account on which she occasionally posts photographs of political figures: Barack Obama offering Michelle his umbrella, President Trump hoarding his, Vladimir Putin not helping Queen Elizabeth down a flight of stairs. Seeing that I was no longer in the shade, Andreea urged me to reposition myself, and, as I did, I noticed that her eyes were wet with tears. "Etiquette is not something you learn for yourself," she continued. "It's something you do for others, and I think that's beautiful."

When Andreea finally excused herself, it was to study. With the exception of some of the older and wealthier students, who elect to stay down the hill at an opulent and airless family-run hotel, most of the women at IVP stay on the grounds of the chalet. Andreea's roommate was from China; their suite, like all the others, was named after a flower. There is a summer-camp-like camaraderie among the students, who repeatedly expressed surprise that they felt so intimate with one another after only a few weeks. But why shouldn't they have bonded? Attending the school at all was a kind of radical act of admission, of social ambition and insecurity, of having identified one's current station and found it wanting.

By Friday, after having spent six hours every day at IVP, smiling and nodding and sitting always very upright, I was exhausted and bored, although by what, exactly, I couldn't say. I hadn't had occasion to play truant in close to a decade, and ditching class elicited a familiar thrill. I made my way down a winding road, past apple trees and timber-framed houses, to the funicular. When I arrived, the station was deserted, and a display screen said the waiting tram would depart in five minutes. Sitting inside the car, which was about the size of a Manhattan restaurant's bathroom, was a man in grass-covered work boots. It was a conspicuously small space to share. I felt my heart rate quicken, and with it the tedious compulsion to pretend otherwise.

The man looked up and smiled. *"Bonjour,"* I said. *"Bonjour,"* he replied, before retracting eye contact. I got in and sat down. He adjusted his body away from mine, crossing his legs in the opposite direction. He did so subtly, in a way he must have hoped I would sense but perhaps not consciously notice. The slight pivot of his torso was meant to increase the distance between us; the crossing of his legs was to make himself small. It was for me that he was doing these things, and I was grateful.

MATT GROSS

How the Chile Pepper
Took Over the World

FROM *Airbnb Magazine*

THIS IS WHAT HAPPENS when you bite into a chile pepper: A full load of the chemical capsaicin—the compound that makes peppers hot—floods your tongue and throat, binding to pain receptors and shooting an insistent SOS message to the brain that, essentially, your mouth is on fire. Then there's sweating. Panting. Maybe some crying. And then, finally, the glorious endorphin rush, which instantly transforms all that pain into the kind of ecstasy that forges lifelong addicts: chileheads.

At least, that's how I became one, ever since I chomped a farmers' market cherry pepper at the age of 10. But chiles aren't just hot. They're head-spinningly versatile. They can be sweet, smoky, lemony, cherryish. The heat can be dry or juicy; it can sidle in, strafe, or scorch; it can strike the tip of your tongue, the insides of your cheeks, the back of your throat, or everywhere all at once.

What chiles do, and how they do it, depends on where in the world you're eating. And you can eat them just about anywhere. Chiles are arguably the hottest fruits in the world—both from a popularity and a heat standpoint. And if sriracha mania and *Hot Ones* are any indication, their world domination hasn't come anywhere close to an apex.

Here's what's astounding: chiles are native only to Central and South America. That means that until Christopher Columbus sailed for the New World in 1492, there were no chiles anywhere else. Not in India. Not in Thailand. Not in China or Korea. Those cuisines we now consider spiciest had many other spices, including black pepper, long pepper, and Sichuan pepper. But the most powerful, pungent, polarizing pepper of all?

Nope!

For the past few years, I've been studying the route(s) chiles took around the globe, with an eye to understanding not just when they arrived in different lands but what happened afterward: How did chiles get so deeply integrated into these cuisines? How did that ferocious shift in food alter their cultures? And what do chiles mean to chile eaters today? This summer, I headed to three countries that were remade by chiles over the past half millennium— Jamaica, Hungary, and Thailand—to find out.

Jamaica

Where our heat seeker begins his journey, on the isle where the almighty Scotch bonnet reigns supreme

Soldier—né Neville Anthony Swire—was 51, fit, and beaming as he darted across the rocky hilltop in San San, on Jamaica's northeast coast. Here, he showed me, were young avocado trees, there young soursop. Gargantuan okra pointed skyward from bushes; cacao pods would soon dangle from other branches. A neat gravel pathway arced around Soldier's farm, passing two broad platform swings where we lazed awhile, watching the Caribbean roll in 250 feet below.

Of all Soldier's crops, the most important—for him and for me—were the pepper plants. Dozens dotted the farm, some cayenne, others "devil" peppers, but the vast majority were Scotch bonnets,[1] the fruity, fragrant, fiery symbol of Jamaican cuisine— the essential ingredient in everything from rice and peas to escovitch fish to jerk chicken. Soldier plucked a Scotchie from a bush. Deep green, it was shaped like a wrinkly Scottish tam-o'-shanter. He bragged that if he didn't turn it into pepper sauce, he could get 10 Jamaican dollars for it at market.

"And how many ten dollars I got here?" he crowed, waving his arms at his four-acre pot of gold.

All around us in the foothills of the John Crow Mountains were the estates of Jamaican multimillionaires—modernist villas, money launderers' castles, rickety midcentury follies—but at that moment Soldier seemed like the richest man on the island, and independently wealthy to boot.

That type of independence—hard-won, pepper-powered—has a history that goes back centuries in Jamaica. There were some things I already knew: that peppers were essentially native here, carried throughout the Caribbean long ago, partly by birds (immune to capsaicin, they spread seeds in their droppings) but also by the Taínos (Arawak Indians) who once populated these islands. And I knew that Christopher Columbus, who'd set sail in search of black pepper (genus *Piper*), had first encountered chile peppers (genus *Capsicum*) not far away, on the neighboring island of Hispaniola, kick-starting not only the fruits' world-conquering voyage but also the era of colonialism and slavery.

But that's history; I could read it. I wanted to taste it.

A few days earlier, at the start of my journey, I'd found myself at an unexceptional industrial park in the middle-class streets of the capital, Kingston, where I'd navigated my little rented Suzuki to meet Winston Stona, a man who's been eating peppers longer and more thoughtfully than just about anyone. Now 76, a rambling storyteller with a neat white beard, Uncle Winnie—as his family calls him—is a legend: not only a former deputy director of tourism but an actor who was in the movies *The Harder They Come* and *Cool Runnings,* and a hot-sauce entrepreneur to boot. His life today is cosmopolitan (cocktails at the club, holidays in France), but he grew up on a farm (albeit his family's estate) and still considers himself "an agrarian."

"My father always sat at the table in the morning, and his Scotch bonnet was right here," Uncle Winnie said, placing an imaginary pepper before him in his Kingston office. "And he would just have it on a saucer and bite it while he had his food."

Again and again I would hear stories like this, from Jamaicans of all stripes—dads and grandpas who carried Scotch bonnets in jacket pockets, pulling them out at meals to nibble or to slice directly, often with a specially designated knife, onto their food. It's this kind of eating that Uncle Winnie prefers to all else: a poached egg on brown toast, accompanied by spinach-like callaloo and "little slivers" of Scotch bonnet.

"There are few things that warm the heart more," he told me dreamily.

While some people eat Scotchies straight, I was craving a hit of them in jerk, the slow-grilled meats that are a cornerstone of island culture. Jerk is everywhere, sold at shacks, street-side drums, and cushy restaurants in the touristy parts of Montego Bay. And it has deep connections to resistance and liberation, having been invented, according to legend, by the Maroons, escaped slaves hiding in the Jamaican mountains, who used the flavors available to them—spicy cinnamon, allspice, pimento wood, hot peppers—to transform the game they hunted into flavorful, healthful, long-lasting sustenance.[2]

I whipped my Suzuki up and around mountain passes to the rough, hurricane-battered northeast coast that once attracted luminaries like Errol Flynn and Ian Fleming. When I arrived at the Boston Jerk Center, a famous cluster of jerk joints and bars on the island, smoke was curling from the broad jerk pits, where whole chickens and pig parts lay on pimento-wood poles. (The oil they secrete adds a sweetly aromatic spice, like allspice, with a subtle bitterness that lands at the back of your throat.) Enthusiastic touts from the joint closest to the main road clamored for the tourist trade, but farther in there were no sales pitches, just cooks tending fires and customers gathering to watch the World Cup.

At Goldteeth's Jerk Centre, I found the pork of my dreams: juicy, smoky, deeply seasoned. The pepper burn was even, slow, never overwhelming. And that's the point: peppers are just one element of a complex marinade, yet utterly indispensable.

"In a jerk, that is the most important thing," said George "Goldteeth" Wilson, who's been getting up at 4 a.m. running this joint for 20 years. He can remember when pig's blood was a regular component of the marinade, which balances the pepper heat with scallions, garlic, ginger, allspice, and thyme. These days he uses traditional wild bird peppers, not Scotchies, but they work the same unifying magic. "The peppers bring everything out," he told me.

But as powerful as peppers are, as both spice and symbol, Jamaica's pepper industry is in deep trouble. Sure, you might visit Coronation Market, the Caribbean's largest farmers' market, and see mountains of green and yellow Scotchies for sale. Sometimes, though, in the winter or if the weather's been rough, you'll see molehills.

Taji Alleyne, who oversees the local produce supply network for the $400 million GraceKennedy Group, a huge conglomerate, one wing of which distributes food, told me by phone that Scotch bonnet pepper crops have "traditionally been plagued by virus, pest infestation, and adverse climatic conditions." As a result, two things happen: supply is inconsistent, and the price erratic.

To maintain supply, many farmers grow a more resistant pepper known as the West Indian Red, spicy like a Scotchie but flat-tasting, without that addictive sweetness. Hot-sauce makers (whose 2017 exports totaled nearly $20 million) have even had to buy pepper mash from Costa Rica and Peru. Yes, Jamaica, home of the matchless Scotchie, can't meet its own demand for its beloved native(ish) son. Farms like Soldier's are not enough.

There are some signs of hope. In Clarendon Parish, west of Kingston, 300 acres of hip-high bushes stretch across a hill-bounded plain, bright orange and yellow Scotch bonnets nestled under their gold-green leaves. They are the work of Gary Coulton, who's taking Soldier-style self-reliance into the future with techniques he developed during decades of farming in Florida, using a custom irrigation system and imported fertilizer. His Scotch bonnet seeds, meanwhile, are extra hardy. "It's a good, pure seed," he said. By the end of the year, he plans to have 120 acres under cultivation, for a potential annual yield of 90 tons. That's a lot of Scotch bonnets in a world, Coulton believes, that truly needs them.

"Scotch bonnet pepper is a great ambassador," he said. One day in Florida, he explained, a home inspector came to examine the house he was building and noticed Scotch bonnets growing out back. "He picked a pepper, smelt it, bit it—it burned him—but he was so impressed that he encouraged me to do it more," he said proudly. "To be honest, he spent more time talking about the Scotch bonnet pepper than he was inspecting! It just preached that it opened the door for dialogue between me and a total stranger."

Hungary

In which our adventurer gives his scorched taste buds a rest in the land of sweet and smoky paprika

In the middle of our deeply traditional dinner at a restaurant just outside Budapest, Ádám Bóday, a researcher described by a mutual friend as a "man of mystery," did something deeply mysterious. We had been eating hearty classics of Hungarian cuisine at a cozy spot called Nosztalgia Étterem—stuffed peppers, fatty-chewy tripe in a tomato-paprika sauce, ratatouille-esque *lecsó*—while discussing the gradations of paprika, the sun-dried, finely ground, relatively mild chile pepper that is Hungary's national spice. The way quality is measured, Bóday was explaining, is by dissolving it in acetone, which extracts the crimson pigment, then shining a 640-nanometer-wavelength beam of light through the liquid.

"The less light that comes through, the higher the ASTA value is," he said, referring to the American Spice Trade Association's grading guidelines. A value of 120 and up is the highest quality; below are two lesser grades.

Then Bóday pulled four small bottles of acetone from his bag, and the trim, mustachioed restaurant owner, Jenő Boross, brought four foil packets of paprika from the kitchen, where they're stored away from the light. "The Hungarian expression is 'The paprika gets blind,'" Bóday explained about the storage. "Of course, because the pigments are photosensitive."

Carefully, I spooned one gram of paprika from each packet into the acetone bottles, then sealed and shook them gently. Bóday tapped on his smartphone's flashlight and shined it through the acetone. Refractions danced on a white piece of paper below, one molten gold, another lava red. Even though we didn't have a professional spectrophotometer on hand, we could see: one was a deeper red than the others! Clearly, this paprika was best! Satisfied, we returned to our dinner, and our wine.

This may seem like a fabulous effort to go through to grade paprika, but the spice is more than just Hungary's favorite flavoring. It's an emblem that adorns everything from market stalls, in the form of dried-chile garlands, to T-shirts (I ♥ BUDAPEST with red peppers forming the heart). It's a luxury export, demanded by New York delis and the Kremlin alike. It's the fire in the forge of Hungarian identity, a taste that for over 300 years helped unify a nation as kingdoms and empires rose and fell and new forms of government took hold and were then displaced.

"We cannot live without paprika," Eszter Palágyi, the head chef at Costes, the first restaurant in Budapest to win a Michelin star, told me over espresso one afternoon. She estimates that 60 to 70 percent of the cuisine contains the spice in some way. The powder can be sweet or spicy(ish)—the upper bounds of paprika heat are a few times that of a jalapeño, but those are less common strains —lending an umami-like richness that helps bind dishes like goulash. Chile pastes bear colorful colloquial names: "Strong Stephen is *Erős Pista,* and Sweet Anna is *Édes Anna,*" Palágyi said. "So the girl is the sweet one, the man is the hot one." These, I was told, are also the two sides of the Hungarian character—on the one hand delicate and refined; on the other, hard and headstrong.

Palágyi is young—just 30—but she's a serious student of food history, with a collection of sixteenth- and seventeenth-century cookbooks that have given her a window onto her cuisine's evolution. Hungarian gastronomy, she said, always borrowed freely from its neighbors—and its occupiers. The Ottoman Empire was one of the latter, ruling most of Hungary during the sixteenth and seventeenth centuries and leaving behind a fondness for thermal baths, a deep and lasting bitterness over the conquest, and, of course, peppers.[3]

To get from Turkish peppers to the Hungarian paprika we know today is, however, a journey of another 200 years—or, as it turns out, a 100-mile drive south from Budapest to Szeged, Hungary's third-largest city and the historic heart of paprika production. The center of Szeged is grand and lovely, dominated by a university, full of intricate Art Nouveau buildings, and cradled by the Tisza River—a wealthy city, much of it built on paprika.

"This was a holy crop here," Albert Molnár told me through his translator, marketing director Anko Reijnders, as we sipped coffee in the offices of PaprikaMolnár, the growing and processing company he'd founded in Szeged in 1992. "Every second family was working in paprika, either on one side or the other side of the continuum," he added, "from growing to processing." At the industry's height, in the early twentieth century, 10,000 people farmed paprika around Szeged, and hundreds more processed the spice.

We got up and walked through the factory, past the red-dusted machinery and workers in head-to-toe red, with Molnár—close-cropped white hair, checked shirt, sun-lined face—leading the way to his beloved paprika museum. Black-and-white photos lined the walls, showing families stringing peppers into garlands to dry in the sun, or hauling them to market. Until about a century ago, Molnár said, Hungarian paprika was actually quite spicy and could only be toned down by carefully plucking out the seeds and membrane, which contained most of the capsaicin. Although Hungarians liked their food spicier than anyone else in Europe, they still didn't like it that spicy. (Intensive cross-breeding after World War I resulted in even sweeter strains, which helped create a massive export market in countries that really couldn't take the heat.) Then, after sun-drying the peppers for weeks, they'd pound them to powder in foot-driven wooden mortars called *kulu,* a couple of which were on display.

Even today, "we do everything with hands," said Agota Hodi, another paprika maker, whose spice is used at Costes (and sold at Zingerman's here in the US). At her suburban Szeged house, where the paprika scent spilled wonderfully into the street, Hodi, 40 and lively, served me slices of bread smeared with lard and dusted with paprika ("You can taste paprika the best in fat or in oil," she told me) and explained the process: Yes, a machine dries the peppers, but first they need a couple weeks in the sun. Yes, machines grind them, but Hodi must add water to maintain the ideal 8 percent moisture. "If not enough water," she said, "then the color is not so red."

Harvesting peppers requires human beings—machines clip too many unpalatable leaves—so each September 50 to 60 laborers come, many from Romania, and get paid $30 for a thousand hours of work to clear the 20-acre farm. Most laborers, she said, won't do that kind of work for that kind of money.

And that's one of the reasons why Hungarian paprika is dying.

Yes, dying. Already, only 10 percent of the paprika consumed in Hungary is produced in the country, said Hodi, who worked at the Ministry of Agriculture before turning full-time to paprika.[4] The rest comes from abroad, mostly China. Even at PaprikaMolnár, many of the peppers processed are grown abroad, in Serbia. Farming peppers, which get a single annual growing cycle, is expensive and risky, and many Hungarians seem willing to put up with substandard paprika as long as it's inexpensive. While Jamaica is striving to modernize pepper farming in the face of climate change, Hungary, challenged by economic shifts, is letting its fire go out.

The standard economic solution to this would be to import cheap labor instead of cheap paprika. But immigration in Hungary has become one of the hottest-button issues in the country—and Szeged, in fact, was a flashpoint for the migration crisis back in 2015, when hundreds were crossing the Serbia-Hungary border daily, not far from Molnár's and Hodi's operations. The government reacted harshly, erecting a double-layered, razor-wire-topped electrified fence along the border. It's an imposing creation, a harbinger of isolationism and a throwback to the days of Hungarian-Soviet communism.

The chance of Hungary accepting migrants to prop up the paprika industry is zero. The government currently allows a mere two asylum seekers per day into its temporary "transit zones," and, as is the case throughout much of Europe these days, xenophobia is in the air. At a cathedral in Szeged, where I'd gone to see a bell adorned with pepper imagery, I met a man who spoke of the need to safeguard "white, Christian Europe." (This Jew was unmoved.)

That Hungary's signature flavor was brought to this country by Turkish Muslims only deepens the already long-running and sad ironies.

So it was heartening to meet Márk Bogár, a 24-year-old who lives in Tetétlen, a village of 1,500 in eastern Hungary, and who represents another path of pepper possibility. Alongside his parents, Bogár is growing tons of the world's spiciest chiles—ghost peppers, Trinidad Scorpions, Carolina Reapers—and turning them into sauces, sold under the name "Sárréti Chilifarm," that are getting attention from local fans and Hungarian TV, and winning awards.

When I stopped in to visit, Bogár and his friends and family were in the backyard, enjoying home-grown jalapeño poppers and grilled chicken wings with a dozen Sárréti sauces, from kiwi-habanero to apple-horseradish to one called Csak Norris, after the *Walker, Texas Ranger* star. (*Csak* means "only," the implication being that only Chuck Norris could handle the heat.) Kids of varying ages were running around, grown-ups were pouring *pálinka,* and soon my mouth was aflame in a way I'd never expected here in Hungary.

As Bogár talked about his love for seriously spicy peppers—no "ish" necessary—it gave me hope. Hungarian cuisine took centuries to get where it is now; maybe another hundred years will see paprika morph again, reinvigorated by Sárréti's strains, and make today's Strong Stephen look like Sweet Anna by comparison. Maybe traditional paprika didn't need to survive. Maybe, I suggested to Bogár, Hungary had erred in breeding out the heat a century ago?

"This was a mistake!" he laughed.

I began to feel my head spin—not from chile-fed endorphins or *pálinka* but from the delicious sense of history repeating itself. Now, though, the chiles were hotter, the influences American, and yet all was still very Hungarian. As Goldteeth had said, "The peppers bring everything out." Everything, yes—and everywhere, too.

Thailand

The final chapter of our journey, in which our hero's mouth, and mind, are set aflame with the possibilities of a globalized, chilefied world

Finally, my face was on fire. My lips burned. My tongue burned. My throat burned. Sweat beaded on my cheekbones, under my eyes. This wasn't just heat—this was electric. My mouth pulsed with incalculable voltage. Pain and pleasure blurred, the distinction irrelevant. I breathed deeply. I smiled like a twelfth-century Buddhist god-king carved in sandstone. I picked up my spoon and my fork, and prepared to take another bite.

For weeks, I had been looking forward to Thailand, the most thoroughly chilefied country in the world, where peppers are everywhere (*everywhere!*), in everything (*almost!*), pounded into curry pastes and papaya salads, sliced into stir-fries, soaked in vinegar or fish sauce, and placed upon seemingly every dining table. And now I was at Err, a cool, comfy restaurant near Bangkok's Grand Palace that specializes in "urban rustic" drinking food, which tends to be spicier than non-drinking food, which, let's be clear, is decently spicy already. Before me were tart ribbons of shaved green mango dusted with ground chiles; a flash-fried egg buried in chiles, shallots, and mint; and a sour and fiery pork-rib curry, plus the house cocktail, made with rum, fresh passion fruit, and—of course!—skinny red chiles.

Together, they lit me up—but they didn't push me over the edge. My palate didn't collapse. I could taste the lush, semiliquid egg yolk and the pork's savory roughness—could taste them even more acutely, I imagined, than if the heat had been dialed down. The chiles were inextricable.

Except, of course, that technically, historically, they are entirely extricable. Because if you went back in time about 500 years, you'd find no chiles in Siam, as Thailand was then known. You'd find ginger and galangal, and black, green, and white pepper, and *makh-waen*, a cousin to Sichuan peppercorn. You'd find cinnamon and cloves and other dried spices, and a panoply of pungent herbs. You'd find coconuts and citrus. You'd find rice and fermented fish and shrimp. You'd find mango and durian. In short, you'd find nearly everything you'd need to make recognizably Thai food to-day—except that without the chiles, it would be unrecognizable.[5]

As with the story of peppers elsewhere in the world, I knew the shorthand version of how they got to Thailand: the Portuguese. Arriving in Siam in 1511 after capturing Malacca, up the Gulf of Thailand, the Portuguese likely brought chiles, along with guns, cannons, and other items for trade.[6] But what happened next re-mains mysterious. How did chiles so thoroughly take over?

"Thai cuisine, you know, it's supposed to hurt a little," Pim Techamuanvivit, the chef at San Francisco's Kin Khao and Bang-kok's Nahm, had told me. "But there's definitely a balance be-tween using chile and allowing the other flavors and the true na-ture of the ingredients to show themselves." I would have to be careful not to let my quest for fire get in the way of my quest for enlightenment. Any dumb *farang*—i.e., "foreigner"—could burn his face off; I wanted something more nuanced, to burn with un-derstanding.

One Sunday morning, a quick ferry ride across the Chao Phraya River from Err, the Church of Santa Cruz was alive with activity. A pale-blue sky hung over the century-old Italianate church— peachy yellow with pink accents and a red-domed steeple—while inside dozens of worshippers sang hymns in Thai and listened to a priest's sermon from the gold-adorned chancel. They were young and old, some dressed up, most casual, all members of the 200 or so families that make up the surrounding community—a commu-nity that is not only Catholic, with crosses and images of the Holy Family adorning their homes, but Portuguese.

Historically, anyway. This neighborhood was Kudichin, and it was about as close as I was going to get to envisioning the first contacts between Thailand and the Portuguese. The neighbor-hood was created in 1769, when King Taksin granted land to three groups that had aided Siam in a war with Burma. It was a war that Siam basically lost: The Burmese looted and burned the royal capital, Ayutthaya, 50 miles north, where the Portuguese and other foreigners had encampments. Siam's leaders retreated to Bangkok, and the Portuguese, along with the Chinese and a group of Muslims, now had land to call their own, here on these flood-prone mudflats.

Two and a half centuries later, the community has managed to preserve some Portuguese culinary traditions. At the airy café of the Baan Kudichin Museum, I snacked on *sappayak*, a light and yummy baked Portuguese bun stuffed with sweet minced pork, potatoes, curry powder, and red flecks of mild chiles. And after Sunday mass, a street stall behind the church sold a very Portuguese beef stew with potatoes and tomatoes (both New World crops!), as well as sweet, Chinese-influenced pork, braised with soy sauce, tofu, and hard-cooked eggs, and a fiery Thai curry of ground pork and pea-size eggplants that popped with tart astringency. Eating all three together felt like communion with history, as if the groups that had created modern Thai cuisine were right there at this folding metal table at the edge of the street.

The exact moment chiles arrived in Siam may have been lost to history. Foreign visitors' accounts offer tantalizing threads. Portuguese apothecary Tomé Pires visited Siam around 1514 and wrote of rice and pepper, and a 1688 account by the French Jesuit Nicolas Gervaise mentions pepper but not peppers. (He also berates Siam's "stupid cooks" and their shrimp paste, "which has such a pungent smell that it nauseates anyone not accustomed to it.")

But what is certain is that over the past 500 years, Thailand's chiles have flourished in dizzying variety. Today, there are *prik kee noo suan*,[7] or "mouse-shit chiles," skinny and hot and known in America simply as "Thai chiles." *Prik chee fah*, or "sky-pointing chiles," are longer and milder, growing up from bushes instead of dangling. *Prik som* are orange and meaty. *Prik kaleang*, the chiles named for the Karen hill tribe, may be the hottest of all, but they were not included in a 2008 Kasetsart University study that measured the pungency of Thai chiles and rated most between 45,000 and 80,000 Scoville units, at least 10 times hotter than jalapeños. Of course, that's just the beginning. Trying to track down every variant, when flavors and names proliferate and overlap, is a fool's errand.

Which is how this fool came to be in Phatthalung, about 500 miles south of Bangkok, closer to Melaka than to the Thai capital. On the west the district was bordered by greenish limestone mountains that erupted from the rice-paddied plains; to the east was Thailand's biggest lake, and beyond the lake the sea. Whichever direction I looked was pure Thai picturesqueness.

Loveliest of all was right before me: two long fields of *prik khao chi*, a relatively rare variety of chile known as "white nuns" because they don't redden when ripe. On the bush, they were a very pale yellow, skinny and wrinkly and crooked, and when I nibbled one it gave off a ton of heat and a fresh, bright aroma that was, I'd been told, essential to southern cuisine, which is known not just for its intense fire but for its sourness and fermented fishiness. The night before, at the quiet lakeside restaurant KiengTalay, I'd dived headlong into those flavors—a tart and crunchy lotus-shoot salad, soupy-shrimpy curries with crabmeat or whisker sheatfish—until a pleasant funk lodged in my nostrils and my throat burned and lips puckered. The heat had taken its time building, a signature southern style derived from local chiles.

These white nuns had been grown by Vichit Janphaleuk, who was 64, with wavy hair just going gray and a loose checked shirt, and who'd specifically chosen to farm chiles 30 years ago. It was a decision born of practicality.

"This area is going to be flooded every year," he said through a translator, "so if I grow something else, it's going to be flooded before I even sell it." With chiles, he can harvest about 100 kilos a week of the fast-growing crop from May until the floods hit in November.

But growing chiles, he'd also come to realize, is more than a business—he sees it as a responsibility. "Because everyone eats chiles in daily life," he told me, "I need to make high-quality chiles, clean chiles, to feed everybody—maybe around the world!"

That's not to say it's an easy business. Currently, Vichit sells his *prik khao chi* for around 45 baht per kilogram, or about $1.50. That seems decent, but a few years back, he said, the price was 200 baht per kilo. Meanwhile, he had a half field of *prik kee noo* he wasn't even bothering to harvest—the price was simply too low.

Because out in the countryside, everyone had chiles already. They'd been planted around the house I rented nearby, and they grew wild, too. A bird poops in your yard, and—boom!—you're growing *prik kee noo*, "wild bird-poop chiles." Maybe you'd farm *prik khao chi* for restaurants or city dwellers, but for many Thais, it doesn't make sense to spend hard-earned money on what's freely available out back. Spice is spice is spice.

Well, sort of. Slightly more than 24 hours later, at the opposite end of Thailand, I was facing down a fundamental challenge to that idea, put together by the young, round-faced chef Weerawat "Num" Triyasenawat in the narrow kitchen of his ambitious restaurant, Samuay & Sons, in Udon Thani.

On the counter before us lay five bowls of *som tam*, the mortar-pounded salad of shredded green papaya, chiles, and fermented fish paste that is an icon of Isaan, this inland region along the northeast border with Laos. *Som tam* is also iconically incendiary: you sometimes order it with a number indicating how many chiles to include.

That night, however, we were not just testing our (okay, my) chile tolerance but trying to figure out which variety of chile worked best. Each bowl had been prepared identically, but with different peppers—*prik kee noo suan, prik leung, prik jinda dang,* and smoked *prik kaleang;* the final bowl contained all of the above. Along with Num and me, the judges included three of his female cooks, who giggled as I reached out with my bare hand, pinched a bundle of papaya from the first *som tam,* and popped it gamely in my mouth. Unlike in the south, with its slow-to-build fire, Isaan-style heat hits you right up front, repeatedly, like a Thai kickboxer out for a quick win. Behind each beautiful capsaicin burst lay subtleties—the invigorating freshness of the *prik leung,* the meaty-smokiness of the *prik kaleang.* By the end, I was dripping sweat.

Heat had been a factor in Isaan cooking for ages, Num told me: "Before the chile came to our region, people in ancient times used pepperwood to spice up the dish," along with *makhwaen,* Krachai, and long pepper. (Southern spices like cinnamon and cloves were too expensive for isolated Isaan.) But heat was never just for heat's sake. It worked in concert with the vast orchestra of ingredients found only in this region, many of which I'd never seen before: herbs that were peppery, astringent, lemony, obscure, addictive; foraged mushrooms as dainty as daisies or as massive as porcini; hairy tomatoes.

In fact, this was the whole point of Samuay & Sons, whose tasting menu I leapt into as soon as I'd finished with the *som tam.* Each of chef Num's seven courses highlighted Isaan-specific ingredients and flavors, alongside the world-class technique he'd honed at San Francisco's Michelin-starred Commonwealth. Meaty, thin-shaved prawns were tiled next to a pool of smoked pineapple curry; a morsel of chicken, mango, and yellow curry punched way above its weight. I adored a dense block of "soured fish confit"—fermenty and rich—and its miraculously cooling accompaniment, rice in a watermelon consommé.

Chiles were in there, too, but harder to pinpoint. At first I worried that the *som tam* taste test had blown out my palate. But no —that spice bath had only sharpened my senses. Chef Num had achieved the type of balance that Pim had described to me before I'd set off, deploying chiles that "hurt a little" but then stood humbly aside to let the true stars shine.

When I returned to Bangkok, I felt like I was finally getting a handle on the chilefication of this country. Peppers likely came to Siam in the sixteenth century, brought by the Portuguese and, later, the Spanish. They took off because people were primed to like spice and because chiles grew easily, even wild, so everyone could afford them. Now they were ubiquitous, essential components of every strain of regional Thai cuisine, and getting more popular by the day.[8] A film director, I'd heard, was planning a movie about chileheads, and a candy company was selling "Hell Spicy Jelly," jelly beans that contained Carolina Reapers, one of the world's spiciest peppers.

The future began to look even more fiery one Friday, when I traveled about 100 miles west from Bangkok to the edge of Kaeng Krachan National Park. Just as a soft rain began to fall, I arrived at the farm of Prew Pirom, the 41-year-old owner of Pla Dib, a Bangkok restaurant that happens to be my all-time favorite. Prew wore a broad hat and a round-cheeked, persistent smile as he showed me around: his small, chic home adapted from shipping containers; a pond for raising catfish. Citrus and other fruit trees surrounded half a dozen airy greenhouses, inside which grew eggplants, cucumbers, tomatoes, lettuces, and chiles. Scotch bonnets, to be precise. I did a double take. Jamaica's pride, here in Thailand?

The seeds, Prew explained, were gifts from two foreign friends who'd picked them up in Jamaica. He grew them, offered the chiles to customers on pizza, integrated them into Thai dishes like braised pork leg, and fermented them into a sparkly, fiery sauce —finally, he had a chile that was hot enough for his taste. His capsaicin tolerance, he said, was above average. (Every other Thai I asked said the exact same thing.)

Scotch bonnets, I figured, should have great potential in Thailand, but could they take off? Whoever tried one, Prew posited, would like it. Perhaps he could let birds feast on his Scotch bonnets and have them spread the seeds far and wide. It worked in the sixteenth century; why not now?

Before that future arrives, though, he's got to stabilize his crops. Some of the pepper plants he showed me were small, their leaves a mottled white and yellow, victims of a disease he said had afflicted all peppers in the area. Just like the farmers in Jamaica, Prew was facing the double-edged sword of a warm, moist climate. But then, I thought, maybe a Thai problem needs a Jamaican solution! Right away, I fired off a WhatsApp message to Gary Coulton—could his high-quality seeds help? Could I put him in touch with Prew?

"As we say in Jamaica," Gary wrote back, "'NO PROBLEM, MAN.'"

Finally, it felt like I was no longer chasing history but right in the middle of it. Chiles may have begun their planet-spanning voyage half a millennium ago, but they were nowhere near finished —there were always new lands to conquer, new palates to convert, new routes to crisscross and double back on, new mash-ups of heat profiles to set afire even the smallest acre of bland land. The world is burning, my friends, and it's our delicious privilege—in my case, a duty!—to add fuel to that fire.

Notes

1. Scotchies are a variety of *Capsicum chinense*, a species that includes habaneros, ghost peppers, Trinidad Scorpions, Carolina Reapers, and many other kinds of the world's most insanely spicy chiles.
2. The West Africans who were taken to the New World as slaves were already familiar with chiles. The Portuguese had introduced them on their fifteenth-century voyages, and they were such a widespread part of the diet that they were a part of the "slabber sauce"—basically flour, oil, and chiles—poured over beans that slaves were fed during the Middle Passage.
3. The Turks probably acquired peppers from Arab traders, who'd acquired them in India, where they'd been brought by the Portuguese. Around the same time, peppers were also coming in through Western Europe as ornamental plants grown by monks.
4. Albert Molnár estimated it at 50 percent, but still, that's a lot of non-Hungarian paprika.
5. To be sure, there's plenty of non-spicy food in Thailand, much of it influenced by the ethnic Chinese minority, but even so, chiles remain

present and available nearly everywhere you might possibly consume a meal.

6. The Spanish likely brought chiles, too, though not before 1565, when their Manila Galleon shipping lines started carrying New World goods —primarily silver—to Asia.

7. English spellings of Thai pepper names may differ depending on source.

8. Sugar may have something to do with this. Since the 1930s, its price has dropped. Sugar tends to tame chile heat, so the sweeter the dish, the more chiles you can add. This theory dovetailed with Pim Techamuanvivit's complaint that the food in Bangkok has gotten too sugary since her childhood.

RAHAWA HAILE

I Walked from Selma to Montgomery

FROM *Buzzfeed*

My arrival in selma, Alabama, on April 4, 2017, was less a choice than a matter of self-preservation. Following years of unarmed shootings, bombings, hate crimes, gentrification, voter suppression tactics, pay gaps, school segregation, dwindling reproductive freedoms, refugee bans, jeopardized health care access, and all of the indignities of life in America as a visible Other, I traveled to Selma because the fury in me had nowhere left to grow.

On February 9, 2017, 20 days after President Donald Trump's inauguration, Alabama senator Jeff Sessions was sworn in by Vice President Mike Pence as attorney general. The travesty of that sentence, the sinister potential of it more than a year later, fuels my anxiety still. It is the reason why, mere months after returning from the Appalachian Trail, I emailed my father on February 22, 2017, to see if he might be interested in meeting me in Alabama for a thru-hike of sorts. I wanted to walk from Selma to Montgomery —following in the footsteps of the civil rights marchers who had come before me—to protest Jeff Sessions's entire political career, specifically his most recent and wildly dangerous appointment as the head of the Department of Justice. It had been five days since Scott Pruitt was confirmed by the Senate to lead the Environmental Protection Agency. A week later, Ryan Zinke and the literal horse he rode in on would seize control of the Department of the Interior. Within a year, both Zinke and Pruitt would be responsible for shrinking national monuments sacred to indigenous communities, forcing the entire National Park Service board to resign, removing pages "detailing the risks of climate change" from online resources, perpetuating environmental racism, and implementing so many other disastrous policies—while squandering financial resources—that the rest of this essay could consist of them alone.

I often think of this day, February 22, 2017, when people ask me how it feels to be a black outdoorswoman, what it means to never shrug the reality of my identity from my shoulders in exchange for a backpack and freedom. While the white hikers I'd shared the Appalachian Trail with from Georgia to Maine were busy planning their next adventures, each day in America under the new administration served as a reminder of the myriad ways I'd never be one of them. My feet were bound tighter and tighter by the dual diseases of vanishing civil rights and threatened public lands. The best I could do most days was stand in the pooling blood. I traveled to Selma, Alabama, because I had to, because no other walk on earth made sense to me, or my rage, at a time when walking was the only activity for which my despair made a small hollow. And fam, let's be clear—I did it for us.

Today, Selma, Alabama, hosts an annual Bridge Crossing Jubilee that sees thousands descend upon the city to commemorate "Bloody Sunday" and reflect on the work ahead. Representative John Lewis and Martin Luther King III were among the many to walk across the Edmund Pettus Bridge earlier this March in tribute to the Americans, mostly black, who risked their lives for the right to vote. Every five years, a full reenactment of the walk takes place, with jubilee participants continuing all the way to Montgomery.

At 54 miles, the Selma to Montgomery National Historic Trail is the shortest of America's 19 National Historic Trails, the majority of which (including this one) are meant to be driven, not hiked. At present, no designated safe path exists for pedestrians hoping to walk between the two cities along the dangerous truck route; the road shoulders repeatedly switch sides or disappear altogether, though perhaps this may change someday.

Regardless, my hope was to walk alone on the margins of US Route 80, also known as the Jefferson Davis Highway, for approximately 10 to 12 miles a day—a leisurely pace for a recent thru-hiker that would allow plenty of time for exploration. My father would then pick me up before sunset and drop me back off in the same spot the next morning. We would stay in Selma for two nights as I walked the first 20 miles, followed by Montgomery for two nights as I walked the middle 20 to 25. After I completed the final 10 miles and climbed the steps of the Alabama State Capitol, my father and I would drive back to Atlanta, where we'd flown into initially, he from Miami, and I from New York City.

But a sketch of a plan, no matter how well-intentioned, is only that—a sketch. And I can credit much of my walk's success to the work of an accomplished Japanese American thru-hiker named Liz Thomas (trail name "Snorkel") who walked the Selma to Montgomery NHT in 2015 and has hiked over 15,000 miles around the United States. Hers was the first website I found when researching what a solo walk of this nature would entail, and her blog posts provided me with a treasure trove of data, including a list of mile markers and notes about places to refill water bottles, grab a snack, or duck behind a shed to pee. Granted, a day with Google Maps might have revealed some of these opportunities. But there is no world in which I could have convinced my father to let me walk on the side of a busy highway for five days had I not been able to point to another hiker's similar desire and subsequent success. It helped greatly that she'd created a trail guide with recognizable landmarks he could see and understand. Thomas's foresight to document and share the logistics of her journey for those seeking to walk the same path someday is the kind of outdoor allyship a person like me dreams about and rarely gets to experience.

"There's something profound about walking a trail that was not created because people wanted to have fun and highlight cool natural features—a trail that people walked because they had to," writes Thomas on her website. The two of us spoke on the phone recently about the aspects of her walk that have stuck with her most over the years. "Walking is a political action," said Thomas. "Many people want to treat hiking or walking like they're getting away from politics, and I think—especially for people like me who are pretty good at walking—there's a privilege that comes with hiking in natural areas, but there's also a statement that can be made walking in the places we choose to walk."

As with most conversations about trails, Thomas and I discussed our shoes and foot pain on the Selma to Montgomery NHT at length. Roadwalking might not offer the same challenges as traversing a scree field or ascending slick granite, but it is far from comfortable over long distances. The hardness of the ground tires feet more rapidly than a natural surface like a forest trail would, while the sun bears down on the asphalt relentlessly, adding to the already substantial heat. That said, roadwalking on most highways beats navigating the grass beyond the shoulder, which can slant even more than the canted asphalt in anticipation of rain. This results in walkers extending one leg farther down than the other, approximating a limp that sacrifices stability and strains the opposite leg.

It might surprise some to learn that roadwalks play a significant role in connecting many sections of America's famous long trails. Between 200 and 300 miles of the Florida Trail's 1,100 miles consist of pavement. The Eastern Continental Trail, which spans 5,400 miles from Key West, Florida, to Newfoundland, Canada, and includes the Florida Trail *and* the Appalachian Trail, involves a section simply called "the Alabama Roadwalk."

The wrong footwear can quickly lead to agony. Before arriving in Selma, Thomas accidentally selected a pair of Altra Olympus trail runners that were light but too small for her feet. By the time she reached Montgomery, most of her toenails had turned black in protest after 50 miles of slamming into the front of her shoe. I, on the other hand, chose a pair of low-cut Oboz Sawtooth hiking boots for my walk—overkill for the road, and twice as heavy as the trail runners I should have brought instead. "Still," emphasized Thomas toward the end of our conversation, "I wore shoes that were actually made for walking long distances. To think of the people who marched from Selma to Montgomery in their Sunday best, in fancy [footwear]—it just blew my mind. To have grandmothers and people of all ages doing that."

Thomas wasn't wrong. I had the privilege of dressing comfortably on my first day on the road, in an airy, navy-blue cotton T-shirt with a fake pocket on the left breast and a pair of khaki-colored convertible hiking pants zipped into shorts, the same ones I'd worn on the Appalachian Trail. A few snacks, some sunscreen, and a tube of ChapStick were stashed into one hip-belt pocket of my pack, a knife and a small coil of Leukotape (in case of blisters) were tucked away in the other. A rain jacket and a liter of water rounded out the remaining contents of my bag, while a lemon-lime Gatorade dangled from a shoulder strap's bungee cord positioned over my chest for easy access.

I cannot begin to imagine what drivers must have made of me during my five days along US 80, as I repeatedly stopped to sob on the shoulder of the highway to the songs on a playlist my friend,

the music critic Chris O'Leary, compiled for me. Many of the usual
suspects for a walk from Selma to Montgomery were present. Ma-
halia. Odetta. Nina. But it was Dorothy Love Coates's "Ninety-Nine
and a Half" that brought me to my knees less than seven miles in.

Earlier that day, I'd stopped at the Selma Interpretive Center
after visiting Brown Chapel AME, where the final march to Montgomery began in 1965. I spoke briefly with the National Park Service employees at the center, snagged a "Selma to Montgomery"
patch to sew onto my pack after completing the trail, and stepped
outside, bracing myself for the humidity. A tornado warning had
been in effect less than an hour before, and the high for the day
was 86°F. I was nervous enough to forget not to smile when my father photographed me on the Edmund Pettus Bridge. Despite my
late start at 3 p.m., I wanted to make it to the campground where
the marchers stayed on their first night. Today, camping is not permitted, and a large sign marking the historic occasion stands in
what is essentially the front yard of someone's private property.

It is difficult for those who have not walked across the Edmund
Pettus Bridge to fully understand just how high it sits above the Alabama River. Looking down into the distant, muddy waters brings
a devastating, visceral understanding of the marchers' vulnerabil-
ity on that expanse of concrete and steel—what they were willing
to risk to reach the other side of freedom.

Shortly after crossing, I spotted four monuments arranged in
a row, dedicated to heroes of the march. One honoring Representative John Lewis, his likeness floating above the words GET IN
THE WAY; another dedicated to Amelia Boynton Robinson and
Marie Foster, MOTHERS OF THE CIVIL RIGHTS MOVEMENT BE-
FORE AND BEYOND THE BRIDGE. These monuments and others
like them, presented by the Evelyn Gibson Lowery Heritage Tour
and SCLC/WOMEN, Inc., would serve as some of the high points
of my 54-mile walk, the majority of which felt like a testament to
infrastructure's power to—at times literally—cement racism into
the lives of black communities, regardless of evolving legislation.

In some ways, the subsequent three days of walking were similar to the first. Guzzling water for miles before running into any
building, school, or gas station that would let me use its bathroom. Wrapping my pylon-print bandanna around my nose and
mouth while walking through endless clouds of gnats. I'd treated
my shoes and socks with permethrin, an effective tick, chigger,

and mosquito repellent, in order to minimize my risk of infection while shuffling through stretches of tall grass. I quickly fell into a rhythm during the non-paved sections, scanning the sloping green footpath ahead of me as best I could for snakes, ant mounds, and freshly rotting carcasses. In the beginning, I shut my eyes every time a semitruck seemed as though it was seconds away from plowing into me. By Montgomery, I barely blinked at terror.

The Viola Liuzzo Memorial sits just five miles east of the Lowndes County Interpretive Center, in what is one of the poorest districts in America. The interpretive center, to its credit, does not mince words, spelling out what many of the black tenant farmers in the South lost after the Voting Rights Act was signed into law. White landowners punished their newly liberated occupants by rendering them homeless, resulting in the rise of tent cities that would house black families for years at a time.

I found that the ritual of walking gave me an opportunity to move meaningfully in the present through a place whose importance was so deeply tied to its past. At my pace, I had time to discover how the Selma to Montgomery NHT continues to be shaped by those whose lives run along its borders. In contrast, many careless drivers treat the highway as their garbage dump, and much of the roadside is littered with the detritus of those hurtling through the state at 60-plus miles per hour. A discarded construction glove, an oil canister, several diapers, a peeling bootleg Yo Gotti CD, Heart's greatest hits, a blue ice cube tray, one decapitated broom. More bottles and cans of beer than I consume in a year, with Budweiser empties the most common offenders.

I repeatedly ran into signs on or near the road that offered no explanation as to their meaning but clearly signified something to locals. A green mile marker sported a white rectangle beneath it that read "Prayer Mile." And in the patch of grass opposite the designator for campsite number three, a large sign with a dramatic orange arrow above it stated: ANNIE MAE'S PLACE. BLACK LIVES MATTER. BLACK HISTORY MATTERS. STOP RACISM AND SEXISM. My father and I followed the arrow in search of Annie Mae's Place, to no avail, down a grid of black excellence. A turn onto Frederick Douglass Road. Another onto Langston Hughes Drive. Some backtracking and another turn onto Harriet Tubman Road. A sharp right onto Ida Wells Way. We would later discover we'd driven right past it. A heat wave in 2000 had killed most of the crops grown in nearby residents' gardens, except for okra, so neighbors Alice Stewart and Barbara Evans started an annual Okra Festival for the community. Evans named the small house containing the art she'd collected from around the country Annie Mae's Place. Many of the works highlight the struggle for civil rights, and the Okra Festival still takes place today.

My last day on the Selma to Montgomery NHT would also be my hardest. If you think walking a highway for 50 miles is difficult, try walking against traffic onto an on-ramp for that highway on the day of an air show. I shook for 10 minutes in the chips aisle of a gas station afterward and tried to remind myself of how close I was to completing my walk. I'd left the smell of cow dung from the farms along US 80 behind and properly entered the outskirts of Montgomery, Alabama. An egret in Catoma Creek watched as I ran screaming across the last bridge I'd brave without a walkway.

Less than a mile from the City of St. Jude, the fourth of the marchers' campsites, I approached a tall, gray slab on the sidewalk that resembled a headstone. The monument read: ENTRANCE TO CRADLE OF THE CONFEDERACY. PLACED BY SOPHIE BIBB CHAPTER U.D.C. 1928. Its location next to a local bus stop—the normalcy of it all—left me shaking with anger. Months later, as Confederate monuments were removed in New Orleans and North Carolina, this ominous slab was the one my mind drifted to. Even in 2017, the Selma to Montgomery National Historic Trail still had to put up with this shit.

Interpretive signs placed by the City of Montgomery lead walkers along the remaining miles toward the state capitol. One sign describes how highway construction destroyed historic black neighborhoods in the area, as it did black communities around the country. The intersection of Mildred and Moore Streets, one of Montgomery's former black business hubs, stood deserted. In a walk predicated on all that the civil rights marchers had gained, everything black communities had lost in the years afterward lay equally apparent.

The Rosa Parks Museum was closed when I walked past. One block separated it from the Jefferson Davis Apartments, a low-income-housing complex for seniors in a city that is more than 55 percent black. Black footsteps had been painted upon the wide, gray crosswalk facing the Alabama State Capitol to honor those who walked from Selma over 50 years ago. Sitting opposite the crosswalk was another monument, built in 1942 and paid for by the Sophie Bibb Chapter of the United Daughters of the Confederacy. It commemorated Jefferson Davis's inauguration as president of the Confederacy. All around me, the distant past fought the near past for dominance. A reckoning was nowhere to be found.

I climbed the steps of the Alabama State Capitol on April 9, 2017, the day Robert E. Lee surrendered to Ulysses S. Grant in 1865—roughly 100 years before Martin Luther King Jr. asked, "How long? Not long"—and blinked back tears. Walking, even when challenging, had been the easy part: I had no idea how we'd endure the rest of the year.

Ultimately, the line between hiking and walking is thinner than most would imagine. Both activities can empower, but only one is accessible to the majority of the American population. We walk to protest. We walk to remember. We walk to demand better. Despite what outdoor magazine covers emphasize, our intentions always matter more than the nature of the terrain that carries them.

When I first told friends of my plan to walk from Selma to Montgomery, most thought I'd lost my mind. It made less sense to them than my desire to thru-hike the Appalachian Trail. A roadwalk along a highway in rural Alabama months into our fresh hell —why? When several of them asked if I was afraid, I did my best to explain the fear was the point. That their fear for me was the fear I lived with every day.

I did not tell anyone that maybe I needed to walk into oncoming traffic for 54 miles—those 54 miles—to see people choosing not to kill me each day. That perhaps I could walk my way to reclaiming enough of an illusion of safety to survive the next four years in this country. And that it would have to be enough for now.

Morsi the Cat

FROM *The New Yorker*

NATASHA WAS THE FIRST of our daughters to get bitten by a rodent. It probably happened while she was sleeping, but she was too small to communicate anything. As with Ariel, her identical twin sister, Natasha's early vocabulary was mostly English, but the girls used Egyptian Arabic for certain things—colors, animals, basic sustenance. *Aish* for "bread," *maya* for "water." If I twirled one of them around, she would laugh and shriek, *"Tani!"*: "Again!" And then her sister would pick up the refrain, because anything that was done to one twin had to be repeated with the other. *Tani, tani, tani.* They weren't yet two years old.

I noticed the mark while changing Natasha. To the right of her navel, there were two pairs of ugly red puncture holes: incisors. Perhaps the animal had been nosing around the top of her diaper. If Natasha had cried out, neither I nor my wife, Leslie, heard.

We had moved to Cairo in October 2011, during the first year of the Arab Spring. We lived in Zamalek, a neighborhood on a long, thin island in the Nile River. Zamalek has traditionally been home to middle- and upper-class Cairenes, and we rented an apartment on the ground floor of an old building that, like many structures on our street, was beautiful but fading. Out in front of the Art Deco façade, the bars of a wrought-iron fence were shaped like spiderwebs.

The spiderweb motif was repeated throughout the building. Little black webs decorated our front door, and the balconies and porches had webbed railings. The elevator was accessed through iron spiderweb gates. Behind the gates, rising and falling in the darkness of an open shaft, was the old-fashioned elevator box, made of heavy carved wood, like some Byzantine sarcophagus. The gaps in the webbed gates were as large as a person's head, and it was possible to reach through and touch the elevator as it drifted past. Not long after we moved in, a child on an upper floor got his leg caught in the elevator, and the limb was broken so badly that he was evacuated to Europe for treatment.

Safety had never been a high priority in old Cairo neighborhoods, but things were especially lax during the revolution. Electricity blackouts were common, and every now and then we had a day without running water. A pile of garbage next to the building attracted mice and rats. Below the windows of my daughters' room, I had seen weasels scurrying into a hole in the building's foundation.

At a medical clinic, a pediatrician examined the marks on Natasha's stomach. "Insect," she said.

I was incredulous. "That's an insect bite?"

"Maybe it was a flea," she said.

I sent a photograph to a family friend at a dermatology clinic in the United States. The response made me nostalgic for the American ability to apply cheerful language to any situation:

> Hi! We discussed in case conference today—all agreed . . . bite as fang by snake/rodent—hope this helps. Hope both are doing well. Hugs, Susie.

Leslie and I took a cab to the west bank of the Nile, where a vaccination center called Vacsera sold us a rabies vaccine. Then we found a new pediatrician. I also bought about a dozen glue traps.

At night, I set traps beneath the cribs. Sometimes I awoke to the sound of the twins' voices: "Daddy, mouse! Daddy, mouse!" Once, something rattled in their toy kitchen, so I opened the tiny refrigerator door, and a mouse popped out. How the hell had it got in there? None of the mice I trapped seemed big enough to have made the bite marks, but they kept coming—*tani, tani, tani.* I drowned them one by one in a bucket of water.

When it was Ariel's turn to get bitten, the mark appeared on her back instead of on her stomach. Otherwise, it was identical to Natasha's: four incisors. We took another cab to Vacsera.

I was finished with traps. Leslie and I visited an expat who was giving away a male and a female cat. The choice was easy: the male was bigger, with a fierce expression, and he stalked lithely around the furniture. On his forehead, tiger stripes formed the shape of an *M*—a mark of the breed that's known as the Egyptian Mau.

We named him Morsi. Egypt had just held its first-ever democratic presidential election, which had been won by Mohamed Morsi, a leader of the Muslim Brotherhood. Not long after Morsi the cat arrived, he bit Leslie's arm hard enough to leave his own set of puncture wounds. *Tani*—back to Vacsera. After a year in Cairo, I was the only member of the family who hadn't received rabies shots.

Leslie and I met in Beijing, where we worked as journalists. We came from very different backgrounds: she was born in New York, the daughter of Chinese immigrants, whereas I had grown up in mid-Missouri. But some similar restlessness had motivated both of us to go abroad, first to Europe and then to Asia. By the time we left China together, in 2007, we had lived almost our entire adult lives overseas.

We made a plan: we would move to rural Colorado, as a break from urban life, and we hoped to have a child. Then we would go to live in the Middle East. We liked the idea of writing about another country with a deep history and a rich language, and we wanted this to be our first experience as a family.

All of it was abstract—the kid, the country. Maybe we'd go to Egypt, maybe Syria. Maybe a boy, maybe a girl. What difference did it make? An editor in New York warned me that Egypt, where Hosni Mubarak had ruled for almost 30 years, might seem too sluggish after China. "Nothing changes in Cairo," he said. But I liked the sound of that. I looked forward to studying Arabic in a country where nothing happened.

The first disruption to our plan occurred when one kid turned into two. In May 2010, Ariel and Natasha were born prematurely, and we wanted to give them 12 months to grow before moving. The schedule didn't matter—a year in a newborn's life is a rush compared with never-changing Cairo. But, when protests broke out on Tahrir Square, our girls were 8 months old, and they were exactly 18 days older when Mubarak was overthrown.

We delayed and reconsidered, but finally we decided to go. We applied for life insurance, and the company carried out a medical screening but then rejected us on account of "extensive travel." We visited a lawyer and wrote up wills. We moved out of our rental house; we put our possessions in storage; we gave away our car. We didn't ship a thing—whatever we took on the plane was whatever we would have.

The day before we left, we got married. Leslie and I had never bothered with formalities; neither of us had any desire to organize a wedding. But we read somewhere that if a couple has different surnames the Egyptian authorities could make it difficult to acquire joint-residence visas. We left the babies with a sitter and drove to the Ouray County Courthouse. As the deputy county clerk started the ceremony, Leslie asked when the department that handled traffic violations would close.

"Four o'clock," the clerk said.

Leslie looked at her watch. "Can you hold on a minute?"

She ran upstairs to pay one last speeding ticket. The marriage license noted that we "did join in the Holy Bonds of Matrimony" at 4:08:44 p.m. I shoved the license into our luggage. The next day, along with our 17-month-old twins, we boarded the plane. Neither Leslie nor I had ever been to Egypt.

After Morsi arrived, the mice vanished. He ate the heads of a couple, leaving the bodies behind, and others stopped showing up. The coat markings of Egyptian Maus resemble those of cats that are portrayed on the walls of ancient tombs, and even the name is old: in pharaonic times, *mau* meant "cat." Maus are agile, and they are characterized by a flap of skin that extends from the flank to the hind leg, which allows for greater extension. These house cats have been clocked at speeds of up to 30 miles per hour.

The toddlers, like the mice, learned to give Morsi a wide berth. He had no patience for their chattering and tail-pulling, and he scratched each of them hard enough to draw blood. This was handled efficiently: one attack on Ariel, one attack on Natasha. Leslie and I thought about having Morsi declawed, but it would have put him at a disadvantage against the neighborhood's rodents and stray cats.

It was impossible to keep him inside. He was strong enough to open screen windows and doors, and he hid around the apartment's entrance, waiting for an opportunity to dart out. Often I'd hear cat screams within minutes of his escape. We had a small garden, where strays liked to gather, but Morsi refused to tolerate them. Many times, I saw him drive some scraggly animal out through a gap in the spiderweb fence.

Sayyid, the neighborhood garbageman, warned me that somebody might grab Morsi. "He's a beautiful cat," Sayyid said. *"Qot beladi."* People often used this phrase—"a cat of the country"—when they saw Morsi and his stripes. Egyptians are believed to have been the first cat breeders in history, and they loved the animals so much that they forbade their export more than 37 centuries ago. They used to call Phoenicians "cat thieves," because the seafarers snatched them for their ships.

In our building, an elderly woman on the fourth floor was the self-appointed cat carer, and she put out bowls of food for the animals. She always greeted me with a smile when I took the girls out for walks in their double stroller. Egyptians are even crazier about small children than they are about cats, and we attracted attention in Zamalek. Certain faces stood out: a one-eyed doorman, a tea deliveryman with a broken nose, a shopkeeper who liked talking to the twins in Arabic.

When the girls got bigger, they started throwing tantrums if their outfits didn't match. Leslie and I didn't want to dress them alike, but we were so overwhelmed by the adjustment to Egypt that we quickly caved. We bought everything in pairs, and when the girls sat side by side in their stroller, wearing matching clothes, it felt like a kind of show.

Foreigners sometimes asked if I had seen "those other Zamalek twins." They were legendary: elderly Egyptian brothers who walked together around the island. They always dressed identically: nice jackets, button-front shirts. A couple of times, I tried to strike up a conversation, but the men ignored me. They never so much as glanced at the girls. Whenever we crossed paths—old twins, young twins; twins on foot, twins on wheels—I wondered how my kids were going to turn out after this odd childhood on the Nile.

Something about Zamalek's geography, and its old-money residents, seemed to draw out an Egyptian flair for eccentricity. The island is situated in the heart of the city, but the river creates a powerful sense of separation. Even on days of major demonstrations, it was easy to forget that Tahrir was only a mile and a half away. I often saw Zamalek residents watching the revolution on television, as if the images had been beamed in from some distant land.

Most people had no interest in getting involved. Sayyid told me cautionary tales about certain figures, like the one-eyed doorman. During a demonstration, the doorman walked to a street near Tahrir, where he decided to watch from an overpass. That was a mistake: when Egyptian police disperse crowds, they often fire their shotguns into the air. The doorman got hit with bird shot and lost his eye, and that was the last time he went to a protest.

"Your Brotherhood cat is doing a terrible job as president," Sayyid often said. The local veterinarian was a Coptic Christian, like approximately 10 percent of the country's population, and he feigned anger the first time Leslie brought Morsi in. "I hate this name," the vet said, grabbing the cat. Morsi fought fiercely whenever the Copt clipped his claws.

Soon the twins started differentiating between "the good Morsi" and "the bad Morsi." They picked this up from their nanny, Atiyat, who was also a Copt. Atiyat's opinion was hardly surprising: years before, Morsi had declared that neither a woman nor a Christian should be allowed to lead Egypt, and the country was a mess under his government. Half a year into his presidency, at the beginning of 2013, we received a notice from the girls' nursery school:

> Due to the heavy smell of tear gas in Zamalek at the moment. We think it is safer for the children not to come to school today . . . We are terribly sorry for the very short notice, but it is strictly out of our hands.

I started stashing large amounts of cash around the apartment. If things got violent, I had plans for an emergency departure: what we would pack, how we would get to the airport. By now, the protests were almost constant, and we lost electricity several times a day. The government announced a policy of dimming the lights in the airport; there were hardly any tourists. Whenever I returned from a trip, I touched down in the Morsi-era twilight zone: darkened hallways, frozen escalators. *It is strictly out of our hands.*

One morning, I went to renew our visas at Mogamma, the government building beside Tahrir. I chose a day when there weren't any protests, but the area still reeked of tear gas; by now, it seemed as if the flagstones had become so soaked with the stuff that they sweated it out in the heat. I handed our applications to an official.

"Where is your marriage license?" he said.

This was what mattered at such a time? Even more absurd was how pleased I felt: I was so happy that we had got married! I returned to Zamalek and retrieved the Ouray County license. The official seemed just as pleased as me; the visas were processed without a hitch.

When the coup finally came, in July 2013, none of my planning mattered. General Abdel Fattah El-Sisi, the minister of defense, issued a statement that gave Morsi 48 hours to respond to the demands of protesters. Morsi had a reputation for stubbornness, and it seemed impossible that he would negotiate.

On the day that everybody knew would be the last of the Morsi presidency, Atiyat arrived with her fingernails painted in the colors of the Egyptian flag. She took out some red, black, and yellow crayons, and she instructed the twins in the production of little flags. Should my three-year-olds be celebrating a military coup in advance? But I was too distracted to think about it; soon I would have to leave to cover the day's events.

Leslie and I ran through scenarios: What if it's impossible to make it home tonight, or if the cell-phone system goes down? What if things get violent? We decided that, in the event of gunfire, the safest place in the apartment was the interior hallway. That was the plan: shut the doors, stay close to the floor.

There was always a plan. Old plans had a way of becoming irrelevant, but new plans were easy to make, and Leslie and I often had other versions of this conversation. Once, the nursery school canceled class because the police found a terrorist dummy bomb a block away. Another time, an ISIS-affiliated group kidnapped a foreigner on the outskirts of Cairo and beheaded him.

Before moving to Egypt, I had imagined that we would establish clear protocols: if *x* happens, then we will respond by doing *y*. This was how embassies operated; during the summer of the coup, the American Embassy in Cairo evacuated all nonessential personnel. But once we were living in the city, without a connection to any institution, I realized that we were more likely to respond as Cairenes did, with flexibility and rationalization. People talked about the events calmly, and they maintained a sense of distance — *it is strictly out of our hands*. They told jokes. They focused on the little things they could control. Even a newcomer learned to normalize almost any situation. It was a dummy bomb, not a real bomb. The kidnapped foreigner was an oil worker, not a journalist. It happened only once. If it happens again, then we'll worry.

And the difficulties of everyday life kept people occupied. Things went wrong all the time, and usually it had nothing to do with politics. Our Arabic teacher died suddenly, because of poor medical care. The shopkeeper who chatted with the girls was shot and killed near his home, reportedly after trying to mediate some dispute. One day not long after the coup, the elderly cat carer on the fourth floor put out some food. She called to a cat on the landing below, but the animal didn't come. So she poked her head through a gap in the spiderweb gate, in order to look down through the elevator shaft. Above her, on one of the upper levels, the Byzantine box was motionless.

At that moment, on the ground floor, somebody pushed the call button.

Afterward, the police interrogated the doorman, and he either quit or was fired. As far as I could tell, he hadn't been at fault, but he made for an easy scapegoat. The landlady also had wire screens installed behind the spiderweb gates. On the fourth floor, the family of the elderly woman played recorded Quranic chants for months, to put her soul at peace. Leslie and I told Atiyat and our other sitters never to allow the twins to go on the landing unattended. During this time of violent headlines, one of the things that scared me most was the elevator outside my front door.

One winter, Morsi left and didn't come back. The morning after he disappeared, five ugly strays were lounging in the sun on our balcony. I wondered if Morsi had finally lost a fight, and I tossed water at the strays until they left. But still he didn't return. I remembered Sayyid's warning about somebody grabbing the cat.

The girls were upset. By now, they were big enough so that Morsi tolerated their presence; occasionally, he even showed affection. In the evenings, I walked the streets, saying, "Morsi! Morsi! Morsi!" People looked at me strangely. I was becoming another Zamalek eccentric, the foreigner who wandered the island at night, calling out for the deposed president.

Around this time, Leslie and I realized that we should stop discussing politics in front of the girls. During one of our trips to see family in the US, an uncle asked Ariel about her pet. "There is another Morsi who is a man, not a cat," Ariel said. "He was the president."

The uncle asked where Morsi was now.

"He is in prison."

"Why?"

"He sent some people to kill some other people," Ariel said, matter-of-factly. "There's another president now. I don't know if he is bad or good. But his name is Sisi."

Morsi, Sisi: I had a theory that it's a bad sign when Egyptian leaders sound like pets. After the great age of pyramid-building ended, in the twenty-fifth century BC, the pharaohs who followed had names that seem "babyish" to our ears, as the Egyptologist Toby Wilkinson noted. During this period of declining authority, many kings could have been cats: Pepi, Teti, Nebi, Izi, Ini, Iti. Ibi built an itty-bitty pyramid, only 60 feet tall, but he didn't even put the stone casing on top. Pepi II ran the country into the ground. When an expedition to the south reported the discovery of a Pygmy, this ineffective pharaoh responded as if he had glimpsed something shiny: "My Majesty wants to see this Pygmy more than the tribute of the Sinai and Punt!"

Someday, I thought, historians would view our current age as another example of bad-cat politics, crude and fable-like. Once upon a time, Morsi was in power, then Sisi drove him out like a stray in the garden. Then more than a thousand protesters were massacred in a brutal crackdown. Then Morsi was placed inside a cage in a courtroom, where he was tried for murder and treason. Could anybody blame a child for confusing these political figures with animals?

On the fifth day after Morsi's disappearance, I heard him mewing weakly. From our garden, I looked up and realized that he was stranded on an upper balcony. He had climbed there on the limb of a tree.

Leslie went up to the apartment. The woman who lived there refused to open the door, and she stood silently on the other side while Leslie introduced herself. Then the woman finally spoke. She threatened to call the police.

"She doesn't like to see people," the doorman told me. He said that the woman was probably afraid of the cat. He made an

Egyptian gesture, tapping his head, rolling his eyes, and whistling: crazy.

The landlady also had no interest in dealing with the recluse. "Let's talk about this tomorrow," she said. For an hour, Leslie and I engaged in intense negotiations with the landlady, her daughter, and two doormen; finally, the six of us gathered outside the recluse's apartment. It was after 9 p.m. The woman opened the door partway.

She pointed at me. "You can come inside," she said. Then she pointed at Leslie and glared: "But not you!"

The place was cleaner than I expected. The woman was nice-looking, and she wore an elaborate dressing gown that made me think of Miss Havisham. I opened the balcony door and Morsi streaked across the apartment and leapt into Leslie's arms. I thanked the woman, but she ignored me. She was still staring fiercely at Leslie. She slammed the door.

"Do you have any idea what that was all about?" I asked.

"No," Leslie said.

At home, Morsi slept for most of three days. Sometimes he went to the sink and sucked on the faucet. The reclusive woman hired some workers to chop down every tree branch that was remotely close to her balcony. For good measure, they left the debris strewn around our garden.

We bought a new Honda sedan. In eastern Cairo, we scheduled a meeting with an agent at the insurance company Allianz, but at the last minute he called to say that he couldn't make it, because he had just totaled his vehicle. Another agent stepped in. While handling our application, she mentioned that she herself no longer qualified for auto insurance from Allianz, because she had had multiple accidents every year for three consecutive years. She handed us a glossy brochure that read "Our own data shows that six out of every ten cars purchased in Egypt will either be crashed, damaged, or stolen."

I paid for the auto insurance. They had a much better sales strategy than the life-insurance people in Colorado.

We took road trips to the Red Sea, to the Mediterranean, to Upper Egypt. The first time we visited ancient sites in Upper Egypt, in the south, the girls were transformed. They became obsessed with Akhenaten and Nefertiti, the king and queen who ruled during the fourteenth century BC. The connection had something to do with the names—one *A*, one *N*—but it was also the twinned iconography. Akhenaten and Nefertiti ruled with unusually equal status, and they were often portrayed together.

Such pairings run throughout ancient Egyptian art, theology, and politics: Osiris and Isis, Horus and Seth, king and queen, male and female, Upper and Lower, life and death. Antony and Cleopatra (and their twin offspring). Ray Johnson, an Egyptologist who directs the University of Chicago's research center in Luxor, told me that he believed the original inspiration was the divided landscape: the lush Nile Valley next to barren desert. Whatever the source, it touches something deep in the human imagination, and after the twins' first visit to ancient sites they suddenly insisted on different outfits. Ariel, as Akhenaten, wore pants; Natasha wore dresses. We never worried about matching outfits again; the Eighteenth Dynasty had convinced the girls in a way that we never could have.

The long drives were as relaxing as anything I did in Egypt. Outside Cairo, politics disappeared; most places had experienced little or no violence during the Arab Spring. The tourist sites were largely abandoned. One year, we drove all the way to Abu Simbel, near the border of Sudan, and for the final stretch the police required us to join an armed convoy. But after 10 minutes the escort sped off, at more than a hundred miles an hour. Probably the officers had become bored; there wasn't any real risk in these remote places.

For nearly three hours, we drove through desert solitude. To the east, I saw bright pools of blue, which I assumed were inlets of Lake Nasser. But then I realized that the pools were mirages—I had never seen natural illusions that looked so real. Some of them had rocks poking up from the center, like islands in a lake.

When we arrived at Abu Simbel, we were the only visitors. The girls ran to the massive statues of Ramses the Great, and they played in the darkened halls of the temple. They were now five, and I had photographed them at ancient sites across the country. In almost every photograph, they were alone. I knew that someday these images would also feel mirage-like—twins in Abydos, twins in Esna, twins in the Valley of the Kings. Two tiny spots of pink on a plain, gazing up at the Colossi of Memnon.

*

As part of the ancient Egyptians' twinned worldview, there were two words for time: *neheh* and *djet*. Scholars told me that modern people probably can't fully grasp these concepts. We're accustomed to linear time, with one event leading to another: a revolution, then a coup. The accumulation of these events, and the actions of the people who matter, is what makes history.

But ancient Egyptians never wrote history in the way that we would define it. Events—*kheperut*—were suspect, because they interrupted natural order. Instead, Egyptians lived in *neheh*, "the time of cycles." *Neheh* is associated with the sun, the seasons, and the annual flooding of the Nile. It repeats; it recurs; it renews. *Djet*, on the other hand, is "time without motion." When a pharaoh dies, he passes into *djet*, which is the time of the gods, the temples, and the pyramids. Mummification is a human response to *djet*, and so is art. Something in *djet* time is finished but not past; it exists forever in the present.

The years I spent in Egypt felt like the longest of my life. Outside in the city, governments came and went; inside the apartment, my children became unrecognizable from the toddlers we had brought to Cairo. As they grew, I realized that small children must come closest to living the time of the ancients. Things are repeated, in the manner of *neheh:* games, words, bedtime routines. *Tani, tani, tani.* And then there's *djet*, the eternal present. My daughters had no concept of our life before Egypt, and they had no sense that it would ever end. They never questioned whether we belonged there. I often felt the stress of wanting to protect them, but their sense of normalcy was also reassuring. In Natasha's first-grade journals, blackouts were simply part of *neheh:*

> December 15, 2015—I was reading a book in night time when the electricity turned off.
> December 20, 2015—I went to the pyramids and we went inside. It was dark.
> December 27, 2015—I was done with breakfast when the lights went away.

The twins often told people that they were Egyptian. They had the body language of little Cairenes: for an emphatic "no," they said *"la'a,"* with a brisk shake of the head and a wave of the hand. Like virtually all Egyptians, they feared cold, rain, and silence.

They talked constantly; it was impossible for the weather to be too hot for them. Once, a friend visited from Germany, and he thought it was hilarious that these Chinese Americans kept saying, "We love Cairo!" But, for them, Egypt was *um al-duniya*, "the mother of the world."

During our last year, we went to Jerusalem, where we toured underground sections of the Western Wall. At the site of some ancient cisterns, the guide asked the girls, "Where does water come from?"

"The Nile," Natasha said. The guide tried to nudge them toward the right answer, but they just stared blankly. According to Toby Wilkinson, in the entire corpus of ancient Egyptian literature the word "cloud" appears twice.

We left Cairo in the summer of 2016. We had lived there for half a decade, and now, in an election year, it seemed right to return to the US. After Morsi and Sisi, I looked forward to living in a country where the president behaved responsibly.

For the last month, the girls cried virtually every day. They cried about saying goodbye to Atiyat, to their school, to their bedroom. They worried about their cat staying behind. As far as they were concerned, leaving Egypt was the worst thing that Leslie and I had ever done to them.

Back in Ridgway, Colorado, we rented a double-wide trailer high in the mountains, surrounded by a forest of cedar. As the evenings grew cooler, field mice streamed into the double-wide. I started buying glue traps.

That fall, the second-grade class at Ridgway Elementary was given a writing assignment in which each student was asked to imagine a new name. Ariel wrote, "I wish my name was Ackananen because it is an old pharose name and it reminds me of Egypt." At an event for parents, a father with a rural accent asked me where we had moved from. He laughed at my answer. "You know, my kid told me there are two Egyptian girls in his class," he said. "I just figured he was lying."

Morsi was extradited from the Republic of Egypt at 2:20 in the morning on November 13, 2016, aboard Lufthansa Flight 581. Prior to transport, he was injected with three milligrams of diazepam and placed in a cat carrier. The veterinarian estimated that he would be unconscious for 10 hours. The product description for the cat carrier included the words "sturdy construction."

After we left Egypt as a family, our flight connected in the United Kingdom, which has strict rules about animals being transported through its airports. So Morsi boarded with a friend in Cairo until Leslie returned for research. Periodically, the friend sent updates. The first read, "I've also found he is a bit of an escape artist, and so I have been making modifications to my apartment." Then: "He can open my windows and balcony doors even with the addition of screens with sliding locks." Finally: "He's had feline company from vaccinated adult cats on and off, but I should warn you that he doesn't seem to like it. Morsi is quite aggressive toward other cats."

After the sedative was administered, Leslie caught a cab. Morsi woke up before they reached the Cairo airport. There was no problem going through security, but now he was making noise.

The flight departed on time. Leslie placed the carrier beneath her seat and fell asleep. At approximately three o'clock in the morning, she was jolted awake by the sound of people yelling, "Get that cat! Somebody grab that cat!" It's unclear how many other passengers were also awakened. But the ones who were conscious saw a small Chinese woman chasing a large Egyptian cat while shouting the name of a Muslim Brother who had been in prison for more than three years.

She caught him near the bathrooms. A German flight attendant was angry in the way that only German flight attendants can be angry. "What if somebody is allergic to cats?" she said repeatedly. But Leslie was more concerned about the carrier. Morsi had completely obliterated the thing.

She sat down with the squirming cat on her lap. After this flight, she was scheduled for a layover of 7 hours and 30 minutes, followed by a flight of 10 hours and 20 minutes, a layover of 6 hours and 30 minutes, a flight of an hour and 5 minutes, and a ride in a van.

The man in the next seat liked cats. He held Morsi for a while. Later he emailed to request Morsi photographs to show his kids.

In Frankfurt airport, Leslie walked around holding the cat until she found a shop that sold a hard-shell carrier. For the final flight, it was necessary to buy a soft container. All told, it took three cat carriers to get Morsi from Cairo to Ridgway.

On Morsi's first day as a Colorado trailer cat, he curled up with the girls on the couch. Soon headless mice started to appear. The first time it snowed, I threw open the door and told Morsi to run as far as he wanted into the forest. He crept up to the powder, sniffed it, and went back to the couch.

A Visit to Chernobyl:
Travel in the Postapocalypse

FROM *Rick Steves' Europe*

"AND NOW WE will stop at the abandoned Kapachi village school
to experience some radiation hot spots." This is something I've
never heard a tour guide say before. And I don't really welcome it
now, truth be told. I'm on a rural road near the Ukrainian town of
Chernobyl, a few short miles from the site of the worst accident in
humankind's brief history of splitting the atom. I came here will-
ingly. I *paid* to come here. But at this moment, I'm questioning the
wisdom of that decision.

The Tour

We hurtle toward Chernobyl on a tightly packed minibus, far faster
than is comfortable on rutted country roads through the dewy
postdawn hours—drawing nearer, ever nearer, to the ominously
named "Exclusion Zone." I think back on a lazy summer barbecue
a few months before, when I casually mentioned to some friends
that I was thinking of visiting Chernobyl. Mouths dropped open
and faces turned white, as our lighthearted evening pivoted into a
full-blown intervention. They pleaded and begged me, for the love
of all that's holy, *not to go.* Only Karl—who I suspect doesn't like
me very much—was supportive of the idea.

Undeterred, I stuck with the plan and booked a $100, all-day
tour by minibus from Kiev to Chernobyl. This morning I had shown
up promptly at 7:30 a.m. at Kiev's gritty train station. In the KFC
parking lot, I met my tour group: a twentysomething couple from

Austria, a gregarious bald Dutchman, a well-to-do retired couple
from Seattle's Eastside, and a tattooed bloke from Manchester who
inexplicably wore shorts in spite of the chilly temperatures.

Now, bouncing recklessly in my springy seat, I look out the
minibus window over a flat landscape with little definition: fields
of wilted, unharvested sunflowers; peekaboo views of the dammed
Dnieper River, which fills its broad basin like a great lake; and the
occasional forest of skinny pine trees that recede infinitely—a
haunting house of mirrors. It feels like we're driving to the very
edge of the civilized world, toward the edge of the treasure map
marked "Here There Be Monsters." At one point, an hour and a
half outside of Kiev, we pass a lonely rural bus stop—so remote it's
hard to imagine who might possibly catch a bus there.

Our guide is dressed in a faux-military uniform. With his fa-
tigues, his furry neck beard, his strong features, and his flat-topped
cap, he's the spitting image of a young Fidel Castro. I assume his
getup is intentional—designed to tinge the experience with even
more Cold War nostalgia.

The Accident

Our guide—who has a generic Ukrainian name like Yuri or
Volodymyr, but whom I've decided to call "Fidel"—is comfortingly
knowledgeable. As we drive, he explains the history of the event:
The V. I. Lenin Nuclear Power Station was built in the 1970s as a
jewel in the crown of USSR technological achievement. A couple
of miles away, they also built the planned workers' town of Pripyat,
where nearly 50,000 people lived in one of Ukraine's most desirable communities.

In the middle of the night of April 25, 1986, a perfect storm of
design flaws and human error brought about a catastrophic systems failure at the Chernobyl plant's Reactor No. 4. A plume of
radioactive matter was ejected high into the air and drifted north,
across Belarus and the Baltics, before finally being detected at a
power plant in Sweden. It was only then—a full two days after the
accident, when the Swedes called Gorbachev and said, "Um, we
think maybe you have a serious problem"—that the Soviet authorities publicly acknowledged the meltdown.

With the catastrophe out of the bag, the USSR scrambled to

contain the damage. They sealed off an "exclusion zone" around the plant—at first 10 kilometers, later expanding to 30 kilometers—and evacuated tens of thousands of people from Pripyat and the surrounding villages. Firefighters, miners, and a half million Soviet soldiers were mobilized. It took them two weeks to extinguish the fire at the core of the reactor; within seven months, a containment "sarcophagus" had been installed over the meltdown site.

An untold number of responders (or, as they're called, "liquidators") spent the rest of their lives grappling with health problems. While the official number of deaths stemming directly from the meltdown is in the double digits, the radiation is thought to be ultimately responsible for deaths numbering in the thousands —or tens of thousands, or perhaps even hundreds of thousands— mostly from increased rates of thyroid cancer, leukemia, and other ailments. To this day, people living within the blast radius, who lack the resources to relocate, raise their children on food and milk contaminated with toxic levels of radiation. The legacy of Chernobyl is far from over.

But the legacy of the liquidators is that today, many parts of the Chernobyl area are safe to visit—provided you're accompanied by a guide who knows which hot spots are best avoided. Fidel outlines the ground rules: avoid touching or setting personal effects down on any surface within the Exclusion Zone; don't take anything home with you; and wear long pants and long sleeves at all times. (Hearing this, the shorts-wearing Mancunian sheepishly reaches into his backpack and pulls on a pair of sweatpants.)

Oh, and if you encounter any cute, curious foxes sniffing around in the woods, keep well clear. Some of them are rabid. There have been some . . . incidents. And, you must understand, it would be best not to repeat these.

The Exclusion Zone

We approach the first checkpoint, at the boundary of the 30-Kilometer Exclusion Zone, and have our passports checked—a mercifully brief exercise in bureaucratic posturing with machine guns. Soon after, we pull over on a gravel shoulder in the middle of nowhere.

Stepping out of the minibus, we're greeted by three gregarious stray dogs. Having been warned about those rabid foxes, I recoil. But Fidel points out that these dogs are healthy: well fed, vaccinated, and with tags in their ears. "You can even pet them," he says. "But, uh, wash your hands after. Their fur may be contaminated."

He means radioactive. Their fur may be *radioactive*. Hands in pockets, hands in pockets.

With our trio of mascots in tow, Fidel walks us through a dense forest. Soon, ruined houses begin to emerge from between the trees. "This was the village of Zalyssa," he tells us. "It was evacuated after the accident, and never repopulated. The three thousand or so inhabitants were resettled to a new village in a different part of Ukraine."

First, radiation overtook Zalyssa. Then came the slow onslaught of nature. It's astonishing to see how quickly a tidy community of businesses and homes, once deserted, is enveloped by brush and trees. If I didn't know better, I'd say this place was abandoned a century ago—and certainly not within my lifetime.

We head up an overgrown path, once a paved street, past rusted cars and ramshackle cabins. The community hall still echoes with an endearing village pride. Stucco garlands ring the ceiling, directing the eye to a little stage at one end of the room. It's easy to imagine this hall, 40 years ago, filled with revelers at a wedding reception, or with concerned farmers at a meeting of the collective. But today, the windows are mostly broken, the decor is weathered, and in a darkened corner of the stage, sinister black mold spreads unchecked. A cheery red banner preaches a sickeningly ironic message: "All hail communism—the bright future of all humankind!"

In the next room, the floorboards have been pried up, revealing a subfloor of chimney-like brick stacks and a few lonely joists. "Looting is a big issue here," Fidel says. "People harvest wood and scrap metal from these buildings to sell on the black market. If you buy certain things at a flea market in Kiev, you have to wonder if it's radioactive." I imagine some poor, unfortunate Ukrainian hipster renovating a stylish urban flat with reclaimed wood floors and vintage fixtures.

As we hop on the bus and wave goodbye to our canine friends, Fidel explains, "The dogs are very nice, as you can see, and local people take care of them as well as they can. In fact, there's a charity for getting Chernobyl's stray dogs adopted in the United States. But . . ." He shrugs, matter-of-factly. "These dogs will probably be eaten by the packs of wolves who roam here in the winter." Driving onward, all I can think is: *wild carnivorous radioactive wolves.*

Just beyond Zalyssa, as we drive past the jaunty WELCOME TO CHERNOBYL sign—topped with the local symbol, a friendly atom —I reflexively check my dosimeter. But the radiation levels here are about the same as in Kiev.

The Radiation

Walking around with a radiation dosimeter clipped to your belt is fascinating. Having spent a day doing it here, I'm inclined to try it at home.

Like most Americans (at least, those barbecue interventionists), I think of radiation in black-and-white terms: It's bad, full stop. But visiting Chernobyl cultivates a more pragmatic way of thinking about radiation: Too much is bad, but a little is okay. And as long as you're keeping track, you'll be fine . . . probably. It's not that different from deciding how many cigarettes or hamburgers you can safely consume. You could swear off smoking or go vegan, but most people don't. They take a calculated risk in order to do something enjoyable . . . like visiting Chernobyl on vacation.

Is Chernobyl safe? Wild carnivorous radioactive wolves aside, the answer seems to be yes. The most hazardous forms of radiation released in the accident also had the shortest half-lives and have already stopped being dangerous. A patina of longer-lasting radioactive particles settled over the entire region, but these sink deeper and deeper into the soil with each passing year. Because of these factors, a daylong visit to Chernobyl will expose me to 10 times *less* gamma radiation than my flight home to Seattle.

Until planning a visit here, I never knew that long-haul, high-cruising-altitude flights expose their passengers to significant loads of cosmic radiation. And that's to say nothing of dental X-rays, CAT scans, mammograms, and other medical testing. If you're truly "worried about radiation" . . . you'll never get on an airplane or go to the dentist again.

Dosimeters track the amount of gamma radiation you are exposed to, in real time. The "safe" level—meaning sustainable in-definitely—is anything under 0.3 microsieverts per hour (µSv/h). That's the reading, more or less, when I get on the bus in Kiev, and it's probably the reading in your hometown. And for most of the day, the dosimeter stays comfortingly below that number, with a few brief spikes to 1 or 2 µSv/h. That seems scary, but a com-mercial airliner at 35,000 feet would make your dosimeter ping at a rate of 2 or 3 µSv/h.

One thing you learn from the Chernobyl experience is just how localized radiation is. It tends to be low inside buildings and higher in overgrown areas. The classic Chernobyl tour-guide gim-mick is demonstrating radiation hot spots: The group is walking on concrete sidewalks through a forest, where radiation levels are normal. But then the guide pauses and holds out a dosimeter near the roots of a tree or a suspicious-looking pothole, and the num-bers shoot up.

The most striking example of this will come later in the day, when we drive across the path of that initial cloud of atomic ejecta that sowed radiation across a swath of Ukrainian and Belarussian countryside. Fidel suggests that we hold our dosimeters up to the bus window. They're reading normal. But then, as we cross that invisible line, they skyrocket at a terrifying pace—up to 38 µSv/h. The bus driver, helpfully extending our adrenaline rush, slows down. While half of the passengers giggle with nervous delight, the rest of us shout, "Okay, we get it—*keep going!*"

All of this is specific to gamma radiation. The Chernobyl site also has alpha and beta radiation, which can be carried by dust and other particles. Your clothes protect you from these, for the most part; that's why visitors to the Exclusion Zone must wear long pants and long sleeves. (Full disclosure: I made a point to shower and wash my clothes when I got back to Kiev that night . . . just in case.)

Because careless visitors may pick up alpha- and beta-radioactive material on their shoes and clothing, everyone is required to pass through three special screening checkpoints: you step awkwardly into a giant contraption that feels like standing sideways in a metal detector, place your hands and feet on special pads, then wait for the green light. The technology seems comically antiquated, and we're told that visitors are almost never flagged. If your shoes did set off the alarm, near as I could tell, they would simply have you wade through a rusty pan of dirty water and try again.

Before my trip, I was nervous about the danger involved in visiting Chernobyl. But ultimately, the most toxic thing we're exposed to all day is the silent, devastating, eye-watering flatulence of the Mancunian, who eventually reveals that drinking the Kiev tap water has been wreaking havoc on his insides.

The Russian Woodpecker

Soon after passing through the second checkpoint—at the 10-Kilometer Exclusion Zone—we turn off the main road at a bus stop colorfully painted with a Ukrainian knockoff of Yogi Bear, collecting mushrooms in the forest. This ostensibly marks the location of a children's camp. But that's just a ruse to throw Cold War–era spies off the scent: A few miles down this road, through a rusted gate adorned with silver, five-pointed stars, stands an impossibly gigantic Soviet-era radar antenna array. Clearly not familiar with the adage about eggs and baskets, the USSR located this top secret surveillance facility next to their top secret nuclear power plant.

This was the receiving station for the Duga-3 over-the-horizon (OTH) radar, which picked up the signal emitted by a transmitting station 60 kilometers away. Fidel scratches a globe in the sandy soil to demonstrate how the radar worked: it bounced its signal three times, hopscotching between the earth and the ionosphere, to reach all the way over the North Pole and deep into North American airspace—allowing operators to detect an ICBM launch up to 10,000 kilometers away. This was the last gasp of the pre-satellite era, and mostly effective; false positives nearly caused global thermonuclear war only about two times—three, tops.

The Duga is nicknamed "the Russian Woodpecker" for the staccato interference it caused in short-wave ham radios and other broadcasts. One day in 1976, hams in North America turned on their radios to find this mysterious new chattering lurking at the edges of their signal. Nobody knew exactly what the Woodpecker was for, and conspiracy theorists believed it was some form of Soviet mind control. But one thing was clear: it drove ham radio operators nuts. They issued formal complaints to the USSR gov-

ernment, and bought "Woodpecker mufflers" in an attempt to filter out the noise. It finally went silent when the Duga radar was
turned off for good in 1989.

While long since decommissioned, the radar installation has
been open to visitors only since 2013. And now, as we stand beneath it and gape up, it fills our entire field of vision. Like all of the
best examples of the Soviet aesthetic, the Woodpecker makes you
feel very, very small. It's more than 30 stories high and stretches
nearly 700 feet—as far as the eye can see toward the horizon. It
looks like a wire frame for a giant dam, rising up from the middle
of a forest. Its precisely located nodes and crisscross support cables
create mesmerizing optical illusions.

Gazing up at this rusting masterpiece of Cold War technology feels like touring the Colosseum: a boldly ambitious, epoch-
defining achievement of engineering that now stands as an artifact
of a toppled civilization.

The Sarcophagus

At a certain point in the day, the nervous gallows humor of visiting a nuclear wasteland on your vacation gives way to the somber
humanity of the tragedy. For me, this happens on our surreal drive
along a cooling canal toward the Chernobyl power plant. We drive
closer. And closer. And—*gulp*—closer. And soon, we're pulling
into a parking lot across the street from Reactor No. 4.

When the reactor exploded on the night of April 25, 1986, the
superheated nuclear fuel inside Reactor No. 4 began melting right
through the floor. Liquidators drained the cooling pools located
below the molten core, to avoid a steam explosion. Coal miners
were brought in to build a protective barrier that would prevent
the core from reaching the water table deep below—which could
cause another massive explosion and widespread contamination.
Helicopter pilots flew thousands of sorties to dump lead, sand, and
boric acid onto Reactor No. 4, smothering the meltdown. And radioactive debris was carefully removed and disposed of. Workers
were exposed to levels of radiation that were permanently injuri-
ous after just a 40-second shift.

To prevent another meltdown, the USSR embarked on the

largest civil engineering project in history: building a concrete "sarcophagus" to safely encase the volatile reactor core. Over the course of six months, a quarter million workers reached their recommended lifetime limit of radiation exposure as they put the sarcophagus in place. Meanwhile, scientists inspecting the meltdown site discovered what's known as "the Elephant's Foot"—a petrified column of molten radioactive material that is considered the most lethal object in the world.

Chernobyl had a pan-European impact. Radioactive rain fell in the Scottish Highlands, and the South of France saw an increase in the rate of thyroid cancer. But even as it's easy to fault the Soviets for allowing the accident to occur in the first place, you have to credit them for saving Europe from something far worse. Ultimately, the cleanup was a success, the worst of the radiation was contained, and further meltdowns were forestalled—all at a cost of somewhere around $18 billion.

Not only did the Chernobyl incident—which is sometimes called "the final battle of the USSR"—contribute to bankrupting the already shaky Soviet economy. It also forced Soviet premier Mikhail Gorbachev to live up to his recently issued pledge of *glasnost* (openness). As details of the accident became public, it eroded trust among Soviet subjects and cast severe doubt on the USSR's much-touted technological achievements. While the fall of the Soviet Union had many causes, Gorbachev himself cites Chernobyl as one of the key dominoes to topple during that critical period.

The original sarcophagus has more recently been itself covered by another, more modern sarcophagus. Designed and built in conjunction with a French company, the new sarcophagus has an elegant arch and a shiny shell that seems designed to instill confidence—a stark contrast to the rusty original. Costing $2.5 billion and taller than the Statue of Liberty, the new sarcophagus was built a few hundred yards away, then slowly moved into place—the largest metal object ever moved by humans.

The meltdown site, now encased in *matryoshka* stacking dolls of sarcophagi, has surprisingly low levels of radiation. Standing at the monument honoring those who lost their lives in the accident, directly in front of the sarcophagus, my dosimeter shows that I'm absorbing about a third as much gamma radiation as I would on a long-haul flight. And yet, it's still above the recommended safe levels for long-term exposure. The soundtrack of a visit here is the high-pitched chattering of dosimeters—like the insistent ticking of a stopwatch, reminding you not to linger.

But work is not done: The next challenge is to dismantle and safely dispose of the inner sarcophagus, to prevent a future collapse. And the long-term goal is to remove the plant entirely. Someday—2065, they hope—this will simply be an open field.

Workers at the facility do shifts—two weeks on, two weeks off —and wear badges that monitor how much radiation they have absorbed. If they hit their annual limit, they're done until next year. We're told that the French workers appreciate the safeguards . . . while the Ukrainian ones, eager for a steady paycheck, would prefer the limits to be increased.

As if to emphasize the safety of the site, we have lunch in the humble canteen for Chernobyl workers, in a building a short walk from the meltdown site. We're told the cafeteria ladies—who pile our plastic trays with mountains of hearty food—don't like having their photo taken. Checking my dosimeter while eating my borscht and chicken schnitzel, I see that the radiation here is no higher than in Kiev.

The Ghost City of Pripyat

The grand finale of our tour is just a couple of miles from the plant: Pripyat, an entire city trapped in a postapocalyptic time warp, and now completely overtaken by nature. Pripyat seizes travelers' imaginations. It's what you picture when you imagine visiting Chernobyl.

Founded along with the plant in 1970, the planned workers' town of Pripyat showcased the ideal Soviet lifestyle. This was as good a place to live as you'd find in the Ukrainian Soviet Socialist Republic. Because of the importance of the plant, Pripyat was directly supplied by the Soviet government, making its shops unusually well stocked. At the time of the accident, Pripyat had just completed work on a new amusement park and sports stadium, and was laying out plans to expand the city across its little river bay. From a dock below the trendy café in Pripyat's town center, you could hop on a public hydrofoil and zip downriver to Kiev faster than driving. The mid-1980s was a prosperous time, with no inkling of the lurking disaster, much less the impending collapse of the Soviet Union. Having a good job at Chernobyl and a flat in Pripyat was a blissful existence that many Ukrainians aspired to.

The 50,000 people of Pripyat (including 17,000 children—the median age was 26) were perhaps the cruelest casualties of the accident. While the firefighters, miners, pilots, soldiers, and scientists who threw themselves into the radioactive cauldron did so with heroism, and more or less knowingly, the civilians of Pripyat were simply not told that they needed to leave until it was too late.

After 36 hours of cover-up and obfuscation, the authorities finally gave the order to evacuate Pripyat. And when it happened, it happened all at once. One night, as irradiated firefighters were slowly dying in the Pripyat hospital, the ballroom in the town's big hotel was hosting a wedding party. The next morning, 50,000 people were carried away from their toxic hometown, in a column of buses 10 kilometers long, within a matter of hours. They were told to turn off the lights, close the windows, and bring along a few supplies for this "temporary" evacuation. They were told they'd be back in three days. They were told many things. But the truth is that nobody will ever live in Pripyat again.

Most of the people of Pripyat survived the initial exposure, but were sentenced to a life of creeping, unpredictable health problems—which, thanks to the cruelly insidious nature of radiation poisoning, are now reverberating well into the next generation.

We set out to explore the forests that have filled in the empty space between buildings. Concrete apartment blocks, standing in formation like platoons of rigid soldiers, are tattered and dilapidated. Just inside the entrance of one, a hand-lettered directory lists each family that resided here, circa 1986.

The apartments are still sort of furnished, with dribs and drabs of vintage furniture. But the wallpaper is peeling off the walls in crooked rolls, and the appliances have been looted of their copper wire. Fidel tells us these apartments are a popular place for squatters to sneak in and hole up for a weekend bender. (Apparently, Ukrainian partiers know how to turn their self-destructive tendencies up to 11.)

At the town's fancy café, once cheery mosaics and stained-glass windows are shattered and scattered around the hauntingly still interior. The indoor swimming pool—recently made famous by one of the first-person shooter video games that have found inspiration in Pripyat—is filled with black muck. The local cinema, which was named for Prometheus, the god who brought fire to humans, is decisively closed for business.

We walk through an open field of sturdy trees and dense brush. Only after Fidel points out the faint echoes of a grandstand do we realize that we're crossing the center line of a soccer pitch—in the middle of what was Pripyat's sports stadium.

Inside a school, a few tattered notices hang on bulletin boards, locker doors gape open, and long-forgotten homework litters the muddy floor. In one room, someone has assembled the creepy dolls into macabre little tableaus—as if this nauseating site needed to have a fine point put on it. A teddy bear wearing a toddler-size respirator mask toasts a doll that winks one dead eye from under wispy, matted hair. It's a postapocalyptic island of misfit toys.

In the town amusement park, which was slated to open just weeks after the accident, stands the icon of Pripyat: its Ferris wheel, a perhaps too-on-the-nose symbol for innocence lost. It looms above Pripyat like a rusted skeleton—childhood joy filtered through a grotesque prism of Cold War nuclear paranoia. The abandoned bumper cars (which, Fidel warns us, are likely "contaminated"—there's that word again) are welded by rust to the mossy floor.

The most notorious corner of Pripyat is the former hospital, where those first responders were treated for radiation sickness —pointlessly, yet humanely. While heroically extinguishing the initial fire, they were not told about the meltdown, and took no special precautions. They noted a metallic taste in their mouths, and a tingling sensation on their faces. Coughing and vomiting came next. And soon it was clear: they had absorbed a lethal, delayed-reaction dose of radiation. They had just enough time to come to the hospital, strip off their gear in the basement, and climb into their deathbeds.

Today, that basement—and those clothes—remain irrevocably contaminated. Jackets and boots sit in heaps, right where they were dropped more than 30 years ago, too dangerous to move —or even get close to. Although it's strictly off-limits, there's a cottage industry of amateur YouTube daredevils who sneak into the basement for a selfie with a summiting dosimeter. Having traveled extensively in Eastern Europe—with its brutal, war-torn history—I am used to hearing a guide say, "That building over there? In the basement, many people were killed." But this is the first time I have been told, "That building over there? If you stay in the basement for too long, it'll kill *you*."

The Liquidators

As we pass through what was the main square of Pripyat, Fidel calls us over to a humble memorial of photographs pinned to a wall. Scanning the faces of those who lost their lives at Chernobyl, we hear their stories:

The middle manager who showed up to deal with the crisis on his day off, even though he was stinking drunk. Fortunately, his high blood-alcohol level helped insulate him from the worst of the radiation (he survived for decades).

The plant worker who stayed as long as he could to help, until he was removed to a hospital for his final days. His wife refused to leave his bedside—until she, too, was doomed to radiation poisoning.

And the firefighters who initially responded to the meltdown, sacrificing their lives in those critical first hours to prevent a catastrophe that could have been far worse. Perhaps it's hyperbole, but local authorities insist that if the liquidators had not acted so quickly—had they allowed the meltdown to worsen—it could have tainted much of the European continent. Imagine all of Europe carrying dosimeters for each hike in the woods.

At this poignant moment, I consider all of the reasons why a traveler would want to visit Chernobyl. Is it simply gruesome rubbernecking at human tragedy? For some, yes. But it's also an opportunity to learn about one of the most dramatic events of the late Cold War era. It's a chance to gain a better understanding of the actual risks of nuclear power—and the unexpected safety of a cleaned-up radioactive site. You see old Soviet bloc towns trapped in time, in their native state, untouched by the modernization and westernization of the post–Cold War world. And you see how rapidly and without hesitation nature overtakes a depopulated civilization.

But standing there, looking into the eyes of the people who contained that first horrible wave of radiation, I think of yet another reason: to honor the memory of those who died to make this area safe for future generations. People may no longer be able to live long-term in certain parts of the meltdown zone. But we don't have to stay half a country away, either—wondering nervously when the next meltdown will come. At Chernobyl, it's humbling to see how human ingenuity can bring about horrifying problems. But it's also inspiring to see how it can solve them.

Paper Tiger

FROM *The New Yorker*

ANDREW ORCHARD LIVES near the northeastern coast of Tasmania, in the same ramshackle farmhouse that his great-grandparents, the first generation of his English family to be born on the Australian island, built in 1906. When I visited Orchard there, in March, he led me past stacks of cardboard boxes filled with bones, skulls, and scat, and then rooted around for a photo album, the kind you'd expect to hold family snapshots. Instead, it contained pictures of the bloody carcasses of Tasmania's native animals: a wombat with its intestines pulled out, a kangaroo missing its face. "A tiger will always eat the jowls and eyes," Orchard explained. "All the good organs." The photos were part of Orchard's arsenal of evidence against a skeptical world—proof of his fervent belief, shared with many in Tasmania, that the island's apex predator, an animal most famous for being extinct, is still alive.

The Tasmanian tiger, known to science as the thylacine, was the only member of its genus of marsupial carnivores to live to modern times. It could grow to six feet long, if you counted its tail, which was stiff and thick at the base, a bit like a kangaroo's, and it raised its young in a pouch. When Orchard was growing up, his father would tell him stories of having snared one, on his property, many years after the last confirmed animal died, in the 1930s. Orchard says that he saw his first tiger when he was 18, while duck hunting, and since then so many that he's lost count. Long before the invention of digital trail cameras, Orchard was out in the bush rigging film cameras to motion sensors, hoping to get a picture of a tiger. He showed me some of the most striking images he'd collected over the decades, sometimes describing teeth and tails and stripes while pointing at what, to my eye, could very well have been shadows or stems. (Another thylacine searcher told me that finding tigers hidden in the grass in camera-trap photos is "a bit like seeing the Virgin Mary in burnt toast.") Orchard estimates that he spends $5,000 a year just on batteries for his trail cams. The larger costs of his fascination are harder to calculate. "That's why my wife left me," he offered at one point, while discussing the habitats tigers like best.

Tasmania, which is sometimes said to hang beneath Australia like a green jewel, shares the country's colonial history. The first English settlers arrived in 1803 and soon began spreading across the island, whose human and animal inhabitants had lived in isolation for more than 10,000 years. Conflict was almost immediate. The year that the Orchard farmhouse was built, the Tasmanian government paid out 58 bounties to trappers and hunters who presented the bodies of thylacines, which were wanted for preying on the settlers' sheep. By then, the number of dead tigers, like the number of live ones, was steeply declining. In 1907, the state treasury paid out for 42 carcasses. In 1908, it paid for 17. The following year, there were 2, and then none the year after, or the year after that, or ever again.

By 1917, when Tasmania put a pair of tigers on its coat of arms, the real thing was rarely seen. By 1930, when a farmer named Wilf Batty shot what was later recognized as the last Tasmanian tiger killed in the wild, it was such a curiosity that people came from all over to look at the body. The last animal in captivity died of exposure in 1936, at a zoo in Hobart, Tasmania's capital, after being locked out of its shelter on a cold night. The Hobart City Council noted the death at a meeting the following week, and authorized £30 to fund the purchase of a replacement. The minutes of the meeting include a postscript to the demise of the species: two months earlier, it had been "added to the list of wholly protected animals in Tasmania."

Like the dodo and the great auk, the tiger found a curious immortality as a global icon of extinction, more renowned for the tragedy of its death than for its life, about which little is known. In the words of the Tasmanian novelist Richard Flanagan, it became "a lost object of awe, one more symbol of our feckless ignorance and stupidity."

But then something unexpected happened. Long after the accepted date of extinction, Tasmanians kept reporting that they'd
seen the animal. There were hundreds of officially recorded sightings, plus many more that remained unofficial, spanning decades.
Tigers were said to dart across roads, hopping "like a dog with sore
feet," or to follow people walking in the bush, yipping. A hotel
housekeeper named Deb Flowers told me that, as a child, in the
1960s, she spent a day by the Arm River watching a whole den of
striped animals with her grandfather, learning only later, in school,
that they were considered extinct. In 1982, an experienced park
ranger, doing surveys near the northwest coast, reported seeing a
tiger in the beam of his flashlight; he even had time to count the
stripes (there were 12). "10 a.m. in the morning in broad daylight
in short grass," a man remembered, describing how he and his
brother startled a tiger in the 1980s while hunting rabbits. "We
were just sitting there with our guns down and our mouths open."
Once, two separate carloads of people, eight witnesses in all, said
that they'd got a close look at a tiger so reluctant to clear the road
that they eventually had to drive around it. Another man recalled
the time, in 1996, when his wife came home white-faced and wide-
eyed. "I've seen something I shouldn't have seen," she said.

"Did you see a murder?" he asked.

"No," she replied. "I've seen a tiger."

As reports accumulated, the state handed out a footprint-identi-
fication guide and gave wildlife officials boxes marked THYLACINE
RESPONSE KIT to keep in their work vehicles should they need to
gather evidence, such as plaster casts of paw prints. Expeditions to
find the rumored survivors were mounted—some by the government, some by private explorers, one by the World Wildlife Fund.
They were hindered by the limits of technology, the sheer scale
of the Tasmanian wilderness, and the fact that Tasmania's other
major carnivore, the devil, is nature's near-perfect destroyer of evidence, known to quickly consume every bit of whatever carcasses
it finds, down to the hair and the bones. Undeterred, searchers
dragged slabs of ham down game trails and baited camera traps
with roadkill or live chickens. They collected footprints, while debating what the footprint of a live tiger would look like, since the
only examples they had were impressions made from the desiccated paws of museum specimens. They gathered scat and hair
samples. They always came back without a definitive answer.

In 1983, Ted Turner commemorated a yacht race by offering a hundred-thousand-dollar reward for proof of the tiger's existence. In 2005, a magazine offered 1.25 million Australian dollars. "Like many others living in a world where mystery is an increasingly rare thing," the editor in chief said, "we wanted to believe." The rewards went unclaimed, but the tiger's fame grew. Nowadays, you can find the thylacine on beer cans and bottles of sparkling water; one northern town replaced its crosswalks with tiger stripes. Tasmania's standard-issue license plate features an image of a thylacine peeking through grass, above the tagline EXPLORE THE POSSIBILITIES.

With the advent of DNA testing and Google Earth and cellphone videos, it became ever more improbable that the Tasmanian tiger was still out there, a large predator somehow surviving just beyond the edge of human knowledge. In Tasmania, the idea gradually turned into a bit of a joke: the island's very own Bigfoot, with its own zany, rivalrous fraternities of seekers and true believers. Still, Tasmanians point out that, unlike Bigfoot, the thylacine *was* a real animal, and it *had* lived, not so very long ago, on their large and rugged and still sparsely populated island. As the decades passed, the number of reports kept going up, not down.

We are many centuries removed from the cartographers who used the phrase "Hic Svnt Leones" ("Here are lions") to mark where their maps approached the unknowable, or who populated their waters with ichthyocentaurs and sea pigs because it was only sensible that the ocean would hold an aquatic animal to match every terrestrial one. We've learned quite a bit, since then, about where and with whom we live. By certain accounts, however, our planet is still full of unverified animals living in unexpected places. The yeti and the Loch Ness monster are famous; less so are the moose rumored to roam New Zealand and the black panthers that supposedly inhabit the English countryside. (The British Big Cat Society claims that there are a few thousand sightings a year.) Panther reports are also common across southern Australia.

Some of these mystery animals may be part of explicable migrations or relict populations—there are active, if marginal, debates about whether mountain lions have reappeared in Maine, and whether grizzlies have survived their elimination in Colorado —while others are said to be menagerie escapees. Australian fauna

are reported abroad so often that there's a name for the phenomenon: phantom kangaroos, which have been seen from Japan to
the UK. In some places (such as Hawaii, and an island in Loch
Lomond), there are actual populations of imported wallabies.
Elsewhere, the kangaroo in question was nine meters tall (New
Zealand, 1831) or eschewed its usual vegetarian diet to kill and
eat at least one German shepherd before disappearing (Tennessee, 1934).

What are we to make of these claims? One possible explanation
is that many of us are so alienated from the natural world that
we're not well equipped to know what we're seeing. Eric Guiler, a
biologist known for his scholarship on thylacine history, was once
asked to investigate a "monster" on Tasmania's west coast, only
to find a large piece of washed-up whale blubber. Mike Williams,
who, with his partner, Rebecca Lang, wrote a book about the Australian big-cat phenomenon, told me that "people's observational
skills are fairly low," a diplomatic way of explaining why someone
can see a panther while looking at a house cat. In April, the New
York Police Department responded to a 911 call about a tiger—
presumably the Bengal, not the Tasmanian, kind—roaming the
streets of Washington Heights. It turned out to be a large raccoon.
Williams, who travels to Tasmania a few times a year to look for thylacines, described the continued sightings as "the most sane fringe
phenomena."

Another explanation is that the natural world is large and complicated, and that we're still far from understanding it. (Tasmania
got a lesson in this recently, when the government spent $50 mil-
lion to eradicate invasive foxes, a scourge of the native animals on
the mainland, even though foxes were never proven to have made
it to the island.) Many scientists believe that even now, in this age
of environmental crisis and ever-increasing technological capability, more animals are discovered each year than go extinct, often
dying off without us even realizing they lived. We have no way to
define extinction—or existence—other than through the limits of
our own perception. For many years, an animal was considered
extinct a half century after the last confirmed sighting. The new
standard, adopted in 1994, is that there should be "no reasonable
doubt that the last individual has died," leaving us to debate which
doubts are reasonable. Because the death of a species is not a simple narrative unfolding conveniently before human eyes, it's likely

that at least some thylacines did survive beyond their official end
at the Hobart Zoo, perhaps even for generations. A museum exhibit in the city now refers to the species as "functionally extinct"
—no longer relevant to the ecosystem, regardless of the status of
possible survivors.

Tiger enthusiasts are quick to bring up Lazarus species—animals that were considered lost but then found—which in Australia
include the mountain pygmy possum (known from fossils dating
from the Pleistocene and long thought to be extinct, it was found
in a ski lodge in 1966); the Adelaide pygmy blue-tongue skink (re-
discovered in a snake's stomach in 1992); and the bridled nailtail
wallaby, which was resurrected in 1973, after a fence builder read
about its extinction in a magazine article and told researchers that
he knew where some lived. In 2013, a photographer captured
17 seconds of footage of the night parrot, whose continued existence had been rumored but unproven for almost a century. Sean
Dooley, the editor of the magazine *BirdLife,* called the rediscov-
ery "the bird-watching equivalent of finding Elvis flipping burg-
ers in an outback roadhouse." The parrots have since been found
from one side of the continent to the other. Is it more foolish to
chase what may be a figment, or to assume that our planet has no
secrets left?

Last year, three men calling themselves the Booth Richardson Tiger Team held a press conference on the eve of Threatened Species Day—which Australia commemorates on the day the Hobart
Zoo thylacine died—to announce new video footage and images
that they said showed the animal. They'd set up cameras after
Greg Booth, a woodcutter and a former tiger nonbeliever, said
that while walking in the bush two years earlier he had spotted a
thylacine only three meters away, close enough to see the pouch.
The videos were shot from a distance, and grainy, but right away
they prompted headlines, from *National Geographic* to the *New York
Post.* By the time I arrived in Tasmania, this spring, the team had
gone to ground. When I reached Greg's father by phone, he told
me that their lawyer had forbidden them from talking to anyone,
because they were seeking a buyer for their recording.

One of Tasmania's most prominent tiger-hunting groups, the
Thylacine Research Unit, or TRU, looked at the images and pronounced the animal a quoll, a marsupial carnivore that looks

vaguely like a weasel. TRU, whose logo is a question mark with tiger stripes, has its own web series and has been featured on Animal Planet. "Every other group is believers, and we're skeptics, so we're heretics," Bill Flowers, one of the group's three members, told me one day in a café in Devonport, on the northern coast. Since Flowers began investigating thylacine sightings, he has been reading about false memories, false confessions, and the psychology of perception—examples, he told me, of the way "the mind fills in gaps" that reality leaves open. He talked about the unreliability of eyewitness testimony in court cases, and pointed out that many people, after spotting a strange animal, will look it up and retroactively decide that it was a thylacine, creating what he calls a "contaminated memory."

It isn't unusual for an interest in thylacines to lead back to the psychology of the humans who see them. "Your brain will justify your investment by defending it," Nick Mooney, a Tasmanian wildlife expert, told me. I met Mooney, who is 64, in his kitchen, which was filled with drying walnuts and fresh-picked apples. In 1982, he was studying raptors and other predators for the state department of wildlife when a colleague, Hans Naarding, reported that he'd seen a thylacine. The department had just been involved in the World Wildlife Fund search, which had found no hard proof but, as the official report by the wildlife scientist Steve Smith put it, "some cause for hope." Naarding's sighting was initially kept secret, a fact that still provides grist for conspiracy theorists. Mooney led the investigation, which took 15 months; he tried to keep out the nosy public by saying that he was studying eagles.

The search again turned up no concrete evidence, but, from 1982 until 2009, when Mooney retired, he became the point person for tiger sightings. The department developed a special form for recording them, noting the weather, the light source, the distance away, the duration of the sighting, the altitude, and so on. Mooney also recorded his assessment of reliability. Some sightings were obvious hoaxes: a German tourist who took a picture of a historical photo; a man who said that he'd got indisputable proof but, whoops, the camera lurched out of his car and fell into a deep cave (he turned out to be trying to stop a nearby logging project); people who painted stripes on greyhounds. Mooney noticed that people who had repeat sightings also tended to prospect for gold, reflecting an inclination toward optimism that he dubbed Lasseter

syndrome, for a mythical gold deposit in central Australia. One
man gave Mooney a diary in which he had recorded the hundred
or so tigers he believed he'd seen over the years. The first sighting
was by far the most credible. Eventually, though, the man would
"see sightings in piles of wood on the back lawn while everybody
else was having a barbecue," Mooney said. "What we're talking
about here is the path to obsession. I know people who've bankrupted themselves and their family . . . wrecked their life almost,
chasing this dream."

But there were always stories that Mooney couldn't dismiss. The
most compelling came from people who had little or no prior
knowledge of the thylacine, and yet described, just as old-timers
had, an awkward gait and a thick, stiff tail that seemed fused to
the spine. There were also the separate groups of people who saw
the same thing at the same time. He often had people bring him
to the scene, and then would reenact the sighting with a dog, taking his own measurements to test the accuracy of people's percep-
tions, their judgment of distance and time.

In the media, Mooney is regularly consulted for his opinion
on new sightings or the species' likelihood of survival. (Extremely
low, he says.) But he won't answer the question everyone wants answered. Flowers told me, "We ponder very often, does Nick believe
or does he not?" Mooney's refusal to be definitive angers those
who accuse him of perpetrating a government cover-up of a relict population and also those who think he's encouraging non-
sense by refusing to admit a dispiriting but obvious reality. Mooney
thinks these views represent a thorough misunderstanding of how
much we actually know about our world. "I don't see the need to
see an absolute when I don't see an absolute," he told me. "Life is
far more complicated than people want it to be." In his eyes, the
ongoing mystery of the thylacine isn't really about the animal at
all. It's about us.

To the outside world, Tasmania has long been a place of wish-
ful thinking. For centuries, legends circulated of a vast unknown
southern continent, Terra Australis Incognita, which was often
said to be a land of riches so great that, as one writer put it, "the
scraps from this table would be sufficient to maintain the power,
dominion, and sovereignty of Britain."

This is the dream that the explorer Abel Tasman was chasing

when he sailed east from Mauritius on behalf of the Dutch East India Company, in 1642. (Mauritius, an island in the Indian Ocean, had become a popular stopover for Dutch sailors, who restocked their larders with a large and easily hunted bird that lived there, the dodo.) Almost seven weeks later, his crew sighted land, which they took for part of a continent, never discovering that it was an island. Onshore, they initially met no people, although they heard music in the forest and saw widely spaced notches carved into trees, which led Tasman to speculate, in his published journal, that giants lived there—a notion that may have inspired Jonathan Swift's Brobdingnagians. Tasman also wrote that a search party "saw the footing of wild Beasts having Claws like a Tyger."

A century and a half later, the first shipload of convicts and settlers arrived. They didn't know what creature—later named for the devil they feared it to be—made the screams they heard in the night. When, a few months after the establishment of a settlement at Hobart, some convicts caught sight of a large striped animal in the forest, it seemed another symbol of this strange and intimidating land. "I make no doubt but here are many wild animals which we have not seen," a chaplain wrote. They encountered creatures like the platypus, an animal so bizarre—venomous, duck-billed, beaver-tailed, with the furry body of an otter but egg-laying—that George Shaw, the author of *The Naturalist's Miscellany,* believed it to be a crude hoax. From the beginning, the thylacine's common names—zebra wolf, tiger wolf, opossum-hyena, Tasmanian dingo—marked it as another chimera, too incongruous to understand on its own terms.

Three years after the colony's founding, Tasmania's surveyor-general wrote a scientific description that was read before the Linnean Society, in London: "Eyes large and full, black, with a nictant membrane, which gives the animal a savage and malicious appearance." More harsh descriptions followed, from the 1830s through the 1960s: "These animals are savage, cowardly, and treacherous"; "badly formed and ungainly and therefore very primitive"; "marsupial quadrupeds are all characterized by a low degree of intelligence"; "belongs to a race of natural born idiots"; "an unproportioned experiment of nature quite unfitted to take its place in competition with the more highly-developed forms of animal life in the world today." The thylacine was stupid and backward and also, somehow, a terrifying menace to the new society, which

blamed it for killing tens of thousands of sheep—an absurd infla-
tion—and sucking its victims' blood like a vampire.

This abuse was part of a larger prejudice against marsupials that
is sometimes called placental chauvinism. The science historian
Adrian Desmond wrote that "civilized Europe, for its part, was
quite content to view Australia as a faunal backwater, a kind of
palaeontological penal colony." As Europeans spread throughout
Australia, killing native animals and displacing them with their
preferred species, their assessments of marsupials were as unflat-
tering as their racist dismissals of the people they were also killing
and displacing.

Aboriginal Tasmanians, who had lived on the land for roughly
35,000 years, were dying in large numbers, succumbing to new
diseases introduced from Europe and attacks by colonists who
wanted to raise livestock on the open land where they, and the
thylacine, hunted. In 1830, just 27 years after colonization, Tasmania's lieutenant governor called on the military, and every able-
bodied male, to join a human chain that would stretch across the
settled areas of the island and sweep the native people into exile.
The operation, which used up more than half the colony's annual
budget, became known as the Black Line, for the people it tar-
geted. That same year, a wool venture in the northwest offered
the first bounties for dead thylacines, and the government of the
island began offering them for living Aboriginal people—later to
be amended to include the dead as well.

By 1869, it was believed that only two Aboriginal Tasmanians,
a man named William Lanne, known as King Billy, and a woman
named Truganini, survived. Scientists suddenly became obsessed
with these "last" individuals. After Lanne died, a Hobart physician
named William Crowther stole his skull and replaced it with one
that he took from a white body. Lanne's feet and hands were also
removed; the historian Lyndall Ryan contends that other parts of
his body, as well as a tobacco pouch made from his skin, ended up
in the possession of other Hobart residents. There was a public
outcry at the "unseemly" acts, but Crowther was soon elected to
the legislature and later served as Tasmania's premier.

In 1871, two years after Lanne's death, the curator of the Australian Museum, in Sydney, wrote to his counterparts in Tasmania
with a warning: "Let us therefore advise our friends to gather their
specimens in time, or it may come to pass when the last Thylacine

dies the scientific men across Bass's Straits will contest as fiercely for its body as they did for that last aboriginal man not long ago." Truganini, who died in 1876, professed her fear of a similar fate. Thanks to a guard who kept watch over her body, she was successfully buried. Eventually, however, her bones were exhumed and displayed at the Tasmanian Museum, along with taxidermied thylacines.

In fact, Lanne and Truganini were not the last Aboriginal Tasmanians. Descendants of the island's first people lived on, mostly on the islands of the northern coast, where Aboriginal women had had children with white sealers; today, though the numbers are contested, some 23,000 people in Tasmania identify as Aboriginal. For decades, they had to fight against the widespread belief that they no longer existed. "It is still much easier for white Tasmanians to regard Tasmanian Aborigines as a dead people rather than confront the problems of an existing community of Aborigines who are victims of a conscious policy of genocide," Ryan has written. In 2016, the Tasmanian government, by constitutional amendment, recognized Aboriginal Tasmanians as the original owners of the island and its waters. As of this writing, the *Encyclopaedia Britannica* defines them as extinct.

The politics and the emotions may have changed, but the thylacine still serves as a proxy for other debates. In March, in the tiny town of Pipers Brook, a group of Tasmanian landowners gathered over tea and quartered sandwiches to learn about how to support native animals on their properties. During the past 200 years, more mammals have gone extinct in Australia than anywhere else in the world; Tasmania, once connected to the continent by a land bridge, has served as a last refuge for animals that are already extinct or endangered on the mainland. In Pipers Brook, the group was shown a picture of a thylacine, accompanied by an acknowledgment of grim responsibility. "A lot of what we do has the soul of the thylacine behind it," David Pemberton, the program manager of the state's Save the Tasmanian Devil Program, said. The devil, Tasmania's other iconic species, is suffering from a contagious and fatal facial cancer that essentially clones itself when the devils bite one another's faces. Pemberton has calculated that the combined weight of the tumors, most of which are genetically a single organism, now exceeds that of a blue whale.

As the group toured an enclosure for a devil-breeding program, a man named John W. Harders told me that the possibility of the thylacine's survival had become a matter of pure belief, like whether there is life after death. Other participants said that they couldn't help but feel some optimism, despite their rational doubt. "There's so much despair in terms of conservation these days," a botanist named Nicky Meeson said. "It would provide that little bit of hope that nature is resilient, that it could come back."

But some people erupted in frustration at the mention of the tiger. "We killed them off a hundred years ago and now, belatedly, we're proud of the thylacine!" Anna Povey, who works in land conservation, nearly shouted. She wanted to know why the government fetishizes the tiger's image when other animals, such as the eastern quoll—cute, fluffy, definitely alive, and definitely endangered—could still make use of the attention. I couldn't help thinking of all the purported thylacine videos that are dismissed as "just" a quoll. "It does piss us off!" Povey said. "It's about time to appreciate the things we have, Australia, my God! We still treat this place as if it was the time of the thylacines—as if it was a frontier and we can carry on taking over."

In the 1970s, Bob Brown, later a leader of the Australian Greens, a political party, spent two years as a member of a thylacine search team. He told me that although he'd like to think the fascination with thylacines is motivated by remorse and a desire for restitution, people's guilt doesn't seem to be reflected in the policies that they actually support. Logging and mining are major industries in Tasmania, and land clearing is rampant; even the forest where Naarding saw his tiger is gone. Throughout Australia, the dire extinction rate is expected to worsen. It is a problem of the human psyche, Brown said, that we seem to get interested in animals only as they slide toward oblivion.

While living Aboriginal Tasmanians were conveniently forgotten, the thylacine underwent an opposite, if equally opportune, transformation. To people convinced of its survival, the animal once derided as clumsy and primitive became almost supernaturally elusive, with heightened senses that allow it to avoid detection. "This is one hell of an animal," Col Bailey, who is writing his fourth book about the thylacine, and claims to have seen one in 1995, told me. He has a simple explanation for why the tiger hasn't been found: "Because it doesn't want to be."

Last year, the thylacine's genome was successfully sequenced from a tiny, wrinkled joey, preserved in alcohol for decades. It was a breakthrough in a long-standing project to revive the species through cloning, an ecological do-over that has been suggested for species from the white rhino to the woolly mammoth. Some critics consider cloning another act of denial in a long line of them—denying even the finality of extinction.

Of all the disagreements among tiger seekers, the most contentious is this: Do they, could they possibly, still live on the Australian mainland? Although thylacines are now synonymous with Tasmania, they lived as far north as New Guinea, and were once found all across Australia. Carbon dating suggests that they have been extinct on the mainland for around 3,000 years. That would be a very long time for a large animal to live without leaving definitive traces of its existence. And yet some Aboriginal stories place the tiger closer to the present, and mainland believers contend that there have been many more sightings—by one count, around 5,000—reported on the mainland than in Tasmania.

Thylacine lore in western Australia is so extensive that the animal has its own local name, the Nannup tiger. A point of particular debate is the age of a thylacine carcass found in a cave on the Nullarbor Plain in 1966, so fresh that it still had an intact tongue, eyeball, and striped fur. Carbon dating indicated that it was in the cave for perhaps 4,000 years, essentially mummified by the dry air, but believers argue that the dating was faulty and the animal was only recently dead.

To many Tasmanian enthusiasts, mainland sightings are a frustrating embarrassment that threatens to undermine their credibility; they can be as scathing about mainland theorists as total non-believers are about them. "Every time a witness on the mainland says, 'I found a tiger!' it looks like they filmed it with a potato and it's a fox or a dog," Mike Williams, the panther researcher, told me. He pointed out that sarcoptic mange, a skin disease caused by infected mite bites, is widespread in Australian animals, and can make tails look stiff and fur look stripy.

Last year, researchers at James Cook University, in Queensland, announced that they would begin looking for the thylacine in a remote tropical region on Cape York Peninsula and elsewhere in Far North Queensland, at the northeastern tip of Australia, about as far from Tasmania as you can get and still be in the country. The search, using 580 cameras capable of taking 20,000 photos each, was prompted by sightings from two reputable observers, an experienced outdoorsman and a former park ranger, both of whom believed that they had spotted the animal in the 1980s but had, in the intervening years, been too embarrassed to tell anyone. "It's important for scientists to have an open mind," Sandra Abell, the lead researcher at JCU, told me as the hunt was beginning. "Anything's possible."

In Adelaide, I met up with Neil Waters, a professional horticulturist, who, on Facebook, started the Thylacine Awareness Group, for believers in mainland tigers. Waters, who was wearing a T-shirt emblazoned with the phrase MAY THE STRIPES BE WITH YOU, told me that he has "a bit more faith in the human condition" than to think that so many people are all deluded or lying. "Narrow-minded approach to life, I call it," he said. He told me that he also felt a certain ecological responsibility, because his ancestors "were the first white trash to get off a ship, so we've been destroying this place for a long time." His family had been woodcutters, and, for him, becoming a horticulturist was a kind of karmic reparation.

In the dry hills outside the city, we stopped in an area called, appropriately or not, Humbug Scrub, and then picked up Mark Taylor, a musician and a thylacine enthusiast who lived nearby. A few months earlier, Taylor said, his son-in-law and grandson had seen what they described as a dog that hopped like a kangaroo, and Taylor was yearning for a sighting of his own. "It's becoming one of the bigger things in my life," he said. Any time we were near dense brush, he would get animated, saying, "There could be a thylacine in there right now and we'd never know!" Once, just as he said this, there was movement on a distant hillside and he jumped, only to realize that it was a group of kangaroos. The world felt overripe with possibility.

Four weeks earlier, Waters had left a road-killed kangaroo next to a camera in a place where he had found a lot of mysterious scat containing bones. "Shitloads of shit!" he exulted. Now he and Taylor were going to find out what glimpses of the forest's private history the camera had recorded. As they walked, Taylor stopped to gather scat samples for a collection that he keeps in his bait freezer for DNA analysis. "My missus hates it," he said.

The kangaroo was gone, except for some rank fur and a bit

of backbone. Waters retrieved the camera from the tree to which he'd strapped it. Taylor was bouncing again. "This is when we hope," he said. Back at the car, we crouched by the open trunk as Waters removed the memory card and inserted it into a laptop. We watched in beautiful clarity as a fox, and then a goshawk, and then a kookaburra fed on the slowly deflating body of the kangaroo. Waters laughed and cursed, but it was clear that no amount of disappointment would dampen his belief. "It's a fucking big country," he said. "There's a lot of needles in that haystack."

I thought of something Bill Flowers, of TRU, told me about the first time he set up camera traps in a Tasmanian reserve called Savage River. In terms of the island, where about half the land is protected, the reserve is relatively small. But the forested hills stretched as far as he could see. He began to consider the island not as it appears on maps—small, contained, all explored and charted—but as it would appear to an animal the size of a Labrador, looking for a place to hide. Suddenly, Tasmania seemed big indeed. "You go out and have a look and you start going from skeptic to agnostic very quickly," he said. I heard something similar from many searchers. "It's all very well and good to look at Google Earth and say, la la la, it's not possible for something to be not seen," Chris Tangey, who interviewed 200 witnesses as part of his own search, in the late 1970s, said. "But then you go to those places . . ." He trailed off, sounding wistful.

For some people, contemplating the possibility of the thylacine's survival seems to make the world feel bigger and wilder and more unpredictable, and humans smaller and less significant. On a planet reeling from the alarming consequences of human activity, it's comforting to think that our mistakes may not be final, that nature is not wholly stripped of its capacity for surprise. "It puts us in our place a little bit," a mainland searcher named David Dickinson told me. "We're not all-knowing."

After dodos disappeared from Mauritius, in the seventeenth century, naturalists came to believe that the bird had only been a legend. There were drawings and records, sure, but where had it suddenly *gone*? Extinction was a new and much-derided idea. Even Thomas Jefferson refused to believe in it for many years—how could the perfection of nature, of creation, allow such a thing? The evidence of departed species mounted until it was undeniable —dinosaur and mastodon bones were pretty difficult to account for—but it took longer to understand that humans, through their own actions, might be able to overwhelm the abundance of nature and wipe out whole species. That's part of why the Tasmanian tiger became famous in the first place. By the time it disappeared —right on the heels of passenger pigeons, which not long before had blocked out the sun with the immensity of their flocks—we were just beginning to confront the terrible magnitude of our destructive power.

We're still just beginning.

Keepers of the Jungle

FROM *Travel + Leisure*

LONG AGO, there lived an ape. The ape had babies, and those babies grew up and had babies of their own, and over time their descendants drifted apart to the point that they could no longer be considered one type of ape, but five. All were highly intelligent, but one was smarter than the rest. With its gift of speech, this supersmart ape gave the others names: "gorilla," "chimpanzee," "bonobo," and "orangutan."

This intelligence, however, came at a cost. Though this talking ape was capable of creating wonders, it was also capable of destroying them. Among the wonders it destroyed were many of the forests in which the other apes lived. One such forest is on the Indonesian island of Sumatra, where members of a unique species of orangutan are clinging to what little remains of their native habitat. Last summer, feeling less confident than usual in the merits of my own species, I went to Sumatra myself, hoping to meet one of these survivors. My destination was the Leuser Ecosystem, a sprawl of jungle in the north of Sumatra, the westernmost of Indonesia's more than 16,000 islands. Orangutans once lived throughout Southeast Asia, but today the only two surviving species are confined to the scattered remnants of rain forest on Sumatra and nearby Borneo. The Sumatran orangutans, almost all of the remaining 7,000 of them, live in the Leuser—a nominally protected stronghold of biological diversity that is growing smaller and less biologically diverse each year. Logging, hunting, and the illegal pet trade have all played a part in the orangutan's demise, but the main culprit is the global demand for palm oil, a commodity often produced on deforested land.

Conservationists warn that the Sumatran orangutan could become the first great ape to reach extinction, with the Borneo species following close behind. Meanwhile, the slash-and-burn conversion of their habitat into palm plantations is helping fill the earth's atmosphere with excess carbon, threatening the existence of us all. Travelers who don't want to spend their vacations contemplating such truths may want to give Sumatra a miss. Bali is nice, I hear. But Bali doesn't have wild orangutans. Or tigers. Or flowers the size of truck tires. Or the vanishingly rare Sumatran rhino. Although Sumatra's tourism infrastructure is improving, this vast, wild, jungle-clad island remains much less developed than a place like Bali. For a certain kind of traveler, that's precisely why it's such an exciting place to go.

On my way to the Leuser I spent a night in Medan, the capital of North Sumatra province, before heading to the jungle the next day. Riding out of town, I found it hard to imagine that in less time than it takes to drive from New York City to Boston, I would arrive at the edge of one of the richest forests in Asia. Medan was a crush of people and motorbikes and trucks and endless rows of street stalls filling economic niches I didn't know existed. We passed a stall selling only kitchen clocks, another selling only birdcages, and a purse vendor who, lacking a stall, had hung her wares from the sprawling limbs of a tree, prompting my travel companion, Stefan Ruiz, who took the photographs for this story, to make one of his trademark observations: "It's literally a money tree."

Finally the traffic thinned and the city faded, and we were rumbling through the palm plantations, acres and acres of them, the tall, spare trees stretching as far as we could see in every direction, in rows as straight as supermarket aisles. Palm oil is the most commonly used vegetable oil in the world, found in snacks, soaps, cosmetics, and a good number of the other products on our shelves, and Indonesia produces more of it than any other country, accounting for about a third of the world's supply. If there is a money tree in Indonesia, it is the oil palm.

As we neared the forest, I asked our driver, Adi, who didn't speak much English, if he had seen a lot of wildlife over the years.

He started talking excitedly about something called a "mina," which I assumed was a kind of monkey, or maybe a local word for orangutan. In fact, Mina was the name given by researchers to one particularly notorious orangutan. As a local would later put it, "She had mental problems." There were rumors that Mina had bitten tourists. It turned out she had a troubled past: captured as a baby, she'd spent years in a cage. Eventually, she was rescued and brought to a rehabilitation center for orangutans in Bukit Lawang, a village on the outskirts of the Leuser rain forest. But by then, her time with humans had taken its toll.

The Bohorok Rehabilitation Center closed in the '90s, but several of the orangutans that passed through it still live in the part of the jungle closest to the village, and so do their progeny, who tend to take after them. Considered "semi-wild," they generally aren't afraid of people, and some of the guides capitalize on this fearlessness, luring them closer to tourists with fried rice.

Green Hill, a company that organizes jungle treks and runs the village guesthouse where we stayed, doesn't go in for that kind of thing. Andrea Molyneaux, who manages Green Hill with her husband, is an Englishwoman with a master's in primate conservation who did her fieldwork at Camp Leakey, on Borneo. The camp was established by the pioneering Lithuanian Canadian conservationist Birutė Mary Galdikas, who is to orangutans what Jane Goodall is to chimps. Andrea's motto is painted on a big sign out front: KEEP WILDLIFE WILD.

For the most part, Bukit Lawang resembles the other towns in the region—humble concrete buildings with rusty corrugated metal roofs. But at its far end, the road gives way to a footpath that meanders through the trees, and if you follow the path along the river, past the shops selling orangutan T-shirts and orangutan carvings, you'll find yourself in the hotel district, a sort of fantasy of an Indonesian village filled with guesthouses made with bamboo, jungle logs, and branches.

That night, Stefan and I slept in rustic rooms overlooking the jungle. The next day, we planned to march right into that seething mass of green. We were to spend the morning close to the village looking for semi-wild orangutans, which we were practically guaranteed to see. Then our guides would take us deeper into the forest, to an area rarely visited by people where the foliage would be thicker, the trails rougher, and the wildlife truly wild. We planned to camp there for two nights. If we saw an orangutan in the deep forest, we'd be among the very few people who ever have.

Early the next morning, as the sun rose above trees across the river, we went into the forest. Stefan and I were joined by our head guide, Anto Cebol; his assistant, Ipan; and a pair of college students from Colorado. Anto, a native of Bukit Lawang, is 38, with the long hair and philosophical outlook of someone who has been exposed from an early age to the beliefs and customs of stoned Australian backpackers. Sitting on a boulder, he said, "No one knows how much longer the earth will be." He smiled defiantly. "Maybe we go to the moon."

We'd been following him for only a few minutes when he pointed out a troop of black-Mohawked Thomas's leaf monkeys in the trees. Though we were still on easy, well-worn paths, sweat started pouring out of me at a rate I'd never imagined possible. Then we saw it: our first orangutan. This was exciting, of course, that flash of orange in the trees, but she clearly wasn't wild. She was stretched out on a limb, unafraid and unimpressed. Anto recognized her; he said he knew her mother. As we stood there staring, a long-tailed macaque walked right past us, not even bothering to glance in our direction. Then a group of *Homo sapiens* approached in flip-flops, taking selfies.

So by the time we got on the motorbikes and headed down the road toward a more remote area, I was ready to go a little deeper. After a bumpy ride through palm plantations, we arrived at Bukit Kencur, a hamlet on the edge of the part of the jungle that the Green Hill staff had described as untouched. It was clear that this place didn't get many foreign visitors. Clusters of reddish palm fruit sat in the dirt outside the sun-bleached wooden huts. The villagers who came over to look at us didn't attempt to speak English, and no one tried to sell us orangutan carvings or anything else.

One of the villagers approached with a basket of supplies. His name was Chilik, and he was going to serve as an extra guide for the rest of our trip. His training, as I'd later learn, had been unconventional. Some years ago, he got lost in the forest while gathering medicinal plants and sustained himself for five days by watching the orangutans to see which fruits they ate. Chilik didn't speak any English. Unlike Anto, he wore his hair short, and did not bother with the rubber trekking shoes worn by the guides in

Bukit Lawang. He led us through the jungle barefoot, scraping leeches off his ankles with a rusty machete, and he carried most of our supplies on his back in a basket made from rattan vines, which the Bukit Lawang guides had long since abandoned for Western-style backpacks. During snack breaks, he would go off by himself and squat on the forest floor, chain-smoking until it was time to leave.

That first day, we hiked only a short distance, maybe a quarter mile. Still, it was tough going, as the rest of the trip would be. The trail rose and fell at such a steep incline that we often had to grab at roots and vines just to stay upright. At times it disappeared completely, at which point Chilik would move to the front of the pack and hack a path through the bush with his machete. At last we came to the campsite. It sat on a slope overlooking a pictur-esque river. As we rinsed off in the cool, clear water, a pair of cooks showed up out of nowhere and built a fire. They boiled a pot of rice, fried some tempeh, sautéed a sackful of tapioca leaves, and whipped up a delicious dish of dried anchovies with wild ginger and chile.

We slept beneath a tarp stretched over a frame of lashed-together bamboo poles. The soundscape was a layered mix of cicada, bird, stream, and rain, with a smattering of monkey howls thrown in. We awoke early the next morning, at the first hint of daylight. Toast, eggs, strong Sumatran coffee, then back on the trail, pausing every 15 minutes so that Anto could pass out pieces of leaves and bark, schooling us on the names and medicinal or culinary uses of each species. There was the hot-pink flower of a tree he called *assam kimchin.* (A lemony herb; goes well with curry.) The woody stalk of *pasak bumi.* (Bitter; defends against malaria.) The glossy leaf of the *satykop* bush. (Per Anto: "To make not broken the first baby when baby is still drinking from mama and mama pregnant.") On we hiked, our eyes lifted to the treetops, when suddenly Anto saw something that made him break into a sprint. *"Mawa!"* he shouted, crashing through the foliage. "Lucky!"

Mawa, I knew by then, is the local word for orangutan.

Seeing a truly wild orangutan does feel different from seeing one that has grown up around humans. You see in his eyes that he is frightened, and in his innocence and awe, he reminds you of a child. You feel a rush of nostalgia for your own childhood, when all the world felt like this corner of the forest, mysterious and full of wonder. At the same time, you can't help suspecting you feel this way primarily because you come from the West, where you and your compatriots, having benefited from centuries of environmentally destructive agricultural and industrial practices, have forgotten the hardships of forest life. This is one of the reasons you can afford to look back at that bygone existence through a romantic lens, much in the way you can afford to romanticize your childhood only after the pain of growing up has receded. You think these things, and you wonder what the orangutan is thinking. And then the screeching ape demonstrates his mastery of simple tools by breaking off a stick and throwing it at you. Knowing what you know about humans, can you blame him?

Eventually the orangutan calmed down and just hung there from the branches staring back at us. Then we heard a rustling of leaves a little way off. "Another one!" Anto cried. Two, in fact —a mother and baby. So that's why the first one hadn't fled at the sight of us: he was protecting his family. The mom and baby were moving slowly through the treetops, not leaping like monkeys but plotting a careful course, shifting their weight from foot to foot, and hand to hand.

My last few days in North Sumatra unfolded at a rambling hotel on the shore of Lake Toba, eight hours southeast of Bukit Lawang. At 436 square miles—about the size of Los Angeles—Lake Toba is the largest volcanic lake in the world, and maybe the nicest. The water is sparkling and calm. Soft green mountains rise all around it. The hotel, Carolina Cottages, is a collection of bungalows with sharply peaked roofs and ornately carved wooden façades, a tribute to the traditional building style of the local people. A breeze blew onto the hotel veranda, ruffling the edges of the batik tablecloths. On the beaches, the Coke came in glass bottles and the coconuts came with straws.

At the center of the lake lies Samosir Island, the heartland of the Batak, an indigenous group known for their love of singing. One night, we partied with a crowd of Batak schoolteachers on their summer break. They fed us boiled eggs with chile paste and passed out cups of herbal liquor and brought out a guitar and sang for us and begged us to dance with them and laughed hysterically when we did. Even Stefan, who has been everywhere and isn't easily impressed, conceded that one of the guests had a solid case when he called Lake Toba "heaven on this earth."

On my way back to Medan, as I boarded a ferry headed across the lake, a stranger handed me a pocket map. He turned out to be a mapmaker from Java who had traveled all over Indonesia for his work. He told me Toba held a special place in his heart. For years, he said, the Indonesian government had done too little to develop the tourism industry in this provincial outpost, but that was beginning to change. An airport had been built nearby, and there were plans to extend the highway from Medan to the lake. "We want people to know the story of Toba," he said.

The story of Toba is one worth knowing. The massive volcanic eruption that created the lake some 70,000 years ago nearly wiped out the entire human species—and may have made us who we are today. According to the "Toba catastrophe theory," originally posited by the science writer Ann Gibbons, the blast plunged the earth into a six-year winter, leaving as few as 3,000 people alive on the planet. Those survivors were the most resourceful of our kind, and they passed on those qualities to their descendants, our ancestors, planting the seeds of human civilization.

It was perhaps because of Toba that our ancestors learned to make fire, and grow crops, and cure diseases, and come up with clever theories about human civilization. And it was perhaps because of Toba that we learned to clear forests, and developed a habit of wiping other species off the face of the earth.

As the ferry pulled into the dock, I said goodbye to the mapmaker and hauled my bags to the driver waiting onshore. Then we began the journey back to Medan, with its truck-clogged streets, passing palm plantations where there used to be forest. With luck, you'll get to visit one of the forests that remain. If you do, keep your eyes raised to the treetops. You might see someone you used to know.

Mother Tongue

FROM *Oxford American*

MY FAMILY IS NO LONGER speaking because of a disagreement over a heap of jewelry, which my grandmother left behind when she died four years ago. My two aunts were given the jewels—in my mind's eye, the great glittering gold cache guarded by the dragon Smaug in *The Hobbit*—as stipulated in my grandmother's will. The will said everything should be split among the five children evenly, save these extra jewels, which the sisters could divide as they saw fit. That didn't go over well; my dad and his two brothers said it wasn't fair, that it wasn't in the spirit of our family to parse Tata's heirlooms so cynically. My two aunts had a will signed by my grandmother telling them exactly what she wanted done—how could they do any different? By now it's all hazy, calcified by the ensuing silence. I only have my dad's account to go on; my aunts, certainly, would have another take. But the result remains: my dad and his siblings can no longer be in the same room, not easily, and we the grandchildren and great-grandchildren have not gotten together with all our aunts and uncles for four years.

Tata would be ashamed of us if she knew our family had clammed up over some shiny objects, considering all we've been through. My father, his four brothers and sisters, and their parents fled the small coastal town of Nicaro, Cuba, during the revolution. The war had come literally to their door, guerrilla fighters braced against the porch columns firing up at President Batista's single-prop planes, and Dad remembers the driveway heavy with spent bullet casings the next morning. Neighbors who spoke out against the government had been spirited away in the night; boys as young as 12 were being conscripted into the army. Out of fear, the Loredos escaped in the summer of 1960 on the second-to-last ferry from Havana to Key West before Fidel Castro choked the border permanently.

In the United States, my grandfather, the assistant director of the hospital in Nicaro, wasn't allowed to practice medicine until he passed the American board exams. He worked as a mortician's assistant in Miami, studying every night for a test riddled with English jargon until he passed. Then he completed a residency meant for new graduates—not assistant directors of hospitals— and earned the right to practice medicine in the States.

Nicaro to Havana to Key West to Miami, motel vacancy signs reading NO PETS, FAMILIES, OR CUBANS. Meridian, Mississippi. Then Texas: El Paso, Waco, Hallettsville, San Antonio, my grand-father chasing work, the family following. Dad threw newspapers to help support the family and has not stopped working—save the year after my mother died unexpectedly in 2002—for all 58 years since he immigrated. Dad got into fistfights: once after he let a black boy go ahead of him in line at a bakery in Mississippi, which the white kids outside didn't like; other times to protect his younger sisters from boys who attempted sexual assault. As a teenager, girls wouldn't date him because he was Cuban—too dark. His principal told him he'd be lucky to get Cs in college. In graduate school, a professor in the University of Texas psychology department refused to approve his dissertation for increasingly ab-surd reasons (including the criticism that the paper had too many instances of the word "the"); Dad eventually had to threaten the man with legal action and a story in the *Statesman* before the pro-fessor begrudgingly stamped his approval.

My grandfather came to be a respected physician in Texas and worked until his dying day in 1994. He saw the birth of half a dozen grandchildren, and after he passed, Tata became our family's sole steward. Under her watch, our numbers grew past 30. Aunts and uncles, cousins, children, all of us a dash of salt across the map of Texas: Austin and Houston, San Antonio and Victoria, Sealy, Hal-lettsville, Plano. And *the* key feature of our family, for half a cen-tury, has been the ubiquitous Loredo Family Reunions: the annual Gulf Coast beach trip and Christmas and Thanksgiving, Easter and

Tata's birthday, baby showers and first communions and beauty contests and middle school graduations. Baseball games, even, can merit a two-hour drive and a glass bowl of pink ambrosia.

Of the original siblings, Dad's the oldest and remembers the most of Cuba. The second-oldest, my aunt, speaks Spanish and is the resident Cuban black beans expert. But the other three barely remember Cuba at all. One mustachioed uncle studied to be a nurse but now repairs power lines, hunts deer on the weekends, and bequeaths mountains of sausage unto us. All—including my dad—have deep Texan drawls.

Picture, in our heyday: a whole Thanksgiving bird, injected with spices via a five-inch syringe, sizzling in a deep fryer; the Cowboys on the tube; Spanish wafting over the scent of black beans and lechón asado; gleaming belt buckles and Stetsons; and stories of Nicaro traded across the table. The one time Dad's horse snapped its lead and chased him into the ocean. The other time one of his cousins, just a toddler, released the emergency brake on the Chevy, which began rolling down the hill, and Tata, in the middle of getting dressed, sprinted half-naked into the yard and dove through the open car window. The royal palms, the one-room church on the hilltop Papa paid to have constructed. The pothos on the children's table my Dad hid nasty foods beneath—and how ferociously that plant grew, Tata not learning why until decades later. In this way, Nicaro had been kept alive; our family had been kept whole through the power of memory and communion.

Know that this is what has been lost with our family's cleaving. The reunions, yes, but all of it—the memory of our family's epic saga at the bottom of a deep well. The family is divided in neat camps: the aunts and their children on one side with Tata's will and a stack of jewels; my dad and his brothers on the other side with their own children and their bitterness. The revolution forgotten, the ferry forgotten, the landing, the assimilation. The family.

Compared to my father's childhood in Nicaro, I felt my own upbringing lacked wonder. He'd tell me about Cuba, and I'd imagine hunting rose-throated parrots in pine forests with a BB gun, or haunting Las Palmas—the club attended by the local American nickel factory workers—until they let me into their fabled chlorinated pool. When I began to write as a teenager, my stories were populated with the broad palms of plantain leaves and the mischief of tobiano colts, and over the years I accumulated a healthy body of work set in revolution-era Cuba. In 2015, I began writing a novel that would tell two stories: the story of a boy's childhood in 1950s Cuba—the magic of it, the violence—and the story of him as an adult in Texas in 2002, trying to find a relationship with his son after the death of the mother.

I'd often thought of going to Cuba, but in the summer of 2017 I was nearing the end of the first draft of the novel, and it became clear I needed to visit the island for research, to see Nicaro for myself. And, though I told no one, I began to dream of the events that might lead to my family's reconciliation, a fantasy in which I was the hero. *Lucas returns to Cuba, the first in his family to do so in six decades. He collects interviews, memories, sucks the marrow of the place. Upon return, he convinces his aunts and uncles to tolerate each other for one hour to view photos and videos of Nicaro. And in his stories of home they remember the importance of family, they arrange the next Christmas reunion, they fall into a sobbing heap of apologies and forgiveness.*

And so, four years after Tata's death, four years after our family stopped speaking, I decided to go to Cuba. The stated goal: to research my novel. The unstated hope: The Great Loredo Salvage Mission.

In May, I called Dad to tell him what I was up to. For so long, Cubans like us could only stare 90 miles across a spit of water wondering why ours was one of only two countries on planet Earth that we could not visit. But in the years since President Obama had relaxed travel restrictions to Cuba in 2011, making possible the prospect of traveling there legally, I'd asked Dad whether or not he was interested in returning to his homeland. He'd always said no, that he'd heard from others who'd made the pilgrimage back home that the country's extreme disrepair did nothing to mend their own hearts; instead, the country they remembered had retreated farther into the murky waters of the long-ago.

So it was much to my surprise that Dad, instead of wishing me safe travels, invited me to a café. *Interesting,* I thought.

He brought with him his yellow legal pad and took notes in immaculate cursive. He sipped espresso and wiped coffee from his white beard. Dad never takes off his black Ray-Bans, which he's worn since the '70s—since his early days as a psychologist when he braided his hair and would arrive at the courthouse on his Harley, to give testimony as an expert witness—and his expression is often inscrutable.

"I'll come with you," he said. "It'll be a father-son adventure."

Double interesting.

On my tablet I pulled up a satellite image of Nicaro. Tata told me their town had once been known as Lengua del Pájaro—*Bird's Tongue*—for the way the sharp peninsula probed north into the Atlantic.

"What? This is it?" He jammed a meaty finger into the screen. "Wow," he said, and kept saying it, until a wet film spilled from the bottom of his shades.

Soon, I'd recruited my brother, who was also uncharacteristically enthusiastic about the idea. He's 14 years older than me and the fairest person I know, and as a marketing executive at a fast-food joint you've definitely heard of, he quickly applied his logistical mind to questions of planes, cars, food, lodging. Hell, we'd invite his wife, my partner, Dad's wife, her son, and his girlfriend. We'd go in December and spend Christmas in Nicaro.

Our cadre grew excited in the ensuing weeks, weighing vans versus a bus, Airbnbs versus hotels, and then: June 16, 2017, when President Trump gave a speech in Miami debuting his new policy for United States–Cuba relations and declared that we would return to the old rules, which more or less said, unless you're a diplomat or a missionary, you can get stuffed. If we wanted to go, we'd have to do it immediately. Instantly, my brother was out—the burger industry needed him—and I have never heard him so obviously downtrodden as when he gave his blessing on the phone for us to go without him. Soon, we cut everyone else from the excursion. It was most important that Dad got to go, so he and I booked a 10-day trip to and from Havana in August; we'd take a bus from the capital to Nicaro.

In the lead-up to our flight, I spent a lot of time not practicing my Spanish, despite the offers of my girlfriend, who had learned the language at cooking school in Peru. Like my uncles, I resisted working toward fluency; I was dimly aware that approaching the language now would start a process I did not want to begin in the States. Instead, I talked to Dad on the phone almost every day, and he recounted all the memories that were returning to him as he spent the evenings poking around Google Earth.

And then, 30 days before the trip, my stepmom emailed me to

say that since Dad left Cuba before 1971, he'd need a special HE-11 visa to get into the country. Otherwise, they'd consider him a long-lost Cuban citizen returned home, and they might keep him there forever. We were advised the visa process would take two months or more; there wasn't enough time.

I left four voice messages with the Cuban consulate in Washington, DC, calling on different days and at varying times to ensure maximum coverage. My father left two messages in Spanish. I emailed three times, in English and Spanish, and wrote an impassioned letter, complete with a scan of the HE-11 form, a facsimile of Dad's passport, and a plea for urgency in the header on each page.

We received not a call, not an email, not a written reply. For all I know, their mail slot went straight to an incinerator. Without the special visa, Dad couldn't come. He had been thwarted, the last domino felled, his mood on the phone despondent.

"I'd just gotten my hopes up so big," he said. Dad had thought he'd closed the door on Cuba forever. Now I'd opened it just enough to slam it on his fingers.

After all that, I'd go alone. The Great Loredo Salvage Mission, indeed.

The plane descended upon Havana, and fear descended upon me. Me, my family's lone emissary. I'd traveled alone plenty, but in the weeks leading up to the trip I had, as I often do, piled on the stakes. Not just a chance to deepen my novel, its make-or-break moment. Not just a chance to collect photos for my family—but a shot at becoming whole. A rising pressure of my own design.

Humidity down the jet stairs. Thickets of plantain trees pressing in on the tarmac. Inside the hangar, the marble-mouthed Cuban Spanish I'd heard around dinner tables since childhood now alive in every throat, the sensation of distant cousins all around, that if I'd shouted *Loredo* a dozen heads would have turned, expectant.

The taxi driver was the ghost of my father at 20 years old. Dark hair, crisp shirt, chewing gum, aviator sunglasses, ready to pilot a puddle jumper. Instead, he commanded, yes, a '50s-vintage ride with tail fins, and asked me where I was from.

The piping of my Spanish plumbing was rusted. I gave the answer that would become my catchall over the next 10 days: "I'm from the United States, but my family is from Cuba, a very small town far from here, called Nicaro. No one has been here in fifty-seven years. I am the first one."

I could have printed business cards.

He dropped me off at my Airbnb in one of the city's nicest neighborhoods, Vedado, whose grids of patinated mansions speak to its history of sugar-trade money. I would spend a week in the capital, then take a 12-hour bus ride to Nicaro and stay three days before returning to Havana to catch my flight home. I wanted a sense of the city, the country's crown jewel, before venturing into the countryside, where the infrastructure would be more challenging. And three days inhabiting my family's shadow felt like plenty.

The Airbnb was owned by two Cubans who were, somehow, visiting family in Miami. I was met at the house's gate by three dogs, a cat, a middle-aged woman, and a teenage girl. I got the distinct feeling that my arrival was the day's excitement. Neither Ileana nor her daughter Melodí spoke a lick of English, but the mother's Spanish was generous—I could understand less than half, but she was happy to prattle on and let my ear wrap slowly around her speech. "Your flight was good? You're hungry? Here's some avocado. Here's mango juice—fresh."

I set my bag in the apartment above the garage, which held an ancient but functional Ford, and sat with my hosts on the outdoor patio under an ivy-strewn roof of corrugated plastic. I had arrived.

For the next seven days I walked—Vedado, Old Havana, the rigid Soviet architectures. I spent hours scoping the seawall that guarded the entire coast of the city—El Malecón—drinking cold Presidentes and watching teenage boys handle fishing lines with the pads of their fingers. Mostly aimless, mostly quiet. I had once traveled to Marrakech, where in the souks I stuck out like a neon dollar sign, but here, if I didn't open my idiot mouth, I blended right in. There were absolutely no advertisements—no FOR SALE signs, commercials, or touts—a welcome casualty of the Communist government. Instead, billboards of Che Guevara and José Martí. A mural of Castro surrounded by fawning children, the caption underneath painted by hand with a fine brush: LA HISTORIA ME ABSOLVERÁ.

On a stroll through downtown I happened upon La Universidad de La Habana, where my grandfather earned his doctorate in medicine and was a peer of, unbelievably, El Comandante himself, whom my grandfather deemed "charismatic but strange." A small square across the street corralled a pasture of cell-phone users. I'd heard of this—pockets of Wi-Fi, digital nomads hunched over at the watering hole. I forked over a dollar to a young man for the password and emailed Dad to tell him I was safe. Lineage of my grandfather, come all this way to bum a signal from the same place he earned his doctorate.

Over time, I learned about waiting. I learned about la cola—*the queue.* Cuba proliferates with queues. One afternoon in the bank waiting to exchange currency, I deduced the rules. When approaching la cola, shout "El último?"—*Who's last?*—and be persistent until someone raises a hand. Lines are not orderly. They are not strictly lines, in any geometric sense. They are a social bond. *That person is first, this person is after that person, that person is after this person, and all I know is I will attach myself by the hip to el último and follow into any darkness this world may hold.*

Half my time in Cuba was trying to figure out what any given cola was for, and half my time in any given cola was discussing who was next in the cola. Rations, bottled water, 10-cent ice cream. Get in line. Wait awhile.

Many days, after my walks, there was nothing to do except sit outside with Ileana on the oxidized patio furniture, attempting conversation or not. I became fond of the yard's menagerie. There was a shivering white Chihuahua called Dolly and a small brown torpedo-looking dog named Lambo. A young cat, Bambina, had just birthed five kittens, who stayed in a plastic, blanket-laden box in the outdoor laundry room. Best of all was Yero, an ancient boxer who had, without a doubt, the ugliest face I have ever seen. He managed only three teeth, all on the bottom row, which jutted from his underbite at impossible angles. His eyes were clouded and cried mucus. His nose—oh, poor Yero—his nose was a craterous crash-landing site on the moon. "Guasaguasa, viejo feo," Ileana would say to him, affectionately. *You dopey, ugly old thing.*

Often, overhead, thunderheads three times black. Rain patter on the corrugated roof. Drops plucking at shallow puddles. The animals would gather near. Then the rain would pass, and I would imitate Melodí's ubiquitous dance practice with a buffoon's ballet, tracing my toe in a semicircle across the wet cement to the tune of laughter.

Every night, we played dominos. It was then that I trod and retrod the landscape of my Spanish. It must be said: Cuba is not the place to learn the language. Cubans tend to give up on each word halfway through, as though the mush-mouthed dialect has just woken up from a nap. At first, I understood only the half they didn't throw away. But, slowly, I too learned to give up on words, to suggest their beginning and let my hands tell about the rest.

One night, Ileana told me about the photos she wanted to have done for Melo's quinceanera. She shuffled into the hallway and rummaged around the kitchen. When she returned, she placed some crumpled pages in my hand. I held what, to me, looked like the airbrushed, bubblegum photos one gets at kiosks at the mall. In the photo, a 15-year-old girl wore a teal dress with dated ruffles. "Melodí wants the Snow White dress," she said. Melo blushed. Ileana told me every girl in Cuba had to have a quince photo, or else. I asked, "Or else what?" and she gave me a dark look. She told me she had been saving up money for two years. They cost 200 CUC, plus another hundred for the Snow White dress.

You can't talk Cuba without talking money. First, there are two currencies on the island: CUC and CUP ("kook" and "koop," respectively). CUC is the foreigner's currency and equates to the US dollar. CUP, on the other hand, is the local currency—moneda nacional—and is worth one twenty-fifth as much, about 4 cents on the dollar. Here's some perspective: I knew by then that Ileana made 20 CUC per month, or 20 American dollars. That's it, and it's pretty standard. I paid $30 per night for my room—a very reasonable price for an American; more than a month's salary for a Cuban. Or think about this: it will take Ileana more than one year of saving—assuming she spends no money on food, clothes, transportation, gifts, *anything*—to pay for photos that would take the average American less than three days to afford. Further: if America's prices were adjusted to reflect Cuba's, based on the median American wage of about $14 per hour, quinceanera photos in the States would cost $36,000. Tata's jewelry would be worth many millions in Cuban spending power. Enough for a hundred thousand quinceanera photos.

On the seventh day, the day I was to leave for Nicaro, Ileana told me that every Cuban has the dream of travel. Of course, visiting other countries is strictly forbidden by the Castro government. I asked her where she'd go, if she were allowed, and she said the state television network had produced a series of documentaries about cities around the world. Rome, Paris, São Paulo. Almost like being there.

I pressed: "But where would you choose?"

Her face warmed. "I would go to the Italian countryside. It is so beautiful there. The wine, the fields, the air."

I didn't know whether or not to tell her I had been to Rome, to the South of France, to Morocco. I felt a shame bloom. I asked her if she thought the rules would relax, if she'd be allowed to leave the country in her lifetime.

"Nos ahogan."

"I don't know the meaning," I said.

Ileana was standing against one of the corroded walls of the house. Suddenly, she took both her hands and began to strangle herself. She stuck out her tongue. She pressed herself against the wall. I sat up and gripped the metal arms of the patio chair. Yero barked, wheezing and rasping like an old man. Abruptly, she stopped.

"Nos ahogan," she repeated. *They choke us.*

That night, I boarded the Vía Azul bus bound for Holguín—11 hours away—where I would meet a taxi to take me the last hour to Nicaro. The back window had a sticker that read NEED FOR SPEED. More stickers of, improbably, bullet holes, riddled the cabin door. On each seat, in the blue fabric decorated with smiling cartoon suns, were written the phrases HAVE A GOOD TRIP!, GOOD ROAD!, and BEST VEHICLE! Ileana had given me four bread rolls for the bus ride, and I quickly ate Number One.

Soon, night came. Condensation on the windows against the peroxide fizz of streetlamps.

The rolling countryside, moon-dusted tobacco fields.

We stopped at a way station. I got out to pee. The bathroom cost 1 CUC. I counted 90 cents from my pocket, dropped two coins, muttered "Fuck," and got back on the bus.

We passed midnight. I ate Bread Roll Number Two. The man in front of me reclined his seat into my lap, so far I could have given him a face massage. I angled my long legs sideways and fell into fitful sleep.

I awoke at 2:45 in the morning for Bread Roll Number Three.

A pothole jostled me awake again at the witching hour.

By the time the sun crept over the windshield in the day's early hours, we had arrived in Holguín.

The station was small and loud, colas everywhere seemingly to no purpose. I had no idea what the driver the Airbnb had sent looked like, only that his name was Tony. I was milling around, making conversation with a backpacker from Australia, scanning the crowd for a likely suspect, when a balding man with glasses tapped me on the shoulder. "To Nicaro?" he asked. "I'm Tony. I heard you speaking English." Tony led me to his car, a beautifully cared-for boxy red sedan, and we drove the final hour toward Nicaro. We passed through Cueto and Mayarí, the same route made famous by the Buena Vista Social Club lyric. Donkey carts and bicycles. The sun rose over a sign that read, BIENVENIDOS A NICARO.

Tony drove me through town, pointing out the hospital, the church. I took a video. All I thought was, *Remember all this, remember that horse, that boy, that hill,* but I was overwhelmed and processed little. The lack of sleep, the magnitude of the occasion.

We made it to the Airbnb, and I staggered to my room, barely greeting my hosts. I showered, drank a Presidente, and ate Bread Roll Number Four looking out the door that led from my bedroom to the back courtyard, which held two avocado trees, a metal swinging bench, and a view of the bay. I passed out and woke much later with sweat pooled in the hollow of my throat.

The whole reason my family ended up in Nicaro was because my grandfather, as a young man, took a job as the assistant director of the town's hospital. Papa did everything from suturing wounds to setting bones to delivering babies. Tata cared for their children, a strict and fiery mother. At that time, the town was hopping; its economic blood pumped from the American nickel factory, where white workers processed the mineral from a nearby mine by day and attempted salsa at Las Palmas by night. The factory was shuttered permanently in 2012, but in the 1950s business was good, and after the revolution Che Guevara, who harbored a passion for the industry, renamed Nicaro's nickel plant after Comandante René Ramos Latour. He even visited in 1961, though my family was long gone by then.

Before I'd left for Cuba, Dad had printed a satellite image of Nicaro and circled key locations. *The church. The American Club—*

Las Palmas. The house. The hospital. The nickel factory. The place Pinto chased Dad into the ocean. I'd studied it. The map told its stories: Dad eating guayaba until he got sick. He and Papa entering the jungle with flashlights to hunt parrots. His brothers and sisters playing in the yard among the rotting avocados (too many to eat). The maids told the children to take care while carrying the trash down the darkened driveway; the night devil was fond of flame trees and spying on children, a red hand grabbing branches. Dad's shitty childish handwriting that, after a teacher shamed him about it in class, he spent days and weeks correcting by moonlight in secret, until, on the next test, he looped his now famous cursive in his composition book. The teacher accused him of cheating, and when Tata heard she dragged Dad to the teacher's office, chewed her out, then demanded her son write something in cursive for his teacher. With a shit-eating grin, Dad wrote, *Me llamo Carlos Miguel Loredo Martínez, y yo escribo con el cursivo del Rey.* That same king's cursive was now scrawled across the map I'd folded and unfolded obsessively since I arrived in Havana, Dad's memories from decades ago now anchored to coordinates, and me on the verge of crossing the threshold between fable and reality.

My first proper day in Nicaro, I was greeted in the morning by my hosts, Xiomara and Omar—Tony's parents—who looked after the guest spaces while the owner was away. I told Xiomara I was the grandson of Dr. Loredo, and did she know him? She'd heard of the family. She told me she'd make some calls and settled into the seat near the telephone and began working the rotor.

Tatico, the cook, gave me breakfast. When I said who I was, he shouted, "Dr. Loredo!" His skin puckered with goose bumps. "He delivered my neighbor's baby. You are a ghost come back from the past."

Tatico served me a thermos of espresso and a saucer of warmed milk. The sugar in Cuba is unrefined and fluffy, as though it has been pumped with air. Next, a coterie of hubcap-size dishes. A full plate of six scrambled eggs, hard cheese, soft cheese, and a cubic creature called jamón rápido—*fast ham*—which I regarded with suspicion. Another plate held half a watermelon. Another, four rolls and four pieces of toast. Another plate held a sweet, fried plantain—plátanos maduros. For dessert, an entire tin of canned peaches. I produced my dad's printout of Nicaro landmarks and asked Tatico if he knew where I could find these places. He took my map in hand.

"We will go for a walk," he said.

The door to the church lay open. In the entryway growled two dogs whom Tatico melted with a series of platitudes. I imagined my grandfather, more than half a century ago, overseeing construction between patients, in a crisp guayabera, a stethoscope around his neck. I found his taste austere but elegant. The pews were hardwood. The ceiling high enough to stand on a friend's shoulders. The generous open windows invited the church's most notable feature: the sound of the ocean, warming the rafters. A house for nothing but God and breaking waves.

We took a shortcut through banana trees to the hospital. Tatico's voice was soft, his words buzzing with friendship. He had dark skin and a shaved head and a leathery stoutness. He lamented the loss of the town's gardens. I told him banana trees were plenty green, but to him, they were pests, evidence of laziness. Anyone with two thumbs could grow a banana tree. What worried him most were the snatches of plastic bags, bottles, and other refuse we passed along the way.

"I wish you could have seen Nicaro when I was a boy," he said. Tatico was the same age as my dad—68. I asked, but Tatico had moved here from another small town right after the revolution. He'd never met my family, but he was adamant that everyone had known their thumbprint.

We reached the hospital. A small two-story structure, sky-blue accents, hives of small windowpanes. Water stains darkened the façade. How many tales had I heard of this place?

Nearby, the site where my family's house once stood. From every doorway I half expected a young couple and their children to emerge, the father bespectacled and egg-headed, the mother elegant and angular, their five kids teasing each other. How close my family felt in these moments, shadows on the other side of the thinnest scrim of time.

Tatico explained that the row of homes off the midsection of the hospital had been torn down and rebuilt after the war. "They used to be very beautiful," he said, as we passed seven houses that looked tacked together with spit.

We reached a small overlook. A hill lined with royal palms stretched a long way down and down, until it reached the bay far below. This was the view I had seen in one of the few photographs my grandmother had managed to smuggle from the island, fronds silhouetted against glimmering ocean. Tatico pointed to the other side of the bay. "I get such nostalgia thinking of the way it used to look. Heartbreaking. Nostalgia will be our death."

I didn't understand at first, but then I noticed his finger tracing a black strip of land between the blue water and the peninsula's green grasses. A fire? No, explained Tatico—the nickel factory. They had dumped all the slag into the ocean, and now the water was 50 feet lower, the exposed land steeped in unused ore. He said they called it la tierra negra—*the black earth*. The shoreline was a decayed gum revealing the root of a rotten tooth.

A handful of dirt roads led us down to sea level, where we found Las Palmas. It lay empty. The roof—whose thatch my dad had described in the most adoring of terms—was now rusted metal. A small ballroom with some chairs laid out. On the back patio stood an outdoor bar. The space felt forgotten; it was impossible to imagine music puncturing the quiet. Tatico greeted the bartender, who polished glasses for no one. The patio abutted shallow ocean. Calm swells lapped at a few ragged piers. Dad had told me he used to fish here, when it was still a dock. Tatico was at my elbow. I asked him why no one had rebuilt it.

"There was an animated cartoon called *The Rockeaters,*" he said. "When they ran out of food and got hungry, instead of going out and finding a new way to eat, they would fill their bellies with rocks. That is the Cuban way. What use is it to fix the dock if it will only break again? Instead, we learn to enjoy sitting on the shore."

Tatico took me down to the old baseball field Dad used to play on. Four heifers munched the outfield. He told me that his mother was a big supporter of the revolution. After the war, Che—*the* Che Guevara—toured the entire country and stopped even in lowly Nicaro. His mother took a photo with Che, the two side by side. "Their arms like this," Tatico said, placing his akimbo proudly. He said the photo was in the town museum, but she'd been cropped out. Only the triangle of her elbow remained.

For dinner, Tatico made me cangrejo—*crab*. I remembered the word by associating it with Congress, imagining a legislative body of suited-and-tied crustaceans writing bills restricting travel. He served me an entire hubcap of rice. Canned peaches again for dessert. I asked Tatico if he ever got time to relax. He said he'd like to go to Cayo Saetía, an island 30 minutes away by car with one of the most beautiful beaches in all of Cuba. I asked why he couldn't go if it was so close, and he said the entry fee was 10 CUC—half a month's salary. Conversions again: imagine $1,200 to swim at Coney Island. The grand irony, that Cubans live in one of the world's most beautiful countries, and they can't afford to see it.

Later, from the backyard patio, under the hand of a large avocado tree, he pointed across the water to the island—it was so close you could skip a rock there without it sinking.

I spent the next day walking alone. I stopped by the natural pool —an area of shallow seawater hemmed in by stacked rubble—and wrote in my journal. I attempted notes for the novel, but it felt far away. More important were the days I'd spent speaking nothing but Spanish, thinking, even, in Spanish. The fire trees felt closer. Pinto the Magic Horse felt closer. More important than a stack of pages written in English a thousand miles away was the sense of becoming something new, and as I lay with my back against the sand I realized the moment I had feared before leaving had come to fruition, and I could name it: I was meeting my second self, my Cuban self. Across the water, another shadow of my father, shirtless in swim trunks, sharing a jug of guayaba juice with a friend. Behind them, spray-painted on the façade of a shack, the red capital A of anarchy. I moved to the water, which was filled with families and children, and lay on my back, allowing the water to hold me up. I imagined myself as my father, half a century ago, floating in this same water. I imagined this as home.

Dad often tells the story of the last moment he saw Cuba. Imagine your country on the brink of revolution, led by a man who was "charismatic but strange." Your neighbor grabbing a rifle and heading into the woods with a rucksack stuffed with resolve. A friend plucked from the night, the only possible explanation that he was a talker. Classmates being conscripted into the army, or being twice-baked in revolutionary fervor, hiking off into the mountains to meet El Comandante. My father was 10—too young for war in normal circumstances, but what is too young when philosophy is at stake?

On the day the battle came to Nicaro, my family covered the

windows with mattresses. Dad fled hand in hand with his siblings to the hospital. A helicopter hovered overhead, a machine gunner in the open flank of the aircraft's belly, the broad hands of palm fronds pushing down under the rotors. My grandfather and the hospital's men dressed the roof in an enormous fabric embroidered with a red cross to protect it from bombs. Inside, a man with his wife and daughter held a gun, saying if the Batistans came to take them, he would shoot first the daughter, then the wife, then himself.

After the battle, my grandfather rode into the forest behind Nicaro on my aunt's horse, Relámpago—*Lightning*—and tended the wounded rebel soldiers.

Soon, my family was at a wharf in Havana, boarding the second-to-last ferry to leave the island before Castro's chokehold. *Nos ahogan*. Tata pressing cash deep into a Vaseline jar. Sewing bills into a diaper. The bathroom so slick with seasickness—halfway up the walls, Dad says—that when the ship rocked, my father went skating. Nervous energies, halfway hewn hearts.

We will return was my grandparents' promise, not yet knowing it would be only me.

And then Cuba was only eyeliner on the horizon.

To hear Dad tell it, he knew he would not see Cuba again. He was 10 years old and vowed to himself that he would erase all memory of Cuba, and then he turned away.

My third and last day in Nicaro, Xiomara announced that her phone calls had yielded fruit; the next-door neighbor had known my grandparents when they were first dating. She had already arranged my meeting with her; in fact, I was already late.

Her name was Nilsa. Tatico walked me over. He shouted her name from the front porch, she responded, and then he made a quick getaway. *Weird,* I thought. I sat on a metal chair. Across from me sat another outdoor chair whose fabric seat had long ago ripped, in its place a mountain of yellowed newspapers. Vines crept up the house and, it appeared, entered in through the open windows. Plantain trees in the yard, a coral honeysuckle.

Nilsa emerged from the screen door, leaning on a walker, her left knee wrapped in an ACE bandage, her shoulders so stooped her neck ran parallel to the cement porch. But as soon as she sat in her chair, a regal formality entered her. Her shoulders unstooped.

Her eyes cleared. I introduced myself. "You knew my grandparents when they were first dating," I said.

"Le voy a decir," Nilsa said, using the formal pronoun, which gave the whole conversation an air of state business. *I shall tell you.*

She had known my grandfather as the one who took over as assistant director of the hospital, the one who had the church built—facts I already knew. She said my grandparents seemed very much in love. Soon, though, her knowledge of the Loredos dried up, which was a disappointment. Instead, I asked about Nicaro, about her family. Nilsa's husband worked as a factory hand for the nickel plant but died after 14 years of marriage. "We gave each other respect," she said. "He did not drink. He did not smoke. Never a bad word, an evil touch. Are you married? Are you Catholic?"

It was, perhaps, the hundred-and-first time I'd been asked of my marital status—by Nilsa, Tatico, and Xiomara; by Ileana and Melo; but also by the coat check worker at the national museum (who later propositioned me) and a random guy who'd asked me for the time. Cubans love being their own personal census bureau.

"I have a girlfriend."

"Do you live together?"

When I hesitated, she raised a hand. "I do not judge. Judging others is not generous. To be generous is to be happy; to be ungenerous is to be unhappy."

"Okay, we do," I said. "In sin!"

Nilsa told me she exchanged letters with a nephew in the United States. She had a brother who lived in Holguín. Her mother had taken ill and lived with her here until her passing. Her nephew had come to help for a time, and she sold everything she owned so her mother could eat.

"Now I have nothing," she said. "No material possessions." Her eyes wobbled, but she refused tears. She straightened her back. "But my mother was able to eat, so I am happy. Nothing is more important, do you understand?"

Later, I explained in mangled Spanish the situation with my family, that my aunts were on one side, my father and uncles on the other, and that they would not speak to each other.

"Here is what I will do," she offered. "Come back after dinner. I will write down my memories of Nicaro. Perhaps then they can remember again what is important."

At dinner, I recounted for Tatico all of what Nilsa had told me. Tatico said Nilsa talked too much.

"But Tatico, she's super-friendly."

"She's not working with a full coconut." He whistled and pointed to his forehead. He said she accused her nephew of stealing all her furniture. That's why he never came to visit anymore. I told him she sold her furniture to feed her mother. Tatico shook his head. Her mother never lived with her, either. It was only after she died that Nilsa starting selling everything.

I was spooked by the discrepancies, but Nilsa was in her 90s, and I figured she'd earned whatever stories she liked to tell herself. Her house was empty, and in her mind she had emptied it out of generosity. To be generous is to be happy. To be ungenerous is to be unhappy.

When I came back, it was dark, but I found Nilsa sitting on her porch under a buzzing halogen lamp reading a newspaper. "Ay, Lucas!" she exclaimed, and told me to come inside. I opened the screen door and followed. She moved into a back room. There was not a rocking chair. Not a dining room table. Not a rug or wall fixture or ceiling fan. The sink drowned in pots. There was only a box fan in the window and a single folding poker table supporting a photograph of a young Nilsa and a man who I assumed was her husband, his thumbs hooked into his belt loops.

Nilsa returned and handed me a folded piece of paper. "Memories of Nicaro," she said. I unfolded the paper and read under a yellow lamp.

Nicaro, 17 August 2017
Many years have passed, but in my mind have remained, still fresh, many memories filled with respect and love for humanity.
Of the families who left a numerous and beautiful legacy are those of the hospital: Guillermo Dumois and his collective, including Dr. Loredo; his brother, Dr. Hipólito Dumois; Dr. Hortensia, stomatology, niece of Guillermo; Dr. Ortega; also including Hernestina, responsible for the laboratory, and

There was nothing else; the letter ended. I looked up.
Nilsa slapped her knee. "Can you believe it? I ran out of ink!"

*

In the morning, Tony drove me back to Holguín, where I picked up the Vía Azul for Havana. The bus ride took 15 hours because we stopped every 20 minutes. Passengers. Lunch. The driver buying Dora the Explorer DVDs at a roadside stand. At one rest stop, I spied an elementary-school-aged boy out the window whose shirt read, simply, FUCK.

Night turned up, and we started letting people off the bus 15 miles from the capital, seemingly at random, on the hips of plantain fields. Ileana and Melo weren't at the Airbnb in Havana when I arrived—it was an unceremonious exit, with only Yero and the rest of the menagerie to bid me goodbye.

I called Dad right when I arrived back in Austin and greeted him in Spanish, wanting to impress him, but we only exchanged a few sentences before he switched to English and told me about recent back pain. I was dying to tell him about my trip, but when I brought it up, he didn't seem interested in talking about it. When I called a few days later, he admitted that imagining me in Nicaro while he sat at home in Austin had made him depressed.

I skirted talk of Cuba for the next week or so until finally my stepmom invited me over for dinner. We shared one of the quieter meals we'd ever eaten together. After we washed the dishes, I sheepishly asked if he was ready to see pictures. "If it's too much, I'll stop," I said. "We can always look later."

"We'll see."

I brought the album up on a computer and ran it through the television. And there it all was: Ileana and Melodí, the patio in storm, a sunny day at the Malecón. A video of '50s Fords puttering down the highway. Dad remained noncommittal, mostly unimpressed. But when I brought up the video I'd taken in the taxi, arriving for the first time in Nicaro, Dad sat up. He started plying me with questions, asking if that was really the nickel plant now, if that was really the hospital, the American Club. He was indignant at the black earth that seeped from the hills, shaken by the absence of his family's home, saddened by the disrepair, the rust, the decay. But in all that there was something else, too. After watching a video of the ruined pier where he had once whiled away the hours fishing with his sister, he said, "It's probably good I didn't go. Nothing's the same."

And then I realized: it was relief. Nothing was as he remembered, to such an extent that, for him, it was not even the same place. Not the Nicaro he knew. Not Nicaro at all. And his memories were safe, preserved in the amber of forever ago.

For months afterward, I waited for my family to express interest in our home country, but no one did. Only at the brothers' Thanksgiving (our uncles and aunts hold separate gatherings now) did one uncle ask offhandedly how my trip was, and when I started to speak, he traveled far away, his hand holding a Lone Star against his sternum, letting my words enter the can instead of what was behind it.

In my fantasies, my family would come to me on the mountain. I'd imagined them suffering a thirst they'd never been aware of until I gave them their first sip of the water of our country. Then they would gorge themselves and with full bellies become docile, wonder where those four years had gone, maybe even dig up some choice morsels of Spanish in their reconciliation. But after a handful of false starts—me hedging into a story or two of my time in Cuba, my relatives unsure how or what to ask me about—there settled a deep sense of futility; I was afraid that if I tried harder to talk about it, I would gather more evidence of my family's disinterest. I began to wonder if the whole enterprise had been a waste of time.

Writers, however, cannot stay quiet forever, and springs will seep even from the most compact earth. Six months after I returned from Cuba, my frustration bubbled into this piece, and I sent my brother the first draft.

"I thought *you* didn't want to talk about it," he said. "You never mentioned it, so I thought it was a shitty trip." He suggested I email the whole family the pictures I'd taken during my time in Cuba. A great idea; if my stories of Nicaro made the family want to off themselves, at least I wouldn't have to watch them resist the urge. So I went through all the photos and videos I'd taken of Havana and Nicaro and created a slide show with all the details and anecdotes I could remember. I attached it to a new email, apologizing for not having written about the trip sooner, and addressed it to every person in the family. The first time my entire family got together since Tata's funeral was in the recipient line of an email. I hit send.

The responses trickled in. Grateful responses, expressions of disbelief at Nicaro's deterioration, minor keys of sadness. My youngest aunt and uncle—fraternal twins—reminded me they came to the States when they were four and remembered nothing of the island. The older aunt said she was brought to tears; the older uncle that it brought back memories on which he did not elaborate.

And then—

Nothing changed.

I realized the homeland wasn't bad medicine. It just wasn't the medicine they needed.

In talking to my dad about writing this essay, I've tried to gain clarity. Was it really the jewelry? Only that? When he saw the first draft, he said I'd gotten it wrong. "It wasn't the jewels. I don't care about that. It was the betrayal." In his version of events, Tata had always wanted everything—*everything*—split five ways. But then in the last vulnerable years of life, when the levees around her mind had started to crumble due to chemotherapy, there'd been a meeting with Tata and her lawyer that only one of the siblings, my aunt, could attend. Then Tata died. Then the will was read, and it wasn't everything five ways, period—it was everything five ways, save the jewels.

"After all that?" Dad says, over and over again. "After I got my ass beat in Mississippi for them? Held their hands running from that helicopter in Nicaro? Really? *Really?*" For him, it's an irreparable betrayal; no amount of talking can fix it. Once my dad is crossed, he's crossed forever.

I know, too, how my aunts feel: that their brothers have accused them of manipulating their own mother in her final years. Another wound not easily healed.

The last time I went to Dad's house, I asked if he could scrounge up a Xeroxed note he claimed Tata wrote in her last couple years saying everything should be split five ways. He didn't find it. Instead, he found a handwritten letter about her will from years earlier, 1996, only two years after my grandfather had died, when the question of death and its resulting mess of logistics must have felt fresh and urgent. I'd never seen it before. It's a short note—all of six sentences—addressed to "Dearest Carlos Miguel" and signed "All my love, Mami." I hesitate to make too much out of it; she lived another 15 years in good health. But one line stands out, the final words underlined so hard the emphasis could gather dirt:

What I really wish is that the five of you get together and <u>make all the decisions together.</u>

It's all fallible. I don't know if the Xerox exists, or if Dad's confusing it for this note, which any lawyer would toss out the window. Dad's memory is porous. So are my aunts' and uncles', and mine. The whole exercise of making an ironclad account of my family's disintegration has felt like sculpting with smoke. It doesn't matter; the result's the same. Dad has settled into his permanent groove — *Really? Really?*—and so have my aunts and uncles.

"Idiotas," Tata might have said. "Greedy, jealous, inconsiderate. Ruining everything over some gold bracelets and a piece of paper."

It's not the story I wanted to tell. But today, I feel like Nilsa; my pen has run out of ink. I wanted to return from Cuba with the One Ingredient to fix our family's amnesia, but it's not a question of recipe; it's a question of our mother tongue. Lengua del Pájaro. The truth is, my family does not speak the same language anymore. Half of it has been thrown away.

ALEX MACGREGOR

Is This the Most Crowded Island in the World? (And Why That Question Matters)

FROM *Longreads*

GEOGRAPHERS HAVE AN AFFINITY for superlatives. Among the millions of named features on earth, if something can claim to be the biggest, tallest, deepest, longest, or otherwise most extreme, it gets a lot of attention.

Asserting any superlative involves a degree of hubris. Our world has been picked over for superlatives, but how sure can we really be about any one claim? Any elementary school class will recite in unison that Mount Everest is the tallest mountain in the world —that is, unless the class happens to contain an Ecuadorian student. Ecuadorians correctly learn that the highest mountain in the world could be measured by distance from the center of the earth, rather than from mean sea level. By this measure, Ecuador's Chimborazo is taller than Everest. An asterisk is warranted for even this basic claim.

Of much less prominence on the globe, but also a tricky superlative to nail down, is the most densely populated island in the world. A handful of the perhaps 100,000 islands on earth have stratospheric population densities: Ultracrowded islands exist in places as disparate as Kenya, Hong Kong, France, and the Maldives, but it's regularly cited that, by the numbers, the densest of all is Santa Cruz del Islote, a three-acre islet of about 1,200 people off the coast of Colombia. This claim has been repeated in numerous publications, most recently by the *New York Times,* and it's even the subject of a short documentary. Journalists usually emphasize the bonds of family and community in a place so radically removed from Western consumerism.

All of which makes for an uplifting read about a fascinating place. But what if the premise is wrong? I can't comment on the experience of life on the island. But we've already learned to be wary of superlative claims, especially when Westerners are the ones keeping score; what about this one? What if this is merely a *very* crowded island, and not *the most* crowded island?

After taking a few trips to other countries as a backpacker, I decided to try my hand traveling in a country that had always fascinated me: Haiti. First I went to the more straightforward northern region of the country, then to Port-au-Prince and other areas. I decided to cut back on time-wasting apps and devote those spare moments to learning Kreyòl instead. I read up on the Haitian Revolution. I made a minor pastime out of studying the country bit by bit on Google Earth.

One day, while poring over the south coast of Haiti on Google Earth—whether I was scouting for places that might be interesting to visit or just killing time I can't recall—I found an island that looked *really* densely crowded. From above, it's difficult to see that it's even an island—just a big clump of houses surrounded by a narrow band of beach. Had I stumbled upon a place that might challenge Santa Cruz del Islote's claim? Could this island really be the world's most crowded?

This far-fetched possibility was tricky to disprove. The internet offers virtually no information about this mystery island, or really about any of Haiti's many fishing islands packed with people. This particular island has dozens of houses and is smaller than a football field, yet Haiti doesn't log a single entry in Wikipedia's list of the most densely populated islands on earth.

Unable to find a sufficiently detailed map of this corner of Haiti, I invested in a navigational chart. After all, this isn't the nineteenth century, and with satellites, airplanes, and 7 billion people wandering the planet, I figured this patch of land must surely be among the millions of features geographers have documented. When the highly detailed map showed up at my house a few days later, I excitedly flattened the monochromatic, water-resistant sheet on the floor. I went straight to the spot where this mystery island sits, and there I found a little islet: Caye de l'Est. Eastern Cay.

Bingo. So Google Earth didn't fabricate a spit of sand covered in houses to troll geography nerds like me. (At least not *again*: in

2013 a glitch caused Google Earth to display a fake island in the South Pacific the size of Manhattan.)

I scoured the internet for information on the island, freshly armed with this somewhat distinctive name. I mostly came up dry. The search results related to this island are all generic web pages without a shred of actual information on the place: automatically generated web pages with skeletal information, but nothing of real value. No news stories, no mission trip reports, no Wikipedia page, no travel blogs. Nothing about its people; nothing indicating its people even exist. A ghost island.

Another, more ominous, revelation of the navigational chart is that Caye de l'Est used to be one of many sandy cays in the Baie des Cayes, the body of water that runs between Île-à-Vache and mainland Haiti. The map shows 15 islands; some named, others unnamed sandbars. Nowadays, per Google Earth, 5 remain: a small island near Île-à-Vache, 2 tiny sandbars, a large island with scores of houses called Caye de l'Eau, and, isolated miles from the others, Caye de l'Est.

Since no other information on the island was forthcoming, my next move was clear: next time I found myself in Haiti, I would make the journey from Port-au-Prince to Caye de l'Est. Or whatever the island is really called—Haitians rarely cooperate with outsiders' names. Most towns, streets, and intersections in Haiti follow an informal but exclusively used nomenclature. I knew that, whatever Haitians call this island, it's probably not Eastern Cay.

Haiti's population density routinely surpasses what other countries consider extreme. The 14 square miles of Port-au-Prince's city proper, a sprawl of mostly one-story houses, hold about a million people: it has a population density equal to Manhattan's. Atlanta's larger metropolitan area covers roughly the same land area as the nation of Haiti, yet Haiti's overwhelmingly rural footprint packs in almost *twice* the total population of heavily suburban metro Atlanta. If the state of Georgia had the population density of Haiti, its population would equal that of California and New York combined.

The high population density that defines the landscape of modern Haiti is a recurring theme from the country's history: too many people on too small of an island. Early Haitian history is, as most people are aware, the story of humans shackled and abducted from their homes in Africa. In the colony of Saint Domingue, which was later to become independent Haiti, France used a brutally efficient supply of slaves to establish one of the most lucrative cash crop colonies earth has ever known. This was not farming; this was a factory plantation economy. The ability of the island to provide food to sustain its population was not a consideration of the French. The goal of Saint Domingue was to maximize sugar and coffee production by whatever means necessary, and this meant a huge supply of slaves—roughly twice as many slaves were imported to Saint Domingue compared with the United States—and a shockingly high mortality rate. The colony became one of the most densely populated places in the colonized Americas; its population quickly dwarfed the Spanish side of the island, the present-day Dominican Republic.

The enslaved population rose up and obliterated the plantation system, seeing in the beginnings of the French Revolution an opportunity to break free from their chains. But before Haiti was even independent of France, the heroes of its slave rebellion debated how a country so packed with people could ever feed itself; surely a return to plantation economics and cash crops was inevitable to feed the overcrowded nation. It was ultimately this unpopular assessment that led to the legendary Toussaint Louverture's downfall.

Haiti's population has grown 20-fold since those days.

The debate over whether Haiti was to focus on food or export crops was never settled, but was instead eclipsed by the second great theme of Haitian history: with disasters natural and human-made, big and small, the deck has been stacked against Haiti from the beginning.

The 2010 earthquake that devastated Port-au-Prince was just the latest in a series of damaging tremors, but the scale of destruction and harm, still widely visible to this day, cannot be overstated. People have often asked me when I mention traveling to Haiti whether it has recovered from the hurricane. I tell them that they're probably mistaking the 2010 earthquake for a hurricane—except, sadly, they might not be. Devastating cyclones came through in 2004, 2008, and 2016, flooding coastal areas, destroying crops and livestock, and spreading disease. Each one would probably be dubbed "the hurricane" in most places; in Haiti, you must be specific.

Diseases have also played prominently in Haitian history. Haiti was, cruelly, a byword for HIV in the 1980s, although changing behaviors and public health efforts have reduced the infection rate significantly. More recently, the UN's peacekeeping force, MINUSTAH, spread cholera to the country through poor sanitation at a base in the center of the country, causing 11,000 deaths and stoking international outrage. Nonetheless, I learned that Haitians are equally angered by a completely different grievance against MINUSTAH: *kadejak,* a word my nascent Kreyòl vocabulary didn't contain. *Kadejak* means "rape."

I could go on about Haiti's misfortunes, but that's not the point of this—that story has been told before, and better than I can tell it. At the root of all these catastrophes is a human-made culprit: debt.

Shortly after independence, France forced Haiti to accept a crippling indemnity at the threat of a blockade or outright invasion. Haiti was to pay 150 million francs that it clearly didn't have. This financial ransoming ultimately left Haiti indebted to French and American banks until after World War II. At one point, 80 percent of Haiti's tax revenue went toward servicing debt on this indemnity, which was ostensibly compensation to France for the theft of French property during the Haitian Revolution, mortgaged all the way into the 1940s and paid for by the children and grandchildren of enslaved people who fought for and won their freedom. The exact toll is incalculable: Haiti's government was, by design, unable to make a single payment on time, and conveniently had to take out loans from French and American banks at predatory terms. This was a much cleaner way of exploiting the island than direct slavery. Estimates place the present-day value of the payments between $20 and $40 billion. And that's not the end of it. It's impossible to know the additional damage caused by the creation of the Haitian police state by the United States during its occupation of Haiti from 1915 to 1934—an occupation to enforce Haiti's debt to the United States, naturally—and by the subsequent deployment of this police state by future regimes against the Haitian people.

The powerful forces of the world ensured that a nation born in a slave rebellion could never stand among them as equals.

*

Haitians must resort to extreme means of survival in light of a densely overcrowded countryside and economic disadvantages. The country has routinely asked too much of its rugged terrain, pushing Haitians to cultivate marginal plots for meager yields. Less visibly, the same thing has happened to its waters. The need to fill hungry bellies yesterday created overfished reefs today. Haitian fishing is done by sailboat or canoe. Fishermen scour the remaining productive reefs. Since speeds are slow, being close to the fish means everything. A sandbar stable enough for thatch houses in the middle of a good reef opens the reef up to intensive fishing that would be impossible otherwise.

Sailing in a Haitian fishing boat sounds like a dicey proposition in theory: a handmade wooden vessel propelled by patched-together sails, out in the ocean without a life jacket in sight. Friends and family seemed especially wary about this part of my admittedly unusual journey. But in the moment, setting off toward azure horizons, my mind was quickly put at ease. The skills of the two-person crew more than made up for the simple craft—I felt safer on one of these than on a hobbyist's motorboat, life jackets and all. These guys are badasses, and not just for their decades of experience dealing with every possible weather condition and vessel mishap that a lifetime of fishing in the Caribbean could throw at them: they used to make clandestine runs to Cuba during the tumultuous wind-down of the Duvalier era, over a hundred miles of open ocean, with perils awaiting them at both ends of the journey.

My errand was humdrum by comparison. We set sail from Île-à-Vache—a picturesque island of rolling hills, beaches, palm trees—on a seven-mile journey across the Baie des Cayes on a clear, calm day. The crew knew our destination well. They even had friends there—this is no ghost island after all! They also had a name for it. A *real* name.

Caye de l'Est is really called Ilet a Brouee.

Apart from a handful of hot spots with enough tourism to be monetized by the locals, Haiti is an intensely emotional place for the independent traveler. A *blan* walking around unchaperoned by the dehumanizing security apparatus which typically accompanies aid workers presents a rare opportunity for real human interaction with a foreigner—and Haitians are often inclined to take it. It's

not uncommon to be invited to sit down and chat, whether taking refuge in a doorway during a rainstorm in Port-au-Prince or
wandering the streets of a small town. Usually, it's friendly banter
—playful, poking fun at the *blan*. This adds another dimension to
the emotional challenge Haiti can present.

On Ilet a Brouee I felt this emotional awareness pushed to an
extreme.

Sure, mixed into my emotional stew was a sense of excitement,
as I was finally getting to see this unacknowledged place after years
of wonder. But my heart also dropped as the island came into focus on the horizon, a larger and larger wedge between the turquoise water and cobalt-blue sky.

I'm certainly aware of the negative image the media exploits
when Haiti makes headlines, but I was holding out hope that this
crowded little island might have a measure of stability, perma-
nence, and—dare I say it—prosperity. Like the stories of its cousin
a few hundred miles to the south in Colombia. Or maybe a story
of people living in harmony with the natural world, like you would
see on *Human Planet*. But another lesson of Haitian history is that
narratives imported by foreigners never hold in Haiti; Haiti writes
its own narratives. Ilet a Brouee appeared, at a glance, to be a
tangle of sticks, tarps, and thatch, of unstable structures huddled
on a sliver of beach.

After we pulled as close as you can get to the island, I scurried
over the side of our boat and waded carefully to shore. Suddenly
more than a little overwhelmed by the situation, the crew navigated my introduction to some of the older residents. I was now
doubly indebted to them. This island, apparently off the edge of
most foreigners' radar, is about as curious a place as any for a *blan*
to wind up unannounced.

They graciously gave me permission to wander around and take
pictures.

Ilet a Brouee is a maze of alleyways through crooked thatch- and
tarp-covered houses—some more permanent than others—with a
handful of turns before you reach the center of town or the shoreline. The main landmarks in town are the two concrete buildings
—the church and the store—and the modest town square in the
middle, outfitted with two solar streetlights: a defunct old one and
a shiny new one.

Men outnumber women and children, but not to the extent

I would have guessed; this is no mere fishermen's retreat. Ilet a Brouee is more like a factory: many people are out fishing during the day, dotting the surrounding horizon with sails and pirogues, but others remain on the island, working all day repairing boats; mending nets, hooks, and traps; processing and preparing thousands of fish for shipment to Île-à-Vache and Haiti. Most of the kids seem to spend their days swimming.

As is sadly common throughout Haiti, the landscape is harsh. Most of the shoreline isn't beach, but rather makeshift levees of conch shells, broken concrete, and old tires, sometimes held together by fishing nets and much too jagged for unaccustomed bare feet. The island's only natural feature, a coconut tree, was snapped in half by Hurricane Matthew. The trunk was used to build a ladder to the toilet, elevated over the sea just off the northern edge of the island.

There are a few wells around the island—perforated plastic buckets dug a couple feet into the sand. They don't provide drinking water, but supply water clean enough for bathing. Drinking water is imported from mainland Haiti in plastic bags. Each bag costs about a nickel, and contains 200 milliliters of clean water. Cisterns are not used.

After a few minutes of walking around, I came across one of the many canopies people congregate under as they work in the midday heat. Except that this one was different: it had an empty chair, right in the middle. A chair meant for me. Welcome to the conversation—time to explain myself.

A man began by telling me he's very happy to see me here because if "someone like me" is coming to their island, it means I must be planning a project to help. He was keen to know my background and my religion—questions I wasn't expecting nor eager to answer, knowing full well my answers probably weren't the ones they were hoping for.

There was that sinking feeling again. If I could have picked any group of people in the world to avoid disappointing, it would have been these people.

I feebly explained that I'm not here to help, at least not right now, and not in that way. I'm not with an organization or a church, and I can't plan a project. I tried to explain the unsatisfying fact that I'm just a guy with a fondness for Haiti who came here partly on a hunch that this might be the most crowded island in the world, and partly out of exasperation that I couldn't learn a damned thing about this place otherwise. After all, I wanted to say, how could anyone plan a project here when the outside world barely knows Ilet a Brouee even exists?

Instead, I asked them, if an NGO *were* to come plan a project, how could they help?

The answer was as simple as it was tragic: metal roofs and a toilet.

The roofs are mostly thatch, and impossible to waterproof. The difficulty of keeping dry—a fundamental problem that plagues contemporary Haiti—is inescapable here. In a thatch house with a sand floor a few feet above sea level, how do you store the precious documents that establish who you are and what you own? Add to that the contribution to disease caused by excessive moisture in the home, and water is, perversely, a major problem for this place that has none to drink. Some people live in tents inside their houses, some put plastic tarps over their houses, and some install metal roofs and hope they hold out against the corrosive sea spray.

The toilet, meanwhile, is a makeshift structure built over the water, so uncomfortable that people often use the adjacent beach instead.

I thought, *Who could be content with a world where these people, living on an island without power, water, sewer, medical care, or schools, complain only about a toilet and leaky roofs to the rare foreigner who passes through?* But that's not a question for these people; that's a question for me.

Instead, I asked: Roughly how many people live here?

As you might guess, it depends. The fish and the rains cause the population to fluctuate during the year. Some children leave the island to board with family elsewhere and attend school; others don't. Some people have family over in Haiti—the name they give the mainland proper. The people who own boats are more likely to have another place to return to; others wind up on Ilet a Brouee to work, and this is it for them.

I was told there are 97 houses on Ilet a Brouee. Adding up all the residents, including the children who stay with family elsewhere to attend school during parts of the year, Ilet a Brouee is home base to around 500 people.

Ilet a Brouee is almost exactly 4,000 square meters, or .004 square kilometer—just under an acre, after losing 20 percent of its landmass during Hurricane Matthew. If the locally given population of 500 is taken at face value, that implies a population density of 125,000 per square kilometer, somewhat ahead of Santa Cruz del Islote's 1,247 people living on .012 square kilometer. I later got in touch with Île-à-Vache's mayor, Jean Yvres Amazan, who estimates the population of Ilet a Brouee at 250. Either way, if you're going to talk about the most crowded island on earth, Ilet a Brouee belongs in the conversation.

Another question I couldn't help asking the islanders: Have you ever heard of Caye de l'Est? They chuckled politely when I told them that's the name by which the world knows their island. Each foreigner must be entitled to a few ridiculous statements.

After asking and answering a few more questions, I returned to wandering around on the island and talking to as many people as I could. The buzz of the foreigner arriving was dying down, and I was only accompanied by a throng of curious children. A *blan* in their tiny world.

I saw people busy processing hundreds of small fish; napping in the church or under canopies in the midday heat; mending nets, lines, and hooks. Powered by private solar panels that have become ubiquitous in Haiti, Western pop music and *kompa* took turns drowning out the soft hum of waves breaking on the levees and the workday banter.

When they think of it at all, developing world poverty bothers most people who live in first world comfort. They react to it differently, but for compassionate people, it's important to hold out hope for improving the lives of the world's poor.

What about the people on Ilet a Brouee? I've racked my brain, before visiting and since, thinking of how to support those living there, of how to make Ilet a Brouee look more like the micro-island success story the papers peddled about Santa Cruz del Islote.

But the contradictions on Ilet a Brouee are intractable. Who can sell a Western-friendly development vision in a place where sewage and trash go into the sea? What economic development plans exist for an island where the only possible economic activity is plucking the ever-smaller fish from an overfished reef? And what about sea level rise, and the fate of most of the other sandy cays in the Canal de l'Est?

To call Ilet a Brouee endangered is neither abstract nor hyperbole. Sandy cays are extremely sensitive to sea level rise; a few extra inches of water can increase erosion and ultimately doom an island. Google Earth shows the tragedy in real time. Off the north coast of Grand Anse, in a different archipelago from Ilet a Brouee, satellite images show that multiple islands inhabited as recently as 2014 have been wiped off the map.

Should outsiders step in to reinforce the sandy banks of the island? Or perhaps restore the island to its former size, while they're at it? This reef is less overfished than the others—that's why people go to such lengths claiming a plot on this island.

The hardest part of Ilet a Brouee for me to confront is the why, on a larger scale. *Why* do people live on a spit of sand in the ocean, with no water, no electricity, no sewer, no medicine, no services of any type? The sad reality is that the conditions on Ilet a Brouee aren't all that different from what Haitians must endure across the country. Most Haitians lack these things; what difference does it make if you're doing it on a sandbar a few miles out in the ocean? At least you're in the middle of a big reef that's a comparative bonanza of protein.

Modern society uniformly condemns the historical kidnapping and enslavement of African people. At times, we're even willing to have conversations about the economic subjugation of developing nations and the blatant extortion of Haiti in the early nineteenth century. However, questioning the ongoing effective imprisonment of Haiti's inhabitants remains the domain of only radical thinkers.

Humans, especially poor ones, *must* remain in their homelands. Haitians need a visa to travel to most nations on earth, let alone work in them—this includes the Dominican Republic and every nation with nonstop flights from Haiti. Haitians are confined to their overcrowded island, forever paying the price of the kidnapping and extortion of their ancestors for the benefit of foreigners.

Faced with life in a land that can barely feed its inhabitants, many Haitians flee to parts of the world where food, water, electricity, and medicine aren't in critically short supply. There's a saying in Haiti: A rich man travels, a poor man leaves. But this option is closed to most, and the peril Haitians face abroad is well documented. From the 1937 Parsley Massacre perpetrated against Haitians in the Dominican borderlands, to the dehumanizing status many Haitian migrants suffer today, especially in the United States and the Dominican Republic, economic migration is a dangerous endeavor, and the supply of Haitians hoping to work abroad overwhelms the willingness of foreign countries to host them.

Ilet a Brouee and islands like it tell another, less visible story of people who fled a country unable to feed itself. Instead of migrating to foreign lands, these people fled Haiti and built a town on one of the last sandbars in a dying archipelago. Suffering from overcrowding, dwindling food sources, and even questions about the viability of sustaining life on the island in an ever-fiercer climate, Ilet a Brouee became a microcosm of Haiti itself. In the long-standing debate about whether foreign aid helps or hurts recipient countries, foreigners smugly assert that Haiti has a "culture of dependence" on foreign aid and charity; the extremes to which the residents of Ilet a Brouee resort to feed themselves and their country debunk this patronizing label.

It is a perversion of conventional human rights that freedom of movement is granted for capital, but not for labor. Anyone who believes that a child born anywhere in the world deserves an opportunity for a stable, healthy life must advocate for steps toward freedom of movement. The only alternative would be a world where all states are truly on an equal footing, and that went out the window with gunboat diplomacy, with systematic looting of the developing world through debt, with colonization, with the slave trade itself. These misdeeds shaped the world as we know it. We cannot ignore this history and assert that feeding Haitians is just Haiti's problem. Humans should have the right to migrate, especially to the places that benefited so much from the historical exploitation of their homelands. By barring free movement, we guarantee countless tales of people resorting to desperate measures to survive.

I'll stop short of claiming a superlative, of claiming that Ilet a Brouee is actually the most crowded island on earth. After all, if as obvious a candidate like Ilet a Brouee is beyond our readily shared knowledge, what else might be out there?

We talk with derision about the "discoveries" of European explorers, and the contradiction of discovering a place already well within current human knowledge. Now, with most of humanity exchanging information in an open-source, global forum, it's tempting to think that we've integrated the knowledge of earth's many places and peoples—that if somebody knows about it, it's probably easily knowable by everyone.

This appears to be untrue. On a smaller scale, "discoveries" are still being made: take Somoto Canyon in Nicaragua, a stunning 150-meter-deep crevice that's only 10 meters wide, which flew under the radar until 2004; or Fort Drouet in Haiti, a military fort and coffee plantation that contains the only known ruins of slave housing in the country, which was forgotten until a road was built nearby in 2009. These are both in densely populated parts of their respective countries, a short walk from farms and villages and well known to generations of locals. Not only is our planet surprisingly poorly understood, but we're also less adept than we might guess at gathering these threads of local knowledge and experience, scattered across the globe and frayed by borders, language, and economics, and weaving them into our collective understanding of the human experience. Our understanding of life on this planet is still mainly projected from narrow, elite corners.

JEFF MACGREGOR

Taming the Lionfish

FROM *Smithsonian*

None of this had to happen. Not Florida. Not the ibis's beak. Not
water. Not the horseshoe crab's empty body and not the living
starfish. Evolution might have turned left at the corner and gone
down another street entirely.
  —Jane Hirshfield

Friday

WE WERE SOMEWHERE around Pensacola Pass, on the edge of
the Gulf of Mexico, when the over-the-counter drugs failed to take
hold.

Just after sunrise the seas are running two or four or six feet
and at the mouth of the Gulf where the bay opens up and the tide
meets the wind from the east and the west and the north and the
south is a washing machine of razorback crests and sub-basement
troughs, waves running horizon to horizon, some as big as houses,
whitecaps peeling off the long rollers, the water every blue and
every green, the rise and fall of our little boat a series of silences,
groans, engine noises, and cymbal crashes as we pitch and roll and
the whole boatload of gear works itself loose from the fittings, the
tanks and the spears and the wet suits and the vests and the fins
and the buckets and the coolers and computers and the compasses
and regulators and the backups to the backups to the backups,
every dive system three times redundant now soaked and stream-
ing, bobbing in the bilges, and the waves coming over the side, the

top, the stern, the bow, all of us pitching and yawing and rolling and moaning and swearing and all that gear floating at our ankles with the bags of white cheddar popcorn and the wasabi and the Red Vines, all of us grabbing for the gunwales or the rails or each other, Captain Andy at the wheel calm as a vicar, Barry with his feet planted, singing at the top of his lungs, "Welcome back, my friends, to the show that never ends," and the planetary surge of 500 quadrillion gallons of angry water pouring through the tiny nautilus of my inner ear on its way to my stomach. I lean over the side and throw up again. Doubled over the transom, John casually does likewise. The motion-sickness tablets do nothing.

We all laugh.

We're here to hunt lionfish.

Before we get to the marine biology, this has to be said: the lionfish is one of the most beautiful animals alive. With its bold stripes and extravagant fins, its regal bearing and magisterial stillness, every lionfish is a hand-lacquered eleventh-century Japanese fan. It is a diva, a glamour-puss, a showoff. If you ran a hedge fund in Greenwich or Geneva or Tokyo, the first fish you'd buy for that 100,000-gallon aquarium in your lobby would be a lionfish. It is in every respect spectacular. And in this hemisphere it is an eco-killer, a destroyer of worlds.

Four hundred twenty-two words of marine biology boilerplate, a NOAA crib sheet, and a warning:

In the southeast US and Caribbean coastal waters the lionfish is an invasive species. It competes for food and space with overfished native populations. Scientists fear lionfish will kill off helpful locals such as algae-eating parrot fish, allowing seaweed to overtake coral reefs already stressed by rising water temperatures and bleaching. Lionfish kill off other small cleaner fish, too, which increases the risk of infection and disease among sport fish and cash fishery populations. In US waters, lionfish stocks continue to grow and increase in range. Lionfish have no known predators here and reproduce all year long; a mature female lionfish releases roughly 2 million eggs a year, which are then widely dispersed by ocean currents.

Two million eggs a year.

Scientific name: *Pterois volitans* (red lionfish)

Unscientific, badass nickname: devil firefish

Identification: Lionfish have distinctive brown and white or maroon and white stripes covering the head and body. Tentacles protrude above the eyes and below the mouth. They have fanlike pectoral fins and long dorsal spines. An adult lionfish can grow as large as 18 inches.

Native range: The South Pacific and Indian Oceans, where natural predators, including grouper, keep their population in check.

Habitat: Lionfish are found in the tropics, in warm water and in most marine habitats. Lionfish have been found in or on hard-bottom ocean floor, mangrove, sea grass, coral, and artificial reefs at depths from 1 to 1,000 feet.

Non-native range: Since the 1980s, lionfish have been reported in growing numbers along the southeastern United States coast from Texas to North Carolina. Juvenile lionfish have been collected in waters as far north as Long Island, New York.

Lionfish are eating machines. They are active hunters that ambush their prey by using their outstretched pectoral fins to corner them. If lionfish are unable to adapt to declines in their prey, their population might decrease. In the short term, however, they will turn to cannibalism.

Warning! Lionfish spines deliver a venomous sting that can last for days and cause extreme pain. Also sweating, respiratory distress, and even paralysis. Lionfish venom glands are located in the spines on the top and the sides and the bottom of the fish. They can sting you even after the fish is dead. The venom is a neurotoxin. Once the spine punctures the skin, the venom enters the wound through grooves in the spine. If stung, seek medical attention immediately.

The guys on the dock will tell you that the sting of a lionfish is like "getting hit hard by a hammer, then injecting the bruise with hot sauce." Wear gloves.

How they got here no one really knows. Like giant shoulder pads and the music of Frank Stallone, some things about the 1980s remain inexplicable. The arrival in American waters of the lionfish is one of these mysteries. There are a couple of recurring stories, but they don't really add up to a truth. The first is that some home aquarium owner emptied a few of them into the ocean one night—the narrative equivalent of the New York City alligator-down-the-toilet story. Another story suggests a big resort hotel in the Caribbean mishandled the filtration setup on its giant destination aquarium and pumped them out into the sea. Or that a breeding pair escaped during Hurricane Andrew. Maybe they arrived here in the water ballast of big cargo ships from the Pacific.

Now they're everywhere. Like locusts. That's the bad news. The lionfish has Florida in a noose, and from Mobile, Alabama, to Cape Hatteras, North Carolina, the lionfish is a blight, a plague, an epidemic. A perfect evolutionary machine for eating and ruin, every lionfish is the lace-collared cutthroat in your underwater Elizabethan costume drama.

The good news? Lionfish is delicious.

All this I learned at the Smithsonian Marine Station in Fort Pierce, Florida. They have a team of molecular scientists and marine biologists there, and benthic ecologists and visiting zoologists and doctoral candidates and postdocs and technicians and reef experts. They have a research laboratory and a public aquarium where a couple of times a day you can watch a little lionfish get fed. This is out on Seaway Drive, and on a hot spring morning the light here is like the aftermath of a blast. In fact, when you drive from here to Pensacola, all of Florida feels like a trick of the light. Overbright or too dark, at once too soft and too sharp, under water or above it, you're never sure what you're seeing. At noon the asphalt shimmers and the sand dazzles and at midnight the stars swim in an ink-black heaven above the cypress and the slash pine. Is that a Disney castle rising in the distant murk, or just a jet of swamp gas? From Daytona to the Everglades to the Keys, from Universal Studios to the Fountain of Youth, Florida is a fever dream, an unreliable narrator. Florida is a fiction. It is an impossible place.

And that's how we all wound up in this little boat at the Lionfish World Championship. One of dozens of lionfish rodeos or derbies or hunts around the state, events like this are the first line of defense against the lionfish takeover. The premise is simple: whoever spears the most lionfish wins. Sponsored by Coast Watch Alliance and the Florida Fish and Wildlife Conservation Commission, Reef Rangers, the Gulf Coast Lionfish Coalition, and about a dozen others, over the last few years this tournament has cleaned thousands of lionfish out of the local ecosystem. In 2016 alone it brought in more than 8,000 fish—in a weekend. I'm here to watch one of five or six teams kill every lionfish it sees.

Even before dawn the marina is loud with gulls and banging halyards and happy obscenity. As the sun rises so does the wind, and wary talk of what a wild, E-ticket ride the day's going to be. Before any of us step aboard, the little boat is already filled with gear and we're still lashing coolers to the deck. There isn't a spare inch anywhere. But off we go.

Captain Andy Ross is a fidget spinner of a man, quiet, apparently motionless, but going a thousand miles an hour. He is fit and tanned and of some glorious sun-worn indeterminate middle age. He is one of the tournament founders, too, and master and commander of the *Niuhi,* a 25-foot catamaran dive boat with a small deckhouse and cabin and twin Yamaha 150s to push us out into the Gulf. Generally soft-spoken, from time to time while I'm redistributing my breakfast over the port-side gunwale, he calls out to me with a small sideways smile, "Sporty today!"

Why yes, Cap'n, yes it is.

On the other hand, Barry Shively, the mate and dive master, never stops talking. Never stops. Never stops singing or storytelling. He is a dynamo, what Grandma would have called a real live wire. He dives and spearfishes mostly for fun. His day job is repairing MRI and CT scanners and other nuclear imaging equipment. He is exactly the kind of charming knucklehead savant you need on a day like today. I was able to sit upright long enough to ask him to describe the early days of the lionfish siege in this part of the Gulf.

"So, we first started seeing them showing up here probably four or five years ago. The first year we seen like one or two. And we'd alert FWC and they were like, 'Well where'd you see it? Let's get some maps going.' Then the science started and every time we came in they wanted to know . . . I mean they were meeting us at the dock asking questions. So, concern was growing and we didn't realize it was going to bloom like this. The next year, it quadrupled. And then the year after that, it was one hundred–fold more than the prior year. It's been an explosion and they have just taken over."

John McCain, smiling a wide smile and vomiting calmly across from me, is a sales manager from Dive Rite, a manufacturer of scuba equipment. Next to him is Carl Molitor, an underwater photographer, calm as the Buddha and somehow eating a breakfast of yogurt and fruit. Next to Carl is Allie ElHage, who has been trying

very hard to light a cigarette in the wind for the last few minutes.
He invented and makes and sells the Zookeeper, a length of wide,
clear PVC pipe with a plastic flange at one end and a Kevlar bag at
the other, into which one stuffs one's speared lionfish. He is smiling, too, and when he leans back and tips his face to the sun he is
a picture of absolute happiness. Alex Page, salon owner and para-
legal and recreational slayer of lionfish, sits on the midships gear
locker with the peaceful mien of a man on his third morning at
the spa. Everyone on this little boat but me is a lionfish serial killer.

The last thing you see of Pensacola as you motor out into the
Gulf are the checkerboard water towers at the naval air station.
That's what the town is famous for, naval aviators. Fighter jocks.
And for prizefighter Roy Jones Jr. Otherwise, the travel posters are
filled with beaches, seafood, board shorts and T-shirts and flip-
flops. It's the Panhandle Eden.

Here's how it works, even on a day as rough as this. You and your
buddies head out past the horizon, about 18 miles. You'll locate by
GPS and by chart and by fish-finder an underwater structure likely
to harbor a population of lionfish. Some of these structures are
known to every charter captain everywhere, and some are jealously
guarded secrets. There aren't many coral reefs in the northern
Gulf—it's mostly a hard sand bottom down there—so these underwater features are almost entirely man-made. Picture a pyramid
of I beams six or eight feet high, or a sphere the same size. The
state sinks them to promote habitat for sportfishing. Most of them,
anyway. There are some shipwrecks down there, too, and some
"habitat" sunk by enterprising locals in less enlightened times, like
rusted school bus bodies and little hillocks of old appliances.

As a charter captain, Andy is a great example of a grassroots
response to an environmental problem. He was taking folks out
spearfishing for snapper and triggerfish and he was seeing more
and more lionfish crowding them out of the habitats.

"It just seemed like a light suddenly came on. I had written in
to someone at one of the local chambers of commerce, I think
we've got a big problem here. We need to probably address it and
I wasn't sure how to go about doing that. The Perdido Key Chamber of Commerce said, 'Well, we've got some funds available for
special projects. Why don't we at least raise some awareness?' I go,
'That's a great idea. How do we go about doing it?' Let's put to-

gether a tournament. It was a little rough at first, but we managed to pull off four or five small tournaments the first year that we had some funding. That just got the whole ball rolling pretty fast."

With the water coming over the bow, you're not going to anchor, you're going to circle while your divers head down in twos and threes. The water out here is between 90 and 120 feet deep, so the divers breathe nitrox from their tanks, a cocktail of nitrogen and oxygen that allows them to make safer trips up and down and stay a little longer on the bottom. Program all that into your dive computer, and it gives back a precise dive profile: how long it takes to descend, how long you can stay, and how fast you can resurface. These are quick "bounce" dives, about 10 minutes descending, 10 minutes on the bottom, 10 minutes back. And these are all very experienced divers. But even for them, it's a bruising proposition trying to pull on gear while being flung from corner to corner, falling, colliding, tripping, swearing. Did I mention they're all carrying spears? You hunt lionfish with what amounts to a modest trident, powered by a short length of surgical tubing.

That's okay, fellas, I'll wait here.

"Are we parked?" the divers yell.

"Yep," says Andy, and the guys wobble the regulators into their mouths and roll backward into the water with a splash.

And that's how we spend the day. Two or three of us always on board and two or three of us almost continually over the side hunting lionfish. Crocs and Kevlar gloves and weapons-grade sunglasses slosh around the bilge. We circle the divers' bubbles until they're ready for pickup. A lot of the exchanges at the stern ladder go like this,

"How many did you get?"

"Twenty-five or thirty."

"How many did you leave?"

"None."

Then empty the Zookeepers into the cooler, get the lionfish on ice, and head for the next spot. Andy peers into the fish-finder; Barry tells another story; Allie lights another cigarette. It's all jawboning and affectionate insult and classic rock on the loudspeaker, "Radar Love" and PG-13 punch lines. Barry hauls the jumbo sandwiches out at midday and the Italian dressing and the peanut butter crackers and I excuse myself to go below. The boys are bringing up fish a dozen or two at a time. At one point, Alex brings up more than 100 fish himself. This is why we came. He is a giant killer.

"Be afraid, lionfish, be very afraid," says Barry.

The rest of the day is a montage of iridescent water and Tintoretto sky, wisecracks and tattoos and lionfish. The coolers slowly fill, and by late afternoon we're surfing back to the pass. The wind is up and the trip home rolls like a motocross track. "I'm tired, man," says Allie to no one in particular.

"But it's addictive, man, like Angry Birds," Barry says, and we rise and fall and ride the crests home.

Somewhere far to the east of us, over the horizon, there is an all-women's team, the first ever, and from what we can make out on the radio, they've been taking many, many fish. But it's hard to know for sure; sandbagging and gamesmanship are a big part of the competition. You never want anyone to know your real numbers until the fish are totaled on Sunday. For now, the women and their lionfish are a distant rumor.

We're back at the dock just before sunset. We might have speared more than 400 lionfish. Or we might not have. I am asked to keep mum on the matter. We are met by a couple of marine biologists. These tournaments are a terrific resource for scientists. Tonight, they're checking the females for egg sacs, researching effective ways to interrupt that prodigious lionfish reproductive cycle. They'll be at it for hours, well into darkness, and will handle every one of those fish.

As it says on Barry's Zookeeper, LEAVE NO LIONFISH BEHIND.

Saturday

It's so windy today, and the surf so much worse, that most teams do not go back out. We do not go back out.

The women's team goes back out. No one has seen them yet. They remain a whisper filled with static, a ghost across the horizon, a figment. Talk of their courage and their madness is a near constant for the day.

For the rest of us, it's a hot sun and calypso on the loudspeakers and 700-horsepower pickup trucks in the parking lot.

The point of the dry land portion of the tournament, the weekend-long lionfish festival in the small park out on the Plaza de Luna, is educational. Informational. And tasty. Once you see the banners in the little park, you begin to understand the statewide strategy for lionfish management.

"Eat 'em to beat 'em"
"Edible Invaders"
"Be the Predator"
"Remove—Eat—Report"

The exhibition tents and displays are evenly divided between things you can read and things you can eat. There are lionfish cooking demonstrations all day, given by well-known local chefs, and long lines to taste the samples. This morning it's Asian wraps done up with lionfish tenders. By noon it's a 10-minute wait to try one. One tent over, Captain Robert Turpin of the Escambia County Marine Resources Division is delivering an informational presentation to the crowd. "Remember folks," he says into the wind noise, "lionfish are venomous, not poisonous."

This is a central tenet of the "Eat 'em to beat 'em" master plan. Consumers don't know lionfish very well. Even though a lionfish sting is sharp and painful, the meat of the fish itself is safe to eat. Unlike fugu, Japan's riskiest delicacy, lionfish is harmless. The fish has to be handled carefully when caught and when filleted, but for customers in a restaurant or at the seafood counter of their local grocery, lionfish is no more of a threat than salmon or flounder or cod. Venomous, not poisonous, is the drumbeat of the whole weekend.

Because the only way to control the lionfish invasion in this hemisphere will be to create a market large enough to turn them into a national cash fish.

But you can't do that by spearing them one at a time. Especially not at depths greater than commercial divers can safely and routinely cull them. You need to start harvesting them in large, dependable numbers. And for that, you need to figure out how to trap them. Or kill them with submersibles, drones, or remote-operated vehicles.

Walk this way to the tent of Steve Gittings, chief scientist for NOAA's National Marine Sanctuary System. If you were asked to paint the portrait of a distinguished, thoughtful, slightly-gray-at-the-temples National Oceanic and Atmospheric Administration PhD, he'd be your guy. On his display table are a number of models of a bell trap, a kind of semiautomated snare that rests on the sea bottom, then closes over, catches, and hoists up lionfish in quantity.

I asked him to thumbnail Florida's lionfish problem, just so we know.

"I think it boils down to two levels of activity that lionfish do. One is eating any small fish that they can eat, but that means those fish are not available for other fish to eat, commercial or otherwise, so that's a whole ecosystem-trophic effect. It's a collapse. Could be a collapse.

"On the other end of the spectrum," he goes on, "they're eating juveniles of the fish that would become commercially available. So, why are people not yet saying, 'There's no more grouper. There's no more snapper'? Well, it might be the juveniles of those species have not reached adulthood—and won't, because they're being eaten by lionfish. So if lionfish are eating a lot of juveniles of snapper, grouper, there's all of a sudden going to be a collapse at the level of species entering the adult phase. That will eventually show up as no more snapper-grouper."

That's it, that's the lionfish apocalypse. But Gittings is an optimist.

"I'm still hopeful that it'll be a non-apocalypse because I hope nature will figure it out. But, at least, as far as the evidence goes . . . so far, apocalypse. It could be.

"But I have to trust in nature, because for a lot of previous invasive species, land or sea, nature eventually figures it out. With disease, with parasites, with predators. So something's going to get these things. Right now, they're taking over. They reproduce better than rabbits, eat like crazy, and nothing eats them.

"There are these places, though, where you just go, 'Where are the lionfish?' So, does that mean non-apocalypse, or does that mean they haven't gotten here yet? Does it mean they will? Does it mean they won't? Does it mean local control is taking care of the problem? I think it's that in large measure.

"Local control does do a lot of good. You hear people here talk about how they are not finding lionfish near shore. That's probably because people are shooting them. The farther offshore you get, the more fish you see.

"So, I think we have to treat it like an apocalypse, but even as a scientist I think it's going to work itself out, and become some kind of balance of nature."

And the deep-water traps?

"You can talk about local control in shallow water using divers. That's doing a good job. I think we ramp it up as much as possible to minimize anything that inhibits that from happening. But that helps us down to that depth.

"But now we've got to tackle the deep-water problem. And do regional control. And how do you do that? You've got to engage lots of people, and maybe lots of different ways. I believe the fishing communities, they answer to that. I don't think that conservation people like myself can buy a bunch of ROVs and go down and shoot them and do things. The fisherman who has a good ROV or some other way of catching lionfish might do that, and that's a good thing, because they get to (A) kill fish and (B) sell fish and make money. And take the pressure off the other species while they're doing it.

"So that's why I got into the thinking about traps to deal with deep-water populations. My logic was, let's design traps that fishermen would be comfortable with, which is mechanical. Fully mechanical, easily deployed, easily retrieved, you can put a bunch of them on a fishing boat. And then we've got to deal with the regulatory matters related to that."

In the next tent over, there's a beautiful mermaid in a chaise longue talking to children about ecology and our collective responsibility to the environment. There's a long line of kids—and their dads—waiting to speak to her.

Around the corner, I talk to Brian Asher, a diver and spearman, and one of the directors of SEALEG, a nonprofit trying to grow the lionfish business into sustainability.

"As a business problem, we have this incredible supply of lionfish. They're breeding rapidly. And on the other end, you have restaurants and grocery stores. You have this huge demand, and there's really no efficient way of connecting the two right now.

"The traps, though, haven't been available until the last two or three months when NOAA published the plans, and that's an inexpensive, easily deployable trap design. Taking commercial fishing operations, and having them focus on this would be . . . I mean, just huge gains can be made out of that. But it's convincing that fishing community, and then, on the flip side of that, convincing the public that, hey, this is something good to eat. And there's still a lot of resistance in the public."

Hence all the tastings. And "venomous, not poisonous."

"Right, and again, we enjoy diving, we enjoy our reefs. The first time I pulled up a lionfish, and it had a shovelhead lobster baby in its stomach, it was like, all right, game on. I want to go down, and I want to spearfish for my allotment of snapper or grouper, or I want to pick up spiny lobster—those little bastards are eating what I am, eating my stuff! Well, someone needs to do something to fix that and it might as well be us."

One of the ways to break through with the public would be to get a big national retailer on board. Guess who's here this weekend with their own tent? Whole Foods Market.

Dave Ventura is the grocery chain's Florida regional seafood coordinator. The stores have been rolling lionfish out on a test basis for the last two years or so. The response has been overwhelmingly positive.

"Our customers here in Florida are very well educated about our ecosystem, our environment, are passionate about protecting them. They're very happy to hear that the Whole Foods in Florida has taken the lead on trying to be part of the solution to remove the lionfish from the water.

"What I can say is we've been selling lionfish for fifteen months and I'm happy to report we've sold over thirty thousand pounds.

"You know, everybody seems to realize that the good news is we scratched the surface. We developed a market, we know there's a market. Now it's like, hey, how do we get it on scale? How do we remove the lionfish in large volume? Once we accomplish that, then I think I can say confidently that we are making a dent, making a difference. Right now, I think we've been very successful in creating a public awareness."

And Whole Foods is developing its own product lines, too, like smoked lionfish. There are a million ways to prepare it. In fact, do an image search for "whole fried lionfish." It's a centerpiece showstopper at several local restaurants, with the fins fanned golden brown in all directions. At the end of the meal, they hand out the spines as toothpicks.

So we're going to fight the rapaciousness of one species with the bottomless appetites of another. Ours. Lionfish in this hemisphere have only one enemy. Us.

But it's going to take some doing.

Because "venomous, not poisonous" sounds like something Truman Capote might have said about Gore Vidal on *The Dick Cavett Show.*

In Which I Speak to the Mermaid

Saturday night, and there's a lionfish tasting.

This is upstairs at the Bodacious Olive, a restaurant and event space on a charming old-town stretch of brick storefronts not far from the park and the tournament tents, across from a Pilates studio.

The wind howls and low clouds worry the rooftops, but inside the Edison bulbs glow and the wineglasses sparkle and the test kitchen is as snug and clean as a catalog layout. There are 40 or so of us here, sponsors and spear hunters and dive masters, wives and husbands and scientists, captains and mates and mermaids. Celebrity Flora-Bama "chef-advocate" Jon Gibson is making lionfish tacos and lionfish sashimi and talking about sustainability and lionfish deliciousness.

There's Captain Andy, and there's Allie and Brian and John and Steve. Barry isn't here. He's across town at Pensacola State for a screening of the documentary *Reef Assassin,* produced by Mark Kwapis and edited by Maribeth Abrams. It's all about the lionfish invasion, but thanks to a scheduling wormhole these two events are happening at the same time. Some of the people *at* the movie should be here. Some of the people *in* the movie are standing right in front of me. Confused, I talk to the mermaid. Her name is Moira Dobbs. She is from Plano, Texas—where she runs a mermaid school.

I'm in italics, and a business suit.

Do you find that the kids retain the things you tell them about lionfish?

"Absolutely. And what's so great is Coast Watch Alliance not only does amazing things for the lionfish invasion issue, but they also are big into marine debris awareness and cleanup. When I do these in-character performances, if they're a birthday party, if they're an event, I bring balloons, straws, fishing line, different things that I pick up at the bottom of the ocean as a diver, and I say, 'Hey, it was so nice to meet you, when I go home, look at all these things that are all over my house,' and I watch it wash over these kids. And it's creating little eco-warriors."

She looks just about exactly how you'd picture a mermaid. Pale. Pretty. Lots of auburn hair. In fact, think of Ariel easing out of her 20s, on her way to a job interview, and you'll have it. But out there under the tent, on her chaise, sun bright and the bay sparkling, wearing the tail and her magnificent fin, talking to children, the illusion is complete.

So how long have you been doing this?

"Professionally, a couple years now. I host a full-time year-round professional mermaid school, that's actually in landlocked DFW, Texas."

Do you get a lot of good turnout, in Dallas–Fort Worth?

"We do, and many walks of life, for mermaid school, and that also allows me to establish a great performance troupe that does the same kind of in-character performances that I do. Birthday parties, ocean education, library readings, stuff like that."

Are you a lionfish hunter on your own time?

"I am, I am. Yes."

So you know all these guys?

"Yes. As a mermaid and a diver."

I was going to say, do a lot of the dads hit on the mermaid, when they bring the kids over?

"We get the 'Hey, speaking mythologically, I don't know if mermaids wear tops!' We call those 'merverts.' But yes, I'm all about the banter."

So the tail . . .

"That thing I was wearing today is a free-diving monofin embedded inside forty pounds of platinum Dragon Skin silicone. Yeah. So you can free dive in the ocean in that thing."

Hot, though, on land.

"Yes. It is hot. It's neutrally buoyant, and really wonderful to swim in the ocean, or pool. But it's a little rough after a few hours. I do dry out. Every two to three hours, I take a thirty-minute break. You need to. Your feet are inside of that really heavy fluke. The fluke is the bottom of the tail that you see. It's kind of like being *en pointe*, in ballet."

So if you could tell America one last thing, as the mermaid spokesperson—

"Yes . . ."

—on behalf of the lionfish invasion awareness—
"Yes . . ."
—what would you say?
"Seek, find, and destroy, man."

Truth is, lionfish tastes pretty great. The raw flesh of the fish is opalescent, fine-grained and smooth and nearly translucent, with a flavor to match. On the tongue, uncooked, it melts fast and tastes faintly of the sea—a memory of salt rather than salt itself. Baked, broiled, fried, poached, grilled, seared, or blackened, the meat of the fish is firm and white and buttery. It takes and holds whatever flavors you throw at it, whether you're making ceviche or fish and chips. It stands up to Cajun rub and to citrus and to wasabi and to remoulade and cilantro and garlic and ginger and cumin and aioli. It won't back down from red peppers or green chiles. It is as fearless as the person cooking it.

Everyone lines up for samples. Lip-smacking ensues.

"Don't be afraid of it," Jon Gibson says low and sweet to us all. "This is a versatile fish." He's slicing fillets so thin you could read a newspaper through them if anyone still read newspapers. "Just remember, everybody, the fish is venomous, not poisonous."

And out we all go into that windy evening.

Sunday

Most of the tents were blown down overnight, so the park looks forlorn as folks work to reset for the big day. There's Captain Andy picking up chairs and tables while Adele rolls in the deep on the PA. The early crowd is sparse, but by midmorning, even under threat of rain, the little plaza is filled again, and the music rises with the smoke from the grills and the waves pound the seawall and the crowd waiting for lionfish-stuffed jalapeño poppers is as long as the line for the crawfish boil.

You hear fragments on the wind, from the chefs and the experts and the kids and their parents . . .

"they reproduce every three or four days"
"these are fantastic"
"it's really good"

"aren't they poisonous?"

"venomous"

"go tell your restaurants you want lionfish"

"there's not much I won't eat"

Early in the afternoon, it's time for the count and the presentations to the winners. Captain Andy handles the microphone and the afternoon is an inventory of his gratitude and his enthusiasm. He and the crowd are stoked.

Biggest fish speared was a little over 17 inches.

Our boat, "Team Niuhi," finishes third, with 539 lionfish. "Full Stringer," a crew from up the road, is second, with 859 fish. "Team Hang On"—the all-women's team—wins going away, with 926 lionfish. The crowd roars and many tears are shed. Allie won't stop hugging people. For several hours.

There's a presentation of plaques and prize money and prizes, many of them quite nice, from dive gear to drones to nights out on the town, but it's pretty clearly pride everyone competes for.

Rachel Bowman is first among equals on the women's team. She is a commercial spearfisher down in the Keys and appears to be the lean, inked, freckled, and clear-eyed apex predator for the entire state of Florida.

She shoots and sells lionfish every day.

"I've got about a forty-mile range that I work, from Alligator Reef to American Shoals, and I have my spots. I have secret spots. I have public spots. The commercial fishermen in the Keys have been amazing as far as sharing their numbers with me, especially the commercial lobster guys. They know where there's big piles of rubble that other people don't know about because their traps get smacked on them. They really appreciate what I'm doing, and they help me out as much as possible. I like to think that the Whole Foods thing has made them more money because now the lionfish in their traps, they're not worth two dollars a pound anymore. Now they're worth six dollars."

You're fighting them to a draw down there.

"Yeah, I've got commercial trap guys that tell me that last year, the lionfish numbers kind of stopped going up, and this year they've actually gone down a little bit.

"I know Dr. Stephanie Green with Oregon State University has been doing some research with the organization REEF. They found, on isolated coral heads in the Bahamas, that not only is there a decline in the lionfish population, but there's actually a resurgence of the native fish populations. What we're doing—we're never going to get rid of them—but I have to believe we're making a difference. She and I measured fish today and the whole table was covered in egg sacs. Those are egg sacs that are never going to have a chance to do any kind of damage."

What do you think of Doc Gittings's traps?

"Well, I've got a brother-in-law who's a commercial lobster trapper, and this year in three months, he pulled up six thousand pounds of lionfish in his lobster traps. That's in sandy bottom, two hundred to three hundred, where divers can't go. So, maybe if he was allowed to deploy those traps when lobster season is closed, then that's another possibility."

Rachel Bowman has a diver-down flag enameled on her big toenail. She is the real reef assassin.

Grayson Shepard is the Panhandle charter captain who masterminded the women's team. Like Captain Andy, it is impossible to judge his age. He is sun-red and fit and rawboned and could be 35 or 235. He is now the Red Auerbach of lionfish, and we sat for a while to talk in the Florida Fish and Wildlife Conservation Commission motor home.

"I put together this little dream team that are just hard-core and fun as hell to hang out with. And they are dedicated and they are killers of the deep. They went with me in four-foot seas the past two days where a lot of men would not have gone. Several of my fellow charter captains canceled trips and they were freaking out. I'm like, I'm going. The girls are like 'Go go go!' My buddies were on the radio like, 'Are you okay?' 'Are you all right?' I'm like, man we're fine. We're kicking ass out here."

I explained to Captain Shepard about the throwing up.

"Well they didn't throw up. The girls suited up and went down. Over and over and over again."

Captain Shepard is himself a little bit of a sentimental badass.

"This crazy little lionfish has brought together so many incredibly cool people. We all have the same screw loose in our head. That same screw makes you an interesting, easygoing kind of person. It's a little community. We all have this common obsession with lionfish. You could put all of us in a van and drive us across the country. We would get along like peas and carrots. We're best friends. When you meet us, we're all like of the same tribe. It gives us the chills."

Even with most teams canceling their Saturday fishing, the tournament still brought in nearly 4,000 lionfish. Turns out the only thing more rapacious on earth than a lionfish is you and me.

So I ask folks as they leave, "You think eating them might be able to help stop the invasion?"

And they'll say, "It's fantastic, I hope it helps."

or

"Fingers crossed!"

or

"It ain't gonna hurt. It's gonna help a little bit, I guess, but I don't know. That's a big Gulf out there. That's all they can do to try and stop it? I don't see how that's going to stop it."

For the last hour or two of the afternoon, everyone puts their feet up. After three days of work and worry and nausea, 6-foot surf and 100-foot bounces, there's finally time to sit around the tents and the trailers and drink spiced rum and tell some lies. This everyone does with great relief.

Music plays and the wind eases and the bay is a luminous green.

Andy says, "I think it went great. We had some tough obstacles and I was a little bit nervous that maybe we wouldn't have the best turnout and you know, under the circumstances, with the tough weather and all, I think we did a fantastic job and everybody really came together and they went out and worked real hard at getting their fish. They came in and they were all very supportive and they all had an awesome time and I think everything went very smoothly. I think it came out fantastic. I've been on the water long enough to know that you cannot predict the weather and even when you do, you're wrong."

Allie is still hugging people.

"Let's go eat," Andy says.

The Big Finish

So, quiet and tired, everyone caravans to the Sake Café, a sushi place a couple of neighborhoods over, eating what they speared, now set out on two long tables full of hand rolls and sashimi, chopsticks and wasabi and cold beer. The kitchen bustles, but the place isn't crowded. It's early yet, even for Sunday dinner in Pensacola. At the head of the longest table Andy's wearing that enigmatic smile, that sidewise Andy smile, but Barry is the one who stands to speak.

He thanks everyone for their hard work and for their excellent spearfishing skills and for fighting this good fight. He thanks the event sponsors for their contributions and the restaurant for making dinner. He talks about what all this means to the environment and to Florida and to him. When he talks about the camaraderie of the divers and the friendship and yes, the love, he surprises himself by choking up. He gathers himself and goes on just a little longer.

"You gotta eat 'em to beat 'em," he says at the end.

And everyone applauds.

Dolly back, roll credits, that's the last scene in your Hollywood movie.

But if you're writing a magazine story, maybe you don't end it there. Not like that. Not with sushi and a speech. Too upbeat. Too certain.

Nor can your story end with that unremarkable wind steady off the bay, not with the striking of the tents and boxing of the leftover brochures, not with the loading of the vans or the vendors rolling up their banners or emptying their grills, and not with the stragglers wandering back to the parking lot under a Sunday sky as flat and gray as gunmetal.

What you want is something to remember them all, a way to think of Florida and that crazy light and that water and those men and those women and those fish.

So maybe you'll look back, no matter where you go or what you do, and see them all forever at the dock that Friday night, the whole wrung-out, laughing, groaning boatload, Andy and Allie and Barry and John and Carl and Alex and those scientists gathered around those big boxes of fish, those big coolers filled with ice and fins and Japanese fans, the sun faltering in the west, tangled in the trees, shadows long on the ground and the sky a low flame up there in the spreaders and the shrouds. One of the marine biologists leans down into the cooler and gingerly plucks up another lionfish. "I've got you now," she says to herself and for a second you don't know if she means one fish or the whole species and anyway you can barely hear her because Andy's got the stereo cranked on the boat and Van Halen is playing "Hot for Teacher." It's all a trick of the light, sure, too sentimental and too droll, but it's also true and that's the beauty of it.

It's a long fight. And maybe the lionfish win.

Maybe that's your ending.

LAUREN MARKHAM

If These Walls Could Talk

FROM *Harper's Magazine*

ACCORDING TO ONE Norse myth, the gods needed a wall. Asgard, their kingdom, had once been surrounded by barricades, but a war had destroyed them. When the gods decided to erect a new wall, a builder appeared out of nowhere and offered his services. Loki, the trickster, suggested that the gods accept his proposal but set an impossible deadline. When time ran out, they could send him on his way, thereby getting the lion's share of the wall for free.

The builder accepted the terms and set to work. Accompanied by his trusty horse, he made quick work of the wall; he was perilously close to completing the stone loop around the kingdom before his time was up. Desperate, Loki transformed himself into a mare to lure away the builder's horse. The builder was outraged. This was when the gods realized, to their horror, that he was actually a giant—their sworn enemy—in disguise.

Thor bludgeoned the interloper to death with his hammer. The wall remained, but the gods' dishonest dealings set in motion Ragnarok: the fall of the empire and the end of the cosmos.

Border walls have been around as long as the gods themselves, guarding our cities and castles. They fell briefly out of favor, but at the moment, they seem to be enjoying increased popularity in such far-flung locations as Myanmar, France, Bulgaria, Pakistan, and, of course, the United States. Unlike those of yore, erected to keep out marauding invaders, today's walls are designed to guard against desperate refugees and migrants. Governments are launching efforts to strengthen overburdened borders as people seek to escape everything from war and famine to drought and rising seas.

This revival comes at a time when the argument against walls seems particularly convincing: experts have found that walls have never really worked, and they often seem to presage not an empire's perpetuity but its collapse. Walls offer the promise of absolute protection, but they almost always fail to deliver. Still, we build them again and again. Last winter, I traveled to Norway to see one of Europe's newest and most infamous projects in hopes of learning what it could tell us about our age-old impulse to both wall ourselves off and wall ourselves in.

The Arctic town of Kirkenes, in Norway, is where land meets sea, where water meets ice, where taiga meets open tundra, where even the membrane between day and night is always shifting. There are days without darkness and other days when the sun barely glimmers at the horizon. The town sits on the border between Norway and Russia, a 121-mile line through rock, river, and permafrost. On a cold, clear day in late winter, I parked in a small lot near the Storskog border checkpoint, nine miles outside town on a well-paved road that cuts through the Arctic hinterlands. Across a frozen lake, I could see Russia, dappled with petite arctic birch and spruce. It looked just like Norway, except it had a sheen of magic simply for being an elsewhere.

In the summer of 2015, migrants—first mostly men from Afghanistan and Syria, then their families, and eventually people from other parts of the Middle East, North Africa, and Asia, too—began arriving at this checkpoint. That June, to help lift the burden on Mediterranean countries on the front lines of the migration crisis, Norway had pledged that it would take in 8,000 refugees. (In total, more than a million people would seek asylum in Europe that year, double the numbers from previous years.) Granting asylum entails a lengthy screening and transfer process, but many migrants took Norway's statement to mean that the border was open—and that they'd better cross before the 8,000 spaces were filled.

Seeking to circumnavigate the clogged routes of the Mediterranean, they chose an alternate way to the safety of Europe. Some migrants had come directly from war zones or refugee camps farther south; others had been living in Russia for months or even years, and feared being sent back to Syria or Afghanistan once their visas expired. Many made their way to the Russian city of Murmansk, where, racing the coming winter, they hid from immigration authorities in local hotels and hired smugglers to get them to the other side. Russia doesn't allow individuals across the border on foot, so the smugglers provided bicycles, charging $500 to get people to Kirkenes. In *The Bicycle Pile,* a documentary about the arrivals, a Russian hotel owner recalls that smugglers covered the city with posters showing Norwegian women holding signs that said COME TO US. WE WILL PROTECT YOU AND YOUR FAMILY. Social media helped the images spread around the world.

Both countries are supposed to check paperwork and make sure crossers have proper visas for the other side, and yet when the asylum seekers showed up, Russia simply let them pass. Norwegian officials felt that by allowing people to cross without permission, Russia was exporting its problem to Norway. A few hundred came to Kirkenes the first month; by the fall, it was thousands, and the community scrambled to accommodate the new arrivals. By November, more than 5,500 migrants from some 50 countries had come to this town of 3,500.

Oslo asked Moscow to take the refugees back, but in the end only some 300 people were returned to Russia. In one chilling scene in *The Bicycle Pile,* a Syrian woman with two children is taken across the border zone back into Russia. It's dark and snowing. She sits down with her kids in the middle of the no-man's-land between the Russian and Norwegian checkpoints, refusing to move.

After several months of debate, the governments agreed that any migrant trying to cross without the proper papers would be stopped by Russian authorities. The word got out on social media, and the flow stopped. "They disappeared," said the mayor of Nikel, a town on the Russian side of the border. Then, four months after the last asylum seeker crossed, Norway's government announced that the nonexistent problem required a bold solution.

"It's important to send signals," Espen Teigen, the political adviser to the minister of immigration and integration, told me. He is also a member of the Progress Party, the Norwegian, and thus relatively liberal, expression of the nativist wave sweeping the globe. Teigen was concerned about the number of migrants coming into Europe, the cost of caring for them, and their failure to assimilate

into society; he believed the barrier would serve as a counter to
the messages of welcome that other leaders on the continent were
sending.

But the signal was faint. The wall—actually a chain-link fence
—would stretch only 600 feet. Still, most people and politicians
in and around Kirkenes were outraged. Residents had rallied to
support the asylum seekers, collecting donations and opening
their homes, schools, and community centers to them. The fence
negated those efforts and alienated the townspeople from their
Russian neighbors. (In the United States, attitudes follow a similar pattern: the closer conservatives live to the US-Mexico border,
the more likely they are to oppose a wall.) "This is an example
of incompetence, historically and politically," Rune Rafaelsen, the
mayor of Kirkenes, told me. The fence cost $830 per foot, about
$500,000 in all—not much for a public-works project. But to most
locals, it was an expensive and abrasive imposition intended to
stop a problem that had been solved.

As it happens, there was already a wall on this very border. Early
in the Cold War, the Soviet Union began erecting fences on its
borders. Rather than keeping people out, they were intended to
prevent those inside from escaping a brutal regime. Norwegians
stayed away, but in 1965, a 27-year-old American walked through
the Storskog checkpoint and up to the Russian authorities, hoping to get a stamp in his passport and bragging rights back home.
Instead he was carted off to a Soviet prison, and died within a year.

Construction on the Storskog fence began in August 2016 and
was finished about a month later. (The project had been delayed
when surveyors realized that the fence had been built an inch
or two into the buffer zone between the countries and had to be
moved.) Now the "wall" stands several miles from the old Soviet
border fence, which was recently updated with surveillance cameras, though its current purpose is unclear. Today, on the frozen
cusp of northern Europe, the two fences stand opposite each
other, as if in a face-off.

Outside the checkpoint, the ground was frozen with ice, which
splintered underfoot like shards of glass. There was an uncanny
atmosphere of temptation, rooted in the forbidden. Signs told me
not to take pictures, which made me nervous that I would forget
and do so all the same. I also worried that I might accidentally step

over the line and violate international law, as if the border had a subliminal pull. Milan Kundera once described vertigo much the same way: not so much the fear of falling but the desire to jump.

My phone pinged with a welcome message from a Russian telecom network, and I stepped inside the checkpoint—a low-set, caramel-colored building with a snow-covered roof. At a conference table decorated with miniature Russian and Norwegian flags, I sat down with Stein Kristian Hansen, the chief of the border station. Tall and blond, he poured coffee into mugs decorated with cartoon elves frolicking on the border. The mugs, he told me, I was allowed to photograph. Hansen explained that he had been asking for a fence ever since he took the job eight years ago. His desire "had nothing to do with migration," he said, "but with security."

In 2017, there were 265,000 crossings at Storskog, mostly Russians coming in to shop. (This was a massive increase from the '90s, when only about 8,000 people crossed at Storskog each year.) When the government announced its plans, Hansen was most interested in the proposal for a retractable gate—one he could open and close with the touch of a button, so that, in an emergency, he could seal the border to stabilize the situation and protect the officers who serve alongside him. But he was certain that the fence would do nothing to curb a future flow of refugees. For one, people could simply walk through the forest and circumvent the checkpoint. Hansen lives in Kirkenes, and he is perplexed by the outrage against the wall. "They think it's a message to Russia," he said. "But Russia is a big country with a powerful army." He gestured to the fence and smiled. "This fence isn't going to stop Putin."

Elf cups drained, Hansen and I walked outside. The fence was slightly burlier than one at a schoolyard, with tight chain link secured to metal posts set some three feet apart. It sliced a path through a low boreal forest, which had been clear-cut about 10 feet on each side to allow for a clear view of anyone approaching. To the west, Lake Neitijärvi formed a natural boundary. To the east, the fence crested a slight hill and disappeared from sight, creating the impression that it continued on forever.

Recently, the border has become a tourist attraction. According to Lars Georg Fordal, the head of the Barents Secretariat, an organization that promotes cross-border cooperation, local tour operators use it as a selling point. In the summer, visitors can lunch on smoked salmon at a nearby restaurant with views of Russia and the lake. Fordal also told me that cruise ships dock at Kirkenes so passengers can travel to the border and say that they saw Russia with their own eyes. The fence promises to draw even more visitors.

Hansen showed me the slatted metal gate. It was open, nestled against the fence; with mechanized wheels, it is designed to slide shut across the tarmac. Unfortunately, he admitted, the design was off. The bottom wasn't high enough to clear the snowpack, so the gate got stuck in place every time there was a freeze. For now, they kept it open at all times. "They'll rebuild it during the summer," he said with a shrug, giving the fence a final little jiggle. We turned our backs toward Russia and, breath freezing against our faces, walked back inside.

Throughout history, humans have folded walls into myths and legends while also erecting walls to buttress geopolitical borders and project imperial grandeur: the wall that separated the lovers Pyramus and Thisbe, the gilded walls of the Incas, and the city of Troy, whose walls were outwitted by a horse. The Great Wall of China, actually nearly 4,000 miles of semi-connected segments and additional barriers, was meant to keep out nomads from the steppe. In the second century AD, the Roman emperor Hadrian conceived of a 70-mile stone fortification at the upper reaches of his empire—now in the United Kingdom—in order to manage trade, keep out the barbarians, and advertise the power of his empire and its ruler. Meanwhile, other walls were designed to keep people from leaving. The Mur de la Peste (Plague Wall) in Marseille, France, was built to contain the disease, and thus the diseased. More recently, repressive regimes such as those of East Germany and North Korea (and, of course, the Soviet Union) built walls to keep people from fleeing. Many of these walls largely failed in their expressed purpose. Guards along the Great Wall of China were often bribed to gain entry; the barbarians breached Hadrian's Wall and killed a general and his troops.

In the Arctic north, borders hardly existed at all. Indigenous nomadic people had lived in the Scandinavian Arctic for thousands of years, believing that land was a communal resource. Today, the Sami people, the descendants of these tribes, fight to herd their reindeer over borders drawn in 1826 in direct opposition to their way of life.

In Norway, border walls weren't erected until feudal times, when it became a bargaining chip for several larger empires. As the kingdom consolidated and began to face threats from outside, Norwegians began building walls, and now the country is dotted with their relics. Last year, Norway celebrated the 450th anniversary of the founding of Fredrikstad, one of Europe's best-preserved fortified towns. In 1567, when Norway was still a part of Denmark (a period now referred to as the "400-year-long night"), the Swedes were at war with the Danes, trying to win key territory and coastline. When the Swedish Army burned down the city of Sarpsborg, King Frederick II ordered that a new city be constructed at the point where the Glomma River bends toward the North Sea. This was a key trading point and also a strategic defensive zone with a 360-degree view of approaching threats.

The rampart walls of Fredrikstad were built in a star shape, according to the Dutch style, with a moat around the perimeter. There were 200 cannons and 2,000 guards—10 soldiers for every cannon—stationed atop the wall, on 24-hour patrol. Each night, the drawbridge was raised, sealing the city, and it was not lowered until the king gave the command the next morning. (He was a known drunk who slept late, often leaving farmers stuck at the city gate as they waited to take their flocks out to pasture.)

From above, Fredrikstad is stunning and resolute; the rippling river forms its western border, and to the east, the three star points of its walls push outward as if taking aim at the green horizon. For nearly 150 years, Fredrikstad was on guard against potential threats, but perhaps because its defensive reputation preceded it, the city was never attacked. Then, in 1814, the Swedes came up the river by boat. After one day of battle, the city waved its white flag.

During the Second World War, the Germans occupied Norway and laid siege to the Finnmark region; Kirkenes became one of the most-bombed towns in the war. It was the Soviet Union that liberated Kirkenes from the Nazis, and when the Germans capitulated, the Russians went home. "They didn't stay. This is still very much remembered," Lars Georg Fordal of Barents Secretariat said, emphasizing a fact that is prominent in the local historical consciousness. The border has always been peaceful; Russia and Norway have never been at war, although in recent years, relations between Russia and Norway—that is, between Moscow and

Oslo—have become frosty, particularly after the annexation of Crimea. The migrant situation only made matters worse.

In 2015, two political scientists from the University of California, Berkeley, surveyed dozens of border walls built around the world since 1990, mapping the fortifications to try to understand common trends. Not only did the rate of wall-building increase over the period, but, they found, the building projects were becoming more ambitious. They also found that walls weren't built in places that suffered from disproportionately high terrorism rates or in areas under territorial dispute. In nearly all cases, they were built on borders between countries with significantly different economic standing, often a non-Muslim country and a Muslim-majority country. Nevertheless, most border walls of the current resurgence were built, the research found, in the name of security.

For those who live in border towns, the boundary is mostly understood as a construct devised by those in power, who often live far away. The distance may lead to a kind of reverse provincialism. "Kirkenes is the geopolitical center of Norway," Mayor Rafaelsen insisted. "There's nothing happening in Oslo."

As Rafaelsen sees it, countries that share economic interests and complex logistical ties are less likely to go to war. He is rooting for joint industrial projects in the Barents Sea, where Norway's oil and gas reserves are located. Given Russia's feeble industrial output and economic challenges, Rafaelsen believes that cross-border cooperation would benefit both parties and, most importantly, strengthen Norwegian national security. "The wall," he declared, "is not the answer."

One evening in Kirkenes, I joined Rafaelsen and the staff of the *Independent Barents Observer*, the local online daily, at their tidy office in the center of town. It was happy hour, and a group of journalists, municipal employees, and neighbors crowded into the small room, pulling up folding chairs and passing around some beer and chips. "Everyone agrees that it's a symbolic fence," insisted Atle Staalesen, the paper's managing editor. "It doesn't have a function at all."

Indeed, my hosts explained, the fence was an affront to their very identity. Crossing the border is not only a fact of life here but also the draw; both Staalesen and his colleague Thomas Nilsen moved to Kirkenes because of its proximity to Russia. People in town frequently go to Russia for shopping, they told me, or to get clothes tailored or shoes cobbled.

"I'd often just go there to meet a friend for a beer," Nilsen said, "then come back that night." The fence and the increased border security have changed that—and then Nilsen found out that his name had recently been added to a no-entry list for Russia, another sign of the friction between Moscow and Oslo.

The border has always been an integral part of the region's identity—indigenous migrations, mutually beneficial commerce, a sense of being at the place where the West meets the high Arctic and Russian Orthodoxy meets Protestantism. Here in the far north it can be difficult, in flat light, to distinguish between land and ice and sea and sky, and the notion of a dividing line seems peculiar. How could it be otherwise? Borderlands dwell in paradox: the landscape might be the same on either side, but the geopolitical reality is vastly different.

Even so, geography encourages cross-border affinities. Oslo is a 23-hour drive from Finnmark, which requires passing through Finland and Sweden. The closest major city is Murmansk, in Russia —which as it happens is 23 hours from Moscow. The average person in Kirkenes, Nilsen explained, doesn't see the border "as a geopolitical designation. In Oslo, they do."

We had consumed many rounds of Russian beer, purchased on the other side for about a dollar a can. (Norwegian beer costs eight times as much.) Brede Sæther, a businessman and the landlord of the *Independent Barents Observer*, suggested a nightcap at his place. Six of us followed him through downtown, where dusk cast pale-cornflower light onto the snow. Sæther led us into his backyard and along a neatly shoveled pathway through hip-high snow. He knelt down and, with a grunt, yanked up a great metal door in the ground. "Here," he bellowed theatrically, with a slight backward sway, "is my bunker!"

A staircase descended more than a story underground and deposited us in a massive cavern of around a thousand square feet, an echoing, apocalyptic ballroom. The main chamber had 20-foot ceilings and connected to half a dozen other rooms, some blocked by metal doors, others accessible via a low-ceilinged hallway. "There are bunkers all over Kirkenes," said an awestruck Staalesen, "but I've never seen anything like this."

During the Second World War, Kirkenes was on the northernmost front, and there's a whole underworld in the city, built by the Nazis—and perhaps by their Russian prisoners of war—to defend against Soviet forces. Sæther tossed us each a beer and called us over to a narrow, circular stone chamber that reached all the way up to the crust of earth above us, where we could see an opening onto the evening light. He had discovered this tubular room only last year, when a crack running beneath an adjacent wall inspired him to take it down with a jackhammer. He soon realized that the room was filled with the garbage that he and his family had been dumping down a mystery hole in their backyard for decades. Because of its shape, he deduced that the room had been a gunner station. "We thought there might be treasure!" Sæther said, laughing. "But it was just my own trash!" He slammed his hand against another wall, which seemed to promise more mystery just beyond. "This summer, I'm going to knock it down."

Sæther's remark reminded me of a conversation I once had with an undocumented family living in a studio apartment in the Tenderloin, in San Francisco. I'd asked why they'd come to the United States. "We just always had this curiosity," the mother said. The border, she suggested, had an appeal that was irrational, almost mystical. "We just wanted to know," she recalled, placing her hand against her forehead as if scouring the horizon, "what is it on the other side?"

Later, I read that while the Nazis were building the bunker network in Kirkenes, Adolf Hitler issued Directive 40, which called for another defensive public-works project: the so-called Atlantikwall, a fortification that would surround the sea perimeter of the Nazi empire. In March 1942, he conscripted 260,000 soldiers and civilians to build the wall, imagining it as a physical barrier between the Third Reich and the rest of the world. In the end, the project was a series of unconnected fortifications along the coasts of Germany, Norway, Denmark, the Netherlands, Belgium, and France. Hitler boasted that the wall was impenetrable, but in 1944 the Allies would manage to breach it in a single day.

When migrants first started crossing the border into Kirkenes, the Norwegian government commissioned a series of social media posts to discourage the influx. "Why would you risk your life?" the posts read in Farsi, Arabic, English, and French. The goal was to "inform people of the dramatic consequences of embarking on such a large journey," explained Teigen, the political adviser. If online rumors helped to facilitate migration along the Arctic route, the thinking went, perhaps the same medium could be used to stop it.

On my last morning in Norway, I went to meet with Edin Krajisnik, who was working as a refugee-resettlement adviser with Norwegian People's Aid, a humanitarian and charity organization. His office in downtown Oslo is a few blocks from the building where, in 2011, Anders Breivik, a radicalized former member of the Progress Party, set off a bomb. He went on to massacre dozens of leftist Labor Party youth leaders on a nearby island, hoping his actions would spark an anti-Muslim, anti-immigrant revolution.

"There are more invisible walls in Norway than visible ones," Krajisnik said. These take the form of repressive, anti-immigrant laws, of government-sponsored Facebook posts discouraging migration, and even of anti-immigrant public opinion. When he came to Norway in 1993 as a young refugee from Bosnia, Krajisnik was met with open arms. Today, he lamented, new arrivals face a different reception. The spike in anti-immigrant fear "coincided with an increase of images of ISIS on the internet," he told me. "They're seeing more images of terrorists than they are of suffering children."

This embrace of the internet—of walls that are essentially virtual, made of algorithms rather than steel and concrete—as a political tool is perhaps understandable. Physical barriers are moving toward obsolescence. Yet we keep building them anyway. Why? In *Walled States, Waning Sovereignty*, the political scientist Wendy Brown asserts that such walls are a reaction to "the dissolving effects of globalization on national sovereignty." The more enmeshed, known, and mutually dependent we are, the more we fear that the nation-state itself is toppling into irrelevance. Meanwhile, the internet also helps propagate fear—of terrorism, of the other —with racist media, hate groups, tweets, and viral content thriving online and further stoking irrational paranoia. The wall craze, like global nationalist movements, can be seen as a backlash, a call for clear, knowable boundaries in an increasingly porous world.

Perhaps in response, walls loom large in contemporary popular culture. In the world of the Hunger Games trilogy, walls protect the bounty of the capital. On *Game of Thrones,* an immense, icy barrier shields civilization from the unknown, sinister evil on the other side.

Politicians, too, invoke this imperiled sense of identity in their calls to close off borders. Forced migrants are moving around the world in record numbers, and the refugee crises are steadily moving toward the global North, into wealthy nations whose fixed borders have traditionally defined them. When millions of refugees cross from one sub-Saharan country to another, there is no threat to the United States and Norway. In such cases, governments offer humanitarian rhetoric, aid packages, and resettlement opportunities, which do little in the face of mass migration. But a mass of refugees clambering over your own borders is something altogether different. Images of these migrants can evoke a humanitarian response but also populist fear. If a nation seems to be coming apart, perhaps a wall can hold it together. We convince ourselves that we're in a state of perpetual siege; we turn the state into a bunker.

After my meeting with Krajisnik, I stopped at Akershus Fortress, the old walled center of Oslo, built in the thirteenth century to defend the city against the Danes and the Swedes. The cobbled grounds, which resembled something between a college campus and a cemetery, led to a hilltop, with the glistening harbor visible over the lip of the wall. In spite of multiple attacks from the Swedes, the Scots, and the Danes, Akershus was never successfully besieged. (It was, however, given up to the Nazis without a fight.)

Up on the rampart, I stood within fortifications used to defend against a knowable enemy. Today, we are assaulted by threats that we cannot always see, and in our fear it's as if we've become sentinels on our own walls, ever ready for battle.

I thought of the fences of yesterday, and the fence of today. There was something absurd about traveling all the way to Norway to see a fence so small. Yet its flimsiness was somehow fitting: it was, after all, no more than a screen onto which anyone could project needs, fears, and dreams.

When I was ready to leave, I somehow took a series of wrong turns and found myself stuck in a maze. *Surely this path will lead me out,* I kept telling myself, but instead, every turn I took led back to the wall itself. There was still something ominous about being trapped amid the looping pathways and the trilling Akershus birds.

My flight was leaving in a few hours, so I pulled out my phone and followed my blue-dot avatar out of the fortress and back into the city, onto the train, through passport control, then finally up into the air. From the plane, everything below was just sea and ice and then land again; the distance rendered the borders invisible.

The Floating World

FROM *The New York Times Magazine*

THE BEST HANDYMAN living among the boat people in Chong
Koh was named Taing Hoarith. Most days, Hoarith woke up at
5 a.m. and bought a bowl of noodle soup from a passing sampan,
the same genre of wandering bodega from which his wife, Vo Thi
Vioh, sold vegetables houseboat to houseboat. When she left for
the day, around six, Hoarith rolled up their floor mat and got to
work.

Chong Koh is one of hundreds of floating villages, comprising
tens of thousands of families, on the Tonle Sap River and the lake
of the same name in Cambodia. Dangers on a floating village mul-
tiply in the rainy season. When I first visited, in late July, there was
always something for Hoarith to do: repairing storm damage in a
wall of thatched palm, clearing the water hyacinths that collected
along the upstream porch. Sometimes the house had to be towed
closer to the receding shoreline so that storms or the waves of
passing ships would not capsize it. Every few months, he got his
ancient air compressor working and swam beneath the house, a
rubber hose between his teeth, to refill the cement jars that kept
the whole thing buoyant. He was mindful of pythons.

The afternoon of my arrival, Hoarith was squatting over an
old butane camp stove, scraping at a rusted gas valve. Rust was
the common enemy on the water. Someone had thrown the stove
away, but he thought he could fix it to sell on his next trip onto
the lake. His wooden long-tail, moored against the house, covered
in tarpaulin, and heavy with cargo, carried him to floating villages
as far as 90 miles away. "I know Tonle Sap like my hand," he said.

There was Prek Tor, a remote village where every family, rich or poor, had a wooden cage for raising crocodiles. And Kbal Taol, where fishermen lived in clustered homes on the open water, risking the daily storms, competing to catch hatchlings with nets up to half a mile long. Hoarith visited them all. He was sometimes on the lake for a month at a stretch, selling pots and stoves, sleeping rough under the long-tail's planked roof.

But he always came back to Chong Koh, his home of several years, where the villagers live on cabin-size houseboats and junks arranged in tidy rows orthogonal to either shore. In the space between houses, some families raise carp and catfish in bamboo cages or keep floating gardens of potted pepper and papaya trees. Other villages are labyrinthine extensions of nearby shore towns, with broad Venetian canals and twisting alleyways, floating temples, churches, schoolrooms, and oil-black ice factories. Chong Koh is relatively small, and shrinking—Cambodian authorities would like it to disappear entirely—but it lies about a mile from the heart of Kampong Chhnang, the large provincial capital, and as Hoarith worked, a steady fleet of peddlers took their boats to and from its markets.

While Hoarith picked at the stove with a screwdriver, a neighbor lay in a hammock, watching him work. The neighbor, like Hoarith and everyone else in the village, was ethnically Vietnamese, and he had a Vietnamese name, Vieng Yang Nang. But most of the time he went by Samnang, which means "lucky" in Khmer, the language of Cambodia's ethnic majority. Both men kept two names on the water—one Khmer, one Vietnamese—and switched between them freely. They felt at home in both worlds, although they weren't always accepted in the first. In Cambodia, where the concepts of nationality and ethnicity are inextricable, members of the ethnic Vietnamese minority are known as *yuon,* a ubiquitous slur that is sometimes translated as "savage."

I sat on the floor listening to Samnang and Hoarith revisit a conversation from earlier in the day. That morning we had visited the school and the Vietnamese pagoda, stilted buildings near the fish market where Chong Koh once stood. Local officials evicted the village in 2015, forcing residents to move more than a mile downriver, and both buildings were now hard to access. Such evictions are frequent and unpredictable, and sometimes lead to other trouble. After Hoarith asked the authorities to help with costs related to the move, the police arrested him and accused him of inciting villagers to resist eviction. He spent three months in a squalid prison cell before Thi Vioh borrowed enough money for his release, after which the charges against him were dropped. They only wanted to send him a message, he thought. "I hadn't committed any crime," he said. "I had a reputation."

Hoarith and Samnang agreed that you can't fight evictions on the water. Floating settlements are technically illegal, and the Vietnamese in particular are powerless against such orders. "The poor will become poorer," Samnang said. Hoarith said nothing, only swept the pile of rust flakes that he amassed into a knothole in the floor. He set a can of butane into the stove's empty chamber and pressed the pilot button. A bull's-eye of blue flame appeared. We laughed. A few houses away, a woman sang love songs on a karaoke system powered by a car battery.

The Mekong River's lower basin is vast, encompassing parts of Myanmar and Thailand, virtually all of Laos and Cambodia, and parts of southern Vietnam, where, after a 3,000-mile journey across five national borders, the mother of rivers divaricates into a complex delta network and drains into the South China Sea. Tonle Sap Lake sits roughly in the middle of this lush expanse. On a map, it appears as a crooked blue finger extending from the Mekong near Phnom Penh. But it is more often described as Cambodia's heart, both for its rhythmic flood pulse and the sustaining role it plays in the country's economy and food supply.

Tonle Sap's unique hydrology makes it one of the most fertile ecosystems on the planet. For half the year, the Tonle Sap River flows southeast from the lake to Phnom Penh. But during the rainy season, the swollen Mekong forces the Tonle Sap to flow in reverse, and the lake engorges to as much as six times its dry-season expanse, two miracles of plenty which over the millennia have drawn fishermen and rice farmers alike to its doubly silted, nutrient-rich shores. Eels, frogs, shrimp, and fish proliferate with tropical abandon, particularly in the fecund bottleneck where, viewed from above, the river appears to fray into dozens of delicate blue fibers before braiding itself back into open water.

The border between Vietnam and Cambodia, which divides the Mekong Delta, has occasioned more battles than nearly any other in Asia. The people living on either side have been in contact for at least a thousand years, an uninterrupted exchange of goods and labor that for the last four centuries has been marked by bold Vietnamese expansion. In the 1630s, a Cambodian king married a Vietnamese princess and allowed the Vietnamese to set up customs ports along the Mekong. The settlers eventually annexed the region, cutting off Cambodia's access to the South China Sea and stranding many Khmer people inside Vietnam, where they developed a distinct ethnic identity as Khmer Krom. This occupation of "Lower Cambodia" has never been forgiven.

Cambodia's borders were formalized when the country became a colonial protectorate in 1863. The French imported Vietnamese workers for its rubber plantations and drew on Saigon's educated elite as administrative clerks. The number of Vietnamese in the country increased 30-fold, to more than 150,000, or 6 percent of the population. By the time Cambodia declared independence in 1953, the country was polyethnic and multinational, with enclaves of hill tribes and other distinct indigenous minorities; populations of Chinese, Lao, and Vietnamese speakers; and boundaries that bore only a loose resemblance to those of its precolonial realm. It fell to Cambodia's first modern leader, Norodom Sihanouk, to unify this haphazardly circumscribed populace.

Sihanouk's grand idea was to redefine the historic term "Khmer" to include a wide range of ethnic identities. The policy rendered most of the nation's indigenous groups, including even its Muslim Cham minority, inheritors of the ancient imperial lineage. But the ethnic Vietnamese had no place in this new national typology. Although small numbers of them had lived in the country for centuries, they were Cambodia's hereditary enemy. After a 1970 coup, they became the targets of pogroms and massacres, adding to the chaos of that decade, which began with civil war and a brutal United States bombing campaign and ended with occupation by the Vietnamese Army. In the interim, during the five-year reign of the Khmer Rouge, millions died from execution, starvation, and disease.

Since 1979, the ruling Cambodian People's Party, or CPP (with the former Khmer Rouge commander Hun Sen at its head), has kept the ethnic Vietnamese in a state of limbo, informally granting and rescinding rights depending on local political climates. The CPP's opposition, the Cambodia National Rescue Party, or CNRP, is more consistently xenophobic, threatening to expel the

Vietnamese invaders and reclaim "Lower Cambodia." The party's
former leader, Sam Rainsy, once proposed to "send the *yuon* immigrants back," and before the 2013 national elections he claimed
that "if we don't rescue our nation, four or five years more is too
late—Cambodia will be full of Vietnamese; we will become slaves
of Vietnam."

Human Rights Watch has described the traditional Cambodian
hatred of the ethnic Vietnamese as "almost pathological." It is
strongest in the cities, particularly in Phnom Penh, where it can
be hard to differentiate between observable corruption and base-
less conspiracy. There are legitimate grievances about illegal logging and fishing by Vietnamese companies, but some people also
insist that the Vietnamese are to blame for the spread of AIDS or
that Pol Pot was a Vietnamese spy sent to annihilate the Khmer
race. The hatred is vernacular. Cambodians undergoing gastroin-
testinal distress say their stomachs are "made in Vietnam," and the
short, prickly tree whose nettles deliver a daylong rash, and which
is known to invade a region and quickly overrun it, is the *ban la
yuon:* "the Vietnamese barb."

It's tempting to view the floating villages, where the highest concentrations of ethnic Vietnamese live, as a consequence of politically waterborne lives. In truth, the villages' history is long and
obscure, and no one knows when the first one appeared in Cambodia. The French naturalist Henri Mouhot—who "discovered"
Angkor Wat in the 1850s, although it had never been lost to locals
—found in Phnom Penh a floating population of 20,000, more
than twice as many as lived on land. He described one village of
Khmer and Vietnamese merchants just outside the capital:

> [T]oward the southern extremity of the city, we passed a floating town,
> composed of more than 500 boats, most of them of large size. They
> serve as an entrepôt for some merchants, and residences for others.
> All their money and the greater part of their merchandize is here kept,
> that, in case of alarm, they may be ready to take flight at a moment's
> warning.

There is also the collective memory, rarely transcribed, of the
floating villagers themselves, who corroborate Mouhot's intuition
that theirs is a lifestyle honed over generations to mitigate against

the bad harvests, marauding bandits, and unfriendly rulers to which minority Vietnamese remain especially vulnerable. Some told me that they had owned land in the early years of independence and that they had lived on the water only seasonally until the land was taken away. Others said they had always lived on boats. Some identified strongly as Cambodian, while others found the question of national allegiance absurd. "We just live on the water, where it's easy to catch fish," a monk in Kampong Chhnang told me. "We lived everywhere."

Hoarith could count at least four generations of ancestors around Tonle Sap. Born at the mouth of the lake, he was nine when the Khmer Rouge marched into Phnom Penh. His family was captured and sent to a labor camp in the mountains. After four months at the camp—where, he said, "they tried to kill at least ten Vietnamese families a day"—the soldiers loaded the prisoners onto ferries to be deported "back" to Vietnam. Hoarith had never been to Vietnam. He didn't know where Vietnam was. He asked his grandmother, but she didn't know, either. The ferry to the border took five days. Anyone who died was thrown overboard.

Around 150,000 ethnic Vietnamese were expelled from the country in this way, joining the 400,000 or so who had already fled pogroms under the ultranationalist Khmer Republic. The Vietnamese were both regimes' preferred scapegoat: "ingrate crocodiles" who wanted to swallow Cambodia whole. Those who survived the journey were traded to Vietnam for salt and rice and lived out the disastrous 1970s on farms in the countryside. Those who stayed in Cambodia—20,000 to 30,000 people—were slaughtered, alongside 90,000 Cham and as many as 100,000 Khmer civilians who were condemned for the crime of having "Khmer bodies and Vietnamese minds."

When the Vietnamese Army marched into Phnom Penh in 1979 and installed the puppet government that would later become the CPP, hundreds of thousands of civilians followed. Many were refugees returning home, but others were immigrants, and their presence revived the same fears of assimilation the Khmer Rouge had stoked. Hoarith and his family resettled in the village where he was born. It was still dangerous. In 1998, during a last gasp of Khmer Rouge resistance, soldiers waded into Chhnok Trou in the middle of the night with RPGs and AK-47s. The village was mixed, so before shooting, they asked: "Are you *yuon* or Khmer?"

There is a tradition of rural pluralism in Cambodia that belies its recent history of racial violence. Most of the floating villages I saw were peaceful mélanges of Vietnamese, Khmer, and Cham fishers, and many of the people I met, including Hoarith, were the product of mixed Khmer and Vietnamese marriages. But everyone seemed to agree that floating villages were traditionally a Vietnamese way of life, enlarged out of economic necessity to include other groups. Today the ethnic Vietnamese live on the water because they are not able to live elsewhere. Neither documented citizen nor, in most cases, immigrant, they are what the government has sometimes described as "nonimmigrant foreigners." They cannot attend public schools or open bank accounts, get a driver's license or a factory job, or own land or property. Their children are not issued birth certificates, precipitating a generational cycle of de facto statelessness.

"Thirty years ago, none of this mattered," Christoph Sperfeldt, a researcher on ethnic Vietnamese citizenship in Cambodia, told me. "No Cambodians had papers. There was no state presence. But the moment the state starts registering people, suddenly it matters." The expansion of services, including education and health care, and entitlements, including landownership, has further marginalized those perceived as foreign.

Last year, fearing a narrowing electoral gap, Hun Sen's government disbanded the CNRP and arrested Rainsy's successor on charges of treason. In an effort to defuse the nativism that had fueled the opposition party, the state also began the process of formalizing the status of ethnic Vietnamese as foreigners. Last October, the Ministry of the Interior identified a minimum of 70,000 mostly Vietnamese "foreigners" who possessed "irregular administrative documents." There may be hundreds of thousands more. Officials began sweeping the country, confiscating IDs and family books and demanding that residents either volunteer to move to Vietnam—where they are similarly considered foreigners—or pay a biannual fee for an immigration card identifying the holder as Vietnamese. "We don't remove their citizenship; they are Vietnamese," the head of the country's immigration department said of the purge. "We just take the Cambodian documents."

With no formal legal identity and few of the rights enjoyed by their Khmer and Cham neighbors, Vietnamese claim to pay large bribes to the fishery police, the environmental police, the maritime police, and other, more ambiguous authority figures, some posing as local journalists. They are subject to evictions, mobs, and capricious imprisonment. Hoarith was released in February 2016, but when I met him nearly a year and a half later, the indignity of arrest, for which he blamed his lack of citizenship, continued to occupy his mind. "I should be recognized as Khmer," he said that afternoon, moving close. His eyes were moss green. "My family has lived in Cambodia for many generations." He pulled back a curtain in the cramped room, revealing a woman asleep in a hammock. "My mother is seventy-six years old," he said. "Even she has no documents." Nor, now, did he. Upon his arrest, the police had confiscated his birth and marriage certificates and the national ID card he received years ago.

It was agreed I would spend the night on the disused houseboat next door. Some of the weathered boards plunged into space when you stepped on them, and most of the floor was taken up by Hoarith's supplies: rust-black sheets of tin, a roll of wire mesh, scales for weighing tubs at market. We cleared a spot for bedding, and Samnang and I chased down a boat woman selling old fabrics for a mosquito net.

Dinner was a leathery fish pounded flat and fried in oil on the camp stove Hoarith had fixed that afternoon. Samnang shouted to his wife over the water that he was staying for the meal. Hoarith's wife and mother ate together on the other houseboat; his mother deftly hopped the gap to retrieve a can of beer from the icebox. She picked up a few grains of rice I spilled from my bowl. "During the Khmer Rouge, this was our entire dinner," she said. "This was all the food we ate in a day."

As night fell, Thi Vioh washed the dishes in a tub of river water, and Hoarith bought bags of bean pudding from the last sampan of the evening, a dessert cruiser strung with colored lights. We listened to the boats roaring up and down the dark channel. Young men in the village liked to modify boats with car engines for night races. Each motor's throat cleared the air of the insects' chirping.

It was in one of these brief pockets of stillness that Samnang explained how his brother had died last year when a night racer collided with his fishing boat. His four-year-old nephew had drowned that year, too, while the parents were both at work. The water has its dangers, including diarrhea (the most common cause of infant death), accidents, and drowning. Most children under five wear life jackets when their parents can afford them, and improvised devices—the grimmest I saw was an empty motor-oil bottle tied to a length of wire looped around an infant's neck—when they can't.

Everyone was in bed by 11 o'clock. From the shoreline came a hollow chorus of empty hulls knocking into mangrove roots. Behind a half wall near my mat, a few alternating floorboards permitted a view of the river between my legs: the facilities. Under the mosquito net, the world was awash in diaphanous pink flowers. Every few seconds, a green light affixed to a roof beam illuminated the room as a warning to nighttime fishermen, whose boats I drowsily mistook for low-flying helicopters.

In the morning, Samnang came back to Hoarith's to take me to an old cemetery in the flooded countryside. He pulled up to the house in a timber-decked dory with an outboard motor whose steering arm he commanded like a limb. Chong Koh was already bustling. Families were gathered on porches playing *xiangqi* and eating breakfast, feeding chickens or exercising pigs and dogs along the waterfront. Women drove their children to market while calling out to neighbors what gleanings they sold, whether gasoline, soup, or Coca-Cola. Two orphan girls were already hard at work, sitting amid great piles of *trei chhlart* and squeezing the guts out of each gleaming fish with iron rolling pins.

We drove past the fish market in Kampong Chhnang, where the dock was being hosed down after the morning rush. The village poor, most of them young boys, had moored their wooden taxi boats in the shoals of churned mud and were halfheartedly looking for fares. The water around us was dotted with the crowns of sunken trees and the rooftops of dry-season market stalls. Fishermen who had been out all night were coming home with coolers filled with *riel*, the silver carp that shares its name with the national currency. The rest were going our way, driving to the systems of nets and bamboo weirs they had installed on the lake according to loose territorial agreements.

Samnang was friendly with everyone we passed, although he did not wave unless his hand already happened to be rising to pluck the cigarette from his lips. He had a fisherman's shrewd economy of movement, and his toes were muscular and permanently splayed, the better to maneuver along the narrow gunwales of a boat in motion. There was an archipelago of pitted skin above his left eyebrow, where he said a drunk Khmer villager had once crushed a glass into his face.

We came to an overgrown graveyard in a raised field. Unlike the Khmer, who cremate their dead, the Vietnamese bury family members in aboveground tombs. Graves thus show a record of Vietnamese residence that no law or loss of document can rescind. Life on the water leaves few ruins, but even families who have immigrated to Vietnam return to Cambodia once a year, usually in March or April, for the annual tomb-sweeping that wards off the wrath of the spirit realm. We drove from cemetery to cemetery, scraping ivy from stones to find the dates beneath, until we arrived at a sunken fen where more gravestones rose from the water like buoys. Samnang pointed to one. "My wife's grandmother's," he said. There had once been a large Vietnamese village here. The stone lay between two converging strands of river. In a few days it would be underwater.

Beyond the cemetery, behind a field of *ban la yuon,* we found a floating shack in the shadow of a ruined stilted house. A group of children waved from the window. Their father was in the abutting field, stomping through peat that came up to his shins, planting beans. He remembered the Vietnamese who used to live here, on the land as well as the water. There was even a Vietnamese temple—a *wat yuon,* he said—in a village not far from here. Samnang didn't know the village, but we decided to go look for it. The farmer warned that we would find no Vietnamese living there. "After the Khmer Rouge," he said, "they were afraid to come back."

We followed the farmer's directions down a narrow stream that meandered for an hour past worm-infested trees from whose branches hung the teardrop nests of tropical birds. Around noon we reached the village, which was called Samraong. There was a dirt road where sickly cows communed with the bovine infinite beneath stilted houses frozen in midcollapse. Children played in the tall grass. Neang Kangrei Mountain loomed overhead, and between the village and the mountain stood an incongruously opulent temple. Its gate was red and gold, framing the mountain's broad green slope. At the entrance stood a banner pillar, which connects heaven and earth in Buddhist cosmology. The pillar was square, in the Vietnamese style. Two stucco warriors stood on either side of the temple, 12 feet tall, pressing their swords into the earth.

We found an old monk in a hammock outside his hut. He woke up as we approached. Like the bean farmer, he remembered the Vietnamese. They had used this land for centuries, he said. Behind the monk's house were two brightly painted tombs, whose caretakers traveled from Ho Chi Minh City every March to sweep them.

A group of men had come up the road as we were talking. Now they approached us. The loudest, Uy Poun, boasted to me that he helped to convert the abandoned pagoda 15 years ago, exchanging the Vietnamese gods for Khmer ones. "I built this pagoda," he said. It had been abandoned for years by then, ever since the Khmer Rouge had moved the whole town to a camp at the foot of the mountain. Some Vietnamese were taken there, and that was the end of their time in the village. "But they weren't killed," he added. "They went to Vietnam."

Another man, Ek Srean, disagreed. Many were killed, he said. "I was an eyewitness. I saw the bones. I saw the bones in the pit."

"There were bones," a third said, "but we don't know if they were Khmer or Vietnamese."

The men fought over the fate of the Vietnamese for a while. Samnang and I listened and ate some boiled peanuts we bought in the market that morning. Conversations about the Khmer Rouge can have a dreamlike quality in Cambodia, drifting back and forth over the same gruesome territory—the crude methods of murder, the pitiful rations of rice and broth—while trading in rumors, jokes, and legends. Facts are overwritten; memories change midsentence. A story is told that contradicts the one preceding it, and both are accepted as passing glimpses of a historical truth too immense to view head-on. After some cajoling, Poun admitted that Vietnamese may have been killed in the camps. "But we didn't know," he added. Then he seemed to change his mind. "The Vietnamese never came to the commune where we were."

We moved on to the question of whether a Vietnamese could ever become Cambodian. As usual, the word "Khmer" was used to denote both ethnicity and nationality. One man in the group put forth a tentative theory: "It depends on their desires, if they want to become Khmer or not. If they give up their Vietnamese nationality, they become Khmer."

Srean again held a different opinion. "They can hold the documents, but they cannot become Khmer. The Vietnamese are still

Vietnamese." He shook his head and was quiet for a while. "Unless the king signs."

This generated murmurs of approval. We had forgotten the king's signature. According to Cambodian law, Prince Sihanouk's son, Norodom Sihamoni, is the final arbiter of Cambodian citizenship. All applicants for naturalization must meet his personal standards of character. None of us knew whether this had ever actually happened. But the men at least agreed that it might, and that the Vietnamese had lived among Cambodians for generations without any trouble. "Vietnamese and Khmer married each other in this very village," Poun said. "But not anymore."

"They were expelled," another said with finality. "And those who decided to stay were all killed. If they had white skin like a Vietnamese, like that"—he pointed at me, not at Samnang, who was keeping his distance—"they would be killed. I saw it."

The man seemed to know what he was talking about. Most soldiers and even senior political leaders who served in the Khmer Rouge melted smoothly back into village life after its demise, sometimes rejoining the very communities where they had once worked as executioners. It is rare for anyone to admit such things. The subject was raised in a tactful way. The man who had spoken thought for a moment, then asked to revise his story.

"Well, I didn't see it exactly," he said. "I heard about it. But someone who had light skin like you would definitely be killed."

I spent the next few weeks traveling through floating villages on Tonle Sap Lake and visiting enclaves of ethnic Vietnamese along the Cambodia-Vietnam border. In one border town, I watched a woman use an old land-mine cap as a chopping block. It had been planted in her yard during the Indochina wars and proved itself a dud. In Chhnok Trou, I watched Khmer and Vietnamese neighbors play rousing midnight games of *cat te* beneath flickering generator light, throwing handfuls of cash into the pot, and everywhere I was the object of extreme village hospitality that knows no ethnic or national distinction: stuffed full of giant river snails and prawn cakes, enticed with can after can of warm Angkor beer.

Wherever I went, I asked local politicians and police officers what they thought of the ethnic Vietnamese living among them. The answer depended on where I happened to be. Officials spoke carefully in the cities, and I was politely bounced from the immigration police headquarters in Kampong Chhnang. But I had no trouble at the immigration police station in Kampong Luong, a sprawling conglomerate of floating villages, both Vietnamese and Khmer, on the southern shore of the lake. More than 3,000 ethnic Vietnamese lived in Kampong Luong, alongside as many Khmer, and everyone said they got along swimmingly.

The police station was near the shore, a tin shed floating in a stream of wet garbage. Deputy Inspector Poa Ven was inside the shed, sweating. He was happy to see me. "We are aware of all foreign visitors," he said, chuckling, when I handed him my business card.

All the foreigners in the village were Vietnamese nationals, he explained. There was no difference between an ethnic Vietnamese and a Vietnamese citizen unless they got a letter signed by the king. "No one here has Khmer nationality."

I explained my confusion. Most of the people I'd met on floating villages could trace their lineage in Cambodia back many generations. They spoke Khmer fluently and had even been issued IDs by previous administrations. They had no ties to Vietnam.

Yes, he said, even they were Vietnamese. Those were the new orders from the Ministry of the Interior.

"But why are they Vietnamese?"

"Because they are still immigrants! Because they came to Cambodia in 1980, they are still immigrants."

"But if they were *originally* from Cambodia, why are they immigrants?"

"Because during the civil war, they went to Vietnam, and after the war they came back."

Nationalism is always in search of an enemy. In Cambodia, the search has a neat circular logic: The Vietnamese are enemies because they are foreign. They are foreign because they are enemies. Their existence here betrays a contradiction between the myth of a pure Khmer empire and the country's lived history of migration and movement along the Mekong. The contradiction has been resolved at times by violence, but it is perpetuated by education. The Khmer Rouge years may be fading from living memory, but children are still taught to resent the loss of "Lower Cambodia," and every student has heard of the rapes, gas attacks, and elaborate acts of torture that Vietnamese soldiers are believed to have committed during the Indochina wars.

"All of that stuff tends to weigh very heavily on Cambodian minds," Craig Etcheson, a Khmer Rouge scholar at Harvard, told me. "And that is very easy for opportunistic politicians to exploit and inflame." Etcheson is a founder of the Documentation Center of Cambodia, which has provided much of the evidence for the Extraordinary Chambers in the Courts of Cambodia, or Khmer Rouge Tribunal, convened in 2006 to try a handful of senior Khmer Rouge leaders for crimes against humanity. The second phase of the trials, concerning genocide against minority groups, including the Vietnamese, concluded its final arguments last summer. A ruling is expected this year.

Lyma Nguyen, an international civil-party counsel at the tribunal, told me she had hoped that one consequence of the trial would be a pathway to a stable legal identity for Vietnamese survivors of the Khmer Rouge. But she encountered insurmountable resistance to the idea. Current plans for reparations include only a watered-down education program for raising awareness about nationality laws. "Many mainstream Cambodians, including some lawyers and academics, actually don't think the Vietnamese victims of the genocide should have a legitimate claim to having suffered genocide, because they're Vietnamese," she said. "They think it's all a big conspiracy by Vietnam to swallow up Cambodia."

Most ethnic Vietnamese in the country continue to feel that they are Cambodians of Vietnamese origin. They refuse to give up hope that someday their Cambodian identity will be accepted in the country they call home. Instead, with somewhere between 400,000 and 1 million members, according to independent scholars, and virtually no international calls for Cambodia to uphold its own nationality laws, they are arguably one of the largest and least-supported stateless populations in the world.

The ethnic Vietnamese have taken to hiding their documents from the police currently sweeping the country. It's not the first time this kind of thing has happened to them. At the Vietnamese pagoda in Kampong Chhnang, I met a diminutive 80-year-old seamstress. Only monks and laypeople are meant to live at the pagoda, but she didn't have any family—her children died before her eyes in a Khmer Rouge labor camp—so the monks took pity on her. I asked whether she ever received any identification papers. She shuffled to her room and came back holding a small packet wrapped in twine. "You're lucky," she said as she untied it. "I've never let anyone look at these before." She began spreading an astonishing half century's worth of documents across the table. There were cards from Sihanouk's Cambodia alongside decades' worth of residency permits from Vietnam, to which she was twice deported. So long as she never showed them to anyone, the documents could never be invalidated or purged. They were her private legal self, a superposition of identities both Vietnamese and Cambodian. She would not give them up. "I'll keep these documents with me until I die," she said, "and then I'll take them to the grave with me."

The monks on the floating pagoda in Kampong Luong were preparing for the ceremony of the drowned, arranging yellow orchids and four-o'clocks beneath a Buddha framed in flashing lights. A rented pavilion had been floated over and stocked with chairs. Young volunteers scattered *riel* and mangos on a picnic table, and all morning long pilgrims from Phnom Penh arrived to give money to the poor and receive blessings. It was August, and the air was torpid.

Drowning is a bad death, the temple laymen explained. The souls of the drowned become water ghosts— *khmoch teuk* in Khmer —causing shipwrecks and pulling swimmers under by their legs. The ceremony coaxes the spirits out of the water so that they may find their way to the next life or proceed to the heavenly plane.

The heat broke with a late-afternoon downpour. The children of supplicants made a game of leaping through the deluge onto an empty fish barge moored to the pagoda, then back again with fearless precision. At dusk, the ceremony began. There was an hour of amplified chanting before the head monk tossed holy water over the crowd and called for the doors of hell to open. As if on cue, the rain slowed, then stopped. The temple emptied into the ferries and sampans outside. At the front of the largest ferry, a monk rang a finger cymbal to wake the drowned, and the boats slipped onto the open lake. There was no moon. The water was black. Webs of distant lightning soundlessly limned the clouds red. Along the sides of the ferries and the gunwales of each boat, families placed paper rafts and plastic lotus flowers into the water.

Each was topped by a burning candle, such that the lake became a field of bobbing orange stars. All was still, save for the families who boated past, singing into the dark. Some of their boats nearly spilled over with children. Some of the paper boats flared up in a flash and sank.

Beyond the scarp that runs along Chong Koh, a new market complex was under construction, and with it came berms of red soil and cement foundations cratered with silted ponds. Once the market was finished, the villagers in Chong Koh would be evicted again, ahead of floating communities across the province. Officials said the villages were illegal and environmentally toxic. Their residents would be squeezed onto marshy rented plots earmarked for immigrants, far from their boats and fish cages.

Neither Hoarith nor Samnang wanted to move. "I can't speak out," Samnang said as we sat drinking coffee in his house. "They claim to give us a choice. But we have no right to buy any other land, so really it's no choice at all."

We paddled next door, where Hoarith was too consumed by boat repair to worry about any new evictions. Last week he had chopped three feet off the back of his long-tail. Now his transmission was spread out before him like a gutted squid.

As he worked, Hoarith's thoughts often went back to his prison cell and to the spot of cold floor next to the toilet where he had slept. "I never discriminate against anyone, Vietnamese or Khmer," he said. "But I was treated so badly." If he were granted Khmer citizenship, he said, all would be forgiven. "My parents were born here, and I was born here," he said. "I have that right."

There was nothing to say. Samnang found a hatchet to sharpen on the rear step over the water. Hoarith turned back to his work. A washer, slick with oil, shot from his hand. It bounced against the floor and off the side of the house before he caught it over the water, hissing in surprise.

The first people to leave Chong Koh went by night as soon as the new immigration cards were announced in 2014. Since then, at least a thousand have shoved off to other provinces or sold their houses and hitched to Vietnam, part of a growing exodus all over Cambodia. In village after village, the immigration police and council leaders said the same thing: "The Vietnamese are leaving."

In a pinch, Hoarith thought he might be able to live with his wife's relatives in Vietnam. Better was the lake. On the open lake it was more dangerous, but he would be close to his ancestors, and the authorities there weren't as strict. The boat people had figured out how to manage them, as they managed the squalls and the waves. They knew how not to challenge the weather but survive it, was how he put it. That was the trick. You had to plan for the storm before the clouds opened up.

DEVON O'NEIL

Irmageddon

FROM *Outside Magazine*

As a KID, you can't control where you grow up. To land somewhere like St. John, in the US Virgin Islands, takes luck—and in
my case an adventurous mother. My fraternal twin brother, Sean,
and I were five years old when our mom decided that she was tired
of commuting from Westport, Connecticut, to New York City. So in
December 1985, she and her boyfriend bought a 41-foot sailboat
named *Yahoo*, we packed everything we owned into 19 duffel bags,
and we headed south.

St. John, half of which is covered by Virgin Islands National
Park, offered singular beauty—and plenty of places to anchor our
new floating home. Mom took a job as a landscaper in Fish Bay
and eventually got her real estate license. Sean and I fell in with a
rat pack of kids who congregated after school to play tackle football, catch tarantulas and lizards, and crawl under barroom floors
in search of quarters. We grew up boogie boarding and surfing on
the south shore. One day we took turns reeling in a 350-pound
shark off the west end of Jost Van Dyke, next door in the British
Virgin Islands.

After two years on the boat, Mom bought a house. A house
that, on September 6, 2017, was completely destroyed by Hurricane Irma. At the time, my mother was on the mainland for a wedding and a visit with Sean and me in Colorado, where we both live
with our families. Four days after the storm, we found a YouTube
video with aerial footage of our neighborhood. It was annihilated;
I didn't recognize our home, a modest two-story structure that had
survived hurricanes for 30 years. It looked like someone had shot

a missile into it. So did our neighbors' houses. I watched the video five times. Despite studying the footage, which covered at least a quarter mile in all directions, I could not locate our roof.

It had been more than 15 years since I'd lived on St. John, but I still considered it home. It's where I learned about the world, everything from fishing to race. When we were nine, my brother and I spent an entire spring glued to a chain-link fence watching St. John's all-black Little League team practice. The West Indian coaches, former pro prospects Orville "Chopper" Brown and Terry "Chino" Chinnery, asked if we'd like to join the team the following year. We did. On September 16, 1989, while practicing in the island's main town of Cruz Bay, I got hit by a pitch and broke my elbow. As the doctor wrapped it in a cast, he said, "Have you heard about the storm coming?"

He said it was called Hugo and that the territory was in line for a direct strike. The Virgin Islands have a long, fatal history with tropical cyclones. The first recorded major hurricane hit the island in 1697. Devastating storms followed in 1772, 1819, 1867, and 1916. It had been decades since a legitimate threat had materialized.

By then we were in our new house a half mile above Cruz Bay; other residents lived in small communities scattered above bays and beaches. We were oblivious to the storm's power. Instead of installing hurricane shutters or armor screens, like people do now, we duct-taped an X over each of the six sliding glass doors and sat on our living room couch as Hugo roared through with 150-mile-per-hour sustained winds. We watched a neighbor's roof peel off, a shed get picked up by a tornado, and a restaurant's roof slam into our yard like a kite. When the glass started to bow, Mom told us to hide under the bed.

In 1995, Hurricane Marilyn landed another roundhouse. Sean and I were in Connecticut when it hit; Mom rode out the storm on a boat in Hurricane Hole, a sheltered bay that offers some protection from the wind. Though the boat held its position, people who hunkered down in more vulnerable locations onshore still insist that the winds were substantially stronger than the 115-mile-per-hour forecast.

I recall images from those storms, but the damage I saw on the Irma video was in a class by itself—three or four times as bad as Hugo and Marilyn combined, locals estimated. "The forces were just incomprehensible compared with previous storms," says Rafe Boulon, a St. John native and retired scientist whose great-grandfather opened the US Weather Bureau office on Puerto Rico in the early 1900s. "Some places lost probably ten thousand years of sand and vegetation in a matter of three hours."

As soon as Irma formed as a tropical storm off the west coast of Africa on August 30, it grabbed scientists' attention. Weak upper-level winds over the Atlantic and sea-surface temperatures that were 2 degrees warmer than average made for an ominous mix as the storm moved toward the Caribbean.

"It's amazing how much difference just one or two degrees can make at that water temperature in terms of how strong a hurricane can get," says Jay Hobgood, an associate professor of atmospheric science at Ohio State University who tracked Irma and has been studying hurricanes since the 1970s.

Despite a roughly 400-mile diameter, Irma had to thread a needle to inflict catastrophic damage on populated places. Most destruction occurs in a hurricane's eyewall, a band of brutally violent wind spinning counterclockwise around the eye; beyond that, winds drop off quickly. This creates a 40-to-60-mile-wide path where you don't want to be. Almost all hurricanes pass between Trinidad, just north of South America, and Bermuda. But most of them track north of the US Virgin Islands, which have only a 3 percent chance of being hit by a hurricane that's Category 3 or stronger.

Irma soon grew to Category 5, with maximum sustained winds of 185 miles per hour—the second-highest speed on record for an Atlantic hurricane. The day before it hit, Chopper got a call from his son, Okyeame, who works in intelligence for the US Navy and is Sean's and my godson. At 61, Chopper is built like a defensive end and remains as imposing as when he served as the island's unofficial patriarch, someone who mothers would bring their sons to for discipline and direction. Okyeame told his father that he had researched the storm and it was a monster—nothing like it had hit St. John in generations, if ever. Chopper felt a wave of fear wash over him.

The same day, I called my closest friend from childhood, Galen Stamford, who was living in the one-bedroom apartment on the first floor of my mom's house with his wife and six-year-old daughter. Sean and I met Galen our first week in the Virgin Islands. He grew up to be one of the top surfers in the region and a beloved island figure. Like everyone else, he had been watching Irma's advance with dread. "I don't think your mom's house is going to survive this one," he said. He had decided to stay at a friend's concrete house in Peter Bay, on the north side of the island, where the windows and doors would be protected by a large armor screen. They had stocked enough food and water to last three months.

Across the 20-square-mile island, the 4,000 residents finalized preparations of their own. In Rendezvous Bay, on the island's south side, Carlos Di Blasi, a 53-year-old restaurant owner, had decided to ride out the storm in the house that he and his wife, Maria, had built 16 years earlier. It had one-foot-thick concrete walls and a roof made of corrugated tin, three-quarter-inch plywood, and half-inch cedar.

Sailors in the area frantically rushed to secure their boats. Longtime skipper Richard Benson, 66, buzzed around in his dinghy helping other people get ready, including his son, Daniel. Benson owned one of St. John's iconic charter boats, the all-black, 84-foot "pirate ship" *Goddess Athena*. He had a long blond beard and gold teeth, and he was known for his stern temperament and reliability. He and Daniel had five boats to prep between them, but as they worked, Daniel was fighting a stomach bug that left him barely able to speak. "I felt terrible," recalls Daniel, a 26-year-old artist and surfer. "All I wanted was to be with my dad and help him."

Before Benson steered the *Goddess Athena* to Coral Bay on September 5, he did something that was rare for him: he admitted regret. "We should've sailed south two days ago," he told a friend.

Benson didn't have as many options as smaller-boat owners did for where to seek shelter. In Hurricane Hole, the National Park Service allots 105 spots across four bays where captains can clip onto a one-inch-thick chain strung across the ocean bottom. But boats longer than 60 feet aren't allowed to use the chain, so Benson positioned the *Goddess Athena* in the shallower water and mud of Sanders Bay, across the harbor.

Just north of where Benson anchored, a 50-year-old lifelong sailor named Adam Hudson tied off his 27-foot Bristol, *Solstice*, in roughly the same spot he always did: in front of the old customhouse on the east side of the bay. The first time he rode out a major hurricane on the water—Hugo, when he was in his early 20s —Hudson escaped a pileup of boats by jumping into chest-deep water and wading to shore as raindrops shelled his skin. He and his dad watched their boat get pounded for the next eight hours, irreparably damaged. This time he figured he'd be fine, if for no other reason than he'd always been fine in this spot—the same rationale Benson seemed to be using.

The night before Irma struck St. John, it mowed down Barbuda —an island three times the size of St. John—leaving 95 percent of its buildings uninhabitable. St. Johnians who watched the radar that night were forced to accept a grim reality.

"Imagine you're skydiving, and you pull the rip cord and nothing happens," Daniel Benson says. "You look at the ground, and the glance that you and the ground exchange, that moment of imminence—that's what it felt like."

On the morning of September 6, the storm ramped up at different times in different places, but it happened quickly everywhere. In Peter Bay, Galen and his storm mates—seven people and six dogs—observed an almost instantaneous change when the eyewall arrived at around 11:15 a.m. "It was like a snap of your fingers," he said. "There was no warning. We went from 70- to 160-mile-per-hour winds like that. The bronze railings started to whistle. You could hear ceramic roof tiles getting ripped off one by one."

Five miles south, Carlos Di Blasi and his family lounged in a bedroom watching a movie, wondering why it was so quiet. Their house faced east and was tucked against a mountain, sheltered from the west winds. Until 12:30 p.m., you could have heard a quarter hit the floor. Then a big gust shook the house, and Di Blasi decided that they should move downstairs to a more secure room. He walked to the closet to get his shoes as Maria and their 11-year-old son, Alejo, looked out the window.

Bang! A deafening explosion rang out—suddenly the dark room was light. Di Blasi looked at his 15-year-old son, Mateo. A long two-by-six beam had pierced the roof like a javelin and missed his son's head by inches, spraying his hair with wood chips.

Bang! A second beam landed on the other side of Mateo. He stood there, frozen, as water gushed through the ceiling holes.

Bang! A third beam came through. Maria started screaming. The four of them raced downstairs to a bathroom under a concrete ceiling and listened as 11 more beams—ripped from another house by a tornado—penetrated their roof.

At the other end of the island, in Coral Bay, six-foot waves crashed down on Hudson's boat, breaking its mast. At 1 p.m., he felt an anchor line snap, and the boat started taking on water. He knew it was only a matter of minutes until it sank, so he grabbed his savings—$5,000 in cash that he kept in a drawer—crawled onto the bow, and waited until the pulpit disappeared into the water. Then he began to swim for his life, greenbacks in one hand, ball cap in the other.

He estimates that he swallowed a gallon of salt water during the swim. He reached the shoreline, crawled up to a rock, and clung to it for five hours in the fetal position, shivering and slurping rainwater.

Several islanders say they felt an earthquake at the height of the hurricane. Water rose through sink and shower drains, then disappeared. Walls expanded and contracted. "I thought ten percent of the people on island were going to die," Daniel Benson told me. "I honestly thought that."

Across most of St. John, the storm simmered down between 5 and 6 p.m. The eyewall had passed, and a hurricane's outer bands usually bring more rain than wind. But high on Bordeaux Mountain, the island's pinnacle at 1,283 feet, the fury was just beginning.

Debby Roberts-Liburd, a grandmother whose family lives on a remote plot above southern Lameshur Bay, counted seven tornadoes between 5:30 p.m. and 1 a.m. She had already watched three relatives' houses get blown apart when her own roof flew away at 10:30 p.m. Then the wind sucked the toilet straight up and out of the bathroom.

"Ma," yelled her son, L.J., "we cannot stay in this room, because we all will be sucked out." As Debby hurried outside to take shelter on the lower floor, L.J. saw a tornado coming and knew she wouldn't make it back inside before it arrived. He ran and grabbed her around the waist as she clung to a water drum. "Don't look up," he said.

The wind lifted Debby's legs off the ground and shook her like a fish. "Just hold on, Ma!" L.J. said. "Don't loose off, 'cause if you loose off, two of us gone!"

When she felt her grip slipping, Debby prayed. *Please, Lord, don't let anything cut off my hands.* Almost instantly, she heard a *ssssssip,* and the air went still. She ran inside.

The morning after felt apocalyptic. Not a leaf remained; the islands were so brown that the color even showed up in images from NASA satellites. Bizarre sights filled the landscape. Chopper came out of his house to find his dog eating his cat. Boats were stacked onshore like sticks in a campfire. Desperation set in. Looters ripped out ATMs. My mom worried that her belongings would be ransacked before she got home. Galen heard stories of people getting robbed at gunpoint, and he began sleeping with a spear.

At first, some 2,700 residents were unaccounted for—more than half the population. "I was getting two to four messages a minute for a while," says Jon Shames, president of St. John Rescue, a volunteer organization.

In the sailing community, boaters shared news of who they'd seen and who they hadn't, in what is known as the Coconut Telegraph. It soon became evident that nobody could find Richard Benson or the *Goddess Athena.* Daniel Benson spent days using a jury-rigged VHF radio to try and hail his dad. He got no response, but he heard the Coast Guard trying, too, which gave him hope.

Unfortunately, the Atlantic hurricane season was far from over. Two weeks after Irma passed, Maria walloped St. Croix and Puerto Rico—major hubs for the relief effort on St. John. Even though St. John dodged a direct strike, its supply chain was broken.

Richard Benson's fate remained a mystery for 19 days, until someone saw a British news story about an unidentified man who was found nine miles northeast of Coral Bay, on Tortola's coast, the day after Irma. "Caucasian, between the ages of 60 and 70, medium build, 5'7 to 5'8 and 160 lbs," read the description. "He had a long blond beard and hair and was wearing blue coveralls like that of a marine engineer when he was found." Daniel took a helicopter to identify his father at the morgue. He was, remarkably, the only St. John resident to die during the storm.

Not long afterward, Daniel located the *Goddess Athena*—or at least the remaining 20 feet of her. The stern, one of 546 shipwrecks left by Irma in the US Virgin Islands, had washed up inside the barrier reef at Johnson Bay, just southwest of Coral Bay. It was a

skeleton. The steering wheel and helm were gone, and the interior
was gutted except for a light bulb and a speaker. The only thing
that Daniel found of his dad's was his old underwater camera.

My mother arrived on St. John three weeks after Irma, the day
the St. Thomas airport reopened. She spent long hours picking
things out of the rubble, which she stored in her car, and doing
laundry at a friend's house where she was staying. She applied for
FEMA aid. She got exhausted quickly and often.

Everyone kept asking what she was going to do, and she didn't
have an answer. Rebuilding at age 68 with a FEMA loan sounded
daunting, but so did the alternative: leaving the island she loved.

I got my first view of St. John two months after Irma, on November 6. Sean and I joined Galen, two friends from Colorado, and
my father-in-law to tear down our house to the foundation. Part of
me feared the job, not for physical reasons but for emotional ones.
Still, the rubble had sat long enough, and we knew Mom would
need it gone if she decided to sell the land. (Before she paid off
her mortgage five years ago, the bank required her to have hurricane insurance, which cost $18,000 a year. She got rid of the
coverage once she settled the debt.)

It's strange to take a sledgehammer to your childhood home—
demolishing the kitchen counter and what's left of your bedroom
walls. But that was better than cleaning out the freezer, which had
sat unopened for two months in 85-degree heat. Thousands of rotting maggots combined with shrimp scampi make a strong case for
the world's foulest smell.

As I broke down walls snared in vines, I couldn't help but imagine how the house had come apart. Assuming that the roof went
first, the west-facing wall must have been flattened by 200-mile-
per-hour winds. The remaining walls likely collapsed after that,
then the south deck and railings, everything swept into the bush.

Iguanas watched from the treetops as we shoveled soggy debris into buckets and piled it eight feet high in the driveway. In
one shovelful, I collected a remote control, part of the kitchen
table, a phone book, chunks of moldy drywall, and a bottle of vinegar. In the next, my high school ID, more moldy drywall, *A River
Runs Through It* on DVD, and a Christmas card to "Gram" from
Sean's kids.

I dug a box out of the mud that contained our grandparents'

Kodachrome slides from the 1950s. Mom found her Woodstock ticket stubs. We discovered a plastic bin full of a hundred framed photos from our childhood and hers, somehow sitting dry next to three bins full of water.

On the third day, a neighbor surveyed our work from his still standing deck. "See!" Mom shouted up to him. "I told you they'd come rescue me." For the first time in weeks, she sounded hopeful.

Despite spending that week on St. John, I knew I had seen only a portion of Irma's impact on the region. So in late November I returned, joining local photographer Steve Simonsen on his boat. We motored all over the British Virgin Islands, which neighbor St. John, visiting people who had survived the eye and were now left to rebuild.

One of our first stops was the world-renowned Bitter End Yacht Club on the east side of Virgin Gorda, a 64-acre resort spread across a mile of sandy coastline. Sixty of its buildings—including 40 rental villas—were destroyed. "It has to be totally reimagined," John Glynn, a marketing executive, told me.

We pulled up to the dock and met Henry Prince, a 20-year employee and Virgin Gorda native who guessed that it would take at least three years for Bitter End to look anything like it did before the storm. "You're not going to rebuild it the way it was. You have to rebuild it for the new type of hurricane," he said.

We headed across North Sound past Necker Island, where Sir Richard Branson has weathered every hurricane for the past 40 years. He told me that 300 of his private island's 600 flamingos survived winds that broke his anemometer when they hit 210 miles per hour. We stopped for lunch at Leverick Bay, one of the most devastated communities, where four out of every five buildings had been blown apart. Marina manager Nick Willis was sipping a beer on his deck when I found him. He told me about the damage but also how Irma had brought out the best in people. Like the rich Czech guy from Nail Bay who had paid hundreds of locals $10 an hour to work on their homes after the storm. Or the man who had boated up to the marina and handed Willis $100, asking only that he give it to someone who needed it. "It just brings you to tears," Willis said.

We drove around Tortola with Chino, my old baseball coach,

who mentors island kids and lives in Cane Garden Bay, a port famous for its beachfront restaurants, all of which were destroyed.
We saw where the ocean had ripped graves out of the earth in
Carrot Bay and flipped a 99-ton ferry upside down on Jost Van
Dyke. We gaped at a battered airplane fuselage—without its wings
or tail—balanced atop a ruined hangar at the Beef Island airport.
I heard rumors that the British military measured gusts up to 285
miles per hour. (The unofficial wind speed record is 318 miles per
hour, set by a 1999 tornado in Oklahoma City.)

None of the sights, however, compared with what we found on
Cooper Island, a tiny cay off the south shore of Tortola. As we
neared a concrete dock, an old West Indian woman walked toward us holding a knife above her head. I got off the boat and
approached her slowly, introducing myself and asking if I could
talk to her about Irma. "Of course. Come in!" she said. She led
me and Simonsen toward a makeshift white tent—actually a sail
draped over some coconut trees. A frail-looking man limped along
the beach to meet us.

Jean and John Leonard explained that they weathered Irma
right here at sea level. Jean, 84, came from Trinidad so long ago
that she'd forgotten the year. John, 90, was born on Cooper Island
and had lived here all his life. Before Irma they had 8 boats and
15 fish pots just offshore. Like many Virgin Islanders, they'd seen
their share of hurricanes and did not fear them, so when a boat
arrived to take them to Tortola, they declined.

Their son, who lives on Tortola, sent his 15-year-old boy to stay
with them during the storm, in case they needed some muscle.
Soon after the deluge began, a sea grape tree fell on their roof,
followed by a coconut palm. The house began to break apart.
Ten-foot waves combined with the fast-rising surge almost pinned
the Leonards to the bed they were hiding under. Their grandson kicked down the door, and they ran outside. As the wind and
ocean raged, John turned to his wife of 54 years. "I can't make it
anymore," he said. He lay down in the water. Jean grabbed a pile
of dry clothes she'd stored in a drum and propped them under his
head to keep him from drowning.

The next day, when their son came to check on them, he was
stunned. "He say he didn't expect to see we alive," Jean told me in
her Trinidadian accent. "He didn't expect to see we *at all.*"

Two dogs and hundreds of ducks, many still limping from Irma, scurried around in the sand next to an outboard motor and various buoys. Bags of corn for their animals—they also have more than 80 goats, which they sell to a butcher on Tortola—were stacked on the dock. I couldn't help but notice a second sail fashioned into an A-frame, 50 feet down the beach. I walked over and peeked inside, seeing two old mattresses on rickety frames under the sail. This was where the Leonards were sleeping. Before the Royal Marines brought them sails, they'd slept in the open.

The Virgin Islands face an uncertain future. The first three months after Irma were focused on solving basic problems and getting electricity restored. It helped that, in addition to local organizations, longtime St. John second-home owners Tom Secunda—a billionaire cofounder of Bloomberg—and country-music star Kenny Chesney launched extensive relief and evacuation assistance. (By the end of the exodus, most believed that St John's population had been cut in half.) FEMA had contributed nearly $300 million to the islands by mid-December, including loans, and at one point Virgin Islands National Park requested $68 million in hopes of catalyzing economic progress on St. John. "The challenge is keeping this place on the radar for the American public and also for Congress," acting park superintendent Darrell Echols told me.

The long-term environmental fallout is unknowable. It took more than three months for the dangerously high levels of bacteria, possibly from runoff tainted by septic backups, to clear up on two popular north-shore beaches, Maho and Oppenheimer. The coral reefs have been stressed by the same runoff. One scientist told me that it could take decades for the red mangroves to recover.

As for reconstruction, David Rosa, an engineer who lives and works on St. John, said that he expects a change in building codes because of Irma. Currently, everything must be constructed to withstand 165-mile-per-hour winds. "It wouldn't surprise me if they went up to 180 or even higher," Rosa said. Still, stronger buildings are more expensive: one-inch rebar, for example, costs six times as much as half-inch.

The most important question is how and when tourism will rebound. Five of the resorts on St. John were still closed in early February, and the two biggest, Caneel Bay and the Westin, don't expect to reopen until 2019. Arthur Jones, owner of Arawak Expeditions, said that he expects to lose two-thirds of his business over the next year. "We are a tourism-based economy, and when tourists don't come, we are going to be hurting," Jones said.

"Things are going to change here," said Miles Stair, an old friend who has lived on St. John for 46 years. "People will go, people will come. Are we going to have fewer restaurants? Are we going to see fewer tourist dollars? Is that good, bad, somewhere in between? I think it'll be years before we really gain a perspective."

Richard Branson, who likened Irma's damage to a nuclear strike, is leading an effort to unite the region so it will be less vulnerable to future storms. It's called the Caribbean Climate-Smart Coalition, and he views it as a sort of Marshall Plan for the region. The goal: get the Caribbean islands—including the US and British Virgin Islands—recategorized as a bloc, so they can receive lower-interest loans faster and better insurance terms. "It's much easier for, say, the World Bank to deal with all the islands at once instead of lots of individual islands," says Branson, who was forced to cancel bookings at his Necker Island resort through September 2018.

As for the likelihood of more megastorms hitting the Virgin Islands, it's one aspect of climate change that scientists disagree about. In general, most believe—and the models agree—that we will see fewer Atlantic cyclones. But when conditions align, they could bring monsters.

Infrastructure aside, Irma's remaining wounds are personal. Galen's wife and daughter left St. John four weeks after the storm and will probably remain off island through the school year. They're far from the only family living a fractured existence.

"Life is hard all over again," said Adam Hudson, the sailor who lost his boat in Hugo and then another in Irma, over a beer on the Coral Bay waterfront.

Daniel Benson was still processing his father's fate when I met him one afternoon at Hart Bay. We walked out to the rocky point and sat next to the break where Sean and I had learned to surf. With his blond dreadlocks tucked under a bandanna and tattoos honoring his roots—U-S-V-I across his left fingers and LOVE CITY, Cruz Bay's nickname, on his thigh—Daniel pondered what happened to his dad.

Benson was believed to have had 10 large anchors securing the roughly 40-ton *Goddess Athena*, so the fact that his boat was found elsewhere means he must have cut his lines. But why? Though friends have differing opinions, Daniel believes his dad lost his dinghy and couldn't get to shore as the storm picked up. And if his anchors then started dragging, he may have decided to fire up the 200-horsepower diesel engine and roll the dice in the open ocean rather than be smashed on the rocks in the bay.

"I think he made it pretty far south, then a wave took him," Daniel said. "I can only imagine hanging on to a steering wheel while duck-diving twenty feet of solid water. I just wonder how many waves he dove through before he finally said fuck it. Or maybe he didn't. Maybe the waves just broke the helm right off."

In late November, a St. John Rescue truck carrying Benson's remains led a procession through Cruz Bay. People lined the streets to say goodbye. "I know everybody says my situation is maybe heavier than what they went through," Daniel said, "but from my perspective, the woman who crawled out from underneath her collapsed house in the middle of the storm, who barely had enough room to breathe, I think she went through something heavier than me in the storm. The girl who had to run out of her house because it exploded and got into a car, then had to go to another car because the first one exploded . . ." He trailed off. "Everybody has experienced a whole different kind of crazy with this hurricane."

Sean and I have tried our best to support our mom after Irma. She put her property up for sale in early December, and she's spending the winter near us in Colorado. In her bedroom, a sign reads DON'T LOOK BACK. YOU'RE NOT GOING THAT WAY.

It was hard for her to admit to people that she was leaving. So much of her identity is tied to St. John and enduring life on a volcanic rock in the middle of the ocean. I tried to remind her that the results were out of her control. As Galen said, "We're like the fleas on a dog, and we got hit by the paw."

A handful of friends whose homes survived told me that they feel ashamed when people ask how they fared. Mom understands, despite landing on the opposite side of that fate. "In some ways, I'm sad that I wasn't actually here for the storms. I've thought of that a lot," she said one night at dinner. "'Missed out' isn't the right phrase, but I've imagined what it must've been like, even though it's unimaginable."

It's a weird feeling to know that I can't go home anymore. I think about sitting on our deck and watching the sunset, picking ripe passion fruit off our vine, hearing the roosters crow each morning. But I remind myself that the island will always be there.

One afternoon in late November, on our way back from the British Virgin Islands, Simonsen and I stopped at the Baths, a famous boulder-strewn beach on Virgin Gorda where you can swim in caves and jump off rocks and nap on soft white sand. Like most beaches in the wake of Irma, it was empty and stunning. I did some bouldering and squeezed through a couple of caves, then jumped into the water to cool off. A family of four, including two boys under 10, snorkeled by. I asked the father where they were from. "Originally the UK," he said, before gesturing toward the lone sailboat in the bay. "Right now we're living aboard."

I smiled to myself and told him they were lucky boys.

Water and the Wall

FROM *The New Yorker*

WHEN DAN REICHER was eight, he became fixated on wolverines. He admired their ferocity but, because they were endangered, feared for their survival. While poring over a catalog of outdoor gear, he came across a parka trimmed in wolverine fur. He was outraged. His mother, a schoolteacher, and his father, an ob-gyn, urged him to put his umbrage to good purpose, so he sent the gear company a letter. After some time, he received a reply: the company was discontinuing the parka. Had his protest made the difference? Probably not, but, still, he inferred that a citizen, even a little one, had the power to effect change. "Boy, was I misled," he said recently.

Reicher, now 61, is a professor at Stanford and the executive director of its Steyer-Taylor Center for Energy Policy and Finance. Previously, he led Google's climate and energy initiatives and served in the Clinton administration as an assistant secretary of energy. He has spent most of his adult life trying to help humankind move past its reliance on fossil fuels. Under President Trump, conservationists have seen decades of gains rolled back in a matter of months. Still, Reicher, like so many environmentalists, goes grimly about his business.

Reicher's real obsession is water. He grew up in Syracuse, paddling on polluted lakes, and liked to collect and test water samples. When he was 11, his parents sent him to Ontario on a canoe trip with a drill sergeant who failed to bring an adequate supply of food. Reicher, getting by on wild blueberries and toothpaste, had never been and would never again be as hungry, but, even so, he loved the whole thing. For a couple of summers in his teens, he attended the Colorado Rocky Mountain School, in Carbondale, where a French champion of the newfangled sport of white-water kayaking taught aspiring river runners the eddy turn and the high brace. Reicher got to spend a week on the Green River, paddling through the vast Dinosaur National Monument. He was captivated by the journals of a predecessor there: John Wesley Powell, the Union Army major who lost an arm at Shiloh and later led the first expedition to navigate the length of the Grand Canyon. As an undergraduate at Dartmouth, Reicher joined the kayaking team and the Ledyard Canoe Club, which is named for John Ledyard, the eighteenth-century American explorer, who dropped out of Dartmouth after a year and paddled down the Connecticut River, from Hanover to the Long Island Sound, in a dugout canoe fashioned from a tree he cut down on campus.

In the spirit of these forebears, in 1977 Reicher and some fellow Ledyardians embarked on an expedition of their own. A classmate, Tony Anella, from Albuquerque, was preoccupied with his hometown river, the Rio Grande, and had determined that no one in documented history had navigated the river's nearly 2,000 miles, from source to sea. He planned to be the first. The students secured backing from the National Geographic Society, which, a dozen years before, had sponsored a Ledyard trip along the Danube. For course credit, Anella, a history major, would compile a history of water rights on the river, while the other principal, Rob Portman, an anthropology major (and now the junior United States senator from Ohio), would take on the subject of mass migration. Reicher, a biology major, would assess the water and whatever life could survive in it.

Generally, the storied river descents, like so many iconic American journeys, have tended to be those which run west, down from the Continental Divide to the sea. And, of those, the torrent that drains the far slope of the southern Rockies, the Colorado, seemed to draw the love and the lore—it had deeper cataracts, bigger flows, gnarlier rapids, bolder boatmen, and fiercer fights over dams and acre-feet.

The Rio Grande had neither a John Wesley Powell nor a Lake Powell. It is typically considered, by those of us who don't depend on it, little more than a boundary separating Mexico from Texas, a squiggly moat on a map. It represents a gateway to opportunity or escape for the migrants and fugitives, in life and in song, who cross it in the hope of a fresh beginning—a kind of baptism by border. Known south of the border as Río Bravo del Norte, and to the indigenous Pueblo people as P'Osoge, its various sections were given an array of now mostly forgotten names by sixteenth-century explorers—Río Caudaloso, Río de la Concepción, Río de las Palmas, Río de Nuestra Señora, Río Guadalquivir, Río Turbio, River of May, Tiguex River. The Rio Grande drops out of the San Juan Mountains, in southern Colorado, bisects New Mexico, north to south, and then, splitting El Paso and Ciudad Juárez, tacks southeast. The majority of its length, from El Paso to the Gulf of Mexico, with the S turn of the Big Bend, forms the southern boundary of Texas, and of the United States. The river empties into the Gulf just past Brownsville, Texas. No part of the river is like any other. Typically, it is treated more as a managed scheme of discrete local parts—Taos Box, Elephant Butte Reservoir, Big Bend, Lower Canyons, Valle—than as an essential artery feeding a vast corner of our continent and a watershed connecting interdependent ecosystems, cultures, and nations.

Reicher, with Portman and Anella and another classmate, a photographer named Pete Lewitt, hiked down from the source, at Stony Pass, just east of Silverton, Colorado, and put in 25 miles later, below the first dam, in fiberglass kayaks, brittle precursors of today's polyethylene creek boats. Two weeks later, they encountered their first great challenge, in the tricky rapids near Taos. The surge of snowmelt was greatly reduced by dams upstream. (And by drought: 1977 was the worst year, in terms of snowpack, in the past half century. The second worst? 2018.) The river was, in kayak-speak, bony. By the time they reached the confluence with the Santa Fe, below Cochiti Dam, there wasn't much water left. Even 40 years ago, the flow south of Albuquerque was so depleted by farmers and by the city's sprawling population that the kayakers had to divert to the network of irrigation ditches that run alongside the river. At one point, a farmer in an El Camino pulled up next to them, unloaded two water skis, strung a rope from the trailer hitch, and towed Reicher along the canal. "First time I ever water-skied with dust in my face," Reicher said.

Farther downriver, in the muddy flats at the head of the Elephant Butte Reservoir, in southern New Mexico, the water would neither support their weight nor allow them to paddle, so they devised a method of pushing their boats with their hands and feet while lying on the stern. Crossing into Texas, where the river meets the Mexican frontier, the Ledyardians switched to bicycles and rode along paved roads until, a couple of hundred miles later, the Río Conchos, running out of the Mexican state of Chihuahua, replenished the ancient riverbed, so that they could saddle up their kayaks again. Because of upstream depletions, the Rio Grande is really two rivers: one that fizzles in southern New Mexico (the locals there refer to it as the Rio Sand) and one that begins in West Texas. In between is the puddled and trenched borderland east of El Paso and Juárez—the Forgotten Reach, which, prior to the big dams, had been regularly revived (and scoured) by seasonal floods from New Mexico. There had even been eels in Albuquerque— 1,500 miles upstream of the Gulf of Mexico.

The Dartmouth expedition, now five strong, made it through the deep canyons and riffles of the Big Bend and then entered the Lower Canyons, the river's most remote leg, which Congress, a year later, designated part of the National Wild and Scenic Rivers System. The desert eventually gave way to a subtropical luxuriance of palms, broccoli farms, and citrus orchards, the riverbanks and wetlands teeming with wildlife. The birds and animals didn't recognize the border. The people, though, were defined by it. The kayakers regularly encountered Mexicans crossing the river with burlap bundles. Near Eagle Pass, they came across a bloated male corpse, with a noose around the neck. ("We tried to report him, but neither side was terribly interested," Reicher recalls.) At night, burrowing into the invasive wild cane to make camp, they set off seismic sensors installed by the US Border Patrol.

After four months on the river, they reached the Gulf. They posed on the beach, five gringos, tan and lean, brandishing the Ledyard flag. Relations among some of them had frayed, amid a clash of egos—endemic to such expeditions. Reicher and Anella have hardly spoken since. But the trip remains a highlight of their lives. To Anella, it was a religious experience. "One-half of the hydrologic cycle—it reached something deep in my soul," he says. He likes to cite Ecclesiastes: "All streams flow into the sea, yet the sea is never full. To the place the streams come from, there they return again."

Reicher prefers Heraclitus: "No man steps in the same river twice, for it is not the same river and he is not the same man." Since 1977, he has been back to the Rio Grande six times; the river may have changed more than he has. Four years ago, a young newspaper reporter in San Antonio named Colin McDonald set out to duplicate the source-to-sea trip, using Reicher's journals as a blueprint. He dubbed it the Disappearing Rio Grande Expedition. He soon discovered that the river was in even worse condition than it had been 40 years earlier. Groundwater depletion, suburban sprawl, periodic droughts (attributable, probably, to climate change): every year, people were asking more of less water. He wound up having to walk a third of the river's length. Reicher, who had helped McDonald raise money and get attention for the trip, joined him for a couple of actual-water segments—in the Big Bend and then the last miles, where the river limps into the Gulf. When McDonald did a slide show in Albuquerque, Anella approached him afterward and said simply, "That was *my* trip."

After Donald Trump was elected, he pursued his campaign promise to build a wall along the nearly 2,000 miles of border between the United States and Mexico. The Rio Grande's "disappearance" took on fresh meaning. As imagined, such an undertaking would be devastating to life along an already threatened river.

Having been determined by the 1848 peace treaty that ended the Mexican-American War, the border traces the river's deepest channel—the thalweg—which, because the riverbed frequently shifts according to the water's whims, is in some respects notional. Of course, no one is proposing that a wall be built in the middle of the river, or for that matter on Mexican soil, even if Mexico is going to pay for it. So the wall would go on the American side, some distance from its banks—miles into US territory, at times. It would cut people off from their own property and wildlife from the main (and sometimes the only) water source in a vast upland desert. The Center for Biological Diversity has determined that 93 listed or proposed endangered species would be adversely affected. The wall could disrupt the flow of what meager water there is, upon which an ecosystem precariously depends. And it would essentially seal the United States off from the river and cede it to Mexico: lopping off our nose to spite their face. It would shrink the size of Texas.

There is also the matter of efficacy. The wall would probably delay a hypothetical crossing by a few minutes, depending on its design and the manner of the breach. There are videos of Mexicans deploying ladders, ramps, ropes, welding torches, and tunnels to get over, through, or under border fences. (There are about 700 miles of fence already, most of it in California and Arizona.) For a great deal of its length, the river is insulated on both sides by hundreds of miles of desert—inhospitable terrain that does more to discourage smugglers and migrants than a wall ever could. (The vast majority of hard drugs intercepted on the southern border is coming through so-called points of entry—the more than 40 official crossings—hidden in vehicles and cargo.) And, while the banks of the river, for much of it, are free of impediments, except for thick stands of invasive cane and salt cedar, which can make life miserable for the Border Patrol, about a hundred miles of it cut through deep canyons far more imposing and prohibitive to a traveler on foot than a slab of concrete or steel. The canyons don't require funding from Congress.

This winter, Reicher put together a trip on the Rio Grande, with American Rivers, an advocacy group, of which he's a board member, to celebrate the 50th anniversary of the Wild and Scenic Rivers Act, and to begin to articulate, in an informal but pertinent setting, a response to Trump's wall. (Last week, American Rivers, for the first time since 2003, included the Rio Grande in its annual list of the 10 most endangered rivers.) This wasn't so much an expedition as a floating Chautauqua, with a missionary bent. He and Bob Irvin, the president of American Rivers, invited me along. Among the guests were two grandees with dynastic connections to environmental conservation: Senator Tom Udall, Democrat of New Mexico, whose father, Stewart Udall, spearheaded the protection of vast tracts of American wilderness and was a crucial proponent of the Wild and Scenic Rivers Act; and Theodore Roosevelt IV, whose great-grandfather, the 26th president, used his bully pulpit, and hundreds of executive orders, to turn the federal government into a force for, and an enforcer of, land and wildlife conservation. Before American Rivers got involved, Reicher had invited Rob Portman, who has the kayak from the 1977 expedition mounted in his office on Capitol Hill, but his schedule was too tight, and he'd been back to the river a year earlier, with his family. "Last thing a Republican needs now is to be seen spending a week on a river with a bunch of tree huggers," Irvin told me with a chuckle.

I'd never given any thought to the Rio Grande, despite its being the fourth-longest river in the United States. My first river trip was a five-night commercial float, on rafts, on the Middle Fork of the Salmon, in Idaho's River of No Return Wilderness. It was 1985. I was a teenager, with my family and about 20 strangers—a group of gay men from Houston and New Orleans, and a biker hippie from Portola, California. The biker, who was a friend of one of the guides, went by Feets (he had got himself listed in the white pages as Amazing Feets) and spent his Middle Fork days aboard the supply boat, in jean cutoffs and a white tank top, rolling and smoking joints. I remember sitting on a sandbank one evening, after a consultation with Feets, watching the river flow—the molecules jostling past, toward the Main Salmon, the Snake, the Columbia, and the Pacific, and then up into the atmosphere and the jet stream and eventually, via cumulonimbus, back to the mountains upstream—and appreciating, really for the first time, the fact that this conveyor belt of snowmelt and runoff never stopped rolling, a quintessence of incessance unlike anything I could conceive of, except maybe time itself. Or an escalator. Then I wandered off in quest of some leftover Dutch-oven apple crisp.

Even in the clear-eyed light of day, the Middle Fork worked its magic. There was something addictive about the unfurling, around every bend, of new vistas. The fellowship, too: by the end of the trip, all of us, clients and guides, vowed to visit one another soon, making what I now know are routine pixie-dust promises that in this case were so unlikely to be kept that it took only a few days for the spell to wear off. (A river trip is a little like summer camp that way.) I passed through Portola a year later and found "Feets, Amazing" in the local phone book. No answer.

Soon afterward, I learned how to do an Eskimo roll, and spent a decade white-water kayaking wherever and whenever I could. Lehigh, Lochsa, Youghiogheny, Ocoee, Gallatin, Tohickon, Penobscot, Payette: the names of the rivers summon up boulder gardens, azure pools, high-speed surf waves, life-threatening keeper holes —and those mesmerizing cellophane stretches where the water, clear and unriffled, accelerates over a rocky bed, getting ever shallower, before dropping into the aerated tumult of a rapid. To

safely navigate big rapids, and to play in them with some assur-
ance, you have to acquaint yourself with a fundamental principle:
water seeks its own level. This is why it flows toward the sea, why it
churns back on itself when it drops steeply, and why, if you lean the
wrong way crossing an eddy line, it flips your boat—and why, if you
fail to roll up and have to swim, it fills your boat (and your sinuses)
as it dashes you against the rocks. Whatever level the water is seeking, you are better off with your head above it.

Work, city life, injuries, and children put an end to my boating.
But, like Ishmael, I intermittently get a strong urge to take to the
ship. Several years ago, I joined a private—unguided—raft trip on
the Colorado River, through the Grand Canyon, put together by
a few friends, some of whom had guided on the river in their 20s.
Most of us were strangers to one another, but the pixie dust was
strong. Two weeks in the canyon, with no connection to the outside world. The rim the edge of your universe, the river your only
way through it. Among the promises I made to myself, down on
the Colorado—promises that were inevitably broken—was that I
would spend a greater portion of my life, or what remained of it,
on swift, wild, and scenic American rivers.

So I signed on to Reicher's trip. At his urging, I started reading
Great River, Paul Horgan's *muy grande* Pulitzer-winning account of
the Rio Grande, which, like *2001: A Space Odyssey,* reaches about as
far back as a history can. It begins:

> Space.
> Abstract movement.
> The elements at large.
> Over warm seas the air is heavy with moisture.

The guy was speaking my language.

This is why, after a five-hour evening drive from El Paso through
the shimmering blood-meridian expanse of West Texas, then a
morning of sorting gear, meeting and greeting, and bouncing in
a shuttle van through the ocotillo-and-yucca high desert of Big
Bend National Park, I found my heart droop upon catching sight
of a sag of umber water, its banks choked with cane. Great river?
It looked more like a polluted tidal lagoon in Flushing, Queens.
The put-in was at the foot of a boat ramp of bulldozed mud. An

empty beer bottle, properly hurled, would have made it over to the Mexican side.

At the edge of this slough sat a flotilla of 12 canoes, 1 kayak, and a supply raft. The lead guide, John LeRoy, a ropy, leathery dude with a gray beard and ponytail, was busy rigging the boats. Eventually, he gathered everyone for an orientation speech—safety, paddling and rigging technique, chain of command. He brought up the urination routine ("Pee in the river, whenever possible. Dilution is the solution to pollution"), but said he'd address the poop question later. Something about LeRoy's edgy forbearance seemed to say *New York City,* and, sure enough, he was from Elmhurst—né Jean-Yves, the son of French immigrants. His father had been a waiter in the theater district. LeRoy had worked blue-collar jobs all over the country, including making tubular sleeves for die-casting foundries at a factory in Milwaukee. In 1996, he quit, moved to Terlingua, Texas, and, having never before worked on a river, set out to become a guide. He'd met his wife, also a river guide, on the Middle Fork of the Salmon. "This is blue-collar work, too, but it's awesome," he said. "Everywhere you go, there's water."

We were a few miles upriver of Boquillas Canyon, where the river cuts through the limestone fortress of the Dead Horse Mountains, by the Sierra del Carmen. That's the stretch we were heading for—four days, three nights, just 33 miles, in one of the most protected sections of the Rio Grande. The water flow was low, the workload light, the dangers few, the rapids negligible. This was a commercial guided float trip, cosseted and catered. Still, we'd be out of touch and off the grid. Four days without cellular coverage can lead to palpitations and debilitating night sweats. So can scorpions and rattlesnakes.

For centuries, Boquillas Canyon was considered impregnable, by boat anyway. There is no record of anyone ever having navigated it when this territory belonged to Spain. In the nineteenth century, numerous survey parties, daunted by the prospect of big rapids and no escape, didn't venture past the entrance. Three Confederate deserters claimed to have floated from El Paso to Brownsville, in 1861, in a pair of lashed-together dugout canoes but left no description of the Big Bend canyons, which would have represented a noteworthy test. In 1899, a boating expedition led by Robert Hill, an officer for the US Geological Survey, set out to explore the canyons. "Every bush and stone was closely scanned for men in ambush," he wrote afterward. The country apparently teemed with bandits, the most fearsome of them a Mexican named Alvarado, who was known as Old White Lip, because his mustache was half-white and half-black. The Mexicans on Hill's expedition were supposed to kill Alvarado if they encountered him, but, at some point, they floated right past him, without realizing who it was, as he watched from the bank with a baby in his arms. Maybe he'd shaved off the mustache. Hill and his men found the going in Boquillas less arduous than expected, and filled in a new section of the map.

One of our guides was named Alvarado—Austin Alvarado. No relation: his parents were from Guatemala. Alvarado had recently returned from a trip led by a 29-year-old filmmaker named Ben Masters; they'd paddled, and ridden horses and mountain bikes, along the Texas border, from El Paso to the Gulf, for a documentary Masters was making, called *The River and the Wall*. Masters, a wry, redheaded horseman with a telegenic Texas drawl, was on this trip, too, along with the film's producer and another cameraman. This time, strictly speaking, Alvarado was a guide and Masters a client. Another client was Colin McDonald, the one who'd done the source-to-sea trip in 2014, and who was now working on endangered-species policy for the Texas state comptroller's office, having capitulated to the looming extinction of his own species, *Reporterus localus.*

All told, there were 20 guests and 4 guides. Reicher, who had his daughter and his son along (one a recent graduate of Dartmouth, the other headed there next fall), made introductions. As people paired up, Udall, unaccompanied by staff or spouse, chose me as his stern man. He is 69 years old, of medium build, and had on a long-billed sun hat, sunglasses, thick sunblock, a long-sleeved fishing shirt tucked into khaki-colored quick-dry pants, and Teva sandals: no Amazing Feets, my bowman. He had a Jimmy Stewart aw-shucks air about him and a way of working my first name into every other sentence, but he wasn't above having a beer on the water or sharing cold-eyed appraisals of his colleagues on Capitol Hill. He is a liberal-voting Democrat with a lifetime score of 96 percent from the League of Conservation Voters, but has some sensitivity to the needs of constituents trying to make a living off the land in the arid West. He'd spent a lot of time outdoors through the years. He'd been an instructor for Outward Bound, in college, and every summer he spends a week or two backpacking in the wilderness of the Wind River Range, in Wyoming. (His cousin—and longtime traveling companion in the Winds—Randy Udall died there five years ago, on a solo hike.)

Udall began to tell the story, over his shoulder, of his family and its roots in the Church of Latter-day Saints. One great-grandfather, David King Udall, was a Mormon bishop and a polygamist, who went to prison for perjury. (He'd lied when Mitt Romney's great-grandfather was being investigated for polygamy; his bail was posted by Barry Goldwater's father.) A great-great-grandfather, John Lee, who had 19 wives, was one of the leaders of the Mountain Meadows Massacre, in 1857, in which a Mormon militia murdered a party of settlers in southwest Utah; Lee was the only one executed for the crime.

The family eventually made its way toward the political mainstream, as the West fell under the sway of Washington. Mo Udall, Tom's uncle, was a liberal congressman who ran for president, in 1976. Mo's son, Mark, spent six years in the Senate. Tom's father, Stewart Udall, was secretary of the interior under Presidents Kennedy and Johnson. "LBJ bullied my dad," Udall said. "He considered him a Kennedy guy." (Stewart had supported Kennedy over Johnson in 1960.) "But my dad had a great relationship with Lady Bird." As a Mormon with deep roots in the Southwest and a dam-happy constituency at home in Arizona, Stewart Udall was constitutionally and politically inclined to develop natural resources, rather than preserve them. "I was born with a shovel in my hand," he liked to say. But his adventures outdoors and his friendship with Rachel Carson and other environmentalists made him increasingly receptive to opposing arguments, and he wound up presiding over the federal government's most prolific spree of land and species protection, including the Wilderness Act, the Endangered Species Preservation Act, and the Wild and Scenic Rivers Act.

The senator and I were getting the hang of our boat. It was an Old Town canoe, almost 17 feet long and piled high with gear. We were approaching the old mining village of Boquillas del Carmen, on the Mexican side. Udall called out *"Hola!"* to some men squatting on the bank with a skiff that they employed to ferry people back and forth across the river, at $5 a head. The Boquillas Crossing, at a shallow and slack stretch of the river, has long been a port of entry. The Border Patrol shut it down in 2002, after the attacks of September 11. This devastated the village, which, on the Mexican side, is about four hours away from the nearest paved road. In the absence of tourism, some hundred remaining residents scraped by for a decade. In 2013, the US opened the crossing again, allowing Big Bend visitors to go over to Boquillas for the day or the night, and Mexicans to go to the other side to sell souvenirs—or to retrieve grazing cattle that might have strayed there.

A little farther downstream, a stretch of fast water steered the boats toward a cut bank and some strainers (as midstream downed limbs and trees are called), and LeRoy pulled up on a gravel bar —Mexico—to supervise, while a *vaquero* in reflector shades and a backward ball cap sat sentry on a burro. *"Buenas tardes,"* the senator said.

"Everyone has a river story," Udall told me. His had to do with a Grand Canyon trip he took with his father, when he was a teenager, in June 1967. As a congressman from Arizona, and then as interior secretary, Stewart Udall had for many years supported two controversial projects in the Grand Canyon: proposed dams in Marble and Bridge Canyons, which would have turned long sections of the Grand Canyon into reservoirs. Eventually, Congress killed the dams. Soon afterward, Udall and his family went on a raft trip in the Grand—what he called his "ride on the wild side."

Tom Udall told me, "My dad wanted, as he put it, to 'let the canyons speak for themselves.'" For the first time, in that wild place, Stewart Udall came to appreciate why his opponents in the dam debates had felt so strongly that the river ought to be left alone. You had to see it to want to save it. He published an article soon afterward taking himself to task for his support of the dams. That year, he also traveled to upstate New York and paddled a canoe with Robert Kennedy in the Hudson River Derby, to promote the pending Wild and Scenic Rivers legislation. It passed the following year. The act now covers more than 12,000 miles of rivers and streams, including two stretches of the Rio Grande—the Lower Canyons and Boquillas. Now his son wanted to hear what this canyon had to say to him.

And here we were. The walls closed in—steep, streaked limestone cliffs with a terra-cotta tinge, pocked high and low with dark openings big and small, made by waterfalls during an era, post-

Ice Age, when these precincts were lush. The water, clearer here, took on the colors of the cliffs, and of the salt cedars that crowded the shore. The air had a prehistoric hush, except for the dip of paddles in the current and the tuneful descending song of the canyon wren.

The first night's camp, called Puerto Rico, was Mile 8, river right, a broad floodplain of sand, stones, and grass. Puerto Rico was in Mexico. (After September 11, Americans were not supposed to pull ashore, much less spend the night, on the Mexican side, but in recent years the authorities have relaxed a bit.) We set up a bucket brigade to offload the accoutrements of our portable hotel: folding tables and chairs, four-burner range, Dutch oven, propane tanks, coolers, water jugs, dozens of duffel-size dry bags, tents, and camping mattresses known as paco pads. You can carry a lot more in a boat than in a backpack. The laws of flotation allow for comfort and encourage excess. As the guides worked, the guests scattered to claim sites to pitch their tents. Dry bags spilled out domestic consolations: clean clothes, toiletries, pillows, headlamps. You could hear some light argument among spouses and siblings amid the clickety-clack of tent poles. LeRoy shooed away some grazing cattle and used a rake to remove cow dung from the prime tent spots. Udall took over for a while. Roosevelt said, "Someone has to get a picture of the senator shoveling shit."

Roosevelt, a 75-year-old investment banker, who served in Vietnam with the Navy SEALs, was dressed like Udall, but with a Stetson hat and a red bandanna around his neck. He had a radio-friendly baritone and a solicitous air. A lifelong conservationist and Republican, by inheritance and practice, he is among those in his party who are dismayed by Trump yet are still striving, against diminishing odds, to find some workable common ground. He's the kind of environmentalist who can acknowledge and regret the occasionally invasive and inflexible nature of a federally enforced regimen. Nonetheless, the rollbacks and predations of this administration appall him.

In 1903, Roosevelt's great-grandfather, as president, established the National Wildlife Refuge system, with the designation of Pelican Island, in Florida—the first instance of the federal government putting aside land for wildlife. As it happens, one of the first sections of the border wall was scheduled to be built on a national wildlife refuge in the lower Rio Grande, the Santa Ana, one of the region's most crucial habitats for migratory birds. Last year, contractors for the Department of Homeland Security arrived there to drill test holes. Just upriver last summer, at the National Butterfly Center, a privately owned refuge, a staff member discovered a crew of workers, sent by US Customs and Border Protection, on the center's property, clearing brush and chopping down trees, in preparation for the wall, which would strand two-thirds of the center's land on the "Mexican" side of the wall. The butterfly center has sued the federal government. "We understand that not everyone in the country may be as interested in butterflies or in the environment as we are," the head of the center told the *Texas Observer*. "But everyone should care when the government thinks it can do whatever it wants on your private property."

This is one of the reasons that the Trump administration has been eyeing federal lands. Thanks to a 2005 Patriot Act provision —the REAL ID waiver—federal agencies were able, under the guise of national security, to ignore environmental and historic-preservation laws in building hundreds of miles of border fencing during the Bush administration. Earlier this year, a lawsuit challenging the waiver, filed by environmental groups and the State of California, came before a federal judge in San Diego, Gonzalo Curiel. Curiel, you'll recall, was the judge in the Trump University case whom Trump, during his campaign, had called "a hater of Donald Trump" who "happens to be, we believe, Mexican." This time, Curiel sided with Trump.

Yet, last month, Congress, in its $1.3 trillion omnibus spending bill, essentially blocked the building of a wall through the Santa Ana refuge—for now, anyway. The bill provided hundreds of millions of dollars to enhance existing fencing and to reinforce levees on both sides but mandated a three-mile gap. (For patrollers, this is the busiest section of Texas's southern border; they apprehended more than 137,000 people crossing there last year, 23 times more than they did in the bigger but far less populous sector of the Big Bend.) Other wildlife refuges along the river were not spared. The South Texas stretch of the Rio Grande was the most affected. Still, Congress provided nowhere near the funds Trump had requested, and so in recent weeks he has started talking about deploying the military to the border, or raiding the military's budget to fund a wall. On April 3, he announced that he was calling in the National

Guard, though, strictly speaking, he doesn't, as president, have the power to do so.

The kayak on the trip, which a few of us took turns paddling, was one of the vessels that had conveyed McDonald from source to sea, a few years before. It still bore traces of the messages that his wife had written all over it, in indelible ink, to keep him company. Lean, bearded, fervid, and quick-spoken, McDonald had brought along some books about the river for people to look through before dinner. He also had a photocopy of Reicher's 1977 journal, in a freezer bag. He seemed to know more about the current state of the Rio Grande than anyone. "The Colorado, always the Colorado—it's like the pretty girl," he said. "The Rio Grande isn't seen, treated, or valued as a river. My wife's from Brownsville, and I introduced *her* to the Rio Grande. People think, *The river is dirty, it's poverty, it's disease.*" He was involved in efforts to address various ills, but, in light of the obstacles (and in spite of his enthusiasm), he did not evince much hope. "We have nineteenth-century laws, twentieth-century infrastructure, and twenty-first-century problems," he liked to say. His focus, in the short term, was finding ways to get kids on the water, to introduce them to its glories, such as they are, and to begin to restore awareness of it, from the ground up.

He pointed to the shrubs that clung to the base of the steep cliff: candelilla, a source of wax used in the production of lip balm, candles, religious figurines, and chewing gum. A hundred years ago, there was a Great Wax Rush here, with factories on both sides of the river, but now it's a small-time affair. He described how people on the Mexican side rip the shrubs out of the soil, boil them with sulfuric acid in vats at a camp downstream, skim the wax off the surface, and then transport it by donkey out of the canyon, up to the mesa, and into Boquillas. On a good day, a *candelillero* can produce about $10 worth of it. "It's either that or running a ferry," McDonald said.

That night, after dinner (tilapia), flashes strobed above the canyon's southern walls. "Heat lightning," someone said, as someone usually does, and there arose a debate about whether there really is such a thing. The wind changed direction and began honking downriver. The camp seemed to be blowing apart. Then came hot pods of rain. I was determined to sleep under the stars, but after an hour of being blasted by sand, amid a light show of indeterminate origin and consequence, I gave in, and Ben Masters and I set up a tent in the dark. As we lay down, he barked, "Scorpion!" We began thrashing around, our headlamps berserking until my beam found a pale spider the size of a silver dollar, which he'd brushed from his leg. Masters got it with his water bottle, and, with the tent flaps slapping around in the wind, we settled down to a night of fitful sleep.

A river trip is a comedy of manners that commences each day with the sheepish, intermittent parade to the groover. The groover is the name of the makeshift portable latrine, which is typically set up at some remove from camp, out of sight and yet often with a stunning outlook, to make up for the flies and the lack of a stall door. It is called the groover because the body of the toilet is an old ammunition can stood on its side—on a wilderness river, you must pack everything out, including human waste, and an ammo can, being sealable and unbreakable, is ready-made—and, when one sits on it, one winds up with a groove on each cheek of one's rear end. Usually, nowadays, a toilet seat is placed atop the opening, to moderate the experience. Still, the old moniker pertains, as does the ritual of campers competing, without demonstrating that they are doing so, to be the first, or at least among the first, to visit the groover, each day after dawn.

Typically, there is a sign indicating that the groover is occupied —a paddle, or a bandanna on a bush. On the Rio Grande, this was a smaller ammo can, like a lunch box, which contained paper, hand cleanser, and (for the lucky camper on groover detail) latex gloves. The smaller box's visible presence, in a designated spot en route to the groover, indicated that the facility was free. The sight of someone carrying a lunch box to the shit box, and the experience of cheerfully passing a fellow boater on the way to and fro (perhaps with a tip of the hat and a "G'morning, ma'am"), become so commonplace that, by day three, any stigma surrounding the procedure is gone. The groover unites us all.

This was not a topic for discussion, however, during the morning coffee conversations initiated by Reicher. The barracks banter typical of other river trips was replaced by a mediated discussion about the Rio Grande and its discontents, chief among them the wall. In the shade of the canyon, as the sunlight gradually made its way down the cliffs on the American side—*There's* your wall! —Reicher asked Austin Alvarado to say a few words to the group, which was seated in a circle of folding chairs.

"The idea of a wall is so un-American to me," Alvarado said. "Is this America first, or America only?" Alvarado, 25, described how his mother, and later his father and brother—all of them Guatemalans—had crossed the river near Brownsville. Udall asked, "Austin, are you a Dreamer?"

"No, I was born here."

Someone joked, "You say 'here,' but we're in Mexico now."

"I was born in Austin, Texas, which is how I got my name," Alvarado said. "I have cousins who are Dreamers, though."

"You're called an anchor baby on the other side," Udall said wryly.

Alvarado and Masters had spent a couple of days with Representative Will Hurd, a Republican from Texas, who strongly opposes the wall—which he has called "a third-century solution to a twenty-first-century problem." He prefers a so-called smart wall, the deployment of camera and drone technology to trace movement on the border, especially in remote areas. You can see instances of this approach here and there in the Big Bend region; a giant unmanned blimp hovers high over the desert south of Marfa. (In the omnibus spending bill, Congress approved about $200 million that could be used for this kind of security.)

The group began to talk about a kind of antidote to the wall, an idea that Reicher had only just heard of the month before but which has been around since Franklin D. Roosevelt's administration discussed it, in the '30s: a binational park, linking the existing Big Bend park and some adjacent public lands, on the American side, with millions of acres of wild country, both public and private, already set aside just across the river. The Mexican government has designated more than 4 million acres as protected. Cemex, the Mexican building-materials behemoth, had bought up ranches along both sides of the river, in the interest of land preservation and the reintroduction of bighorn sheep. (When Trump was elected, Cemex was assumed to be a likely provider of cement for the wall, but the company has stated that it wouldn't be bidding on the job.) As it is, the Chihuahuan ecosystem straddles the border and exceeds the limits of any existing park. Why shouldn't

the parks and preserves be integrated somehow? One precedent
is Waterton-Glacier International Peace Park, along the mountainous border between Montana and Alberta. But no one had ever
thought of putting up a wall to keep out the Canadians.

The next day, we paddled 11 miles in the canyon. Several guests
flipped their canoes. It doesn't take much, once you get caught
broadside against a rock in swift water. Roosevelt, in a boat with
Masters, hit a submerged boulder, and into the drink they went,
along with Masters's fancy camera. Everyone had a laugh.

Camp was on the Mexican side again, just upriver of a two-
pronged tower of limestone known as Rabbit Ears. Again the rituals: the load-in, the scramble for good ground, dry shorts, groover.
Bob Irvin broke out a fly rod, in the hope of catching a longnose
gar, a prehistoric fish native to these waters. McDonald brought
out his books. There was swimming and beer-drinking in the sun,
some exploration of a slot canyon, and then later, after dinner
(Dutch-oven lasagna), in the dark, more Chautauqua—more
schemes and dreams. Another storm blew in, and at night's end
a group of us lingered under the kitchen tarp, telling river tales.
Killer holes, unfamiliar beasts, mysterious strangers. Reichel recalled finding, in a hot springs in the Lower Canyons, a new genus
of isopod crustacean, one that glowed in the dark, which is unusual for a freshwater bug. He took some pickled samples back to
Dartmouth and got a grant to do more research, but by the time
he returned to the hot springs a flood had washed out the pools
and the bugs were gone.

Masters and Alvarado told a story, from their Rio Grande adventure, about a mischievous friend of Masters's who secretly served
the two of them and a cat-loving friend an elaborate taco breakfast
made with bobcat meat. I was thinking of laying out my paco pad
under the tarp, but as the rain intensified, a phalanx of those big
pale spiders came up over the sand, eyes goggling in the beams of
our headlamps. They kept converging on Masters, as though to
avenge the one from the night before. We pitched a tent.

In the Grand Canyon, my friends had, after a week, got into a
mode of talking to one another almost exclusively in the diction
and cadence of a nineteenth-century explorer's journals: "Cabbage stores are mostly depleted and what is left is sodden and ran-
cid. The men grow restless." I found myself the next morning, over

pancakes and coffee, privately lapsing into it. *Morale high, weather improving, Masters unbowed.*

"Hey, I have an idea," someone said.

"I have one, too," Masters said.

"Sweet!"

"Double sweet."

It was a bluebird morning. A tailwind, a blessing in these parts, sped us out of the canyon and into an open desert basin—out of what was, on the American side, Big Bend National Park and into the Black Gap Wildlife Management Area. (It was amazing to consider that the Big Bend park is the southern terminus, geologically speaking, of both the Appalachians and the Rockies—that the ranges, or at least the rock that distinguishes them, almost touch here.) For hours, the river tunneled lazily through the cane and wound around until Mexico, confusingly, was to our north. We camped on that side again, along a run where Irvin spent another hour in midstream, backlit amid the riffles, as if in some fishing magazine, tossing a fly line toward the American side, to no avail—no gar. Udall passed around some Cohibas, then sat half-submerged and shirtless in an eddy, smoking one of them: a ride on the wild side. Someone put out Fritos and guacamole. A group hiked to the top of a nearby mesa just before sunset and took in hundreds of square miles of mountainous desert—a good chunk of a would-be peace park. You could also see a lot of this from the groover—of which the returning mesa hikers had an unobstructed view.

This was the first clear night, eagerly anticipated, since the area is a so-called dark-sky preserve, advantageous for gazing at the stars. The sky was soon full. After dinner (steak), a dozen or so of the group gathered by a fire and passed around a bottle of whisky while playing what they called a drinking game, initiated by Masters: "If you were President, which fifty-mile stretch of unprotected river, anywhere in the United States, would you designate as wild and scenic?" One by one, people spoke of their favorite threatened waterways—the Pecos, the Pigeon, the Crow—until, under the spell of the whisky and the stars and the rustle of the Rio Grande, it seemed possible that each pronouncement had the force of law. I slept outside and woke up with a headache. *Dover's powder depleted. The men complain of ague.*

There's something forlorn about the last run of a river trip,

when you know it ends in a shuttle van rather than at a camp.
A cold front washed in, bringing drizzle and a chilly headwind,
and, as the flotilla passed through some slack water and a rapid
that a guide called Eat Shit Rock, you could begin to see, along
the banks, evidence of harder use. Abandoned infrastructure: an
old mining tram, a pier improvised out of a rusting truck chassis.
The big lode around here had been fluorspar. Dow Chemical once
had an operation in La Linda, on the Mexican side, connected to
the American side by a steel-and-concrete bridge, high above the
river. This had been a busy crossing. But the mines shut down in
the early '90s, and then, soon afterward, the bridge did, too, after
a drug smuggler killed a Mexican customs agent. Now La Linda
was a ghost town, with a ghost bridge, in the middle of the longest
stretch of the river with no active border crossing.

This is where the trip came to an end, on a sandbar across from
the ruins of La Linda. The vans were waiting, with trailers for the
boats. Just before we got there, we passed beneath the defunct
bridge, its underbelly warted up with swallows' nests. On the road-
bed above, the array of median barriers and fences, including a
reinforced-mesh overhang in the shape of a backstop, brought to
mind the collection of wall prototypes that Trump had recently
gone to see in San Diego—the disembodied slabs that some had
likened to conceptual art. Would they work? Had these? We loaded
the canoes onto the trailers. From up on the bank, the river didn't
look like much.

ANNE HELEN PETERSEN

How Nashville Became One Big Bachelorette Party

FROM *Buzzfeed*

IT'S A MILD, early March Saturday in Nashville: the first real weekend of bachelorette season. By 10 a.m., they've already descended on The Gulch, a neighborhood that looks like it was constructed in *The Sims:* everything built at the same time, in the same slick, clean-lined style. Fifteen years ago, it was a rail yard—an actual gulch. Today, it's a collection of brunch spots (the most popular is Biscuit Love, included in every respectable bachelorette blog post), a Frye boots store, an Urban Outfitters, a Google office, a place called Two Old Hippies selling $200 dresses and tea towels printed with spunky messages, a blowout bar, a juice bar, and an actual bar.

The easiest way to identify a bachelorette party is by their matching T-shirts, emblazoned with Nashville-inflected slogans in twee calligraphy (WHEN I SIP YOU SIP WE SIP; BOOTS AND BOOZE AND THE BRIDE). The attendees—bridesmaids, friends, moms, sisters-in-law, anyone who's affiliated with the bride and willing to throw down for a weekend—wear identical tees in black or bright colors. The bride's, of course, is white.

Sometimes, they wear matching flannels, or jackets, or shoes (one group I encountered sported white high-top sneakers; another, pink windbreakers, like a millennial update of the Pink Ladies from *Grease*). I met one group from Manhattan who refused to wear matching shirts, opting instead for blue fanny packs emblazoned with BABE in fluorescent pink. "Our bride hates tacky shit," one of the attendees told me, right before they hopped on a foot-powered Pedal Tavern, where they'd spend the next two

hours pedaling around downtown and obeying the command-
ment to chug every time someone on the street took a picture.

Even without the matching clothing, you can spot a likely bachelorette party from 100 yards away: a group of (almost entirely)
white women, wearing nice jeans, cute tops, and fashionable boots,
their hair styled in the long, beachy waves that the Blowout Co.,
which services dozens of bachelorette parties every weekend, says
is currently their most requested look. They travel in packs, usually between 6 and 16. They always look mildly lost yet resolutely
determined. They tend to be spilling out of or piling into Lyfts or
Ubers. And they *love* murals.

More precisely: they love taking pictures in front of murals,
which, over the last decade, have come to dot every gentrifying
section of the city. What started as a covertly capitalist art form (an
I BELIEVE IN NASHVILLE mural designed by a merch company)
has become overtly so, as business owners all over town realize the
free advertising potential of Instagram location tags. During peak
bachelorette season, the photo line at the most popular Nashville
mural—artist Kelsey Montague's "angel wings," just a block away
from Biscuit Love—can take 90 minutes.

When a group reaches the mural, they snap solo shots before
asking the next person in line to take a group picture. On Saturday morning, a woman in a maroon shirt that reads BRIDE'S
LAST RIDE poses with one leg tucked behind her, her head cocked
to the side. Then she scuttles away to join the rest of the group.
"Tara, are you *so happy?*" one of them asks.

They huddle together to scrutinize the photos. Someone, not
Tara, finds them lacking. "Can I just squeeze back in and do it one
more time?" she asks. But two Ubers have already pulled up to
bring the group to their next destination. A pole dancing class, a
bicycle bar, a pedicure, a wine tasting tour—and, by the end of the
night, a trip to the honky-tonks on Broadway, where bachelorettes
have become conspicuous, ubiquitous, and unavoidable.

Depending on whom you ask, these groups are either a symbol
of all that's wrong with Nashville's recent, astronomical growth,
or exactly the sort of people necessary to sustain it: young, armed
with disposable income, en route to the upper middle class. They
are not the Nashville tourists of our parents' generation. Most
have little interest in visiting the Grand Ole Opry; if they listen to

country music at all, it's a mix of what's become known as "classic" (read: '90s) country and contemporary pop/hip-hop hybrids.

The majority of these bachelorette parties are from the Midwest, but they also come from New York, Seattle, California, and Boston. Most don't own cowboy boots and have never set foot in a honky-tonk. That's part of the allure: the ability to try on a culture while avoiding accusations of appropriation.

The current tourism uptick—which includes the bachelorette parties—can be dated to two different events. The first, which has become a sort of urban legend, was when the Chicago Bears came to play the Titans, and visiting fans drained the entire downtown supply of beer. The second was two articles—one in *GQ* in 2012, and another in the *New York Times* in 2013—that painted Nashville as the hip, artist-friendly home to Jack White and the Black Keys: the latest "it" city, as the *Times* put it.

The overarching argument of these articles was the same: Nashville is cool now. Which is to say, there are parts of Nashville that serve and appeal to and are filled with members of the so-called creative class and promise a different "experience" than your day-to-day life. The draw isn't major attractions, like the Opry, but attending a quaint show at the Bluebird Café. Like Austin or Portland, the draw to Nashville isn't to go and be a tourist, but to go and spend a weekend sort of pretending that you live there—and, who knows, maybe one day make it a reality, and bring your friends and business along with you.

"Weekend visits are key to the growth of the city," Steven Hale, who wrote a locally beloved piece about the bachelorettes for the *Nashville Scene*, told me. "If you come here at twenty-two, twenty-four, twenty-six, and you fall in love with the city, then you can move here and put down roots." That's why the economic development groups in Nashville *adore* "bach parties," as bachelor and bachelorette parties have become collectively known: these women are at precisely the point in their lives when a move to Nashville is possible.

Some Nashville residents fixate on the unignorable blow-up penises, which, as one Uber driver told me, showed up in the pool at a local hotel when she was trying to celebrate her grandson's birthday. Others are annoyed with drunk girls knocking on their doors when they can't find their Airbnb in a residential neighborhood.

254 ANNE HELEN PETERSEN

"It's mostly located in downtown Nashville, but it's spreading out to other 'hip' neighborhoods now, which is a weird feeling, because you can't escape it," one longtime resident told me. "Like, you can't go to brunch in most areas without running into a gaggle of women in matching outfits." Servers dread the large, demanding groups and their checks split 14 ways.

"They've gone from being all over downtown to all over anywhere worth getting drinks in this city on a Friday or Saturday night," said one woman who moved to Nashville five years ago. "It's like the bach industry ruins any 'hot new local spot' within a year."

But the larger issue with the bachelorettes is one few will articulate: What does this influx of young, moneyed women, and the web of industries that have popped up to cater to them, suggest about the town that Nashville is rapidly gentrifying into? And what might it signal about the future—and the impact—of intranational tourism throughout the US?

Tourists always went to the honky-tonks on Broadway. They always went to the Opry. But this new type of tourism, centered on Instagram-friendly experiences—and the mobility and capital it requires—means it's touching more areas of the city, and accelerating the already rapid transformation of a sleepy, artsy southern town into a cluster of "destinations." As that happens, attention to the past—and the things that made and continue to make Nashville feel unique and vibrant and desirable—is swallowed by the desire to document the present. None of these developments are novel to Nashville; at least a dozen people told me "Nashville feels like Austin, ten years ago." But that decade is telling: Austin's ghost has largely been bulldozed and built over with box condos. Nashville's is still just visible enough to haunt it.

"You've come to the right place," yells Todd, a thirtysomething with a buzz cut and sports sunglasses, from across the parking lot of Losers Bar and Grill. "We've had more girls come through here than Bed Bath and Beyond."

Every weekend, Todd "captains" one of four Party Barges—an F-150 pickup truck outfitted with boat seats, a few life jackets, and the general look, if not actual capability, of a boat—from Midtown, up and around honky-tonk-lined Broadway, and back to Losers.

Todd works for Ray Smitherman, a retired police officer who

started the Party Barge four years ago after watching Pedal Taverns —the first type of "transportainment" in the area—take off. Smitherman first came to Nashville from Alabama as a singer-songwriter, and he's found most of his drivers through the music community.

A group of women spill out of a pair of Ubers and pass cases of beer to Smitherman, who then places them in a cooler that'll come along for the ride (all transportainment vehicles in Nashville are currently BYOB). "On a scale of one to Randy Travis, how drunk are you now?" Todd asks the group. They're from Fort Worth, Texas ("We do *not* live in Dallas!") and slightly more classed-up than the group that came before, one of whom had made a point to show me her penis straw: "Isn't it girthy?"

Unlike some other providers, the Party Barge has a firm rule: no standing up. They don't go through residential neighborhoods. They discourage their riders from shouting obscenities. They play "clean" music. They keep the penises "down." The city hasn't figured out how to regulate these transportainment companies, so they try to regulate themselves.

The owners of the Pedal Tavern, which now operates a total of 10 group bikes out of their airy, exposed brick Midtown offices, told me the same. "We begged the city council to regulate us. Because if we're not regulated, then it means that others can come in here and give us a bad name," said Angie Gleason, who moved from Minneapolis to run the Pedal Tavern. "Others" meaning operators like the Nashville Party Wagon (a hay wagon, filled with up to two dozen passengers, towed behind a John Deere tractor), which has faced off with the city over its right to drive a farm vehicle on city streets.

"We want to protect our business," Gleason said. That means no musical chairs, and instructions to yell "Predator danger!" whenever someone on the street tries to hop aboard. On a weekend night on Broadway, the sheer number of drink-while-someone-else-drives mobiles make the street feel like a Disneyland ride. But most operate in respectful, inebriated harmony, united by the rest of Nashville's dislike for them.

Back at the Losers parking lot, one of the Party Barges sets off onto the street, Kenny Chesney blaring. "The girls come here, and they're not necessarily thinking of the effect on the community," Smitherman told me. "There's some stuff they'd just never do in their hometown."

Smitherman's not judgmental; none of the drivers seem to be. One, retired from the Air Force, told me he gets a lot of joy from just driving people around while they have fun. They recognize that the locals are annoyed, but argue that bachelorettes are just the most visible manifestations of what residents, the majority of them recent transplants themselves, are mad about.

The *idea* of Nashville as the cradle of country music might not be changing—in fact, the endurance of that idea is what brings so many tourists here. But the actual makeup of the city—the sort of people who can afford to live here, and what they have to do to be able to afford it—is.

Tourism has been a central tenet of the American economy since World War II: our parents and grandparents drove the expanding web of interstates to destinations like Disneyland, the Catskills, the Grand Canyon, and Niagara Falls. In this old model, there was an infrastructure specifically built for the tourist experience: hotels, tour guides, package deals, all cordoned off from where residents conducted their day-to-day lives. But the bachelorettes in Nashville represent a different *type* of tourist: ravenous for an "experience," especially if there are photos to prove it, and far more willing to spend money on a trip with friends than, say, a couch or a down payment.

That experience can involve something wild and out of the way (say, skydiving) but its most common iteration is deceptively destructive, and usually involves "living like the locals" (staying in neighborhoods, eating in neighborhood spots) without any of the constrictions (not wanting to disturb neighbors, not inconveniencing others, not taking up more space than necessary) that accompany actual residency.

Nashville—or whatever city they're visiting—becomes their playground. And in the case of the bachelorette parties, they get away with it (and have entire industries cater to them) in large part because they are white, and because they have money. Restaurants create rooms and reservation systems to accommodate them. The *New York Times* writes "36 Hours" itineraries for them. New businesses paint murals to attract them. New companies figure out new ways to get crazy while being contained in a kind of organized chaos.

At the same time, the people who make those experiences possible—the Uber drivers, the Airbnb cleaners, the dance teachers, the barbacks, the backup musicians—get pushed farther and farther away from the city, unable to "experience" it themselves in a context that doesn't involve serving others.

Nashville's history is one of settlement, of segregation, of forced relocation, of white flight, of rebranding and regeneration. You can see a palimpsest of that history in the area of Nashville recently rebranded as 12 South, which is less of a neighborhood and more of a long street lined with shops catering to young people with money. There's a vintage shop selling old taxidermied animals and overpriced, worn tees, a high-end denim retailer housed in an old car repair shop, a Sprinkles bakery with a cupcake ATM, and an old VW flatbed truck repurposed as a mobile "flower truck." The entire neighborhood is, as one bachelorette advice blog post put it, "really cute."

At its heart is the flagship store for Draper James, Reese Witherspoon's lifestyle brand named for her maternal grandparents, both of whom grew up in Tennessee. The Draper James building is whitewashed, with baby-blue-and-white awnings and eight-foot photos of Witherspoon hugging her look-alike daughter, Ava Phillippe, positioned like adorable sentries on either side of the entrance. When you walk in, employees—slender, in heels—inquire if you'd like some sweet tea, which is smartly served in petite plastic cups with lids and straws.

The store, like so much of 12 South, is at a price point that makes it aspirational for most of the bachelorettes who come to browse, shop, and grab photos with the various murals that dot the neighborhood. A package of pencils embossed with HELLO SUGAR and THANK YOU MA'AM runs $16; a conservatively cut ponte dress in "Bermuda blue" stripes, which, according to designer notes, is "instantly timeless, polished, but super easy," costs $125. But shopping on a girls trip is less about purchasing and more about browsing and imagining: *Is this the dining room table I'd buy when I have my own townhouse?*

Many of the women who buy clothes at Draper James embrace an old-fashioned understanding of southern femininity, the sort that finds nothing wrong with a T-shirt printed with the imperative KEEP IT PRETTY, PLEASE ($38). As one woman in her mid-20s from South Carolina told me, "My mom's crazy about that store. It's the sort of thing rich moms from the suburbs love."

Those rich moms from the suburbs are the sort of people who
are moving back into the area now called 12 South, which, until
20 years ago, was considered "the bad side of Belmont"—which is
to say, the black side of Belmont: for decades, it served as a community for black residents who stayed in Nashville as their white
counterparts began to decamp to the suburbs. Over the '70s and
'80s, the neighborhood was primarily known for its numbers
joints, drug deals, and prostitution. Sevier Park—now a sprawling,
verdant, family-filled neighborhood hub—was dubbed "Needle
Park."

In the late '90s, the first tendrils of gentrification began to
spread. The "12 South Master Plan," initiated in 1996, improved
streetlights and added bike lanes. Vanderbilt and Belmont University art students competed to design public art for the area; the
eventual plan involved a bunch of sculpted benches. An upscale
restaurant moved in, as did a bike shop, an anarchist bookstore,
and a thrift shop named Katy K Designs and Ranch Dressing. In
other words, Stuff White People Liked. The neighborhood's Victorians and bungalows were bought up, flipped, and/or transformed
—often by artists, musicians, and new families.

Two decades later, that first wave of gentrifiers has been gentri-
fied out of the neighborhood they helped transform. Katy K's shut
its doors in 2015 due to rent increases; the anarchists and their
bookstore are long gone. The median house price in the most
desirable swath of the neighborhood is $633,000. The houses that
don't look like they've been through a rinse cycle of HGTV stick
out; their residents eye the hordes of weekend visitors, parking on
their streets, with a sort of bewilderment.

And the wave of gentrification just keeps expanding. On the
northern border of 12 South, the black population of Edgehill,
long home to middle-class black professionals, has fallen from 67
percent to 50 percent over the last four years. It's a familiar cycle
for so many cities: The people who stuck with the city during the
'70s and '80s, often people of color and/or the working class, are
pushed out by incoming artists and creatives whose incomes neces-
sitate finding cheaper housing. Then the artists get pushed out by
the yuppies, who will pay skyrocketing prices to live in a neighborhood that's "cool" and "historical" and "safe."

When a Lyft driver picked me up in 12 South, driving up

through Edgehill into downtown, she shook her head at what she saw. "Every time I drive through here, I can't believe it," she told me, unprompted. "I grew up here, and I don't even recognize a thing." Like so many black Nashvillians, she's moved to the northern suburbs, making the 40-to-60-minute commute into the city where, especially on weekends, her primary customers are tourists. She doesn't mind the bachelorette parties, in part because she only drives them during the day, when "they haven't gotten wild yet."

Outside Draper James, a cluster of women has surrounded a temporarily installed sculpture of the Rolling Stones' "tongue and lips" logo, set up just feet away from the Draper James mural: a promotion for an exhibit opening soon at the Nashville Musicians Hall of Fame and Museum. One of the women, holding out her phone for a selfie, attempts to hoist herself onto the sculpture, only to slide, ungracefully, down the tongue. She laughs at herself but makes sure to keep the phone steady: it's prime Instagram Stories material. Across the alleyway, six women stand a foot apart from one another in front of a mural that says I BELIEVE IN NASHVILLE painted on the side of a dental "studio."

When asked why they chose Nashville as their bachelorette destination, most groups defer to a single member of the group (sometimes the bride, often not) who'd heard about, or seen pictures of, another group's trip. "Oh my God, this is a *great* location for a bachelorette party. My brother came down here for his bachelor party, and had so much fun," one bride-to-be from Bergen County, New Jersey, told me in the line for the angel wings mural. "And my own fiancé is coming down for his own party later this month."

They say Nashville feels safer than New Orleans, even though statistics indicate otherwise; it's less of a scene than Las Vegas. "I didn't want some club experience where we wore tiny dresses and stood in line," one attendee from Los Angeles told me. "This is so much more chill." As for what makes it chill, what makes it fun, what made them feel the necessity of a destination bachelorette, answers were vague. The possibility that what makes Nashville so appealing is the culture developed and maintained over decades by people now being priced out to make room for them to brunch and get drunk, and that that culture might be gradually, steadily eroded by their presence, didn't seem to occur—at least in terms they could articulate—to any of them.

Robbie Goldsmith is the founder of Bach Weekend, one of a half dozen companies that plans bachelor and bachelorette parties in the area. He saw just how many visitors there were—and their spending potential—during his years at the Nashville Entrepreneur Center, where he helped launch its music "accelerator." In person, Goldsmith, who grew up in the Chicago area, presents like a business major, casually mentioning that the sushi bar where we met, on the second floor of Acme Feed & Seed, "was where I closed my last big deal, so that's awesome." In his online avatar, he's wearing reflective Ray-Bans, sticking his tongue out, and pointing at the camera: a human bachelor party.

But Goldsmith didn't start Bach Weekend to live a debauched lifestyle on repeat. After moving to the area in 2010, he started fielding requests from friends and family for recommendations on what to do in the city, especially for "girls' weekends." He calculated what the average bachelorette party attendee was paying (around $850) and figured he could provide the same services, bundled, for less—and take out the stress of planning.

Over the last five years, Goldsmith's side job has morphed into a company with four employees, and two complementary businesses: Rocket Experiences, which plans pub crawls and scavenger hunts for visiting corporate groups, and Hustle Media, a social media marketing firm "built on badass customer service, innovative strategy, and winning the attention game."

"Sixty to seventy percent of our groups are funneling in from the Midwest, within a day's drive," Goldsmith told me. "We've got a ton from Chicago. Others coming from the Twin Cities, Michigan, Missouri. It's not such a thing with people from the South—everyone who grew up in the South knows country, knows Nashville, has been here at some point in their childhoods for something. It's just not as special for them."

Or as Elizabeth Allison, who helps run the Pontoon Saloon—which, unlike the Party Barge, actually operates on the river—told me, "My South Carolina friends and I would *never* come to Nashville on a bachelorette. It's way too cliché."

To reach potential clients, Goldsmith funnels a few hundred dollars into Facebook ads that surface for women, between the ages of 22 and 31, who've recently switched their status to "engaged." A post from their account will often accumulate hundreds of comments, the vast majority of them just women tagging their friends. "The hard part is conversion," he says. "We get thousands of people who go to our website and fill out our forms, but just hundreds who decide to do it."

Still, those hundreds are paying anywhere between $199 (a base package) to $479 (the Platinum VIP Package, which includes lodging) per person. Bach Weekend customizes the weekend according to the party's desires, planning pedal pub tours, line dancing classes, and open-bar nights at the honky-tonks. (Also included: hangover kits, bachelorette sashes, and room decoration.)

"When they buy, everyone's really tentative about being at the same open bar as other bachelorette groups," Goldsmith told me. "What they don't realize is that whether they go with us or not, they're going to be going to a bar with dozens of other bachelorette parties. Why not go with one with an open-bar package, where everyone's there to celebrate the same thing?" There's less risk, too, of annoying everyone around you: at the heart of the bachelorette ethos, after all, is the notion that every space, every restaurant, every service should accommodate you. During your visit, you bend the city to your needs.

"I understand the objections to the bachelorettes," Goldsmith said. "But I'm not the reason they're here. They're coming no matter what. We're just trying to make it a little less crazy."

Bach Weekend recently expanded to New Orleans and has tentative plans to set up in Austin. But Goldsmith's plans expand much wider: "For one trip, we'd take over an entire condo building, with ten units, ten different groups, and there's a bonfire on the beach at night with drinks—it'd be a real true experience they're never gonna forget." He's also thought about setting up groups who've aged out of bachelorette parties for trips in fully stocked RVs, "exploring the coolest places in America: Glacier, Yosemite, the Rockies."

Bach Weekend attracts repeat customers—Goldsmith told me one woman has now been on four different weekends with four different friend groups. Once they've done the Nashville scene, they need something *new*. "Two years ago, everyone wanted to do Pedal Tavern," Goldsmith said. "Now a lot of groups are like, 'Well, we did that when we came *last* summer.' So now we're thinking of putting them on country music tour buses, the super-nice kind the artists ride in—and we'll bring a songwriter on, have them play and hang out. We're talking super-high-end, highly customizable experiences."

It's about novelty, but it's also about the ability to capture and post that novelty. On *Sips and Sequins,* one of dozens of personal blogs offering detailed Nashville bachelorette itineraries, the author suggests the first thing to do is download the Glimpse app, which "allows you to record 1 to 3 second video clips the entire weekend and add that perfect song!" She also advises setting up a photo booth ("Everyone loves a good photo op!") and creating a custom Snapchat filter (which, if you open the app in the vicinity of The Gulch, you can see in abundance).

Photo ops have long provided the unspoken structure of tourism: Thorstein Veblen, one of the first scholars to theorize the performance of leisure, argued that travel is always, at least in part, about being *seen* traveling. But this feels like something different. "The girls will wait in line for an hour, just for these mural pictures," said Goldsmith. "Next year, we're gonna be prepared with the locations, videographers, the photographers, they're always on call. We're going to build in the experiences—and make sure they get those photos."

You might think that the labor of documenting all these experiences could threaten to overshadow the experience itself. But that's not how Goldsmith sees it.

"Earlier this year, we filmed all the girls pouring champagne into a girl's mouth, and it was just amazing," he continued. "What we really need to focus on now is creating that for every group. We're gonna create great images those girls are going to remember forever.

"And then they Instagram them," he said, nodding, "which, you know, is huge."

It used to be easy to avoid tourists in Nashville: just don't go downtown on a weekend. But over the last five years, locals have ceded other neighborhoods and spaces to the bachelorette parties. Pinewood Social functions as a casual workspace during the week, but transitions into a hipster country club during the weekends, with brunch, bowling, drinks, a pool, and a rooftop patio, which make it one of the "Best Spots in Nashville to Take a Picture."

At 7 p.m. on a Saturday, a woozy bachelorette group had set up shop in the corner of the bowling alley. They ate fancy mac 'n' cheese and tried to stay awake; their bowling game never made it past the fourth frame. It was the point in the night when the friends start to get protective of the bride, who was just a bit further gone than the rest, and very eager to talk about her queer fantasies involving Rashida Jones.

"Most of the people who go to a place like Pinewood Social are the type that would never belong to a country club, even if their parents did," historian Rachel Louise Martin told me. "But how else are you going to demonstrate you're the sort of person that *could* belong to one?" That's one function of a place like Pinewood Social: its image, once Instagrammed, is the new signification of a certain type of leisure and, by extension, a kind of class.

Martin grew up in and around Nashville, went east for graduate school, where she specialized in oral histories of segregation and took a professor job at a liberal arts school in New England. Then she left it all to come back home. These days, she sings soprano in the church she grew up in, waitresses to make ends meet, and writes about the things she knows best, like how "hot chicken" transformed from its origins in the Nashville black community to a must-eat white tourist food.

"When I was growing up, Nashville was considered *so* dorky," she told me. "It was everything you wanted to escape as a southerner." But it still drew people from all over. "Up until ten years ago, you could still live the Nashville dream," she said. "Move here when you're twenty-two, put in your time, and by the age of thirty-two, you'd be a studio musician. You could survive. You can't do that anymore. And that's going to change what the city is."

That change, of course, has already happened: the core of Nashville is increasingly white, increasingly rich, increasingly polished. "I look at the transplants, and I've been surprised by how airbrushed and packaged they seem," Martin said. "A few years ago, I was interviewing a white supremacist for a piece, and when he found out where I was from, he told me, 'Oh, I love Nashville, it's such a beautiful town.' And I said, 'Oh, yes, the river, and the parks, and the . . .' And he cut me off, and said, 'No, no, *I mean the women.*'"

The women aren't white supremacists. But they are very white. Same for the bachelorette parties and Draper James. "It's all a

packaged experience of how to be female: what you're supposed
to look like, what you're supposed to act like, how to perform sexuality and hotness," Martin told me. "It's a cartoon of southern
white sexuality."

Each vendor that partners with companies like Bach Weekend
receives slightly less than they normally would for services (drinking, transportation, line dancing). In return, they get a steady
stream of customers. Kristen Nicole Hall, the owner of Studio
Goddess, doesn't have to take that deal. She has more bachelorette customers than she can handle.

Hall wears her hair in a high topknot and has the centered,
soothing demeanor of a power yoga teacher. But she also has the
arms and back of a competitive swimmer—the direct result of years
learning how to hold her body above the ground on the pole.

Unlike the rest of the bachelorette providers I spoke with, Hall
was born and raised in Nashville. "I'm a unicorn," she said. "Most
people don't even know anyone who's from here." She attended
Middle Tennessee State University, majoring in chemistry and biology, but graduated smack into the economic downturn. She started
doing "pole," as practitioners put it, in a back studio frequented by
exotic dancers, plus a handful of others who pole danced for fun
and exercise. One of them, a district attorney, asked her, "What if
we had a space just for this?"

Recreational pole dancing had already spread to urban areas
across the country, but, as Hall told me, its sexualized connotation
was harder to shake in the South. "I just tell people, 'It's okay to
move your body in a way that feels honest.'" The studio's offerings
have expanded to aerial, acroyoga, and dance classes like "Shake
Your Abs," which run throughout the week. But it's the bachelorette parties—taking classes in pole dancing, "Southern Swagger,"
and burlesque—that keep the doors open.

Studio Goddess has hosted as many as 32 groups in a single
weekend, but the average during bachelorette season is between
20 and 25. One from Louisville, Kentucky, is currently in the studio, wearing purple shirts (NASH BASH JUST DRINK) and very ten-
tatively dancing in the general vicinity of the poles.

The teacher has a blond bob, a classic Wasp look, and very un-
Waspy dance moves. She's a graduate of the New England Circus
Arts School, and works as a performance artist during the week.
"Put your back to the pole," she tells the group. "Now raise your

arm above, grab the pole, then slide your hands down, and swing that hair forward." The song playing is by Beyoncé. The soundtrack is almost always Beyoncé. There's a lot of nervous giggling.

Most enter the room bashful and tentative, but exit in a very different state. "There's something about these classes," Hall said. "We're told that we have to be sexy *for men,* but in the room, you're not doing it for others. It's for us."

The bachelorette party streams out of the studio, glowing with a fine sheen of sweat, and picks up champagne glasses filled with mimosas. "People post pictures on social media complaining about the bachelorettes—their plastic cowboy hats, their Steve Madden cowboy boots," Hall said. "And I always comment on their posts: 'These bachelorettes are paying for my future kids to go to college.'" They help her teachers pay off student loans, help them cover child care, help them pursue artistic dreams during the rest of the week. As Hall tells her weekday students when they bemoan the lack of weekend offerings: "Listen: these girls make *your* classes possible."

Back on Broadway, the sun is setting, and the streets are beginning to clot with crowds. A different country cover band blasts through the open windows of each honky-tonk. Out of one, you can hear the guitar line of Kid Rock's "All Summer Long," which is actually the guitar line from "Sweet Home Alabama," lifted and repackaged. It's a fitting metaphor for what's become of the street in general, as stages that once served as spaces for original music have metamorphosed into Epcot versions of their former selves. This is the future of Broadway: less Robert's Western World, more Redneck Riviera (the new project from Big & Rich's John Rich) or FGL House, centered around the brand of Florida Georgia Line. These multilevel, choose-your-own-adventure bars, built on the *idea* of Nashville, are boxing out the places that composed that idea in the first place.

But this is the blissful part of the night—when you're drunk enough to lean into spectacle, forget whatever article you've read on the side effects of gentrification, and neglect your best intentions to only go to the "authentic" honky-tonks, rather than the ones that have the best call-and-response drinking games.

On the street, traffic has ceded almost entirely to party transportation. A Redneck Riviera open-air bus is filled with women dancing to "Single Ladies" and holding up cutout photos of the absent groom-to-be's face. Down the street, a group of Peoria nurses is stalled on a Party Wagon on the side of the street. When our photographer steps toward them to get a shot, they start to *woo!* as if on cue. "When the girls go downtown, and everyone takes pictures of them," the owner of the Party Barge told me, "they tell us it makes them feel like Britney."

Unlike the traditional bachelor party, whose stated allure is a final, debauched moment of release before settling into monogamy, the bachelorette party—at least in its contemporary iteration— offers a last chance to be a public center of attention in a socially acceptable way. Crucially, that unruly spectacle—the moment when you get to feel like Britney, or believe you can dance like Beyoncé—is a plane ride, a long drive, and a world away from your "normal" life. Some of what happens in Nashville stays on Instagram, but most of what happens gets mothballed in the memory of your friends as that weekend when shit got crazy.

When the freeways of the mid-twentieth century first began to take shape, they were celebrated as great connectors: a way to introduce Americans to so much more of what our vast and diverse country had to offer. Freeways, like cars, and railroads before them, helped democratize travel, but also personalized it. Cheap gas made the entire nation your potential destination. Cheap airfare has only accelerated the process: for $300, you can fly nearly anywhere in the US, then leave it behind after three days and a handful of Instagrams, a public notch on your conspicuous leisure belt.

Like so many others of my age and professional class, I've taken these weekend trips. I've posted these Instagrams. I've been on similar bachelorette parties. I've had fun and I've documented myself doing it, providing proof of something for both myself and others. I don't think women claiming time for themselves is wrong; I don't necessarily think women taking up public space is, either. But watching the bachelorettes of Nashville against the backdrop of citywide gentrification reminded me of how mindlessly I did all of it. Friction, resistance of any kind—whiteness, youth, and money removed it all. Which again begs the question: Who can have a city bend to their will, and whose will is bent or blatantly ignored in the service of others?

That night, waiting to cross Broadway, I find myself sandwiched next to an older couple, dressed up for a dinner on the town. At the stoplight, a Pedal Tavern has just coasted through a red light, holding up traffic in all directions.

"I guess they just have the right-a-way, don't they," the husband says. "They just go whatever speed they want, yell whatever they want, do whatever they want."

The wife stares at the women in the Pedal Tavern, who are seated facing inward, so that they look only at one another. "I guess they do," she responds. "I guess they do."

These Brazilians Traveled 18 Hours on a Riverboat to Vote. I Went with Them.

FROM *Pacific Standard*

EVERYONE ABOARD the *Michael* was there for one reason: they were going to vote in the Brazilian presidential election. It was early morning, and the passengers streamed up the wobbly gangplank and onto the boat docked at the chaotic port in Santarem, smack in the middle of the Amazon. They carried with them big duffel bags and babies, and families jostled through the crowd to reach the most desirable spots and hang up their hammocks. Enterprising vendors boarded as well, shouting offers of three-for-one pastries and ice-cold water, adding their enthusiastic weight to the sway of the rocking boat. The *Michael* is one of the oldest boats to dock at Santarem; its sky-blue paint had chipped away many trips ago, and the wooden floor of its top deck was riddled with splintery cracks and rusty exposed nails. The bathroom—it was likely what you're imagining.

But none of the other passengers overloading the boat seemed fazed by the conditions, and, unlike me, none of them seemed daunted when we set out onto the wide river finally. It was close to 100 degrees, and we were facing nine hours on a rickety boat full of crying children, far from cell signal or signs of industrialized civilization. I couldn't believe that people were taking this hot, long, uncomfortable voyage just to vote in the election. The captain turned up the volume on his cheesy Brazilian soundtrack, adding a background thump to the human racket. It was going to be a long nine hours.

If you've followed any recent news from Brazil, you've heard about the all-important election coming up this weekend. The

stakes are high: if the polls are right, Jair Bolsonaro, a far-right, ho-
mophobic demagogue, will become leader of the world's fourth-
largest democracy. As Bolsonaro's polling figures have risen, his
campaigning style has become cocksure, and he expounds an
alarming vision, one in which the government does away with
the "coddling" of blacks and gays and women and "banishes" left-
ists from Brazil. The only man who can stop Bolsonaro is former
São Paulo mayor Fernando Haddad, a political stand-in for ex-
president and leftist rabble-rouser Luiz Inácio "Lula" da Silva, who
has been jailed for corruption.

But Haddad's party, the Workers' Party, has failed to confound
the mythos that Bolsonaro has created for himself as an anticorruption warrior. The result is a battle between two starkly different
visions for Brazil's future.

What hasn't made the news, though, is a portrait of a different
Brazil from the one seen at the protests in Rio de Janeiro or the
political rallies in São Paulo. It's a Brazil that even most Brazilians
don't know, one that takes hours to reach by boat. In the village
of São Pedro, deep in the Amazon, along the banks of the Arapiuns River, life could hardly be more removed from life in the
cities. It's a place where there's no Wi-Fi and no real economy, a
place where the dominant sound, besides the river, is the loud roar
of the generator in the town square. But these citizens' votes will
count just as much as the votes in the big cities—and here, some
communities' long-term survival could be directly threatened by a
Bolsonaro victory.

So that's where I headed, for the first round of the election, on
a trip that would reveal the contours of the place, and the country,
in ways I could not have foreseen.

São Pedro is one of thousands of riverside villages throughout
the Amazon region whose residents—called *ribeirinhos,* or, roughly,
"riverside folk"—are only vaguely connected to the rest of Brazil.
Saude e Alegria, a nonprofit organization that monitors riverside
communities in the Amazon, estimates that, in the four municipalities the group studies in the western part of the state of Pará,
70,000 people live in 250 *ribeirinho* communities. The curving Arapiuns River, on which São Pedro lies, hosts 68 communities along
its banks; São Pedro, home to about 200 families, is one of the
largest. Most of the other communities along the river are smaller,
populated by not more than a few hundred people. The lives of

these *ribeirinhos,* their struggles and hopes, represent some of the most overlooked stories in all of Brazil.

Part of why *ribeirinhos* are so easily overlooked by both government and media is because they don't fit into simple categories. Their narratives are complex, and even determining the ethnic identity of *ribeirinhos* is a challenge. Some *ribeirinhos* identify as indigenous, some don't. Some speak Portuguese, some don't. The only commonality is that all of them are, by almost any standard, very poor.

The forefathers of many of the Brazilians living in the *ribeirinho* communities in this part of the Amazon moved here during the rubber boom, in the late 1800s and early 1900s, when latex drove the northern Brazilian economy and Henry Ford made his millions, establishing his Fordlandia outpost in the jungle to better access the rubber trees. The laborers during the boom made improvised homes along the banks of the rivers that braid into the Amazon. Once the industry went bust, many of the rubber workers moved to coastal cities; the *ribeirinhos* were the ones who stayed. Some of the communities they formed are nestled deep within the river forests and can only be reached by motorized canoes. Political campaigning here is done by boat, or water bike.

São Pedro, in fact, is one of the few *ribeirinho* communities directly accessible by the iconic double-decker boats that look like colorful toys and function like Amazonian buses: they make stops at all the riverside communities along a route, picking up and dropping off passengers, and bringing supplies and messages (the communities are often far out of any cell-phone-signal range, so messages are sent by word of mouth). On the boats, many of the passengers already know each other; they're neighbors or family, or they've met on the boat route before.

These passenger boats, some of which journey for multiple days to reach *ribeirinho* communities isolated in the forest, become temporary residences for the passengers through all those hours of swaying, as the boat slowly makes its way upriver. They sleep beside one another in hammocks, swinging into each other when the waters get rough. On the boat's one table near the bathroom, they play dominoes when even the hammocks get too sweaty in the afternoon heat. They cook lunch and dinners together, communal meals of rice and beans that are evenly portioned out so that everyone eats at once. At the different riverside stops, the men help unload supplies, while the women care for each other's babies. These boats are at once public and intimate. They lack the amenities of modern life, but they also feel like a sanctuary from workaday routines; the most popular activity on board is simply staring out at the forest as it passes by, hour by slow hour. Being on one of these boats is like being in a place that seems to float outside of Brazil, away from the difficulties that you find once the boat lands in the sands of the *ribeirinho* villages.

I wanted to see what the election was like for people who live in this overlooked Brazil. So I boarded the *Michael,* hooked up my dark green hammock, and joined the crowded ride upriver, into the belly of the Amazon.

In the United States, it sometimes makes the news if people have to stand for more than an hour to vote. But it didn't seem so inconvenient or strange to the people on the *Michael* that they were having to commute nine hours in order to vote. In a way, they're used to it. Because the *ribeirinho* communities have no real economies to speak of, many *ribeirinhos* today live a life in transition: Many say they moved to the city to work or study, but their voting residence is still back home in the *ribeirinho* community. Others still live in the *ribeirinho* village and take the *Michael* nine hours twice a week just to go to university or work for a day. Time ticks by slowly on the boat, but the passengers seem altogether unruffled by the commute.

And voting in Brazil is mandatory. If you don't vote, and haven't obtained prior permission to skip the election, you face a cascade of problems: you get flagged across government systems, and paying taxes or even buying a microwave becomes complicated. But voting also doesn't seem like such an inconvenience when everyone is doing it. Election day is always Sunday, and so if you're not standing in line to vote on that day, you're out of the loop. As in the US, Brazilians are registered in their local municipalities, and so they must return to those locations on election day—even if it takes them 18 hours round-trip to do so.

By the time we embarked out of Santarem, the *Michael* was packed. A baby had been slung inside a hammock above me, a man was sleeping in a hammock below me, and the floor of the boat had no room to step between the coolers and duffel bags con-

taining the city hauls of the passengers. I was on the upper level of
the double-decker, where a hard breeze off the river kept us cool.
But the floor below was dark and hot, and full of people.

In this year's Brazilian election, protections for the Amazon rain
forest are on the chopping block. Bolsonaro, the man almost certain to win, is floating proposals that terrify environmental advo-
cates and supporters of indigenous land rights in Brazil. Bolsonaro
has vowed to do away with the legislation that creates indigenous
territories, the essential land rights tool for indigenous communities in the Amazon and a proxy for preventing deforestation. He's
also *promised* to open indigenous lands to mining.

São Pedro has always been a hot spot for the conflict over indigenous land rights. Years ago, the people here rallied together and
set fire to the barges that were running illegally cut logs out of the
forest. If Bolsonaro wins, São Pedro could see a real uptick in the
pressure on its surrounding forests.

Today, São Pedro is one of many poor villages along the river,
communities so poor that they've been called "Amazonian fave-
las." In the village, bread is a luxury. "There used to be a bakery,"
Margareth told me with a shrug. Margareth and her husband,
Livaldo Sarmento, would be my hosts in São Pedro, and as we rode
the *Michael* together, they told me about how things used to be in
the town. Livaldo had been one of the community leaders who
fought back against the loggers decades ago. Now, he was headed
home to vote.

As we arrived in São Pedro—a spit of sand jutting out into the
Arapiuns River in a way that forces the boats to curve at almost a
right angle to keep along the river—I realized I'd been sleeping
quite a lot. The warmth of the boat, the cradle of the hammock,
and the steady sway of the water had knocked me out for much
of the voyage to São Pedro. But now, upon arrival, I was still tired.
Margareth showed me to a dark room in her home, without a door
or much more than hammock hooks, to which she tied my green
hammock. I slept 12 hours that night, even though a block away
there was a barbecue party hosted by the local politician, in an
effort to drum up last-minute support, blaring country music all
night long.

By the morning, I felt feverish, and Margareth moved my hammock outside into the yard so I could get fresh air. Livaldo sat on

a piece of wood next to me and watched me. I realized he was frightened for my health.

Before I had left Santarem and embarked toward São Pedro, I'd asked my local contact about what I should do if I got sick or hurt while in São Pedro. "There's a *posto de saude* there" (a health clinic), he'd told me. "And in case of emergency, you can take an *ambulancha*"—the local nickname for a boat ambulance—"and it can get you back to the city in two and a half hours."

I remembered that conversation when I saw Livaldo's worried face. I asked him where the health clinic was; I thought I should probably be seen by a doctor. "The health clinic?" he asked, visibly surprised. Margareth chimed in. "There's no doctor here. There's only a nurse. But she's in the city. And she's only here one day a week. On Wednesdays." It was Friday.

Margareth told me I wouldn't want to go to the clinic, even if the nurse was in town. A while ago, she said, the government claimed that it had been sending resources out to the health clinic. "But we never saw them. We never got any medicines or vaccinations," she said, visibly disgusted, and went on to explain that, in response, the community had gathered together and broken into the clinic's back room.

"We found hundreds of medications piled up there, all expired," she said. "They'd been expired for years!" I felt a warm wave come over my face and sensed incoming panic. I took a deep breath.

"Okay, well what about the *ambulancha*?" I asked. "Could I take that?"

Margareth laughed in response. "That hasn't worked for three years." I closed my eyes, took a few more deep breaths, and fell back asleep.

That's right around when the dog started talking to me.

"Hot, right?" he asked. I agreed that it was, indeed, quite hot. He'd been dying beneath me for a while, seemingly forever. His hind hipbones were raw and red and exposed to the flies. I fell asleep while he was midsentence and felt a bit bad about it, but I was just too tired.

I woke up as Margareth offered me a plate of bruised yellow cashew fruit. "You need to eat," she said, and handed me the plate before leaving again. I tried to eat the cashew fruit, but couldn't, so I tossed the rest of the fruit to the dog, who ate it up in a second. The dog then sat back, as if to smoke a pipe, and adjusted his spectacles. "Those frame your face really well," I told him. "Thank you," he said with a smile. A short while later, a helicopter made a slow landing in my hammock. I moved my legs a bit to the side, so they wouldn't be cut by the propellers.

When I woke up, I was soaking wet. Margareth touched me and said I felt like ice and insisted that I eat the fish broth she had cooked by boiling the local *charutinho* fish in water with a few bits of tomato, onion, and cilantro. I told her I didn't think I could eat fish—the thought of it made me faint—so she offered me something else, in a white plastic bag. It was heavy and pokey. When I opened the bag, the nails on a foot scratched my hand. A beige shell covered in shiny hexagons had black grill marks on it, and there was no head; it appeared to be just the hindquarters of something, about the size of a volleyball. I pulled off some of the white meat inside the shell. It came off like Thanksgiving turkey breast, and tasted like it, too. It was endangered armadillo.

"I think you should leave on the next boat," Livaldo declared. He told me later with a kind of morbid humor that he had been worried about having a dead *gringa* on his hands. Coincidentally, the next boat to leave was the *Michael,* and it was scheduled to depart São Pedro halfway through election day, making stops along the Arapiuns on its route back to Santarem, picking up voters who wanted to get back to the city in time for work the next morning. Livaldo helped me string up my hammock on the upper deck of the *Michael,* and then sent me off with a three-gallon bottle of water, some biscuits, and a nervous wave from the shore.

When I would finally make it back to the mainland and to the public hospital many, many hours later, a new sort of delusional nightmare began. Several people in the waiting room of the Municipal Hospital of Santarem were missing limbs. Skinny elderly people were draped across chairs, sleeping or dying. A man with a gash down his back and burn marks—the results of a motorcycle accident, I guessed—bumped against me as he walked into the nurse's office. I went to the bathroom to wash his blood off my arm, but the door was locked. A woman waiting outside of it spit on the ground in front of me. It was a hot room full of human need.

By the time I made it to the doctor, hours later, she told me my diagnosis was one of four options: malaria, dengue, chikungunya, or Zika. I was sent to the lab to get my blood drawn, and as the needle went into my arm, I was suddenly nauseous. The exasperated nurse handed me a trash can half-full with someone else's orange vomit. Hours later, my malaria test came back negative. The result was communicated via a handwritten note, with my name very misspelled, and the birth date of a 21-year-old in place of my own.

The people of São Pedro travel nine hours by boat for these health services—just as they do to vote.

When I set out on this assignment, I didn't anticipate getting so sick, but the experience sent me into the depths of what life is really like for the riverside people in the Amazon; I saw their lives in a way I never would have had I remained healthy. At various points during my illness, I would awake in a sweat with a wave of anxiety and dark thoughts rolling over me: *Am I going to die here?* I wondered many times as I lay in my hammock in São Pedro, too weak to be able to seek out help. Death lurked in the corners of my mind like a shadow on a hot afternoon, and with it came a kind of primal fear, one that is regular in these communities, where help is so many hours away. During my time there, the community was abuzz with worry about a 14-year-old girl who had given birth a week earlier and now seemed in poor health, having lost all feeling in one leg.

Even before the *Michael* pushed off from the sands of São Pedro, and before I made it all the way to the hospital, I summoned the strength to roam my way around the wooden deck of the *Michael* to ask my fellow passengers which presidential candidate they'd voted for that morning. Most had voted for the leftist Fernando Haddad, but there were some exceptions.

Messias Gama dos Santos is a 20-year-old from São Joao, a community of 25 families up the Arapiuns River. He told me he had cast his presidential ballot for the former governor of São Paulo, Geraldo Alckmin, the man who—with his fancy suit and career of catering to the pro-business wealthy—seemed like the least likely candidate to get dos Santos's vote. But dos Santos said that he saw Alckmin as "capable": "He did good things in São Paulo, and so he could be the one to get Brazil out of this situation." Not enough Brazilians agreed with him: Alckmin ended up being knocked out in the first round of voting.

Dos Santos was also in the minority on the vote boat: he was the only voter I encountered on the *Michael* in either direction who admitted to voting for anyone other than Haddad. In fact, in the first round of voting, in Pará state, Haddad ended up with 41 percent of the vote, beating Bolsonaro's 36 percent; in most of Brazil, though, Haddad had fewer votes than Bolsonaro.

The reason has a lot to do with economics. Most of the people on the boat voluntarily offered to me that they identified as "poor" or "very poor," and said they saw Haddad as the best defender of poor people like them.

That's the case for Maria Aparecida de Aquino, a schoolteacher who takes the boat twice a month so she can restock supplies for her students. "I think Haddad is a supporter of the poorest people," Aquino said, adding that she was voting for Haddad also because she was frightened by the way Bolsonaro seemed to endorse violence in his campaign, with calls for increased gun ownership and overtures to military rule.

The boat's captain, 31-year-old Robson Souza, lives in a riverside settlement of the Landless Workers' Movement, a land-rights movement that thrived in the 1980s in Brazil and that still drives the politics of many rural voters across the country. The settlement where Souza lives, called Bom Futuro, or "Good Future," was one of about 10 stops the *Michael* made on the way back to Santarem from São Pedro. We waited on the boat as Souza ran up the banks of the river to vote and then, 15 minutes later, ran back. He'd cast his ballot for Haddad.

"I think Bolsonaro will end the welfare program, and I think he won't let us live in the settlement anymore," Souza said. Even though Souza said he was not on welfare, thanks to the boat job, he said he had family members who were. He added: "I think he would end up being the worst president in the history of Brazil."

And then there was Zica Lopes Ferreira, who goes by Diva. The 59-year-old resident of São Pedro twisted her mouth and anxiously breathed in through her nose when I asked her who she had voted for. "Look," she said. "I'm going to be sincere with you." She fiddled with a stray domino on the boat's table. "I didn't know which numbers to press," she said, "so I just guessed."

Years ago, Brazil moved to a system of assigning numbers to each candidate, as a way of allowing people who were illiterate and unable to read the names to still be able to vote. But Diva's level of electoral literacy is so elementary, that even the numbers assigned to the candidates got scrambled for her. After taking the boat nine hours to the voting station, she ended up pushing random numbers just to get out of the voting booth.

Diva looked at me sheepishly as she told me this, but her answer broke my heart. Here was this woman, way out in the middle of the Arapiuns River, on this creaky old boat *Michael*, on her way to places that most people would describe as "nowhere," and she was still trying to somehow play a part in this national election with global consequences.

"I would have voted for Haddad," Diva continued, looking across at the riverbank drifting by. "I think he would offer a lot to the riverside people. The *ribeirinhos* could use the help."

NOAH SNEIDER

Cursed Fields

FROM *Harper's Magazine*

THE YAMAL PENINSULA juts up from the northern edge of Russia like a thumb sticking out into the Kara Sea. A matrix of lakes and streams stretches across the barren surface, beneath which lie layers of permafrost that can reach deeper into the ground than Moscow's tallest buildings rise into the sky. When the temperatures drop in the winter, the waterways freeze over and the sun recedes, leaving the region shrouded in darkness for 20 hours a day. During the summer, the ice splinters, and the tundra turns into a boggy, mosquito-infested maze.

In the language of the native Nenets people, *yamal* means "the edge of the world." In medieval times, outsiders took to calling the surrounding lands "midnight country." Early travelers wrote of mountains, as high as the heavens, that sloped down to the sea and emitted unintelligible cries. Others told of a savage local tribe who served their children to guests for dinner. Explorers from the Novgorod Republic, who arrived in the eleventh century to trade iron for furs, took back with them tales of a place where little reindeer fell from the clouds and scattered across the earth.

Neither Yamal's remoteness nor winters during which temperatures can reach −55°F drove the Nenets south to warmer ground. Instead, they developed a lifestyle dependent on the reindeer, which were as plentiful as the stories suggested, and well suited to the harsh northern environs. Native legend has it that the gods created reindeer just after they created man; the spirit responsible for the animals is known as Ilebyam pertya, which translates literally to "giving life." The reindeer serve as a mode of transport, as well as a source of sustenance, warmth, and meaning. Soviet anthropologists came to study Yamal's tribes in the early 1920s and remarked on this relationship. As one observer wrote, everyone he met there

> dreams of owning his own herd and never stops collecting reindeer, he does not treat his herd as capital, as a means of obtaining profit and exploiting others (he has no notion of rational economy) . . . The nomad's reindeer herd is his guarantee against hunger and the elements.

To this day, Nenets herders will follow their reindeer hundreds of miles each year, up and down the peninsula in search of new pastures. They come to know their animals so well that they can identify individuals in a herd of thousands. These grueling journeys along the reindeer trail have taught the Nenets to be wary of long-term plans, to recognize the fragility of their existence. Ethnographers note that they often add the phrase *ta eltsyand tevba na* (if we live till then) when discussing the future.

As the Nenets made their yearly migration north in July 2016, Andrei Listishenko, the head of Yamal's veterinary service for the past 15 years, began receiving puzzling messages. "It all begins with the fact that it was a very hot summer," he told me when I visited him in Salekhard, the regional capital. Herders reported that their reindeer had become groggy and sluggish; they were falling behind and had stopped reacting to commands. "They come and immediately lie down," one herder told local media. "They're sleepy." Another, Alexander Serotteto, recalled walking nine hours to reach a camp with a working satellite phone, hoping to alert the authorities that the reindeer were dying.

Initially, local officials paid the news little mind. "They're extreme animals, they can live in almost any conditions, but extreme heat is much tougher on them than extreme cold," Listishenko told me. His wide, flat nose, full cheeks, and rounded forehead lend his face the gentle aura of an otter. He grew up in a farming town in central Russia, surrounded by cows, pigs, and chickens, and enjoyed physics, chemistry, and biology, as well as the popular Soviet-era magazine *Science and Life*. His hands are so calloused that they have become soft. "We thought it was heatstroke," he recalled.

As reports from the tundra grew more urgent, Listishenko took off for Yar-Sale, a small town some 120 miles northeast of Sale-khard. He made his way to the surrounding camps and saw a scene that shocked him: reindeer clustered on the ground, shaking and panting. Patches of their fur seemed to have fallen off, leaving them splotchy; the animals were emaciated, their ribs visible. "The reindeer grows feeble and exhales sharply," Listishenko said. "The pain is visible, he drops his head because it hurts, his temperature starts rising rapidly, he's breathing heavily, he sticks his tongue out, and, in a fit of convulsions, he dies."

Listishenko began to suspect that he was not facing a case of simple heatstroke. "We didn't know the scale of it," he said. "Every day it kept growing." Dozens of dead reindeer became hundreds, then a thousand. The infrastructure of the region—or the lack thereof—complicated the process. "You have to understand, we're not in Europe, where there are roads everywhere, or in Moscow, where you can get anywhere within an hour," Listishenko continued. "Once you're in the tundra, and your helicopter has left, that's it—you're one-on-one with nature." He gathered a team and began collecting samples. They told the herders to avoid contact with the sick reindeer and tried to limit the animals' movement while waiting for answers from laboratories in Tyumen and Moscow.

On July 25, the results arrived. They were unequivocal: anthrax.

For most of us, anthrax evokes fearful memories of white powder in envelopes. The disease, however, is an ancient one. God's fifth plague upon the Egyptians—"Behold, the hand of the Lord is upon thy cattle which is in the field, upon the horses, upon the asses, upon the camels, upon the oxen, and upon the sheep: there shall be a very grievous murrain," Moses told Pharaoh—may well have been an anthrax outbreak. The same goes for Apollo's bane upon the Greeks at the beginning of the *Iliad*. (Homer dubbed the disease "the burning wind of plague.") Perhaps the most striking description from antiquity of what we now know as *Bacillus anthracis* comes from Virgil's *Georgics:*

> Nor was the manner of dying a simple matter:
> After the thirsty slake-seeking fever had gone
> All through the veins and withered the pitiful limbs,

Then a fluid welled up in the suffering body, and
Piece by piece absorbed the melting bones.

B. anthracis is a cruel organism. In their passive form, the bacteria live as hard, oval-shaped spores with thick, nearly indestructible walls that allow them to survive for decades. When the spores colonize a victim's bloodstream, they enter a vegetative state, dissolving their walls and gathering into neat chains that Robert Koch, the nineteenth-century German scientist whose pioneering work helped identify the disease, described as "graceful, artificially ordered strings of pearls." In order to survive, the bacteria must kill the host and reproduce inside it before escaping back into the world and returning to a resting state.

Anthrax bacteria produce two lethal toxins in tandem, akin to those that cause tetanus and cholera. The process tends to be swift, and the chances of fatality high. The early symptoms resemble those of the common flu: your head begins to ache; your temperature rises; a general sense of weakness envelops your body; your stomach starts rumbling; you begin to cough incessantly. Then things get serious: you may go into seizures; your organs begin failing; boils break out across your skin, swelling red pustules with a trademark black center. In the fifth century BC, Hippocrates dubbed the disease *anthrakes,* from the ancient Greek for "charcoal."

The disease has triumphed once the blood begins spilling from your orifices. When the medical examiners or the veterinarians cut you open, they will find that your blood has gone black, and that certain organs, particularly the spleen, have turned into masses of melting flesh.

In the nineteenth century, anthrax wreaked such havoc on cattle that the French scientist Louis Pasteur was hailed as a national hero when he developed the first vaccine. "If he succeeds," wrote the *Veterinary Press*, a respected trade publication, ahead of a demonstration at the Pouilly-le-Fort fields outside Paris in 1881,

> he will have endowed his country with a great benefit, and his adversaries should, as in the days of antiquity, wreathe their brows with laurel leaves and prepare to follow, chained and prostrate, the chariot of the immortal Victor.

*

In Yamal, the authorities were certain that they had defeated anthrax long ago. The last major outbreak took place in 1941. Surveys of some 250,000 soil samples over the past 12 years had revealed no signs of dormant spores. The regional government had stopped vaccinating reindeer in 2007—it was a costly process that required wrangling the vast herds across a territory larger than France. "An extended period of good fortune leads people to let their guard down, their sense of worry and danger disappears, and they think that since everything has been good, it will continue to be good," mused Yuri Selyaninov, the microbiologist whose laboratory confirmed the anthrax diagnosis.

As word of the outbreak spread across the peninsula, so did ever-wilder theories regarding its origins. Some suggested that the anthrax was the work of foreign agents aiming to weaken Russia's defenses in the Arctic. "They say that foreigners spread the infection from an airplane," one local told *Novaya Gazeta,* an opposition newspaper. Another widespread idea held that there was no anthrax at all, and in fact, the state gas giant, Gazprom, had poisoned the reindeer in an effort to drive the herders off potentially lucrative lands.

On the day the diagnosis was delivered, the Yamal regional governor, Dmitry Kobylkin, declared a state of emergency and called in the Russian Army's Radiological, Chemical, and Biological Defense forces to impose a quarantine. Hundreds of soldiers arrived on the peninsula on four-engine IL-76 military transport planes with blue stripes painted across their bellies and the Russian Army's red star stamped on their tail fins. They brought mobile laboratories and drones. Donning gray hazmat suits and gas masks, they took off in helicopters, scouring the tundra for dead reindeer. When they found one, small teams would descend to light bonfires of burning tires around the body.

The disease, doctors found, had also spread beyond the reindeer, infecting the herders themselves. The Nenets' customs had played a trick on them: when they kill a reindeer, rather than slitting its throat, they strangle it, carefully slice it open, and drink the still-warm blood pooled inside. The blood is an important source of nutrients in their meager diet, but it may have also given the anthrax bacteria a pathway into the human body.

Those inside the infected areas had to give up their possessions —clothes, sleighs, tents, boots—to be disinfected or incinerated.

Officials set up aid stations in villages across the peninsula. Galina Mataras, a local activist, spent her days distributing supplies in herders' camps deep in the tundra. "Imagine you have an apartment," she told me. "And suddenly, from above, your neighbor floods you, having left the faucet on. You return home, and all of your property is not even ninety percent, but one hundred percent useless," she continued. "You open the door, and you understand that, at that moment, you're no one, you have nothing. That's what these people went through. In a moment, they lost everything."

Volunteers collected supplies—food, clothes, and tools—to help replace what was lost. Well-wishers from around the region, perhaps unaware of the conditions inside the quarantine zone, sent electric teakettles, sets of shot glasses, and summer dresses. Someone even sent an old electric meat grinder. Sandra Serotteto, Mataras's daughter and a youth activist, helped lead the aid-collection efforts. During the early days, she barely slept. "There was panic," she recalled. "Then that guy, Russia's main anthrax specialist, showed up," she said. "The Jolly Milkman."

Vasily Seliverstov had just begun a shift as the in-house veterinarian at an Auchan supermarket on the outskirts of Moscow when he learned that the situation in Yamal had turned critical. An old comrade from the national veterinary service called to alert him. "He said, 'Get ready and get over here.' I flew that evening," he told me.

True to the nickname Sandra Serotteto used, Seliverstov vaguely resembles the Jolly Milkman, the mascot of a popular Siberian dairy brand. He has a bowling ball of a head, with silvery tufts of hair around the edges, and sports a voluminous white handlebar mustache, as thick as a young reindeer's antlers. The style has been a fixture for him since the late 1970s, when he returned, unshaven, from a month in the mountains of Tuva, in southern Siberia. "My grandmother told me, 'Don't shave your beard, you look like Jesus, it's a good look for you.'" Sanitary restrictions forbade beards in his laboratory, so the stubborn vet stopped going to work for a month or two, until the director called and said, "Stop being an idiot, shave your beard." Seliverstov shaved his beard but left the mustache.

Despite his stubbornness, or perhaps because of it, Seliverstov built a successful career in the Soviet and then the Russian national veterinary services, eventually rising to become deputy director. He specialized in anthrax, known in Russian as *sibirskaya yazva*, or the "Siberian sore." As a young researcher, he had been called in to help with a 1979 anthrax outbreak in Sverdlovsk, where the government was conducting top secret experiments with chemical weapons. "Lots of people died there," Seliverstov told me. "Who and how many died, only the KGB knows."

Yet the new outbreak stunned even him. How could a disease that had not touched the region for three-quarters of a century suddenly reemerge? "I was certain that *sibirka* wouldn't appear there anymore," he said.

After he arrived in Salekhard, Seliverstov spent 17 days circling the tundra, overseeing vaccinations and attempting to trace the path of the outbreak. On the second day, he met Listishenko at a herders' camp and suggested that they walk along the route that the diseased reindeer had trodden. "We walked some five kilometers that way," Seliverstov said. They found dozens of reindeer lying dead in a row. "The thing about reindeer is that they don't stand in place. They're constantly moving . . . So when the animals begin to die, they fall like a trail behind the moving herd," he went on. "Those become future infection sites." They're known as *morovie polya*, or "cursed fields."

Workdays in the cursed fields began at seven. The helicopters took off, and "we returned to sleep when God allowed," Seliverstov said. Specialists set up mobile corrals, some 300 meters of canvas fencing, and wrangled the healthy reindeer toward veterinarians waiting with the vaccine. They tried to explain to the herders that anthrax could be prevented. "I always say, you don't need to blow on cold milk—you won't get burned," Seliverstov told me. The state replaced the reindeer and equipment the herders had lost, and also restored mandatory vaccinations, hoping to fend off future episodes. In Salekhard, officials held regular meetings, reporting back to Moscow. According to Grigory Ledkov, the head of the Russian Association of Indigenous Peoples of the North and Yamal's representative in the Duma, even President Vladimir Putin kept tabs on the situation.

Around the world, anthrax outbreaks are not uncommon, but most affect only a handful of animals, and very rarely do they infect any humans. (Even newsworthy cases, such as a recent spate of hippo deaths in Namibia, involve at most a few hundred creatures.) By the time the Yamal infection had been neutralized and the quarantine lifted, in late August 2016, more than 2,300 reindeer had fallen across the peninsula. Scores of humans had been hospitalized. A 12-year-old boy, Denis, died on August 1. "God knows, from the first day, we took no chances. We did everything possible to save the lives of everyone who found themselves in trouble," Governor Kobylkin told local media. "But the infection proved wily."

I arrived in Yamal in March 2017, during a yearly holiday known as Den' Olenevoda, or "Reindeer Herder's Day," which is celebrated in towns and cities across the peninsula over several weeks in March and April, as the Arctic begins to emerge from its winter slumber. On a cold day in the tundra, all you can see are swaths of white with no horizon. Frost seems to emanate from somewhere deep in the ground. Mikhail Sumgin, the Soviet researcher responsible for the term "permafrost," also referred to it as the "Russian sphinx," a metaphor that, as the historian Pey-Yi Chu writes, "cast nature simultaneously as an enemy to be conquered, a mystery to be unraveled, and a trove of wealth to be unlocked."

In Salekhard, herders came from miles around to mingle with city folk, oilmen, and curious visitors along a stretch of frozen river south of the city. The gathering felt like a cross between a bazaar and a county fair. From a central stage perched atop the riverbank, an emcee addressed revelers: "The scientists say that it's becoming warmer because of global warming! But the warmth is in our hearts and our souls! We're all here, and the sun is here, too!" A thumping EDM soundtrack warmed up the crowd for an appearance by Kobylkin. "We are always proud to say that Yamal has the largest herd of reindeer in the world!" he crowed, to thunderous applause.

Close to the stage, a line of Nenets women hawked the wares of the far north: fox pelts, fur boots, and whole white hares. One offered me a black-and-gray wolf hide for 20,000 rubles (some $350). "We slew it ourselves," she boasted, revealing a row of silver and gold teeth. I asked what the holiday meant for the herders, expecting an answer about family or community or the spirit world. "A chance to trade!" she replied. In the tundra, there are no country stores.

Beyond the merchants stood an Angry Birds carnival game, where young children used a slingshot twice their size to fling inflatable bird heads at a target. Men grilled pork shashlik over open coals. Frozen fish with glazed eyes—muksun, mostly—rested in buckets inside idle trucks. At the outer edge of the festival grounds, toward the middle of the river, stood a ring of traditional Nenets tents, conical constructions made by wrapping reindeer hides around long wooden poles.

Nearby, I met the head of a reindeer herders' union, who had dressed up for the occasion, donning a full set of traditional robes —navy blue with red, white, and turquoise trim. He wore them over a thick coat of reindeer fur, which makes a North Face parka feel like a windbreaker. I asked him and his wife what they thought the previous summer meant for the region's future. "If the reindeer start going, life itself will disappear," she said wistfully.

Many others, however, reacted to the outbreak with incredulity. I asked a group of students how they had been affected. Alisa, a law student from Yar-Sale whose parents had been herding near the infection zone, scoffed. "There was no anthrax," she said with certainty. Her theory was that Gazprom wanted to build a road. I heard echoes of this skepticism throughout the week: "They spread powder from helicopters," another student told me. "There's oil there," declared a third. Even a veteran of the local forestry service answered my question about the outbreak with scorn: "Do you really believe in the anthrax?"

There was little doubt about one element of the saga: as Listishenko had told me, the summer had been hot. It was, in fact, the hottest in Yamal since monitoring began in 1861, with temperatures peaking at 100°F. (Typically, summer temperatures hover around 60°F.) Russia has been warming since the mid-1970s, at a rate some 2.5 times faster than the global average, and the acceleration has been most pronounced in the Arctic regions. Unsurprisingly, the landscape has responded. The herders "understand that something's happening to nature," said Roza Laptander, a Nenets ethnographer. "The herders say, 'Something strange is happening to the tundra.'"

Some of the changes have been subtle, such as shifts in feeding and migration patterns, or the texture of the snow. Others have been impossible to miss, such as bits of land that have started to ripple—imagine your backyard suddenly attaining the quality of an air mattress. Locals have taken to calling the phenomenon *zhivaya zemlya*, or "living earth." Then there are the giant sinkholes that have opened up across the peninsula in recent years, some as wide as a hundred feet and deeper than a 20-story building. Scientists reckon that these result from "methane bombs," pockets of greenhouse gases that build up in the permafrost as a result of rising temperatures—a feedback loop that could drastically increase the rate of climate change. From above, the earth appears to be collapsing in on itself.

Climate change also lies behind the most credible explanation for anthrax's return. You might call it the zombie theory. It goes something like this: The corpses of reindeer infected with the disease decades or centuries ago were preserved in the upper layers of the peninsula's permafrost, keeping the resilient spores alive. As temperatures have soared, the permafrost has begun to thaw ever deeper, exposing the ancient grave sites and giving the spores a pathway back to the surface, where they can once again rise up to infect the living.

Researchers caution against blaming the Yamal outbreak wholly on rising temperatures, noting that a number of factors had to converge. Native traditions, the poor infrastructure, and a lack of vaccination—all somewhat specific to the region—each played a role. Yet there is no denying that absent the abnormal heat, anthrax would not have returned to Yamal. As Yuri Selyaninov and his colleagues wrote in the definitive report on the Yamal outbreak and its origins,

> It has been established that the appearance of anthrax was stimulated by the activation of "old" infection sites following anomalously high air temperature and the melting of the sites to a depth beyond normal levels.

Normally, the upper layer of permafrost melts about 20 to 30 centimeters; in 2016, it receded more than a meter and a half in certain areas of Yamal. "The bacteria sleep as if they're frozen," Selyaninov explained to me. "Then the temperature went up, and the bacteria received a signal that the surroundings had become favorable. It was warm, and there was something to eat."

In a sense, these auspicious conditions had their roots in the region's booming petroleum industry. The depths of Yamal contain, in addition to sleeping spores, some of the world's largest known gas reserves—perhaps as much as one-quarter of the global deposits—and a large chunk of the planet's oil, too. The Soviet Union began inspecting potential deposits in the late 1950s, and early prospectors marveled at the untold riches. "The generosity of the bowels of the Yamal tundra turned out to be truly limitless!" wrote Arkady Kraev, a geophysicist who helped drill many of the first probes for the Soviet Ministry of Gas Industry. Development of the Yamal fields continued, often to the detriment of reindeer pastures. Following the collapse of the Soviet Union, the ministry morphed into Gazprom, one of the world's largest energy companies and a crown jewel of the modern Russian state. Gazprom now pumps some 67.5 billion cubic meters of gas from Yamal each year, with plans to expand to 360 billion as new fields are tapped.

Russia is one of the world's largest producers of oil and gas, its fourth-largest carbon emitter, and its largest Arctic nation. While Moscow has reluctantly accepted the science of climate change, the Kremlin is hardly clamoring to do much in response. Vladimir Putin signed the Paris climate accord, but Russia has yet to ratify it. What's more, the targets that the government set for itself are little more than a sleight of hand: as a baseline standard from which to reduce emissions, Russia chose the year 1990, when the centrally planned Soviet economy kept heavy industry running at an inordinate clip. Cutting emissions by 25 to 30 percent from those levels by 2030 would actually mean an increase from today's output.

Russia's reluctance to act is in large part a function of the economy's overdependence on fossil fuels, which account for more than 60 percent of the country's exports. But it also reflects the sense that climate change may actually prove to be a boon for the country. Researchers at Stanford and UC Berkeley have predicted that while climate change will shrink global GDP per capita by 23 percent by the end of the century, Russia's GDP will grow by more than 400 percent—more than for any country other than Finland, Iceland, and Mongolia. As the far north melts, the theory goes, it will become more hospitable, and its treasures more accessible. "Climate change provides more favorable conditions for economic activity in this region," Putin told a group of business and government bigwigs at a forum on Arctic issues in early 2017.

But if warming temperatures herald a windfall for Russia's oil and gas industries, they also threaten further epidemics for the inhabitants of the far north. In a prescient 2011 article, Boris Revich, an environmental epidemiologist at the Russian Academy of Sciences, warned of this bizarre but potentially lethal development:

> As a consequence of permafrost melting, the vectors of deadly infections of the eighteenth and nineteenth centuries may come back, especially near the cemeteries where the victims of these infections were buried.

Recent research has uncovered a number of specific threats. From mass graves in the Alaskan tundra, scientists have uncovered fragments of the virus that caused the 1918 outbreak of the Spanish flu. In 2013, the French microbiologists Jean-Michel Claverie and Chantal Abergel discovered still-active viruses in a 30,000-year-old slice of Siberian permafrost. Though their sample could not affect humans, their study suggests that other, more infectious viruses may be lurking. Some frozen microbes may even carry diseases that our immune systems no longer know how to fight. Specialists also caution that devastating eradicated diseases such as smallpox could be preserved in the ice. Many researchers see the Yamal outbreak as a sign of things to come. "It's a warning of sorts that the situation with preserved infections infiltrating our modern world may get much worse if we do not address the problem," argued Boris Kershengoltz, the chief of research at the Russian Institute for Biological Problems of the Permafrost Zone.

An uncanny symmetry links this problem to the traditional Nenets understanding of the origins of disease. Nenets shamans speak of a world split into three realms: the upper world is home to Noom, the creator spirit; the middle world is the earth itself, home to humans and animals; the lower world belongs to Nga, Noom's brother, the spirit of death and disease. This lower world consists of seven layers of ice, and during times of trouble, the spirits of sickness rise from the frost. The Russian term for permafrost —*vechnaya merzlota*—literally means "the eternally frozen ground." Revich has stopped using it. "It's clearly not eternal anymore," he told me.

*

Most of those I met in Yamal acknowledged that their surroundings were changing, and probably not for the best. But that seldom
extended to linking those processes with the oil and gas apparatus
that now extends across the peninsula. Few people entertained the
notion that after decades of drilling into the earth's heart and laying pipes under her skin, she might be beginning to fight back.

Even the herders, who bemoan the oil industry's expansion, are
not immune to the allure of capital. Inside traditional tents in the
tundra, one can often find TVs glowing and teenagers glued to cell
phones. At Den' Olenevoda, most of the reindeer I saw had had
their antlers axed off. The fresh scars felt like the bark of a knotty
tree, or the scab on a child's scraped knee. I asked one herder why
he had done it. "Money," he said with a smile. "Hard currency." A
kilo of antler bone, he told me, brought him 650 rubles (roughly
$11), and each set of antlers he sold weighs about five. (The main
buyers are Chinese, he added, who use powdered reindeer antler,
among other things, as an aphrodisiac; they also make up most of
the market for reindeer penis and tail, which they co-opt for similar purposes—or so the herder told me with a snicker.)

Midway through the festival, I approached a racetrack that
stretched along the river, between the stage and the tents. Solemn-
looking men and women wrapped in fur steered their sleighs toward the starting line. They directed the writhing reindeer, five
to a team, with reins and long poles that they used to poke at
their legs, urging them to gallop ever faster. Sometimes the riders howled, imitating wolves. The sleighs careered across the snow,
and the elongated torsos of the reindeer rippled like flags in a stiff
wind. They have immense eyes, the reindeer, the size of golf balls,
and long pink tongues that protrude when they get tired. Their
legs are skinny, considering the distances they cover each year. In
barely more than a minute, the first teams had already completed
the kilometer-long circuit. They had been racing, I later learned,
for the grand prize of a brand-new Stels snowmobile.

After the last of the sleighs had crossed the finish line, after the
tents had been dismantled and the herders had returned to the
tundra, I went for a drink in town. Perhaps unsurprisingly, I was
recommended a place called Bar Neft, "Oil Bar." Bar Neft sits on
the outskirts of Salekhard, in an old industrial neighborhood. The
entrance resembles a giant black oil barrel, with a door carved into
the right-hand side. The employees all wore black balaclavas. "Do

you have a pistol?" the bouncer asked at the entrance. I shook my head. "You're not from here, are you?" he replied.

A message had been posted on the door inside: SANCTIONS! US PRESIDENT BARACK OBAMA IS FORBIDDEN FROM ENTER-ING. Yet behind the bar hung a string of vintage American license plates: Illinois, Alabama, Delaware, New Mexico. On one wall was a homey sign written in English: MONEY CAN'T BUY HAPPINESS BUT IT CAN BUY MARSHMALLOWS, WHICH ARE ALMOST THE SAME THING. On another wall, imposing black graffiti declared, without a hint of irony, OIL IS OUR EVERYTHING. The cognitive dissonance seemed lost on the patrons. The speakers spit out a string of aughts classics, heavy on the 50 Cent:

My flow, my show brought me the dough
That bought me all my fancy things

The crowd stirred, and I could not help joining in. We all swayed, oblivious to the air around us and the ground below us.

WILLIAM T. VOLLMANN

The End of the Line

FROM *Smithsonian*

And men will not understand us . . . and the war will be forgotten.
— Erich Maria Remarque, *All Quiet on the Western Front* (1928)

ONE SUNDAY MORNING in the 11th Arrondissement of Paris, lured by hydrangeas, roses, and pigeons, I strolled past a playground filled with children's voices. The cool white Parisian sky made me want to sit on a bench and do nothing. Behind the playground a church bell tolled the hour, a crow told time in its own voice, and a breeze suddenly hissed through the maples.

It was a hundred years since the First World War had come to an end. Earlier that morning, approaching Paris by taxi, I passed an exit sign for the Marne, reminding me that in one of the many emergencies of that war thousands of soldiers were rushed from Paris by taxi to fight the First Battle of the Marne. Now a couple sat down on the bench next to me and began kissing. Who is to say that what they were doing wasn't a better use of their time than studying and carefully remembering war? And how then shall I recommend the Great War to you? Let me try: its hideous set pieces retain their power to balefully dazzle us right through the earthen darkness of a hundred years! Let its symbol be the 198-pound German *Minenwerfer*, which a Canadian eyewitness described as follows: "At night it has a tail of fire like a rocket. It kills by concussion."

This essay, my attempt at remembrance, is, like any of our efforts, peculiar, accidental, and limited. I should have visited Berlin, London, Vienna, Flanders, the city formerly known as Brest-Litovsk, and the various territories of the warring colonial empires. (For instance, the 295,000 Australians who fought, and the 46,000 who died, will be barely mentioned here.) I would also have liked to see my own country as it was in 1918.

Instead, to see where the conclusive fighting was done, I went to France to find what battle graves I could: the Marne, the Somme, the Meuse-Argonne, Verdun, the St. Quentin Canal. The "fountains of mud and iron," in Remarque's phrase, had run dry; what about the hatreds and memories?

Beginnings, Raptures, Robberies

You might think Europe and its 40 million finally dead or wounded were dragged into the muck by a series of insults and bumbling miscommunications, a whole continent at the mercy of foolhardy monarchs and military strategists who, "goaded by their relentless timetables," as Barbara Tuchman relates in *The Guns of August,* "were pounding the table for the signal to move lest their opponents gain an hour's head start." Not so, according to many participants. "The struggle of the year 1914 was not forced on the masses — no, by the living God — it was desired by the whole people." Thus the recollection of a young Austrian soldier named Adolf Hitler, who enlisted with a Bavarian infantry regiment as quickly as he could, and served almost to the end. "Overpowered by stormy enthusiasm, I fell down on my knees and thanked Heaven from an overflowing heart for granting me the good fortune of being permitted to live at such a time." Could the war truly have been *desired*? That sounds as fatuous as the grinning death's-head emblem on a German A7V tank. But a German historian who despised the Führer likewise remembered the "exaltation of spirit experienced during the August days of 1914." For him, the war was one "of defense and self-protection."

Like Hitler, the aspiring British poet Robert Graves joined the colors almost immediately. He enlisted to delay going to Oxford ("which I dreaded"), because Germany's defiance of Belgian neutrality incensed him, and because he had a German middle name and German relatives, which caused him to be suspected. Other Britons were as enthusiastic as Hitler. "Anticipation of carnage was delightful to something like ninety percent of the population," observed Bertrand Russell, the Nobel Prize–winning philosopher. Trotsky, witnessing the jubilation in Vienna, remarked that for "the people whose lives, day in and day out, pass in a monotony of hopelessness," the "alarm of mobilization breaks into their lives like a promise."

One might equally well blame diplomatic incompetence, Austro-Hungarian hubris, or the partially accidental multiplier effect of a certain assassination in Sarajevo. And then there was Kaiser Wilhelm, with his mercurial insecurities, military fetish, and withered arm—to what extent was he the cause? In a photograph taken New Year's Day 1913, we see him on parade, beaming in outright exultation and taking clear kindred pleasure in wearing a British admiral's uniform. (He was, after all, the eldest grandchild of Queen Victoria.) Twelve years after the armistice, the British military theoretician Liddell Hart, who was shelled and gassed as a young infantry officer at the front, made the case against the kaiser bluntly: "By the distrust and alarm which his bellicose utterances and attitude created everywhere he filled Europe with gunpowder."

The historian John Keegan, in his classic account *The First World War,* called it "a tragic, unnecessary conflict." If that fails to satisfy you, let me quote Gary Sheffield, a revisionist: "A tragic conflict, but it was neither futile nor meaningless," his idea being that liberal democracy in Europe depended on it. Meanwhile, in came the Russian autocracy and Turkish sultanate to complement the empires of Germany and Austria-Hungary; however necessary they thought the war, by entering it they utterly erased themselves.

Some war tourists may be disposed to amble along a more fatalistic line, so here it is: three years before the slaughter, a certain General Friedrich von Bernhardi explained the birds and the bees in *Germany and the Next War:* "Without war, inferior or decaying races would easily choke the growth of healthy, budding elements, and a universal decadence would follow."

Reader, have you ever read more inspiring words to live by?

The Static

1

A certain influential treatise entitled *Weapons and Tactics,* published in 1943 by the British military historian and man of letters Tom Wintringham and updated 30 years later, divides military history into alternating armored and unarmored periods. The Great War was something in between. Those glorious unarmored days when a sufficiently frenetic cavalry or bayonet charge could break through enemy lines still dazzled the generals. Yet the "defensive power" of machine guns, of barbed wire, and of the spade (for digging) "had ended mobility in war." Meanwhile, the future belonged to tanks: "a brood of slug-shaped monsters, purring, or roaring and panting, and even emitting flames as they slid or pivoted over the ground."

Underestimating this armoring trend, German strategists prepared to follow the "Schlieffen Plan," named for Alfred von Schlieffen, chief of Germany's Imperial General Staff from 1891 to 1905, who conceived a rapid flank attack around French firepower. It had to be rapid, in order to defeat France and swing round against Russia before the latter completed mobilization. Well, why not?

To strike France according to timetable, one had to set aside the trifling matter of Belgium's neutrality. But who dreaded *their* armor, their dog-pulled machine guns? So the Germans put on their knee-high, red-brown leather jackboots and, in the first days of August 1914, marched on Belgium.

The First Battle of the Marne began in early September. At this point the opposing armies still enjoyed some freedom of movement. The tale runs thus: an over-rapid advance (à la Schlieffen) of an already disequilibrated German Army beyond its line of supply was answered by French troops—some of whom, as you already know, were frantically delivered to the front by Parisian cabs—and a strong attack on the German right flank led finally to a so-called "failure of nerve," which caused the Germans to retreat to the Aisne River. Here they settled into trenches until 1918.

As one General Heinz Guderian put it: "The positions ultimately evolved into wired, dug-in machine-gun nests which were secured by outposts and communication trenches." Take note of this German, if you would. He was young enough and flexible enough to learn from his defeats. We will meet him again and again.

2

Upon his arrival at the front, Robert Graves's commander explained that trenches were temporary inconveniences. "Now we work here all the time, not only for safety but for health," Graves writes. How healthy do you suppose they were, for men sleeping in slime, fighting lice and rats, wearing their boots for a week straight? The parapet of one trench was "built up with ammunition-boxes and corpses." Others, Graves wrote, "stank with a gas-blood-lyddite-latrine smell." From an Englishman at Gallipoli: "The flies entered the trenches at night and lined them with a density which was like moving cloth."

Let the little village of Vauquois, 15 miles from Verdun, represent the trenches. The Germans took it on September 4, 1914. In March of the following year, the French regained the southern half, so the Germans dug in at the hillcrest and in the cemetery. In September 1918 the Americans finally cleared the place. During those three static years, a mere 25 feet separated the battle lines in Vauquois—surely close enough for the adversaries to hear each other.

Ascending a short steep path through thick forest, where strands of ivy ran up verdant trees approaching the white sky with its sprinkle of rain, I found on the summit near an unimpressive monument the ruins of Vauquois's town hall, which were forbidden to the public by means of red-and-white-striped tape. Twisted rusted relics of agricultural equipment lay on display in a kind of sandbox. Here one could look down over a checkerboard of forest and field to faraway Montfaucon, one of the enemy strongpoints that General John J. Pershing's "doughboys" would face in the great Meuse-Argonne Offensive of 1918. And just below me lay a great crater in the grass, its depth maybe 100 feet or more, where at one point the Germans had detonated 60 tons of subterranean explosives, killing 108 French infantrymen in an instant.

I descended into no-man's-land, passing the hole where the church used to be, then up into the German positions where a steel-faced hole, almost filled in, grinned below the grass. Ahead rose more forest—none of it old growth, of course, for by 1915 Vauquois and its trees had been improved into mucky craters.

The fact that everything was now overgrown I had thought to be a blessing, but taking a step into the greenness I encountered waist-high tangles of barbed wire or dangerous bunker holes whose lips for all I knew might collapse beneath me.

To pulverize positions at so near a distance, a soldier was well served by the so-called trench mortar, which fired its projectile almost straight up, so that it would come down with great force upon one's neighbors. And just here I found a trench mortar excavated from its concrete-and-steel-lined pit. Like most of the ordnance still remaining on the Western Front, it wore a black finish —the work, said the local historian Sylvestre Bresson, who was my battlefield guide for a part of my travels, of postwar preservationists, for during its working career it would have sported field-gray paint. The thing came up to my navel. Its barrel was more than large enough for me to put both arms in.

I proceeded farther into the German lines, whose lineaments were mostly disguised by dandelions, daisies, goldenrod, nettles, and other weeds. The humid coolness was pleasant. How could I even hope to envision the reputed 10 miles of burrows on this side? One of the trenches wound conveniently before me, between belly- and chest-high, its concrete softened by moss, and its next turning celebrated by a rusty bracket—maybe the rung of a ladder.

I clambered down into its clamminess. I followed a dandelion-crowned mossy, winding trench whose side tunnels went darkly down. Here gaped a square pit like a chimney with double-braided strands of rusty barbed wire at ankle height in the creepers just beyond. I drew prudently back. A collector might have liked that German barbed wire, which was thicker than the French version. (Bresson told me that French-issued cutters of the period could not break it.) With its long alternating spikes it looked more primitive and more vegetally "organic" than the barbed wire of today. How many French assaulters with twisted and bloody ankles had it held up long enough for the defenders to machine-gun them?

Returning to the path, I found more dark, filthy, stone-faced and metal-faced dugouts. Stooping down to peer into a mucky tunnel, I braced my hands upon a perimeter of sandbags whose canvas had rotted, the concrete remaining in the shape of each bag.

Every known World War I veteran has died; the very notion of "remembering" the war felt problematic. How could I even imagine the hellish noise? What about the smells? A Frenchman left this description: "Shells disinter the bodies, then reinter them, chop them to pieces, play with them as a cat does a mouse."

3

By the close of 1914, with the war less than half a year old, the Western Front stretched static, thick, and deep for 450 miles. The Eastern Front took on a similar if less definitive character, finally hardening between Romania and the Baltic in 1915. In a photo from November 1915 we see a line of German soldiers in great-coats and flat-topped caps shoveling muck out of a winding narrow trench, grave-deep, somewhere in the Argonne Forest. The surface is nothing but wire, rock, sticks, and dirt.

The generals thought to break the stasis using massive concentrations of artillery. Somehow, surely, the enemy positions could be pulverized, allowing charges to succeed? *Weapons and Tactics:* "Most of the history of the War of 1914–18 is the history of the failure of this idea."

You see, artillery barrages, to say the least, called attention to themselves. The enemy then thickened its defenses where needed. Furthermore, the shelling tore up no-man's-land, so that assault parties, instead of rushing forward, floundered in shell holes, while the enemy shot them down. In one typical outcome, Graves's comrades "were stopped by machine-gun fire before they had got through our own entanglements."

However perilous it was to "go over the top," the defensive positions were themselves hardly safe. Graves writes time and time again about witnessing the deaths of his comrades right there in the earthworks. He feared rifle bullets more than shells, because they "gave no warning." On the opposite side of the front, Hitler emoted: "In these months I felt for the first time the whole malice of Destiny which kept me at the front in a position where every n— — might accidentally shoot me to bits."

And so their various armored immobilities stalemated the belligerents. The British were losing as many as 5,000 soldiers a week in what they called "normal wastage." Unable to go forward, unwilling to retreat, the adversaries tried to speed up normal wastage. That is why, as early as the fall of 1915, the French and British decided on a quota of 200,000 Germans killed or wounded per month.

"Thus it went on year after year; but the romance of battle had been replaced by horror." That was Hitler again. He, of course, remained "calm and determined."

4

The German assault at Verdun announced itself on February 21, 1916, with the detonation of more than a thousand cannons. Something like 33 German munitions trains rolled in *each day*. In a photo of a second-line casualty station, we see a wounded Frenchman sitting crookedly on his crude stretcher, which rests in the dark mud. His boots are black with filth; likewise his coat up to his waist and beyond. A white bandage goes bonnet-like around his head, the top of it dark with blood. His slender, grubby hands are part folded across his waist. His head is leaning, his eyes almost closed.

In a bunker near Verdun 100 years later I came upon a chamber whose rusty ladder ascended to a cone outlined with light, which silhouetted something like a giant mantis's desiccated corpse: the under chassis of a machine gun. Nearby ran another emplacement that Sylvestre Bresson thought must be part of the Maginot Line, thanks to its newer concrete. (I should remind the reader that this latter imposing bulwark was intended, decades later, to use all of World War I's advantages of entrenched defense against that World War II aggressor, Hitler. For why wouldn't war haunt this same ground over and over again?)

A Russian offensive against the Austrians in the east, followed by a French attack at the Somme in July, finally forced the Germans to disengage from Verdun. In October the French retook its most massive fort. The battle, the longest of World War I, finally ended on December 15. Then what? Mud, corpses, duckboards, trenches, broken trees. French and German casualties each exceeded 300,000 men.

But why disparage all this mutual effort? If its object was to kill multitudes of human beings, let's call it a triumph, as evidenced by the French National Necropolis at Fleury-devant-Douaumont. Driving down the hill, we came upon 15,000 white crosses flashing in the sun. I went out to wander those tombstones on the down-slanting grass where crimson-petaled rose beds ran along each row. Up at the chapel, French soldiers in uniform stood gazing down across the stones, the occasion being a change of commander. "For us this is the most sacred site," Bresson remarked. "If

France could keep only one memorial to World War I, it would be this one."

These 15,000 dead men were all French, but nearly 10 times the amount of remains, both French and German, broken and commingled, lay in the nearby ossuary. Looking in through the many ground-level windows, I saw heaps of bones and skulls in the darkness. Some yellow-brown fragments had been combined into almost decorative columns, as in the Paris catacombs.

In the edifice above them stood a Catholic chapel with stained-glass windows, and in a glass case, relics from the churches of destroyed villages. This forest meadow bore stone markers to commemorate the former farm buildings, washhouses, grocery stores. Maples and cypresses had grown 102 years high. I saw dark water in the deeper shell holes, grass in the shallower ones. The grass was ingrown with daisies, dandelions, and clover. Birds were singing.

5

As for the First Battle of the Somme—which was, more accurately, a dozen smaller battles, playing out over 141 days in 1916, from July to November—that accomplished kindred wonders. Liddell Hart remembered the year as "the nadir of infantry attacks," the assaulters being "almost shoulder to shoulder, in a symmetrical, well-dressed alignment, and taught to advance steadily upright at a slow walk." How convenient for the artillerists!

In 2018, Bresson, who lived in the Somme, enlightened me about the residue: "The bomb disposal squad comes twice a week. Twice a week, even now! You know, if there was some live shell in Paris, it would be on the news. But in the country, nobody cares. The farmers, they just carry it into the road."

The Battle of the Somme marked the war's first deployment of tanks (on September 15, by the British), but they were introduced in dribs and drabs, their surprise effect mostly wasted, their potential nearly invisible. On October 7, Hitler, his potential equally unforeseeable, was wounded in the thigh, but he was not out of action long.

The Somme came to be referred to as "the muddy grave of the German field army," for German casualties were up to 650,000 killed, wounded, and missing. But the muddy grave was more international than that. Its local commemorators called it *un espace mondial,* "a world-inclusive space." The British took 420,000 casualties; the battle's first day has been called "the bloodiest day in British history." The French lost 200,000 men. Although General Douglas Haig, commander of the British Expeditionary Force, claimed an attritional victory, David Lloyd George, Britain's soon-to-be prime minister, called it "a bloody and disastrous failure."

In 1918 this churned-up wasteland, well irrigated with trench-blood and fertilized with flesh, would be viciously contested all over again.

6

You may recall that 1916 was the year when the Russians broke through the Austrian defenses on the Eastern Front, causing the Germans to halt their assault on Verdun. But the Russians could only get so far. The czar's army had already lost half its strength in the previous year, and the new assault cost them more than a million casualties. According to Liddell Hart, this latest bloodbath "completed the virtual ruin of Russia's military power." In July 1917, the Russian Army shot its last bolt.

That previous winter, bled weak by Verdun and the Somme, the Germans prepared a strategic withdrawal from a 20-mile salient between Arras and Soissons in northern France. A salient is in essence a bulge into enemy lines—a reified hope of breakthrough. Abandoning one may be a sad business, but also prudent, because any such position is vulnerable on two or three sides.

Hence Operation Alberich, whose first step would be the construction of the best-fortified redoubt in Europe: the Siegfried Line, or, as the British called it, the Hindenburg Line, Field Marshal Paul von Hindenburg being the new German commander in chief: grizzled, calm, soldierly-looking, maybe even statesmanlike. (In 1933, the same Hindenburg, now a grandly senile old figurehead—and president of the young, doomed Weimar Republic—would appoint Hitler as chancellor.)

Hindenburg's First Quartermaster, and in many ways the guiding partner, was General Erich von Ludendorff, humorless and irascible, who five years after the war would march beside Hitler in the sordid "Beer Hall Putsch." (Hitler later proclaimed Ludendorff "leader, and chief with dictatorial power, of the German national army.") Since it is to Ludendorff that accounts of this period generally assign agency, I shall do the same.

The Hindenburg Line has been called "the war's greatest feat of engineering." Its various belts, which bore such mythological names as "Kriemhild" and "Freya," ran for 300 miles. Half a million laborers toiled for four months to make them, dispersing the cargoes of 1,250 trains. The line began with an antitank ditch, followed by "at least" five walls of barbed wire; "next came a line of defense anchored by forts and blockhouses bristling with machine guns, and the final major barrier boasted an intricate system of zigzag trenches designed to prevent enfilading fire"—and this ominous description, courtesy of *The Oxford Companion to Military History*, leaves out the St. Quentin Canal, a waterway that was up to 35 feet wide and 50 to 60 feet deep. Two artillery lines brooded in the rear.

The withdrawal took place in February 1917. The Germans left behind them what one officer called "a desolate, dead desert," Ludendorff having determined to make it into "a totally barren land" in which Allied "maneuverability was to be critically impaired." First they removed anything they could use. Then they razed every building, mined every street, poisoned every well, dammed every creek, burned everything that would burn. The vileness of this policy remains a matter of opinion. Bresson assured me: "You know, we did the same thing when we left Gallipoli, in 1915." Hart described the withdrawal as "a consummate maneuver, if unnecessarily brutal in application." But he was one of those realists who did not consider chlorine gas especially cruel.

And so the front was not merely frozen, but steel-frozen. Thus it went through most of 1917, the year when President Woodrow Wilson proposed, and the kaiser rejected, "peace without victory."

Unlocking the Front

I

What finally destroyed the long primacy of immobile armored defense? First of all, a British naval blockade, which had been in effect since before the first battle of 1914, began to starve the two adjacent Central Powers of essential materials like rubber and brass. By 1916 the starvation was becoming literal. In a German photo from the late war years we see kerchiefed, long-skirted women bending over a rubbish heap, pickaxing its filth in search of anything nourishing to go in a grimy bucket. The protagonists of the German veteran Remarque's *All Quiet on the Western Front,* weakening on their "turnip jam," count themselves lucky whenever they can snatch up butter and corned beef from the French positions they've assaulted.

Attack technologies now also began to render machine-gun nests and barbed-wired trenches, if not yet obsolete, at least penetrable. Planes had barely begun to prove themselves, but the prospect of a pack of high-flying bombing and strafing machines took on nerve-racking plausibility.

Tanks, after their first faltering foray at the Somme, had been improved. One innovator recognized that the fuel tanks should be less vulnerable to direct hits. The British and French commenced mass production. Still, Germany deployed no tanks of its own manufacture until the war's last year, by which time its enemies possessed 5,000; it had just 45.

Here is how the German officer Guderian remembered the First Battle of Cambrai, from 1917: "In a few hours the strongest position on the Western Front had been broken," he lamented. "The bells rang out in London for the first time in the war."

One of the British monsters that so obsessed Guderian was named "Deborah," designated female because "she" sported machine guns instead of six-pounders. I have seen her all alone at the Cambrai Tank 1917 Museum. The poor girl had been buried in muck until 1998. Her rounded-tipped quadrilateral shape challenges description: sort of like a riveted roach or crocodile, but not exactly.

The museum staff had tastefully enclosed her snout in genuine Great War barbed wire. Her bow and starboard side gaped jaggedly open, offering darkness and the smell of oil; her guts were partly shattered and twisted by the German fire that killed four of her crewmen, who lay in the adjacent cemetery. But in her port flank two service-holes remained, one rectangular, the other perfectly round, so that the gray light of that concrete room shined right through her. Her ripped, rusted, yet surprisingly durable carapace made the horror of the war itself more durable. At her backside lay two wreaths.

Immediately adjacent to her public sepulcher I found the Flesquières Hill British Cemetery, whose ground had been captured in the Cambrai battle, lost soon after, then retaken in September 1918, at which point it came in handy for new deposits. After looking out from the stone pavilion across the green lawn to the great cross and past two lovely trees toward cloud-shaded fields with wind turbines on the horizon, I opened the heavy door that protected the visitors' book. One inscription read: *To those who gave their lives, and those who keep their memories so well.* Another: *Thank you all boys RIP.* Four days before me, someone had come to visit his fallen grandfather. The most recent inscription was in French: *We will never forget you.*

The registry book told another story. This place once lay behind the German Flesquières Soldiers' Cemetery No. 2. After the armistice, the German graves were moved to a "cemetery extension" (which would itself be relocated in 1924). In their place British plots were erected. Such disrespect must have increased the vanquished's hatred for the victors, but that was hardly the fault of 28259 PRIVATE JOHN DAVEY CARTER ROYAL LANCASTER REGIMENT 8TH OCTOBER 1918 AGE 27, ON WHOSE SOUL SWEET JESUS HAVE MERCY. I copied these words from his tombstone. Then I stood and took in the red roses, black-eyed Susans, and purple flowers.

2

In the judgment of *All Quiet on the Western Front,* "The summer of 1918 is the most bloody and the most terrible." Not knowing the outcome as we do, Germany tried to see the sunny side of the barbed wire. "The whole army took fresh hope and fresh courage after the Russian collapse," Hitler remembered. For after Russia's soldiers declined to continue prosecuting the war, the weak-willed czar abdicated, and the newly empowered Bolsheviks sued for peace, which the Germans granted at a stringent price in resources and territory. (Thus the infamous Treaty of Brest-Litovsk.)

And so the kaiser could credit himself with the first great conquest of that War to End All Wars. "Out of the wreckage of the czar's dominions," as Gary Sheffield wrote in his history *Forgotten Victory,* grew "a network of client states and spheres of influences that added up to a new German colonial empire with enormous economic potential."

Now, wasn't *that* something worth invading Belgium for? With Russia imploding into civil war, Ludendorff and Hindenburg could now transfer multitudes of German troops to the Western Front, build new assault groups, strike the French and British at just the right spot, and at long last smash through the stasis of 1914–1917.

As always, haste would be called for. The operation depended on quick success—before General Pershing got his American troops trained and mobilized.

3

The United States, goaded into it by the repeated sea-murder (so we not unreasonably saw it) of our own nationals by U-boats, had declared war on Germany in 1917. American soldiers entered the trenches that October, but didn't begin leading large-scale operations until 1918, the year when the actors Lawrence Grant starred in *To Hell with the Kaiser!* and Norman Kaiser changed his name to Norman Kerry. Meanwhile, thanks to Operation Alberich, the Germans had had a year to recuperate their energies and thicken the Hindenburg Line. Secure in defense, they prepared to strike.

On March 21, 1918, only 18 days after Brest-Litovsk, the Germans began a new campaign, code-named "Michael," whose artillery barrage could be heard even in England. A German soldier called the noise "incessant and almost musical," while a British rifleman thought it sounded like "sheer hell."

Since massed attacks preannounced by artillery barrages had accomplished so little throughout the war, Ludendorff essayed what had worked so well for T. E. Lawrence against the Turks: *infiltration,* seeking points of least resistance. The idea was to break the British Army, and thus Allied morale, and so bring about an end to the war.

Concentrating their forces secretly by night, then advancing through fog and their own fresh-laid poison gas in small groups of storm troopers over 60 miles of front, the Germans achieved full surprise. A desirable punch-through point was the town of Arras, birthplace of the French Revolution's ruthlessly "incorruptible" Robespierre, who in obedience to some form of golden rule was himself finally guillotined.

The train from Amiens droned past an emerald field of white cows, which gave way to rippled ponds, gray clouds, mown grass, white churches, trees. Here came the town of Albert, with a golden figure on its high brickwork tower; then our tracks entered a cut between the trees, came out again, and we glided through that kind of landscape that cliché-mongers call idyllic.

Disembarking in Arras, I found myself in a cobbled square, walled in by four-story buildings, facing the ornate sweep of the town hall and the pale-yellow Hôtel de Ville, then a clock tower whose hands and Roman numerals were gold, and finally the famous belfry. Outside the Hôtel a monument memorialized Germany's victims of 1940 and 1944, in this case Resistance fighters; on the square itself two plaques dryly explained that the original belfry dated from 1463 to 1914 and the Hôtel de Ville from 1502 to 1914.

"Michael" quickly gained a miraculous 37-odd miles, so that it began to seem that the stasis was broken at last. Guderian called the feat "the greatest success achieved on the Western Front since trench warfare had begun." On March 23 the invaders set up shop in the Laon Salient, close upon Crépy, and began bombarding Paris. The artillerists fired payloads of 200 to 230 pounds every 20 minutes for 139 days. They killed a thousand people and more. Smelling total victory, the kaiser declared a holiday.

4

Yet failing to reduce Arras on the 26th and again on the 28th, Ludendorff was compelled to release his straining grasp on the city. The date was March 30, two days after go-it-alone "Black Jack" Pershing had finally agreed to shore up the front with American troops.

On April 4, Ludendorff called on fresh reserves to resume the advance, this time turning toward Amiens, "the hinge of the Allies' front," where Jules Verne used to write his nineteenth-century science-fiction novels. The Germans had occupied this town for 11 days in August–September 1914, and with their customary humanitarianism took local officials hostage. At some point before or after, the locals fortified their cathedral's ancient treasures with 2,200 sandbags. As for other prizes, Robert Graves remembers a "Blue Lamp" brothel for officers and a "Red Lamp" for enlisted men.

In this centennial year 2018, massive photo-enlargements of Great War soldiers, some in the beekeeper-esque gas masks of the period, most of them young, grim, and handsome, stared down from the walls of the train station and the department stores and apartment buildings all around the cathedral square.

The first attempt to take Amiens began on March 27. (The

reader is reminded that the dates of battles, offensives, et cetera, vary extremely according to source. I have done my shallow best to rationalize these inconsistencies.) Ludendorff's troops penetrated the Allied front southward of the Somme River, 10 miles from the city. The Germans were driven back, but continued to shell Amiens until June. According to a Michelin Guide from that time, "ruins accumulated in the town and suburbs," but a hundred years later, those ruins had been nicely smoothed over.

On April 9 the Germans won another local success at Armentières—at which point the French and British, as ever, began to dig in. General Haig was worried enough to warn, with uncharacteristic gloom, "With our backs to the wall and believing in the justice of our cause each one of us must fight on to the end."

Finally the anxious Allies began to coordinate their efforts better, and appointed the French marshal Ferdinand Foch Supreme Allied Commander over their joint forces.

5

By now the Kaiser's troops had reached the town of Villers-Bretonneux, a "Franco-British junction" some 10 miles from Amiens. Two Australian brigades stopped them, but 20 days later, employing tanks and gas, the Germans succeeded. As Sylvestre Bresson, my guide, tells the tale, "The Allies now found themselves in trouble, for Villers-Bretonneux was the last defensive bulwark on the Amiens road. The following night, the Australian battalions led a magnificent headlong attack," which ultimately repelled the invaders. In a "2018 special edition" commemorative pamphlet published by the Communes of the Somme Valley, this organization's president wrote: "Let's never forget Australia."

The memorial to the victors (1,200 of whom died on that night) lies not far from a little roadside sign marking the place where "the Red Baron," Manfred von Richthofen, Germany's ace fighter pilot, was shot dead on April 21, 1918. Beneath the sign I saw a Styrofoam "100" and some fake flowers left by Australians; this I knew because my taxi driver, whose family hailed from the west, had chauffeured them out here just a few days before. He had never heard of this site until then. He had grandparents in the Resistance, in the Second World War, but as for the First World War, that was too long a time ago, he remarked, flashing one tanned skinny arm away from the steering wheel.

"People around here don't even talk about it very much," he said of the Great War. He thought that I and my sister, who had accompanied me on this trip and served, when needed, as my French translator, were Australians. "Every family from Australia has some question about the war," he remarked.

At the Villers-Bretonneux Military Cemetery and Memorial roses bloomed on a rolling hillcrest sowed with tombstones. The inscriptions were more personalized than many, DEARLY LOVED SON being in frequent evidence. This complex was inaugurated in 1938, just in time to be shot up in the next war—or, as a plaque explained, "on the firing line." (The culprit was a Nazi tank.) There was a grand tower erected TO THE GLORY OF GOD AND IN MEMORY OF THE AUSTRALIAN IMPERIAL FORCE IN FRANCE AND FLANDERS 1916–1918 AND OF ELEVEN THOUSAND WHO FELL IN FRANCE AND HAVE NO KNOWN GRAVE.

Had they all been properly cataloged, would it have been any better for them? For a fact, their survivors might have gained what we now call "closure," although one question does arise: How much information about the fallen is too much?

"I do a lot of research for the families when they come," Bresson told me. "Sometimes the stories told in the families are different from the truth, thanks to embellishment, exaggeration, and after one, two, or three generations especially. But the archives tell the truth.

"A couple of years ago I had a tour with a couple from Australia. They wanted to visit the grave of a great-uncle. Before they came they gave us the name and I was able to find a lot of information about the great-uncle. But he wasn't killed in action. He was killed in a stupid accident. He was at rest with his regiment and he was shooting ducks with one of his friends and his friend shot him by accident. It was literally written *killed shooting ducks by accident.*

"So on the day of the tour I met them and the story they knew was: he was killed on the battlefield, killed by German snipers when crawling under the barbed wire. Well, they were very moved to come. We went to the cemetery and left flowers there, and I told them they could get more information. I did not tell them directly. They were coming from the other side of the world."

In one of ever so many rows in that cemetery, beneath the emblem of the Australian Imperial Forces, lay 6733 PRIVATE H. J. GIBB 14TH BN. AUSTRALIAN INF. 7TH JUNE 1918 AGE 45, and after a cross came the motto that someone had chosen for him: PEACE AFTER STRIFE. Whatever the circumstances of that untimely death, whether he had bravely held a position, saved a comrade, bayoneted three Germans, or died while shooting ducks, untimely it was, and I felt sorry.

6

The Germans, having been frustrated at Amiens (but never mind: they would break through on a June day in 1940), swung toward Paris, eventually coming within 37 miles of the city. They had drilled a deep salient into French and British lines, but it wasn't enough. The historian Gordon Craig writes that the German offensive "was bound to be disastrous after the enemy had recovered," and that indeed it "degenerated by June into a series of separate thrusts, uncoordinated and unproductive."

Declining to give up, Ludendorff's troops commenced Operation Blücher, assisted by almost 4,000 Krupp guns, shelling and shattering the French Sixth Army. Unfortunately for the Germans, their newest enemy was now in the field. The day after Blücher began, the Americans counterattacked. The US First Infantry captured 200 Germans and buried 199 Americans, and immediately won a victory in the village of Cantigny.

At observation post "Pennsylvania," First Lieutenant Daniel Sargent of the Fifth Field Artillery Regiment reported, "The ground was pounded to dust by our shells—all that was visible was the heavy smoke." The division's commander, General Robert Lee Bullard, called this "the first serious fight made by American troops in France," which was "greeted enthusiastically as a wonderful success." Why not? There were lots of corpses. As a certain Captain Austin wrote home: "When the wind is right you can smell Cantigny two miles away."

7

For Ludendorff this "wonderful success" must have been an incitement to hurry up. On the first day of Blücher his troops gained 13 miles, unheard of in the former static years. Having crossed the Vesle, they took Soissons—although they now kept facing more tank attacks. "Just think a moment!" cried Guderian, wisening up. "Five tanks with crews amounting to ten men had been able to reduce an entire division to disorder."

By June 4, with 30 miles now to their credit, they had reached
the Marne at Château-Thierry. What must they have felt upon finding themselves back where they had been in 1914? But that was
the way of the Great War: Fight and die along static lines. Then
do it all over. Thus July's offering: the Second Battle of the Marne.
The Oxford Companion to Military History remarks: "Just as the Marne
had proved the high water mark of German success in 1914, so it
did in 1918."

Happily unaware of how their offensive would play out, the Germans still imagined themselves on course for the capital. To and
fro in the trenches rushed that busy dispatch runner Adolf Hitler. But now the French rushed up tanks, accompanied by rapid
mobile truckloads of infantry. As the American Battle Monuments
Commission told it: "Responding to urgent pleas from the French,
Pershing ordered the American 2nd and 3rd Divisions into the
line in relief of the French Sixth Army."

8

"Nothing on earth," wrote infantryman Percy Clare of Britain's
Seventh East Surrey Regiment, "is as melancholy as a journey over
a recently-fought battlefield, especially on the day of action . . .
The lust of killing has burned out . . . Here is a young Second
Lieutenant on his back . . . the jagged ends of his thigh bones protruding through his torn breeches. No, he felt no pain. Sticking
from his pocket is a letter to a woman." That diary entry dates back
to the Battle of Arras, in April 1917. Comparable horrors filled
Château-Thierry 13 months later.

A century after that, the melancholy kept everywhere green.
Here at the bank of the gentle gray-green Marne, where white
swans were floating and very occasionally ducking in their heads, I
looked across the water to houses, apartments, and industrial edi-
fices, once more hardly able to *feel* that the war had come here.
The river was barely swirling. It appeared an easy swim to the other
side of town.

Beside me stood an inconspicuous waist-high granite marker
erected in 1921: a tapering plinth with a helmet on top. One of
many fashioned by the sculptor Paul Moreau-Vauthier, it marked
the limit of the enemy advance. There had been a whole line of
these memory stones. In 1940, when the Germans returned thanks

to Hitler, certain German commanders chose to remove them entirely. Others, evidently proud of what the kaiser's troops had accomplished in the Great War, left them but erased the inscriptions.

When I came upon the Château-Thierry American monument, a white stone colonnaded edifice honoring the American divisions that helped repel the German advance, it felt just like coming home, for here alone of all the Western Front sites I visited the entrant had to empty his pockets and pass through a metal detector. As they say, freedom isn't free.

Myself, I preferred the simpler, sadder truth of the Aisne-Marne American Cemetery. Summer green, summer clouds, so many birds. Driving up a long avenue lined with rosebushes, we met a blue-capped gardener who was breaking out a lawn mower. From the burial registry in the visitors' room, I chose for remembrance Plot A Row 3 Grave 72, the grave where lay Edmond P Maes, Private, from Massachusetts. He served in the 101st Field Artillery Regiment, 26th Division, and fell on 23 July 1918.

Lines of marble crosses curved in parallels on the rich green grass, wrapping around a hill of dark green forest. The pigeons were calling, the lawn mower droning far away. Overlooking the graves was a chapel (slightly scarred by the following world war) whose walls were engraved with the names of the missing. Once in a great while there would be a rosette made to the left of the name of someone who was "found," such as LUPO FRANCIS PVT 18th INF 1st DIV JULY 21 1918 OHIO.

In a poem from the month when the slaughter finally stopped, the decorated British soldier Siegfried Sassoon advised his British readers, "when you are standing at your hero's grave," to remember "the German soldiers who were loyal and brave." I asked to see a cemetery of our former enemies. "The German cemeteries are different," explained Bresson. "There was a strong animosity toward them, so in that time the German cemeteries were always set away, on a back road, whereas our cemeteries were set on the top of the hill so they can be seen from miles away. From the German perspective the First and Second World Wars are so linked, like one war. The Germans still feel ashamed of what they did to the Jews, so they don't have any motivation to visit their soldiers."

Indeed the nearby German cemetery was discrete, out of sight from the victors' graves, and instead of white, the crosses, thicker-armed than ours, were gray (in some cemeteries they were black). I saw a very few oval-tipped slabs with the Jewish star, as for Fritz Stern, grenadier. (As a special reward for their service in the Great War, the Nazis would deport some Jewish veterans in passenger train carriages rather than freight cars, their destination of course being the same as for the others.)

Not far away stood a cross for Unteroffizier Peter Latour and Infanterist Ulrich Lederer and on the other side Ein unbekannter Deutscher Soldat (an unknown German soldier) and for Vizefeld-webel Franz Stiefvater—yes, four men buried under one cross. In this soil lay 8,630 bodies. In the sprawling American cemetery adjacent there were not quite 2,300.

Leafing through the visitors' book, my sister discovered that an American with a military affiliation (I will not give his name) had made a fingerprint in what appeared to be real blood, and left a sneering English-language inscription.

9

A German attack of July 14 was hopefully named the *Sieggesturm,* or "Turn of Victory," but Ludendorff was fresh out of victories. The next day he launched his final offensive, aiming at Reims. Three days after that, Generals Foch and Pétain counterattacked on the Marne, close by Villers-Cotterêts—by surprise, with tanks again, and to good effect.

July 18 marked the beginning of Marshal Foch's counteroffensive. "Although the Germans fought stubbornly to the end, they were henceforth always on the defensive," recalled Lieutenant John Clark, an American eyewitness to the battle for Soissons.

On August 8 came what Ludendorff would call "the black day of the German Army," when he realized "the war must be ended." By then a British tank brigade had helped reduce the German-held stronghold of Moreuil. One British major took a spin "in one of those huge armoured cars, and found it most disagreeably hot; but I felt a sense of delightful security when I heard the bullets rattling against the steel walls."

Now began the Battle of Amiens: Australians, Canadians, French, and British all fighting together. General Haig commenced with a tank attack 20 miles wide and 456 (or if you like 552) metal monsters thick; he achieved utter surprise. German casualties may have been three times the Allied ones. In his memoirs, Guderian wrote: "Even now old-timers like us relive that feeling of impending doom which overtook us on that day in August."

On August 21 the British drove toward Bapaume and Albert, reducing both; on September 1 Péronne fell to the Australians. How would all this captured territory have appeared in early autumn 1918? "Deserted," recalled Captain C. N. Littleboy, a British commander of the Sherwood Foresters. "Bleak, devastated." Continuing eastward, Littleboy saw "a derelict Tank, a dead horse, a rifle stuck upright in the ground."

In 2018, driving over this same sad old Somme country, I thought the rolling hills and sky could almost have been somewhere in eastern Washington State, maybe around Pullman. We ascended what appeared to be the curvature of the earth itself, everything gently, evenly falling off; here came Morlancourt; we kept on Highway D42; then ahead stood three trees, to guard the edge of the world.

10

The shelling of Paris finally ended on August 9.

On September 14, after continued Allied gains, the Austrians sent a peace note. Five days later, the Turkish front collapsed in Palestine. On the 21st, the Croatians hung out their flag. On the 24th, the Hungarians rose up and called for independence from Austria. On the 28th, Bulgaria fell. A day after that, Ludendorff had a "fit"—perhaps a minor stroke.

Now at last Marshal Foch called for a coordinated series of assaults upon the creaking Hindenburg Line: on September 26 in the Meuse-Argonne Forest, the Americans with 411 tanks and the French with 654; on the 27th, the British, launching the Second Battle of Cambrai (they would take their objective on the 9th); on the 28th, the Belgians in Flanders; on the 29th, more French and British attacks.

The Meuse-Argonne Offensive, fought by Pershing's First Army under Foch's overall coordination, was intended to breach the Hindenburg Line westward of Verdun. One history calls it "the biggest logistical undertaking in the history of the US Army, before or since."

Six French divisions assisted 22 American infantry divisions, most of which had not yet proven themselves in battle. (By the end, more than 90 Allied divisions participated in the fight.) "The

Germans," the previous source continues, "had created four successive, mutually supporting defensive lines, linked by trenches and interlocking arcs of fire."

The attack began at 5:30 in the morning on September 26. Its logical result was the Meuse-Argonne American Cemetery, the most populated American necropolis in Europe, with 14,246 burials. Which should I single out? In one row of marbled crosses on a field walled in by trees, accompanied by another field of crosses and then more of the same, HERE RESTS IN HONORED GLORY AN AMERICAN SOLDIER KNOWN BUT TO GOD—though never to his hoping, wondering, finally despairing family, who when I read this inscription in 2018 must have all gone underground themselves.

The US 35th Division managed to take that ghastly old concretion of trench-line stasis, Vauquois, bombarding, machine-gunning, and gassing the Germans while overrunning them from behind, and even continuing another 1.5 miles north-northwest, toward Varennes and Cheppy. Yes, they broke that horror and hurried on.

But now, when from a prominence of fossilized sandbags at Vauquois I gaze down into a steep narrow dugout connected to a tunnel, a beech tree outgrasping from the top and a cloud of midges expanding above my head, it seems the nightmare remains. In the grass around me, crowded by trees with singing birds, in dugouts with their side tunnels going who knows where, how much human craft, cunningly, maliciously employed to maim and murder still lies ready to harm? Yet I feel grateful that this is so. Here is one of the Great War's most accurate monuments.

At Cheppy, where there is now a Missouri Memorial, the 35th Division, assisted by Colonel George S. Patton's 304th Tank Brigade (Patton was wounded here), smashed through the Hindenburg Line. Varennes, where in 1791 Louis XVI and his family were captured in their coach, fell to the Americans by about 2 p.m., with the help of infantry, Renault tanks, and the 28th National Guard Division, known as the Pennsylvanians.

Hence the Pennsylvania Monument, a courtyardlike structure of white stone and concrete with a dark bell on an eagle-cornered plinth. Its motto runs: THE RIGHT IS MORE PRECIOUS THAN PEACE. It's a very pretty monument. Had I fought in the 28th, or wished to show appreciation for its men, I would doubtless be pleased. As it is, my preference on war memorials is this: Give me an honest graveyard anytime. Or give me that foul, barbed-wire-toothed hole in the ground, Vauquois. I don't want any sentiments.

11

At the beginning of the war, taking and holding territory up to the Meuse River involved "the toughest fighting" faced by Germany's northern armies. Now defending that ground against the advancing Allies, Ludendorff tried to return the favor. On September 27–28 he reinforced the sector with artillery and 20 new divisions. (Meanwhile he and Hindenburg informed the kaiser that it was most definitely time for an armistice.)

In 2018 a car carried me smoothly across the Meuse, which from the bridge appeared as flat and reflective as a pond. Time, work, and capital had smoothed out this place—twice. Doubtless there were relics to find not far off the road. American losses here had been horrendous, inciting brutal adaptations. For example, it cost "several thousand casualties" for one division to reduce Côte Dame Marie, "a central strongpoint of the *Kriemhilde Stellung*." And so we read of "squirrel squads" a hundred yards behind the first wave, to shoot snipers in the trees; of soldiers who bayoneted each German corpse to make sure it wasn't faking death.

The historian Edward Lengel describes what happened when a certain Major General Morton sent the 116th Regiment against "the worst death trap east of the Meuse," meeting German machine guns, artillery, and the new Fokker strafing planes: the heavy casualties "seemed to indicate that a change of tactics was in order, but Morton could think of only three solutions—more artillery, more men, and greater drive."

Pershing, his drive temporarily stalled, resumed the attack on October 4, fighting "hard." On October 29, the enemy withdrew finally to the west bank of the Meuse—yet another victory for all time. (Hitler's troops would return exactly there in 1940.)

All told, 1.2 million American soldiers suffered 122,000 casualties from the beginning of the offensive to the armistice. For me, at least, this detail casts a certain chill on the following sententious words from a book about the offensive: "Midwestern farm boys had become men. Men had become soldiers. And soldiers had become comrades." Well, they were all comrades here, for a fact. Had their war actually ended all wars, their deaths would have felt less futile to me.

But let's be cheerful: Back when the War would surely end all wars, the Allies broke through at Salonika, finally defeating the Bulgarians, and the Italians penetrated the Austrian lines.

On October 26, Ludendorff, who wished to fight on, discovered that his resignation had been accepted. On October 30 the kaiser, laying the groundwork for a narrative about a leftist-Jewish plot, said: "I would not dream of abandoning the throne because of a few hundred Jews and a thousand workers." He now got an even nastier shock than Ludendorff, being forced to flee that crude, cramped old wooden crown with its ribs like the remnant of a dissected onion and the squat cross on top. He lived in the Netherlands until his death in 1941—just long enough to enjoy a German honor guard posted outside his moated residence.

12

On November 1, the Germans fell back to their final position on the Hindenburg Line. On November 6, the Allies finally reduced Sedan, and sometime that month the Americans liberated Verdun!

And so finally came the armistice: November 11, 1918.

The event certainly deserves a celebratory citation. Here it is, courtesy of Corporal Harold Pierce, 28th Division, Second Army: "It seems so foolish to keep up the killing till the last minute. But the killing the artillery does is so impersonal and miles away. He [sic] cannot see the tortured, horrible looks of the slaughtered or feel the remorse the doughboy feels when he sees a man he has shot."

The Harvest

1

What brought about the happy victory? Shall we be reductionist? We could thank General Haig for attrition, or say "hurrah" to the Americans, or praise Marshal Foch's unifying command, or speak of technical developments, organizational learning, accidents. We all center the world around our own preoccupations. Lawrence of Arabia for his part asserted that "when Damascus fell, the Eastern War—probably the whole war—drew to an end." My own taste is drawn to *Weapons and Tactics'* particular simplification: "In 1918 tanks won a great war."

What then did the Great War accomplish? At least 8.5 million belligerents died, not to mention a mere 12 million or 13 million civilians. Some optimist somewhere must have pointed out that it kept the population down. The survivors had their own difficulties. In the words of *All Quiet on the Western Front*, "The war has ruined us for everything."

Am I too cynical about this war? In October 1918, a Croatian insurrectionist cried out: "The people rise in order to deliver freedom with their blood and over the whole world Wilson's principles enjoy victory." An independent Czechoslovakia came into being that same month; soon after, a free Poland. But in these nations, and likewise in the "new Romania swollen with ex-Hungarian territory," one-third of the people were deemed ethnically "other." (One result: continuing hatreds and atrocities.)

A hundred years later, Croatia had flickered through bygone Yugoslavia; Czechoslovakia had split; Poland, Hungary, and Romania had gone in and out of bondage, altered shape, and begun to swell with right-wing nationalisms. I see no guarantee of stability in their respective futures; in their pasts I cannot avoid seeing the Great War's heirs, Hitler and Stalin.

2

The victors did everything possible to prevent German rearmament. They did not stop there. Churchill, acknowledging that "the mortal need was Security at all costs and by all methods," still called certain terms of the Treaty of Versailles "malignant and silly . . . Nothing was reaped except ill-will."

It is human nature to demand vengeance for the killings of one's own, and the provocations of Germany's ruthlessness approached intolerability. The British diplomat Harold Nicholson reminds us that shortly after commencing peace negotiations with President Wilson, the Germans torpedoed the Irish mail boat *Leinster*, drowning more than 450 civilians. "This eleventh hour atrocity was fresh in people's minds," writes Nicholson. A month after the armistice, prominent British newspapers were calling for the kaiser's execution. Yet whatever its causes and excuses, the Treaty of Versailles, signed in 1919, was not diplomacy's finest hour. "The historian, with every justification, will come to the conclusion that we were very stupid men," Nicholson remarks. "I think we were."

Possibly worst of all was the treaty's infamous Article 231, the so-called War Guilt Clause, which made Germany accept all the blame. As late as 2001, Gary Sheffield insisted, "The German leadership wanted hegemony in Europe, and was prepared to go to war to achieve it." And so the War Guilt Clause "was, therefore, fundamentally correct." Whether or not that was so (what about Austria-Hungary?), it was certainly impolitic. For his part, Hitler in his speeches hammered away at the treaty and the traitorous Germans who had agreed to it. "You felt like dashing your head against the wall in despair over such people! They did not want to understand that Versailles was a shame and a disgrace." (Well, he sure straightened *them* out.)

Guderian, plausibly believing the Treaty of Versailles as being "conceived in a spirit of hate," was one of those who illicitly defied it. Lacking the opportunity to peer inside a tank before 1928, he made do with ersatz, drilling for the next war with tractors. "With this machine we essayed our tank company tactics," he wrote in his magnum opus, *Achtung-Panzer!*

He was on the spot in May 1940, urging Hitler to rush armored tank divisions back across the Meuse ahead of infantry and artillery. Over ground that had so recently sucked down the blood of General Pershing's soldiers drove the new "lightning war" the Blitzkrieg. As in Schlieffen's day, the watchword was haste. There was so much to do: liquidate hostages and Jews in Poland, prepare to invade England, then turn against the gullible Russian ally.

The First World War would be done over. The French were stunned. The Parisian filmmaker Ludovic Cantais, who had three great-uncles die in the First World War and a grandfather who lost an eye fighting it but gained a lifelong alcohol problem, told me: "The Second World War, it was not even like a war for the French —it was so quick." What he said next was particularly thought-provoking, because I had read so much about the allegedly self-deluded "appeasement" of Hitler by the Western democracies in 1938–1939. Hindsight's prophets loved to point out that resisting Hitler early could have saved lives and treasure.

Cantais said, "The First World War traumatized people so much. That was why they absolutely did not want to go to fight Hitler; they were so traumatized. The generation of 1914 was decimated, so they did not want to go. The conditions in the trenches were really sordid. There were rats, disease, fear. These young men, who had just started their own families, they came back crazy because of these crazy conditions they had lived in."

On June 22, 1940, Hitler, having taken France in six weeks behind Guderian's Panzer tank divisions and strafing aircraft, forced the French to sign a humiliating armistice in Marshal Foch's old railroad carriage, the very same one in which the armistice of 1918 had been signed, right there in the bucolic Compiègne Forest.

It may well be that no war is ever over. My French interviewees expressed horror when I asked when the next war with Germany might occur. But our species' abominable record suggests that sometime in the next 800 or even 200 years (if human beings persist on this earth so long) there will be another one, at which time the iron ghosts of the trenches will come shrieking back.

JASON WILSON

"The Greatest"

FROM *The Washington Post Magazine*

IT'S JUST AFTER DARK in Vancouver's downtown financial district, on a chilly autumn evening, and I'm gazing up at the twisting, triangular, neo-futurist Trump International Hotel & Tower, rising 63 stories and 616 feet into the air. If you're impressed by tall things, the Trump tower is pretty tall. But then I glance across West Georgia Street, at the Living Shangri-La tower, rising 62 stories but standing 659 feet tall. Which means that the Living Shangri-La is the tallest building here. For someone like Donald Trump who is obsessed with superlatives, it must be tough to have your name emblazoned on the second-tallest building in Vancouver.

From where I stand, the Trump International Hotel & Tower is not particularly welcoming. It's 7:30 p.m., but I see very few lights on the higher floors, and I wonder who lives in the darkened condominiums in the upper parts of the tower. Below the condos, the hotel occupies the first 15 floors. All over the outside of the property, there are large white bloblike sculptures, as if a giant sneezed.

I'm paying nearly $300 per night to stay in one of the 147 five-star hotel rooms in the tower. When I arrived to check in, I gawked at the two Lamborghini Diablos parked in front of the hotel entrance. After I got to my room, I tried on the robe embroidered with TRUMP, along with the Trump-branded shower cap, in my marble-tiled bathroom. At the Trump Champagne Lounge, I ate a "delectable playful bite"—a trio of not-all-that-delectable toothpicked sliders—and ended up only ordering a cheap by-the-glass sparkling wine, since bottles on the Trump Champagne Lounge's list range from $150 to $1,350. Throughout the lounge, which is interspersed with pillars that look like huge, gold-plated Jenga stacks, everyone else seemed to be speaking Chinese.

Earlier, I had a swim in the strange indoor pool that, late at night, transforms into a Vegas-style nightclub called Drai's; I draped a towel on an upholstered lounge banquette. Later, I was given very professional, very invigorating massage treatment at The Spa by Ivanka Trump™ (which "personifies her lifestyle, embarking on every endeavor with energy and passion, but always taking the time to pause, heal and recharge"). At the spa, a woman with an Eastern European accent asked me about my "intention" for today's treatment. "Calm, restore, or energize?" she asked.

"Energize?" I answered.

The notion of my "intention" had, frankly, been nagging at me. Not just at The Spa by Ivanka Trump™, but existentially. Over the past six weeks, I'd been traveling to Trump vacation properties around the world. I'd been to the Trump golf resort near Aberdeen, Scotland, to Trump Winery in Virginia, to the Trump hotel and tower in Panama City, and now here in Vancouver. Before that tour, over the summer, I'd visited the former Trump Taj Mahal in Atlantic City.

I wasn't traveling as an investigative reporter or a salacious Michael Wolff type. As a food and travel writer, my role as a contributor to the *Washington Post* has always been a minor, lighter-weight one. I'm someone who roves around and writes about craft beverages or artisan cheese or cigar culture or Spanish tapas or Scandinavian culinary movements—someone you'd turn to for a cocktail recipe or a bar recommendation, not political commentary. But at this point, Trump has been written about in every other genre of journalism: political, entertainment, financial, fashion, sports. Why not look at Trump, promiser of luxury experiences, through the eyes of a travel writer? My plan was to sleep in the various Trump hotels, experience the Trump amenities, wear the Trump robe and shower cap, eat in the Trump restaurants, drink in the Trump bars—no differently than when I anonymously visit and review any other establishment in the course of a travel or food article. Given the state of things, this might have been naive, but that's what I ended up doing.

On my second night in Vancouver—my final stop on this journey—I'm planning to eat at Mott 32, the "luxury Chinese" spot on the ground floor of the Trump hotel. Just as I'm about to walk back inside for dinner, a black SUV drives past with its passenger window lowered. A young woman leans out, waving two middle fingers and screaming at the top of her lungs: "F— you, Trump! F— you! F— you! F— you, Trump!" It's like the primal shriek of a banshee. I am one of only two people standing outside the entrance, so it feels like much of her hate is being directed at me. Since I am a paying customer here, perhaps that's her point.

After the SUV cruises on, the street is quiet again. A Trump employee standing nearby shrugs and opens the lobby door for me. His body language is similar to that of the bartender I chatted with at the Trump Champagne Lounge earlier, who grimaced when the name "Donald Trump" was uttered. "The property is actually owned by TA Global," the bartender said, making clear that the Trump brand is licensed. "It's like a franchise."

The $360 million hotel and condominium development was, in fact, funded by 38-year-old Joo Kim Tiah, whose family presides over the Malaysia-based financial and real estate empire TA Global. It's not clear exactly how much Tiah pays in fees to the Trump Organization. When the tower opened in February 2017, it was the first new Trump property since he assumed the presidency and announced he was stepping aside from day-to-day control to let his sons run the Trump Organization. Eric, Donald Jr., and even Tiffany joined Tiah at the ribbon cutting, along with a group of protesters singing "O Canada" and carrying signs reading DUMP TRUMP outside amid the white blobs.

Who was not in attendance was the mayor of Vancouver and other prominent officials. "Trump's name and brand have no more place on Vancouver's skyline than his ignorant ideas have in the modern world," Mayor Gregor Robertson wrote in a letter to Tiah. A city council member, Kerry Jang, called the tower "a beacon of intolerance" and said it had "bad karma."

At Mott 32, the dining room is completely full and I'm seated at the bar. Mott 32 is the North American outpost of a famous Hong Kong restaurant, which has another location forthcoming in Bangkok. A critic for the *Globe and Mail* newspaper called it "the most noteworthy restaurant to open in Vancouver for many years." The Filipino bartender explains that the majority of the clientele in Mott 32 speaks Mandarin and is wealthy. Scanning the full dining room, I can believe it. At the table in front of me, a waiter carves the $95 Peking duck for a Chinese family, with several chil-

dren playing on their iPads. That Peking duck is not even close to
the most expensive dish on the menu: A whole suckling pig costs
$495; braised whole dried fish maw, in abalone sauce, is listed
at $580. (Canadian dollars, but still.) I order a few of the more
affordable small dishes from the "Evening Dim Sum" menu: an
unexceptional duck spring roll, some hot-and-sour Shanghai-style
soup dumplings, which are surprisingly tasty, and a black truffle
siu mai with Ibérico pork and a soft quail egg, served at room temperature, that is just too ambitious to be anything but disappointing. The bartender makes a little joke when he serves the *siu mai:*
"Be careful about the egg inside. It's a soft yolk and you don't want
it all over your shirt."

I tell the bartender about the screaming protester who'd driven
by outside, and he looks pained. "Ah, politics," he says with a sigh.
"I have friends that tell me, 'Well, we can't visit you now because
you work at that place.'" He adds, somberly: "This property is
owned by TA Global, not Trump."

Back in my room, still hungry, I open a container of honey
roasted peanuts ($8) and a Mexican beer ($11) from the mini-
bar, flip on CNN, and lie on the bed watching reports on the first
indictments in the Mueller investigation. As a jaded travel writer,
someone who has stayed in many soulless hotels and eaten in
many overpriced restaurants in many disappointing places, I'm
completely at ease with a certain exquisite idleness and ennui. But
there's something profoundly unsettling about the sort of boredom that I've been feeling in the Trump properties over the past
many weeks.

To be clear, none of my experience has been terrible, and some
of it has been pleasant. Mostly, though, I've been overwhelmed by
a relentless, insistent, in-your-face mediocrity: the scolding "Notice
to Guests" in my room at the Trump MacLeod House & Lodge
in Scotland, warning that I will be charged punitively if I take the
lint brush, shoehorn, coasters, or other Trump-branded amenities;
the strange card displayed in my room at the Albemarle Estate in
Charlottesville explaining that "countryside stink bugs" will "occasionally be found" inside; the jar of stale chocolate chip cookies
I'm told was the only food available later at night; the eerie near
emptiness and peeling paint of the Trump International Hotel &
Tower in Panama, touted as the tallest building in Central America. And it's this mediocrity that's the most disquieting.

I think about the woman earlier this evening who screamed from her SUV, yelling at those of us who happened to be standing in front of the silent, cold, glistening tower. It was a little over-the-top. I suspect that this type of white-hot outrage and hysteria will eventually cool. I also suspect that the era of Trump will pass soon enough. When that happens, what terrifies me is not that Trump's presidency will have ended up as an exploding, burning disaster —but rather that it will have become something dangerously luke-warm, seeping into our identity. Kind of like that black truffle *siu mai* with the quail egg inside, served room temperature, with the soft yolk that threatens to ooze down the shirt of the person who ordered it.

I'm wandering the ghostly hallway of the 50th floor, the high roll-ers' floor, of what was once the Trump Taj Mahal Hotel and Casino in Atlantic City. Tables, lampshades, hangers, broken chairs, and other pieces of furniture line the peeling walls. In some places the carpet is soaked.

The penthouse suite has been emptied of all its contents, save for an ironing board. A window treatment is dangling from its rod, and the wallpaper is separating from the wall, revealing what seems to be black mold. The mirrored fireplace and two faux-classical pil-lars stand pathetically naked in the center of the suite.

It's July 2017, nine months after the Taj shut its doors in Oc-tober 2016. This is the third week of a liquidation sale run by National Content Liquidators, and the public has been invited to rummage around the 1,200 guest rooms, to buy anything with a yellow tag. Men are loading furniture into Ryder trucks near the entrance, close to the gilded elephants, in the shadow of the Taj's onion-domed towers that always looked more Russian than Indian.

Inside, it's clear that most everything of value went in the early days of the sale. Apparently, I've missed out on several "Hand Embroidered Burmese Thai Kalaga Tapestries" and a baby grand piano. HIDE-A-BED SOLD OUT, a handwritten sign announces. But there are still plenty of cheetah-print dining chairs, $16 each.

Near the old casino floor, I walk by a large man wearing a TRUMP-PENCE T-shirt, reclining on a leopard-print fainting couch tagged for $125. "Comfortable?" I ask.

"Yeah, not too bad," he says. "But the really comfortable ones are over there. The ones where you lay all the way back." He points a few feet away. "See, that one. Sit on that."

It's hard to believe that this place was hyped as the "eighth wonder of the world" when it opened back in 1990. At the time it was the world's largest casino, as well as the tallest building in New Jersey. But within 15 months of its opening, the Taj filed for Chapter 11 bankruptcy protection. By 2009, after another bankruptcy, Trump had sold most of his ownership in the casinos that bore his name. After another bankruptcy filing by the company that ran the Taj Mahal, Trump finally sold his remaining ownership, reported to be less than 10 percent.

Now, from the 50th floor, through the dirt-smudged windows, you can look all the way down the Boardwalk at what casinos remain in Atlantic City. Five of the 12 closed between 2014 and 2016. From this high up, looking out past the beach, toward the ocean, things don't look so bad. But the view on the ground is of a different, grimmer reality.

I'm from southern New Jersey, and standing in the ruins of the Taj Mahal is profoundly depressing for me. I think about all of the jobs in this vacant building that have been lost; some of my family members have worked for the Trump casinos. One relative won't talk openly about it with me, still fearing a nondisclosure agreement she signed two decades ago. I actually began my journalism career, in 1992, as a reporter at the *Press of Atlantic City.* This was the moment when the Trump casinos had just emerged from the first of their bankruptcy reorganizations, and Trump still presented himself as a sort of ruling monarch of Atlantic City, helicoptering in from Manhattan occasionally to express his disapproval with how the town was being run. It's mostly forgotten now, but Trump's second Atlantic City casino, opened in 1985, was originally, and unironically, named Trump's Castle.

I remember one speech he gave at a local business luncheon in the spring of 1992, right when I started my job. He told the gathering that Atlantic City needed to "clean up its act" and excoriated officials for funneling money into "unneeded low-income housing" rather than beautifying the entrance to the city "so it won't look like you're coming into a slum." Trump hated us at the *Press.* "They kill us every day," he told the business gathering, bemoaning that we couldn't be more like the newspapers in Las

Vegas; the Vegas papers, he said, "didn't talk about most casinos losing money." Trump was always looking for someone to blame for his casinos' lack of profitability. He was obsessed with the rising competition from legalized gambling in other parts of the country —from Louisiana, from Connecticut, and especially from Native American casinos. "I think I might have more Indian blood than a lot of the so-called Indians that are trying to open up the reservations," he once told radio host Don Imus. Perhaps it's perfect irony that the Taj Mahal will soon be replaced by a Hard Rock Hotel & Casino, owned by the Seminole Tribe of Florida.

I exit the Taj Mahal and cross the Boardwalk to the Steel Pier. It's pretty quiet for a sunny July afternoon, with the amusement rides about a third full. A young woman with a Russian accent at the Krazyballs game holds a microphone and says, "Everyone's a winner!" over and over again, but no one comes to play.

As anyone who has seen HBO's *Boardwalk Empire* knows, the Steel Pier, opened in 1898, was once the classic landmark of Atlantic City—hosting Miss America pageants, dance marathons, and musical acts ranging from John Philip Sousa to Diana Ross. But the diving horse act—that is, a horse diving off the pier into the ocean—is what the Steel Pier's fame, or infamy, rested upon.

The pier closed in 1978, was destroyed by a fire in 1982, and a decade later was reopened, by Donald Trump, who suggested with much fanfare that he was reviving Atlantic City's glory days. Then, during the summer of 1993, it was announced that the diving horse act would be revived. The world, however, had changed. The diving horse act was now met by an angry crowd of animal rights activists, carrying signs that read DONALD TRUMP PROMOTES ANIMAL CRUELTY and chanting "Donald Trump, stop the jump!"

I covered one of the opening nights of the diving horse act for the *Press,* getting reaction from activists, from pier workers, and from people on the Boardwalk. I walked to the end of the Steel Pier to watch the act. All of us in the crowd looked skyward at a raised platform. That's where we saw a "horse" slowly led out onto a plank. It soon became clear that the diving horse was not actually a horse. It was a mule. And it was not going to jump into the ocean, but rather 15 feet down into a pool of water.

The diving mule act went on throughout the summer. Then, with only three days left before the season ended, Trump blew into town to hold a news conference at the pier. He told the assembled television cameras that the diving mule act would be canceled, never to return. Further, Trump claimed to have never really liked the act anyway. Though, he said, "from a purely money standpoint, it was successful." Even People for the Ethical Treatment of Animals joined him at the news conference, with a sign that read DON-ALD, THE ANIMALS THANK YOU.

The following summer, when the Taj Mahal hosted the Moscow Circus for a six-week run, the mob of animal rights activists returned, angry as ever at Trump—now over the alleged mistreatment of the circus's elephants and bears. This time, protesters dropped a half ton of animal feces at the entrance to the Taj Mahal.

Early the next morning, I walk from the Taj Mahal down the Boardwalk to the completely abandoned Trump Plaza. Here, every mention of Trump has long been removed from the building, and grass now grows up through the pavement of the empty parking lots and entranceways. The Plaza will soon be demolished. At the ground floor, from the Boardwalk, you can still look into the dirty windows of Evo Restaurant and see that the tables—now covered with debris—were set for a dinner service in 2014 that never happened. I sit on a bench in a little area across from Boardwalk Hall, which is right next to the former Trump Plaza. There's a monument here erected by the local unions in the 1980s to remember "those who lost their lives while working on the redevelopment of Atlantic City." Legalized casino gaming was supposed to be the city's savior. Sitting here looking at the ghostly shell of Trump Plaza is like the final word, showing once and for all that the casinos were not the savior. Today, Atlantic City just limps along as always, dazed and confused by endless promises, sales pitches, and big talk. It was the perfect place for Donald Trump, someone who would promise you the spectacle of a horse diving into the ocean, and then deliver a mule diving into a swimming pool.

David Milne flies the Mexican flag from atop his home, a former coast guard station that sits on a hill above Trump International Golf Links in Aberdeenshire, Scotland. Milne identifies with Mexico's current plight because adjacent to his yard is a fence that Trump built and then sent him the bill for (more than $3,500, which he threw in the trash). This was back in 2009, when Trump was constructing his golf course on the environmentally sensitive sand dunes and harassing several of his neighbors in the village of Balmedie.

It's a September day in Scotland, sunny one moment, overcast and drizzling the next, with waves of driving rain in between, all of it buffeted by a cold wind off the North Sea. In the distance, we can see working ships, likely heading back and forth to oil rigs. Milne, a health-and-safety consultant for the oil industry who has been living here for 25 years, says the area's been hit hard. Nearly 100,000 people have lost their jobs since oil prices tanked.

The course at Trump International Golf Links is nearly empty. Milne says it's like this almost every day. We see one foursome and some maintenance workers on a hole in the distance. I note that the parking lot still looks half-full. Milne corrects me. "That's actually only half the parking area," he says. "There's another half over there." That half is empty. So only a quarter of the parking lot is full. "And there's actually more cars here today than usual."

Trump came to Aberdeenshire with a lot of promises: 6,000 jobs, 1,450 homes, and millions for the local economy. Nothing near that has happened, and Trump's two golf courses in Scotland are losing a lot of money. Neither has turned a profit since he poured more than $200 million into both Trump International Golf Links and the famed Turnberry course (which he acquired in 2014) on the Ayrshire coast, an hour from Glasgow. The course here in Aberdeenshire lost nearly $2 million in 2016, and the Scottish government recently blocked Trump's attempt to build a new course on the dunes, according to multiple news sources. (The Trump Organization did not respond to a request for comment.)

The employees at Trump's MacLeod House & Lodge, the baronial mansion on the property that's been turned into a five-star hotel, tell me the season is "winding down"—even though I'm paying what the website terms a "High Season" rate of nearly $350 per night. In any case, the hotel has few guests and is unnervingly quiet. Everyone else I talk to in Aberdeenshire says that in Scotland the golf season never really ends, and many of the more than 50 other golf courses in Aberdeenshire stay open all winter.

The few people who have paid to play Trump's course today are mostly inside the Dunes Restaurant & Bar, which is sparsely filled. I order a lunch of "haggis bonbons" with "whisky mayonnaise"; the

Golf Channel is on mute in the background. It's so quiet in the Dunes that I can clearly hear a foursome of older American men a few tables away, involved in a numbingly boring conversation about the rain during their round, which apparently really started coming down on their back nine.

"It wasn't so bad," says one guy. "At least I didn't shoot a fifty!" (Which apparently he had shot on the front nine.)

"Yeah," says his friend. "But I just don't want my handicap to go up."

"Well," says another, "it's hard to convert what you do over here."

"Really? I don't see how it's any different to swing a golf club here as at home."

I'm not a golfer, but I've been to enough golf clubs to know that the 19th hole at the Dunes isn't really all that impressive. Not that there's anything particularly wrong with it (with the possible exception of the haggis bonbons, which are wrong in several ways). Mostly, it's just sort of crushingly average. Maybe it's the generic newness of the place, which was built a little over five years ago —all browns and maroons and sea foam green. It looks no different than plenty of similar golf clubs I've been to for weddings and youth sports banquets back home in South Jersey.

After I finish my haggis bonbons, I zip up my jacket and head outside into the wind and drizzle, wandering up a path toward the tees. As I look out over the dunes toward the sea, I see no one on the course. But I do see a gold-lettered plaque, affixed to a pole, commemorating the opening of this course "conceived and built by Donald J. Trump" in 2012. The plaque reads: "Encompassing the world's largest dunes, The Great Dunes of Scotland, Mr. Trump and his architect, Dr. Martin Hawtree, delicately wove these magnificent golf holes through this unparalleled 600 acre site running along the majestic North Sea. The unprecedented end result is, according to many, the greatest golf course anywhere in the world!"

To be clear, in the latest rankings by both *Golf* and *Golf Digest* magazines, Trump's course in Aberdeenshire is listed, respectively, at 46th and 54th in the world—certainly pretty good, but far enough from what most people would term "the greatest." Further, the "Great Dunes" referenced are part of a natural area called the

Sands of Forvie, which is actually the fifth-largest dune system in
Britain. It is not even close to the world's tallest dunes—Namibia,
Chile, Peru, and several other countries have dunes that are five
or more times as tall.

Since his business arrived in Scotland, Trump has clashed with
locals over an offshore wind farm project and been mired in con-
troversy over whether he's damaged the environment. But oddly,
after reading so much about the Scottish disdain for Trump, I
didn't find too many people beyond Milne and his neighbors who
expressed negativity toward him. "Regardless of what you think of
the man, the golf course is beautiful," said a manager at the White
Horse Inn, about five minutes down the road, where I stayed one
night before checking into my lavish Trump room. "Yes, it's an
American's interpretation of a traditional Scottish links course.
But it's a beautiful course. I love playing there. The man loves golf
and knows golf." This was a prevalent sentiment I heard: Trump's
owning a course in Aberdeenshire was good for everyone's business. "He's been a good boy here," said the taxi driver who took
me to a pub called Brig O' Don in a nearby town. "He's done what
he said he'd do."

The only other person I'd encountered with a truly negative
word for Trump was the Pakistani taxi driver who drove me to
MacLeod House. "I think he's rubbish. He's a crazy man. Why did
you Americans vote for him?" And then, as if to answer his own
question, he said: "Do you know that sixteen million Americans
actually believe that chocolate milk comes from brown cows?"

Back at my room at MacLeod House & Lodge, I lie under a
gaudy, crown-shaped headboard, on a tartan pillow and a shiny
gold bedspread, and watch CNN coverage of the Russia investigation. Right outside my room, there is a framed photo on the wall
of Donald Trump on the cover of the Russian-language edition of
Rolling Stone. The name "Trump" is branded on so many things
in my room: slippers, coasters, lint brush, toiletries in the pink-
marbled bathroom.

That evening I have a few drinks in the clubby whisky bar in the
cozy lobby of the main guesthouse. There are shelves with dozens
of fine Scotch whiskies here, truly an amazing selection. The guy
who drives the shuttle bus to the golf course is also the bartender,
and he pours me an Isle of Jura 16, a Highland Park 18, and a

special Royal Lochnagar "distillers edition" that's finished in old muscat casks.

I'm joined in the whisky bar by four blokes from Liverpool who are here on a golf holiday. They're the only other people in the hotel besides a couple I overheard speaking Russian in the breakfast room. All of them are enthusiastic about the course; after a couple of whiskies, I ask one guy if the Trump association with the course bothered him at all. "My wife said, 'Why would you give that man any of your money?' And I told her, 'Because it's a really nice place!' Honestly, I don't like him, but what was the choice anyway? Hillary Clinton?"

"I own, actually, one of the largest wineries in the United States. It's in Charlottesville." Thus boasted President Trump after a news conference at Trump Tower in August, in which he addressed questions about the clash between white supremacists and those protesting a statue of Robert E. Lee that resulted in a neo-Nazi allegedly killing a woman with his car. There were "very fine people on both sides," he said.

Perhaps unsurprisingly, Trump does not in fact own one of the largest wineries in the country. His is one of about 9,000 wineries in the United States that produce less than 50,000 cases per year. By contrast, at least 65 American wineries produce more than 500,000 cases a year.

A month after my time in Scotland, I'm standing at the bar of the Trump Winery tasting room, just 14 minutes down the road from Jefferson's Monticello and a half mile up Blenheim Road from Dave Matthews's Blenheim Vineyards. It's a sunny autumn Sunday, and plenty of people are taking advantage of the winery's "designated picnic area" and its lovely views. The tasting room is packed, and there's a security guard scanning the crowd. Behind me, a man has spilled a bottle of red wine down the front of him, and a woman is spritzing him with a water bottle. "Can I taste the sparkling rosé?" the young woman next to me asks. No, she's told. She has to be a member of Trump Winery's Wine Club to taste the sparkling rosé.

I've paid $15 for a tasting of five wines. The wine, as *Washington Post* wine critic Dave McIntyre has written, is "pretty good." Though certainly not all of it. The sparkling blanc de blancs and the mildly oaked chardonnay are the most promising; the "meritage" Bordeaux blend and the cabernet sauvignon are fruit bombs and sort of meh; and the cru dessert wine that's aged in Jack Daniel's barrels is a sweet-toothache disaster.

I'm having trouble concentrating on the wines because the big screen above the tasting bar is playing a series of videos. The volume is muted, but there is sweeping footage of the vines, glamorous images of weddings, and shots of the winemakers. Every once in a while, Eric Trump pops onto the screen—arriving at the estate in the Trump helicopter, touring the grounds, or talking to the camera. I recall that Eric and his siblings have been put in charge of the day-to-day operations of the Trump Organization. When the videos end and switch to the next, you can see the video file names. One of them clearly reads "DJT edited out."

After the tasting, I drive up to the Albemarle Estate, the 26,000-square-foot, 45-room manor house that Trump has converted into a luxury boutique hotel. The Albemarle Estate was built in the 1980s by the late billionaire John Kluge (at one time the richest man in America) and his third wife, Patricia Kluge, who also owned the winery. After a divorce and John Kluge's death, Patricia fell on hard times, defaulted on loans, and was facing foreclosure. Though she had originally been asking $100 million for the estate, in 2012 Trump swooped in and picked up the place for a mere $6.2 million.

The guest rooms are all named after US presidents from Virginia, and I'm staying in Monroe (there's also Washington, Jefferson, Madison, and so on). The rooms at the Albemarle Estate are even more over-the-top than at the other Trump properties: an ornate gold-trimmed bed with the same crownlike headboard as in Scotland; shelves with such knickknacks as a leather satchel, an old pipe, and a pewter goblet. Gold accents, such as a gold soap dish, glisten throughout the bathroom. And the branding, even for a Trump property, borders on absurd. Here, besides the robe, the slippers, and the toiletries, I get Trump mouthwash and a Trump hair comb.

Then, on the desk, is the pièce de résistance: the huge, lavishly illustrated *Trump Magazine*. Amid the breathless travel features—on the Trump golf courses, on "A Day in the Life of a Trump Bride," on food and drink at Trump-owned destinations, on the Trump Cookie at the golf club in Bedminster, New Jersey, on Wine by the

Crystal Spoon at the lounge at the Trump hotel in Washington
—there are "exclusive interviews" with Donald Trump Jr. and Eric
Trump. In the Q&A with Donald Jr., he's asked: "If you had to
give advice to a high school student, what would it be?" His reply:
"If you always go with your instincts and never second-guess yourself, you will set yourself up for enormous success." Don Jr. is then
asked, "What would you change about your life if you could?" He
says, "I am really lucky so I would not change anything. But if I did
change anything, I would add more hours to the day."

At 6 p.m., there is a tour of the estate grounds, given by the
hotel manager; I gather with a half dozen other guests. The tour
mixes practicalities with what I guess we might call the "historical."
Since the Albemarle Estate dates to only the 1980s and has had
one owner before Trump, the big themes espoused by the guide
appear to be: (A) how crazily spendthrift the Kluges were, and how
that led to their financial ruin; and (B) what a cunning and opportunistic businessman Donald Trump is for acquiring this $100 mil-
lion mansion for only $6.2 million. "Mrs. Kluge tried to build the
winery all at once, and it bankrupted her," says our guide. "She's a
very tragic woman." ("She is neither tragic nor a spendthrift, and
the vineyard and winery were built over many years," said William
Moses, Kluge's current husband, in a response.)

We walk through hallways plastered with gaudy wallpaper that
looks like a Roman toga hanging on a curtain rod, and we gaze out
the big windows at the faux-classical sculptures and faux-English
hedges and fountains in a garden that appears as if it were dreamt
up by a Mafia don pretending to be a British aristocrat. We wander
down a grand hallway that looks like a Jersey McMansion version
of Versailles imagined by Donatella Versace, and our guide shows
us busts of Jefferson and Washington. "They're working on busts
of all the Virginia presidents," he says.

Someone asks, with a chuckle, "Is one of Trump next?" The
manager smiles and shrugs his shoulders. Later, in the theater,
we see framed photos of Trump with celebrities like Sylvester Stallone, Christian Bale, and Michael Douglas—as well as Trump on
the covers of a *Billionaire* magazine from 2004 and a Forbes 400
"Richest People in America" issue from 2003. It doesn't seem impossible that a Trump bust is forthcoming.

Numerous times throughout the tour, the manager says things
like "Trump did this" or "Trump did that" in renovating the man-

sion. At one point, one of the men on the tour speaks up and says, "Now, you mean Eric Trump, right? Doesn't he run this property now?"

"Yes, yes," says the manager. "Of course."

The tour ends at the pool house, and the manager asks if we have any questions. "Pool towels?" says one woman. "Where are those?"

"Oh, there's a restroom right around the corner, and there's a bunch of pool towels in the closet," he says. "Basically, this is y'all's house while you're here." That may be because the Albemarle Estate is being run on a skeleton staff, and we're sort of on our own.

When someone asks if we can eat here this evening, we're told no, the closest restaurants are 20 minutes away in downtown Charlottesville. A couple, who presumably have been tasting wine all afternoon—and have likely paid anywhere from $350 to $500 per night—look at each other with exasperated expressions. The only food made available that evening was a jar of chocolate chip cookies, offered by the lone night manager.

After I return later from Charlottesville, I grab a pool cue from under a bust of Julius Caesar and shoot some billiards on the big red table while I watch a football game on television. I'm surrounded by bookshelves that seem to have been curated by a decorator who just said, "Get me some books!" There are leather-bound volumes of Virginia law codes dating to the 1950s and Reader's Digest Condensed Books filling some shelves. Novels by Tom Clancy, John Grisham, Dan Brown, and David Baldacci stand on the same shelf as Colin Powell's *My American Journey*. *Robert E. Lee: The Man and the Soldier* is stacked between *The Complete Vegetable & Herb Gardener* and *The Home Book of Trees and Shrubs*. Dinesh D'Souza's *Obama's America: Unmaking the American Dream* and William McGowan's *Coloring the News: How Crusading for Diversity Has Corrupted American Journalism* are shelved near *America's Women* by Gail Collins and, by B. H. Sumner, *A Short History of Russia*.

It's a balmy night in Panama City, and I'm having a rum at the bar of the largely empty Ocean Sun Casino, which is next door to the largely empty Trump International Hotel & Tower Panama, where I'm staying. I'm talking with a friendly young Frenchman who's telling me about his life here as a bitcoin trader. Apparently, he's moved to Panama because of the favorable tax situation for his line of work. Tomorrow, he says, he'll be moving into a condo in the Trump tower, which he says he's rented very cheaply. (The Trump Organization is not the owner of this tower, but it has managed the hotel property since its opening.)

I met him a little earlier at the blackjack table—the only table where there was much buzz or activity. I sat between him and a Russian guy in a white jacket who kept giving everyone at the table unsolicited advice on when to take a hit and when to stay. At the other end of the table was a silent, serious-faced Asian man. In between the Asian man and my French friend was a woman who may or may not have been a prostitute. Prostitution is legal in Panama, and my French friend tells me that "every woman in this bar is probably a prostitute."

He shows me various market trackers on his smartphone. "I buy on leverage," he says. "Some days I spend thirty hours looking at the screen. If I see the market dip, even if I've had a lot to drink, I'll have to go home and start trading.

"Banking is crazy here," he says.

"So is it like Switzerland?" I ask.

"Switzerland? This is way worse than Switzerland. There are over two hundred banks in this city. There's so much money flowing through here."

I have no idea if what my French friend is telling me is true —and I'll never see him again during my stay in Panama—but if he is really moving into a condo in the Trump tower, he'll be one of the few who will actually be residing there.

The Trump tower is just one of numerous looming, mostly empty-looking towers in this city. In the evenings, the tropical darkness falls quickly, and even at seven or eight, there are many 50- or 60-story buildings that have fewer than a dozen lights on. Looking from the balcony of my Trump hotel room, the darkened Panama City skyline looks very much like a futuristic dystopia or a malevolent city-state in a sci-fi film, perhaps the metropolis in *Blade Runner*.

Every time I come up or down to my hotel floor, I see no one except cleaning people. The pool bar is completely empty, all day long. At dinner in the cavernous Tejas seafood restaurant, where I am served possibly the most embarrassing ceviche I've ever seen —rather than ceviche, it was like a Central American version of that rubbery suburban country-club classic, the shrimp cocktail—I sit at the empty long bar while diners occupy only a smattering of tables. About the only places with any activity are the fitness room, where I saw a half dozen women working out, and the infinity pool, overlooking the Pacific, where a handful of women lay out in the sun, some watching their children swim.

On the ground floor is an arcade of stores, with at least a dozen vacant spaces. Walking the arcade by day, I count nine real estate offices, two travel agencies, a Mail Boxes Etc., a beauty salon, an "Italian spa," a jewelry store, a cigar shop, Deluca Euro Café, and a gift shop selling snacks, booze, souvenirs, and "Genuine Panama Hats." I see no customers at any of the establishments. A sign is posted in the window of the Trump Ocean Club office that reads: "Hot Deals . . . Divorce Sale . . . Investor Must Liquidate Trump Ocean Club Portfolio . . . Take advantage of this one-time fire sale of assets in Trump Ocean Club. Prices start in the $200,000s."

Outside, I sit on a seawall. All I can hear is the gentle ripple of the Pacific Ocean. I have the same feeling I had on the Boardwalk in Atlantic City, at the golf course at Balmedie, and tasting the oaky wines in Virginia. Nothing was bad, and much of what I was experiencing was even pleasurable. But these were not great places. These places didn't even seem like they were trying to be great. I look up at the tower itself. It's extremely worn for a six-year-old building, with cracks, black smudges, and what looks like rust and mold. I wonder how much longer the Trump name will be emblazoned on this tower in Panama. Only six weeks from now, the Trump name will be removed from its hotel in New York's SoHo. And in late February an ongoing legal dispute between the Trump Organization and the Panama City building's majority owner will turn into an ugly physical altercation, with Panamanian police storming the tower.

So many people make dire warnings and predictions about Trump, about what will happen to the country once he's finished being president, full of apocalyptic gloom and doom. But what if all that happens is that the country becomes more like his vacation properties? What happens if, after all the shouting and crying and offending and accusing and bragging and deregulating and delegitimizing, America's reputation simply becomes defined as relentlessly mediocre? Perhaps in the great *Golf Digest*–like ranking of nations, the United States drops from being one of the top countries to being, say, the 46th or 54th best in the world.

I don't have sunglasses, and I'm getting sunburned, so I wander back inside the tower. It's lunchtime, so I take the elevator up to the BARcelona Tapas Restaurant & Bar, which, according to the Trump marketing copy, offers "an experience unparalleled in all of Latin America." The outdoor garden patio is closed today, and inside it's empty except for one other table of four. I order the same basic albariño I could have ordered back home, followed by a trio of pork sliders. Middling at best.

JESSICA YEN

Tributary

FROM *Fourth Genre*

WHEN DAD WAS in elementary school in central Taiwan, he would sometimes recite, *"Woshi Zhejiangsheng Yuyaoxian ren."* My family is from Yuyao County, Zhejiang Province, China. Xiahe Yanjia. The "village Yen," next to the "river Xia." I can see him now, wearing what I imagine to be the standard Taiwanese school uniform of the 1950s: blue shorts, grubby white shirt, skin dark from summers spent outside, hands clasped behind his back. He stands next to a peeling desk as he chants out his paternal lineage, the teacher ready with a ruler in case he misbehaves. According to family lore, we sprang from a well-to-do branch of the Yen family tree when a wealthy merchant married off a daughter to a man in a neighboring village. Upon hearing her new town lacked a convenient source of water, he bragged, "I'll bring the water to you." For her dowry, he commissioned a canal to siphon water from the neighboring river and divert it to her new home. The village was thus named Yen Family Village, and it was in this town in southeastern China that we originated.

My grandparents fled China when the Communists took over in 1949, and for years Dad longed to seek out the family village. In particular, he wished to pay tribute to the village shrine where the members of each generation are recorded. He wanted to fill in the lineage of Yens transplanted to American soil, and to inscribe female names within the shrine for the first time. He mentioned this in passing every couple of years, and as my brother, Michael, grew older, the idea took hold with him as well. Michael had romantic visions of a triumphant return to the village, and to a land none of us had known (Dad was born just as his parents left China). Yet I was the first in our nuclear family to live within geographic proximity to the family village, when I accepted a research fellowship in China in 2005, straight out of college.

My interest in Chinese began early, when my parents enrolled me in a bilingual immersion program to learn a language my mother barely knew and which we thus did not speak at home. It was the 1980s, when Japan held America's interest and China was the boonies, and my parents were lucky to find one of the nation's first Mandarin immersion programs, a school so young there were just 56 students spread over eight grades. Thanks in part to my early introduction to the language, I have always loved Chinese.

Yet I was also drawn to it because our household was so much more assimilated than those of my first- and second-generation Chinese American peers, and learning Chinese felt like the single component I could control. In the Bay Area it felt like everyone else's parents cooked Chinese food, spoke to their children in Chinese, went to temple or Chinese-language church, and got their news from Chinese TV channels or newspapers. And for all that my peers scoffed at their parents for being "so Asian!" they also scorned those who were "not Asian enough," who didn't speak Chinese well or know which non-Americanized dishes to order. This assumption of shared experience, though intended to build community through commonality, served to flatten the Chinese American experience, for it narrowed the archetypes and paths that were expected, or even allowed.

None of my peers understood the third-generation quandary. Once you're several generations removed from your cultural heritage, how much connection is truly possible? Bits and pieces might be integrated into home life—a cultural event here, some ethnic food there—but for the most part the upbringing is American. I craved acceptance, and thus Chinese slowly became the center of my universe as I attempted to study my way to a cultural fluency that others osmosed from their home environment. I majored in Chinese literature and then, still seeking to become Chinese enough, I moved to China.

Thus presented with an opportunity to resurrect the dream of finding the ancestral village, Michael and Dad flew out to visit me.

Although I had little interest in the village itself, by this point I was nearing one year in China and had realized my best adventures came from unexpected missions and random opportunities. A trip to the family village seemed ripe with possibility.

When I met them at the Beijing airport, I'd recently had my hair cut and styled by the neighborhood barber, and Michael had to point me out in the crowd. "Where, where?" Dad kept asking. Michael rolled his eyes at me over Dad's head as he punched Dad in mock horror, then leaned forward to give me a hug.

This was Dad's first time backpacking in China, so we decided to take him to the shop my Chinese friend had recommended, not the tourist trap filled with the cheap knockoff packs that most Westerners used, but a local store with Chinese brands. Dad looked around for a cab. Michael feigned embarrassment at his actions and pushed him down the road instead. "Bus or subway?" Michael asked me.

I led them through the intricate maze of narrow streets surrounding my apartment. Michael had visited me before, so the chaos of neighborhood life was a familiar sight, but Dad had only ever seen China from tour buses cruising the main boulevards. We passed cyclo drivers playing cards out of the back of a bicycle cart, laborers jackhammering in the middle of the street, aunties fanning themselves in the afternoon heat. Dad ogled glistening red candied haw strung 10 to a stick. We passed a vendor making Beijing crepes smothered in green onion, egg, sesame seeds, and hot sauce, then folded around a slab of crispy fried dough. "Oh . . . but diarrhea," Dad mumbled sadly, patting his stomach and looking about hopefully, perhaps wondering how soon the bacteria in his gut would acclimate.

As I watched Dad's reactions, I realized how much China had become home. Bareheaded construction workers who padded along bamboo scaffolding in canvas shoes seemed normal to me, but Dad kept commenting about the lack of protective headgear; how this soft, pliable, cheap footwear would offer no shield from an errant blade or nail.

We ducked down a side street filled with small stalls. Around the time I left for college, Michael and Dad developed a clowning relationship built on snarky banter, and they always made me laugh, but now I noticed how their presence overtook the entire sidewalk. Their laughter was too loud for China, their speech too forceful. Even their manner of walking seemed overly confident, aggressive even. I wondered if I'd once moved through Beijing like this, and if that's what natives had reacted to in my early weeks here, when everyone stared at me wherever I went.

Slightly embarrassed at their American way of moving through this Chinese space, I slowly allowed myself to drift behind them.

An auntie in a bright blue polyester vest rushed at Dad. "Hello!" She waved a fake-silver watch. "Very good price!"

They kept moving. When she was out of earshot, Michael turned to me. "How come she didn't attack you?"

Dad nodded in confusion as he looked me over. I shrugged. "Maybe it's the haircut and clothing," I offered as an excuse. It seemed the gentler—perhaps more Chinese—thing to do, provide a half-truth to spare their feelings. Yet it startled me that I could pass for Chinese in ways Dad could not, and that his antennae had not yet picked up on these distinctions. Dad had always been my benchmark for the degree of Chineseness I could hope to attain. He was the one who helped me with my Chinese homework, and he'd always understood the parts of Chinese movies that I did not.

We had almost reached our destination when we stepped into a small store that sold Great Wall replicas and miniature Chairman Mao busts. The vendor swooped over to greet us.

"It's so hot outside—you really should buy one of these fans." She prodded Dad toward a row of gaudy accordion fans marketed to tourists.

"Oh, but this one is so much better," he said as he stationed himself in front of an electric fan that cooled the store, opening his arms wide in exuberant relief.

"But you can't bring my fan outside!"

"Then I'd better stand here a little bit longer." And they both laughed.

I had but two responses to pushy vendors, the rude brush-off and the silent treatment; I had none of Dad's easygoing charm or ready wit. Watching them, I was hit once again with the apprehension that always haunted me growing up, that my lifetime of study would forever pale in comparison to his intuitive understanding of this nation and its people. I knew which hole-in-the-wall restaurants had the best spicy delicacies and could eat anything off their menus. I knew where to find Chinese guidebooks and how to score cheap transportation. But he still had a feel for aspects of the deep culture that I lacked. What else could I do, and would it ever be enough?

Our destination, Yuyao County, was a tiny dot on the map, lodged between two behemoth cities in the northeastern part of Zhejiang Province. Back in my apartment, Michael and I huddled over my worn English-language guidebook and a map.

"Yuyao is between Ningbo and Hangzhou, but Hangzhou is bigger and probably has more rail lines." I traced my finger along the map. "Maybe we could get an overnight train to Hangzhou."

"Hm . . . but Ningbo is closer. Shouldn't we use Ningbo as a base?"

"How will we get to Ningbo? Can you look up if there's a bus from Shanghai to Ningbo? Maybe we fly to Shanghai?"

Dad looked up from the Chinese guidebook. "Did you know Yuyao is known as the 'land of scholars'?" He grinned. Yuyao received passing mention in most English guidebooks, if it received mention at all, but the Chinese guidebook devoted a narrow chapter to the intellectuals who emerged from the region of our ancestors.

I think this description tickled Dad's fancy because it reminded him of his father. The founding of the Yen Family Village may have originated from a wealthy merchant, but by the time Grandpa was born in the early twentieth century, his family had fallen on hard times and migrated out of the province in search of better luck. According to Dad, Grandpa had an uncle with no sons, and when Grandpa came of age at 13 his uncle offered him a modest lump sum as seed money to make his way in the world. "You can use it to start a business. Or get some education—I know you like to study. The choice is yours."

It was enough for three years of education, and Grandpa leveraged those three years to cover all of primary and secondary school. When civil war and the Japanese invasion threw the nation into chaos in the 1920s and 1930s, he tested into university by scoring well on the entrance exam. The upheaval meant many students had no copy of their high school diploma, so Grandpa's lack of a diploma went unquestioned.

While Michael and I plotted a path toward the Yen Family Village, Dad traced the scholarly lineage of Yuyao, from Han dynasty scholars (circa AD 20) through every subsequent century up to the present. China's civil exam system dates back to the 600s and expanded under Empress Wu Zetian; for centuries passing this exam was the surest path for social mobility within China. Nearly every region boasts at least one poor scholar who studied their way into the scholar elite, thereby lifting themselves and their families out of poverty. It is China's rags-to-riches narrative and one Dad could locate Grandpa within.

I believe it is also one reason Chinese immigrants in America place so much emphasis on education, as it transposes well to the American Dream: enter a profession that requires many years of education, and thereby secure prestige, wealth, security, and their many accoutrements. Dad followed this path into medicine, but I was noncommittal. Becoming Chinese "enough" had defined so many years of my life that I needed to keep plunging into my obsession to determine if China was my true *dao* or ultimately a passing phase.

We flew to Shanghai and then hopped a bus to Ningbo, the behemoth city that neighbors Yuyao. If Beijing and Shanghai were the two pearls of the new Chinese economy—Beijing as the center of political power and Shanghai as the center of commerce—then Ningbo exemplified the crop of up-and-coming cities on the eastern seaboard. When Deng Xiaoping opened China in 1978 and ushered in a series of economic reforms, he famously said, "Let some regions and some people prosper first." Beijing and Shanghai would receive the country's initial economic investments so that their experiences might eventually pave the way for everyone else to prosper. In the 1990s, investment widened to include large eastern cities around Shanghai like Ningbo and Hangzhou. Although Ningbo lacked the hypermodern glitz of Shanghai, the avenues were wide and clean, the high-rise apartments were relatively new, and students on mopeds buzzed through the streets. The city had a middle-class feel, whereas Shanghai felt simultaneously ultrarich and extremely poor.

Dad's eyes shone with excitement as he took in our fellow passengers on the bus to Ningbo, and it occurred to me that this was his first experience riding with the natives. I'd worried how he'd take to this style of travel, but he seemed enthusiastic.

Flooded rice fields whipped by our windows, interspersed with sprawling towns of concrete buildings—spare, one-story, utilitar-

ian. Bursts of purple and aqua and pink and gold glistened in unexpected clusters along the highway: nouveau riche mansions of
multistory concrete structures topped by brightly glazed ceramic
roofs, their curved eaves molded in the tradition of Ming dynasty
architecture.

Somewhere in here was the Yen Family Village. Michael poked
me. "We might be passing it right *now* and not even know it!"

He raised his eyebrows, the enthusiasm in his voice coasting
past excitement and into a parody of nervous anticipation. I
laughed. I wondered if he, too, speculated whether our family village was now filled with those hideously ostentatious homes, or if
it was still buried in squalor. Michael's dry humor had emerged
when he entered college; a couple of years before that, when I left
for college, he blossomed into a social butterfly who rarely stayed
home (facilitated by a driver's license), so that I was continually
reacquainting myself with him, this brother who had once been
my closest playmate.

Earlier that day at a breakfast joint, Dad had leaned over to kiss
me on the cheek, which was normal for our family, if abnormal for
stereotypical immigrant ones. I recoiled, alarmed. "People don't
do that here!" I hissed.

Dad jerked upright, looking guilty. An awkward silence fell between us.

"He's just happy to see you," Michael said, his eyes simultaneously reproachful and sympathetic. I looked away, awash with
shame but too irritated and proud to apologize. For the rest of
the day I sought to make it up to Dad by joking and laughing with
him, and when Michael's ribbing became too incessant and Dad's
frustration started showing through, I diverted their conversation,
again and again, to safer ground.

Our second bus from Ningbo to Yuyao was smaller and dirtier
and lacked air-conditioning, for Yuyao was poorer and smaller
than Ningbo. The land was just as densely settled but had fewer
ostentatious homes, and then the mansions disappeared entirely.
The bus bumped and jostled. It creaked to a stop to let a peasant
off at the side of the road. Occasionally we passed a small group
of women sitting together by a roadside stall, gossiping as they
fanned themselves with folded accordions of paper. An old woman
wearing flowered pajamas eased herself over the metal divide to
cross the road.

Yuyao was a nondescript city, the same endless miles of dingy concrete buildings, the same four-lane thoroughfare cutting through its heart. China had hundreds of cities like this, places that housed over a million people and that yet felt oddly reminiscent of old-time small-town America, forgotten by the rest of the world as the standard of living slowly improved and life churned along at its slow but satisfactory pace. The city lacked the hustle of Shanghai, but there was the sense it had done well for itself, likely pulling itself up from dirt roads not 10 years earlier.

Finally, we reached the end of the line. We were the last passengers to exit the bus, and emerged to find a cluster of small red cabs quivering in an impatient line. We looked around. Our fellow passengers had already dispersed into the surrounding streets. So this was Yuyao.

Michael and I shifted uncomfortably in the heat. We'd figured out how to get us this far, but neither of us had thought beyond finding our way to Yuyao. Unsure what to do next, I shaded my eyes and looked toward the bus depot, as though deep in thought.

"Isn't this fun?" Dad asked, looking at nobody in particular. Michael and I avoided looking at one another. Neither of us looked at him.

"Well! I'm having fun!" Dad disappeared into the bus depot.

My backpack, loaded with three water bottles and a guidebook, pulled at my shoulders. Michael's forehead beaded with sweat. An old man ambled across the empty station with a bamboo stick slung over his shoulder, a bundle balanced from each end of the stick. His silhouette evoked bucolic images of the Chinese peasantry, except that his bags were jammed with dirty plastic bottles intended for the recycling center, a man in retirement earning a few extra *kuai* by poking about trash cans.

Dad reappeared. He'd asked the station attendants about the neighboring villages: Was there one named Yen, and which bus could take us there? They shook their heads and laughed, asking for additional details. He had none. He led us toward the cabbies and made inquiries, but they, too, had never heard of a village named Yen. There was nothing to do but kick at the curb and wait for the next bus back.

We were a family of dreamers on a journey born of dreams. Michael dreaming of the triumphant return to the family village; Dad

dreaming of the modernization of our ancestral shrine. I dreamt
of adventures in a land of 1.3 billion, as though by scouring the
countryside I might discover the place, deep within myself, where
I could latch onto the certainty that I was Chinese enough. That
I was enough. But the real dreamer, the one most responsible
for this journey, was Grandpa. It was of his home village that we
dreamt, and it was his dream of a PhD that had brought the family
to the "land of opportunity" in 1963, where we would eventually
prosper enough for a return visit to the motherland.

My memories of him are vague. He passed away from Alzheim-
er's when I was 12. I remember a quiet man of slight build with
kind eyes, gentle with children but shy. Grandpa never finished his
PhD; he left with a master's degree to support Grandma and their
seven children, eventually landing in Lockheed Martin's engineering department. Dad had once been a faculty member at two
different medical schools, and he hoped my fellowship research
would eventually lead to a professorship, where I would be the one
to finally live out Grandpa's dreams.

When I entered Michael and Dad's hotel room later that night,
they were seated across from each other on a bed, a large map
of Yuyao County spread between them. Dad scratched his calf. "I
don't know what it is, but I'm itching all over."

"Itchy . . ." Michael mused. "Like when the body rejects a trans-
plant—"

"Your province is rejecting you!" I said. Dad shook his fist, first
at me and then at Michael, before laughing.

We hovered over the map. Yuyao County held no village named
Yen, only a constellation of unmarked towns that must have been
too small to warrant detailed census. There was also no river named
Xia, although it could have dried up in the intervening years.

"I don't know!" Dad's voice was tight with frustration. "I just
remember being a kid in Taiwan and reciting, *Woshi Zhejiangsheng,
Yuyaoxian ren.*" Dad looked off into space. "Maybe Grandpa got it
wrong. But how could he?"

He bent over the map again. "He couldn't have given us another clue?"

When we met for breakfast the following morning, Dad calmly
announced, "I'm no longer allergic to my province. It's bug bites."
Over steaming bowls of rice porridge with pickled vegetables and
preserved egg, he recounted the tiny village Michael had spotted

on the map, buried deep in the heart of the province. It was not in Yuyao County nor was it near the faintest trickle of water, but it was named Yen Family Village and it was in Zhejiang.

"Are you sure?" I asked. The thread seemed tenuous at best; I was ready to abandon the effort and settle into sightseeing.

"You never know." Michael picked carefully at a plate of tiny pickled fish.

Dad shot me a warning glance. "I think we should do it. We're here anyways."

I shrugged and slouched in my chair. My skin felt grimy from the southern humidity, and I missed the spontaneity of my solo travels, where I could wander down alleyways or befriend children as I journaled. Dad and Michael, much as I loved them, reminded me of the person I'd been before China. Traveling solo was simpler, freer.

Michael unfolded the map and peered at it again. Silence blanketed our table.

"I'd hate to come all this way and miss it," said Dad. "What if that's it?"

So we headed for Jinhua, the largest city within striking distance of our new target. As with the rest of the province, this no-name city of 4 million was booming. This entire time Dad had been voraciously reading guidebooks and newspapers, and he told us that because Beijing and Shanghai had succeeded in establishing themselves, the Communist Party was now starting the second half of Deng Xiaoping's vision, which was to let the prosperity of those "first cities and people" trickle down. The plan was to shift development funds away from the largest cities and instead invest in each province's second-, third-, fourth-, fifth-, etc., largest cities. Jinhua did not make the top five in Zhejiang Province, but even here we could see that the ripple effects of development had begun to alter the landscape.

As Dad acclimated to traveling without a tour guide, he took on more and more of the travel arrangements, flipping through guidebooks to find hotels and map public-transportation options. I hated myself for ceding responsibility for logistics and slipping back into child mode, but it was so easy to be lazy in these small ways.

He booked us into a three-star hotel that stood beyond the edge of town in anticipation of the future growth of the city limits. It was so far out that we had to try several cabbies before one agreed to take us. The hotel was staffed by an army of interns, and when we presented our blue passports for identification verification, we caused a minor uproar. "Americans!" they whispered. "Come look!" Our bedsheets were such a crisp white, I suspected we were the first to use them. We were their only guests that evening.

The hotel connected us with a cabbie who agreed to drive us the 100 miles or so to the Yen Family Village. When he quoted the equivalent of a week's earnings, Dad tried halfheartedly to talk him down. I never had the willingness to raise my voice, insult the product, walk away at least twice, or enter into heated argument, just to reach a price that locals would pay, and Dad was equally soft. I realize now we should have let Michael bargain for us. He would have gotten us to within 10 percent of the local price. Whereas Dad and I rationalized that between the standard-of-living differential and the favorable exchange rate it was not worth the trouble, Michael was driven by the principle of the matter.

The next morning, our cabbie plunged us deep into the heart of Zhejiang. We entered a region so remote it was likely that just one or two buses plied this route each day, the type of place where a regular might ask the driver to deliver a cardboard box of baby chicks to a friend. We climbed into the mountains, the car skating wildly across the narrow highway. Rectangular fields of green, yellow, and brown flashed by our window. Intermittent heaps of trash glistened in the sun. In the passenger seat Dad fell silent, fighting motion sickness. Michael slumped. I closed my eyes, hoping to ignore my stomach's strong protests.

Finally, our cabbie nosed us down a rock-strewn dirt path and pulled up to a row of houses connected by a dirt path. There was no stream in sight. A mangy dog shuffled toward us. There could not have been more than 10 houses in the entire village. Most were made of concrete but covered in a thick layer of dirt, and were surrounded by dirt fences that had never been fully built or were partially washed away by rain (it was unclear which), creating the impression that dirt overran the village. We stared blankly through the windows, unsure of the next step. To stall, I closed my eyes and focused on dispelling my nausea. I imagine Dad and Michael did the same.

Our cabbie waited for us for three heartbeats and then flung open the car door. We hesitated, then followed suit. A middle-aged woman was perched on a low stool in the sun, and as we approached, she aroused herself from her stupor and made small talk with our cabbie in the local dialect, while eyeing us with faint curiosity. She pointed to a house in the back where, our cabbie translated, we would find the oldest person here. He might have answers for us. Nobody appeared under the age of 40.

We stepped into a concrete building with dirt floors and dingy whitewashed walls. A couple of squares cut into the concrete served as windows. A man in his 70s drooped on a rickety chair as he watched a television drama. Flies buzzed about the walls.

He rose. We introduced ourselves. He rumbled his family lineage and confirmed no Yens lived here. Everybody had moved away, he told us, the young gone to the cities in search of opportunity. If Yens once lived here, they had left by the time he was born.

As he spoke, the television drama ended and the credits began to roll, a weeping violin playing in the background. A couple of flies landed on the old man's back and began exploring the holes in his shirt. A tinny cello joined the violin, and their harmony reached a mournful crescendo.

How many people does it take to preserve critical mass in a village? One neighbor passes away; another is brought to the city to live with their children. At what point are villages abandoned entirely, to be swallowed up by dirt and reclaimed by the mountainside, and how often had this story played out across China in the past 20 years? Was this the fate that befell the tiny, unmarked cities within Yuyao County that dotted our map? Had our own Yen Family Village fallen into such disrepair? Or had it simply been swallowed up by the county as development brought the edge of Yuyao to meet the village Yen that stood next to the river Xia, much as the city of Jinhua, with its sterile new hotels staffed by student interns, steadily marched outward?

Our journey had traced China's latest wave of development. We'd hopped from Beijing to a string of increasingly less-developed cities, ultimately landing in a village made up of just 10 households. Whereas mid-twentieth-century China had sought to become a shining model of socialism, an alternative vision for modernity that could compete with the West, by the early twenty-first century China wanted nothing more than to adapt the Western model to its purposes. This village had likely been built during the former, and was one of thousands of casualties that came from altering the course of the world's most populous nation. Yet were these choices so different from the ones third-generation Chinese Americans faced regarding assimilation—what to keep, what to discard, how to marry tradition with modernity?

I didn't mind that we hadn't found the ancestral village. For me, the experience of traversing this dizzying spectrum of economic development, as illuminated by Dad's readings, reinforced a lesson China had taught me time and again. So often I was clueless about my desired destination, let alone the path to take, that I pursued what ultimately proved to be a red herring solely because I needed an impetus to begin, and it was only through trusting the *dao* that I found my way.

Later, Michael told me he hadn't minded the unexpected twist, either. For him, visiting the village was one of the few times he'd been truly off the grid, faced with poverty as he could never know it in America. And yet, he thought, there was a plan for these people. He hadn't seen them as left behind, as I had; he didn't view them as masses to be pitied by outsiders. In the last 20 years, China had lifted more people out of extreme poverty than the rest of the world combined. You could focus on the squalor and decay, or you could see the historical context, the complexities of bringing a billion people out of poverty.

When I first arrived in China I was frequently confronted with the question *"Nali ren?"* which roughly translates as "Where do you come from?" It took me a couple of tries to realize they were not curious about where I lived in Beijing or even that I came from America; they were asking where my ancestors originated. The bilingual immersion program had taught us much, but it did not teach us that phrase. When I remember that the immersion program was so young and experimental that my fourth-grade science teacher was also my creative-writing/drama teacher, and when I think about the strong emphasis my parents have placed on education throughout my life, I am amazed they were willing to take such a gamble on our formative years. Yet they viewed language as a window into another culture, and they wanted us to be proud of our Chinese heritage.

We spent our final days sightseeing throughout the province, and somewhere during this time Dad began responding to the question *Nali ren?* by identifying himself as *Yuyao ren*, that he was originally from Yuyao even though he was now an American citizen, a *huayi*. It seemed important to him to have seen Yuyao, if only briefly. I think it made him feel closer to Grandpa.

Language was indeed a window into another culture, but it was only through understanding a culture that language could be leveraged to its full potential, and Dad understood the power of *tongxiang*, the way a shared hometown is one of the strongest markers of group identity that exists in China, no matter how many generations removed that connection might be.

Dad loved traveling like the locals. As he chatted up cabbies and shopkeepers with this line, I continually admired his amicable bantering style. He only slipped up once or twice. A cabbie turned to him once at the end of a ride and asked, *"Fapiao?"*

"Hunh?" Dad said, unfamiliar with the phrase and bereft of any context from which to guess its meaning.

Michael grabbed the receipt that dangled from the machine. "Pay!" he commanded as he slapped Dad on the arm, a bemused grin on his face.

"What—oh! Oh!" Dad fumbled for his wallet. Michael waggled his eyebrows at me and then vacated the cab.

We'd stopped by the former house of a local scholar that was now a museum. We wandered through bright white rooms filled with low, dark furniture, where large calligraphy scrolls hung from the walls. Dad rambled about excelling at calligraphy as a child, how it took as much discipline as a martial art. I nodded, eyes roaming the room so as not to encourage him, but not interrupting his well-worn account, either. "There were female scholars," he said at last.

"Not many," I said.

"But some. Just like there were female generals and historians and rebels," he said. I tilted my head and looked at him, a question. "Mulan?" he said.

I recalled the picture in my elementary school textbook, a daughter embracing her parents as she left home to fill her aging father's conscripted shoes, a classic tale of filial piety.

"But built like an Amazonian," Dad said. He squared his shoulders and flexed. In the traditional telling of Mulan, she was already well trained in martial arts before she left home. "Not like Disney."

A long, shallow pool of water lay beneath the black, curved eaves, and as it began to drizzle, the droplets slid off the concave tiles and fell in a line in the rectangular pool below. "See how they designed these gardens for both rain and sun," Dad said. "It's a different experience, depending on the weather. These pools create a musical tinkling that scholars listened to as they wrote poetry in their study."

"Just like poets used to talk about the delicate tinkling of jade against jade," I said, latching onto a memory from a Chinese literature class. "That sound was the epitome of womanliness." Michael turned away but I could see him rolling his eyes.

Perhaps Dad knew these kinds of details through close perusal of the guidebook. Or perhaps he had read them in a novel, just as he once told me of a short story that described the distinctive smell of *paocai*, or "pickled cabbage," that overtook Beijing every fall as the city prepared for winter. He wanted to know if this still happened. Not so, I said. I had a friend, a native Beijinger, who could remember when cabbage was the only vegetable that lined the streets each autumn. But at some point all that changed, though she couldn't remember when the transition occurred.

At the time, I thought her comment exemplified the destructive nature of Beijing's rapid development, personal histories obliterated as the city destroyed the vessels of its denizens' memories. But as I stood there in the museum, this memory collided with our recent interaction with the cabbie, and I saw Dad and I both had different, both incomplete, ways of accessing Chinese culture, both cobbled together through a combination of book learning, popular culture, and personal experience.

I had spent my entire life facing east. That entire time, China had been engaged in a race toward the west. I saw then that the third generation's conundrum—perhaps I should say *my* third-generation conundrum—was unsolvable. I had become Chinese enough by my own standards. Somewhere inside the path shifted, and China, though part of my *dao* for a long period, slipped from the horizon, and, with it, Grandpa's dream of professorship, a family legacy that could only be fulfilled by a different Yen. It was time to go home.

A couple of years after this trip, Dad mentioned in passing that he relearned his mother tongue when we attended the bilingual school. He sometimes read a couple of chapters ahead in our textbook so he could answer our questions, because a quarter century in his adopted country had eliminated Chinese from his daily life.

We had given him the opportunity to fall in love with the language, culture, and history all over again.

The last day of our trip we booked Dad on a train back to Shanghai, where he would fly to Beijing and return home. Michael and I were headed to Hangzhou to see the West Lake. Dad stood in front of us, white floppy-brimmed hiking hat on his head, waterproof sandals purchased specially for this trip bound to his feet, gray backpack on his shoulders. He was excited for the soft sleeper bed we'd secured for him, his first ever. Michael gave him a brief one-armed hug. I flung my arms around him. He waved, then turned and slipped into the crowd.

Tourist Trap

FROM *The New Yorker*

RECENTLY, THE BEIJING POLICE took my brother sightseeing again. Nine days, two guards, chauffeured tours through a national park that's a World Heritage Site, visits to Taoist temples and to the Three Gorges, expenses fully covered, all courtesy of the Ministry of Public Security. The point was to get him out of town during the 2018 Forum on China-Africa Cooperation, held in early September. The capital had to be in a state of perfect order; no trace of trouble was permissible. And Zha Jianguo, a veteran democracy activist, is considered a professional troublemaker.

While President Xi Jinping played host to African dignitaries in the Great Hall of the People, the police played host to my big brother at various scenic spots in the province of Hubei, about a thousand kilometers away. A number of other Beijing activists and civil rights lawyers, including several whom Jianguo knows well, were treated to similar trips. Pu Zhiqiang headed for Sichuan, Hu Jia to the port city of Tianjin, He Depu to the grasslands of Inner Mongolia, and Zhang Baocheng to Sanya, a beach resort on Hainan Island. Kept busy in the midst of natural beauty and attended to closely, they had no chance to speak to members of the foreign media or post provocative remarks online.

This practice is known as *bei lüyou*, "to be touristed." The term is one of those sly inventions favored by Chinese netizens: whenever law enforcement frames people, or otherwise conscripts them into an activity, the prefix *bei* is used to indicate the passive tense. Hence: *bei loushui* (to be tax-evaded), *bei zisha* (to be suicided), *bei piaochang* (to be johned), and so on. In the past few years, the *bei* list has been growing longer, the acts more imaginative and color-ful. "To be touristed" is no doubt the most appealing of these sce-narios, and it is available only to a select number of troublemak-ers. In Beijing, perhaps dozens of people a year are whisked off on these exotic trips, typically die-hard dissidents who have served time and are on the radar of Western human rights organizations and media outlets. Outside the capital, the list includes not just ac-tivists but also petitioners (*fangmin*) —ordinary people from rural villages or small towns who travel to voice their grievances to high government officials about local malfeasances they have suffered from.

Jianguo became a tourist only in recent years, but he has been a target of governmental attention for more than two decades. In 1999, he was given a nine-year prison sentence for helping to found a small opposition group, the Democracy Party of China, the year before. Since his release, in 2008, he has lived under constant police surveillance, which is ratcheted up during "sensi-tive" periods. For three months surrounding the Beijing Summer Olympics that year, the police parked in front of his apartment building night and day. Officers periodically knocked on his door to search his home, and followed him everywhere he went. Just as polluting factories were shut down and a barrage of rain-dispelling rockets were launched to ensure clear skies during the Games, po-litical irritants were vigorously contained.

China has grown wealthier and more powerful in the ensuing years, and, as it hosts more global forums, there are more sensitive dates on the state's calendar—Party congresses, trade summits, multinational meetings. Old imperial powers, with deep pockets and grand ambitions, tend to be fastidious about their image as host and benefactor, and China has always set great store by cer-emony. Each occasion is vulnerable to disruption by protesters, so care is taken to sweep them out of sight. All major state functions have so far run without a hitch: perfect weather, perfect banquets, and perfect citizens waving glow sticks. Since 2011, China's annual spending on domestic *weiwen*, or "stability maintenance," has, ac-cording to some reports, surpassed defense spending.

But how serious is the threat of a disruption? After Jianguo and his comrades launched the Democracy Party, all its leaders were swiftly sent to prison, and, for the past 10 years, Jianguo has been a solitary critic, with no party affiliation, no NGO membership, no local or foreign patron. Now 67 years old, he lives alone, having moved to a ground-floor apartment because he tires when climbing stairs. He eats and drinks modestly: mostly vegetables, a light beer or two. Having lost a lot of hair during his prison years, he shaves his head. He used to hold forth at meals; now he listens more than he talks. His smile is serene, as if to convey that all under heaven is forgiven. Someone remarked to me once, "Your brother looks like a Buddha now."

Yet, in recent years, the Chinese government has come to see him as more, not less, of a security threat. The authorities monitor his phone, block some of his messages, and bar him from certain gatherings. During sensitive periods, he is watched and followed around the clock. On *bei lüyou* trips, three officers usually accompany him, often including one who sleeps in his hotel room.

Why do they think he is so dangerous? My brother may no longer operate a party cell, but—like more than a billion other Chinese citizens—he does have a cell phone. He regularly posts his analyses of current events in online groups, and he has become an increasingly prominent pundit on the Chinese internet. Since 2012, Jianguo has trained his criticism chiefly on one target: the *Global Times* (*Huanqiu Shibao*), a pro-government, strongly nationalistic, and influential tabloid daily, which is distributed widely under the auspices of the *People's Daily*. In a series labeled "Debating the *Global Times*," Jianguo took up editorials and scrutinized them point by point.

Looking at his posts, I used to marvel at his bullheadedness, but the whole thing seemed to me like playing a game of solitaire; the posts appeared to go unnoticed. Gradually, however, I saw that Jianguo was honing a new voice, and gaining a following. From 2012 to 2017, he produced, with accelerating frequency, a total of 456 "Debating the *Global Times*" posts. He was helped by the explosive growth of WeChat, the messaging and social media app: by 2015, Jianguo was sending a new post every other day to between 50 and 70 WeChat groups, reaching tens of thousands of readers.

He's part of a broader trend. Since organized opposition is impossible, protest and resistance have increasingly shifted to the internet. Spotlighting abuse and corruption, online critics and bloggers have often succeeded in rallying public opinion and pressuring authorities to act. Online platforms like WeChat and Weibo, in their fragmented immensity, can still provide badly needed

public spaces for critical exchange, as well as bonding and camaraderie, all with the advantage of speed and influence.

Back in the late 1990s, the Democracy Party of China was a
fringe group of radicals whom the government could easily quarantine. Reformist intellectuals, who supported a path of incremen-
tal change, viewed men like Jianguo as politically naive and their
mission as suicidal. Few people even knew that his party existed.
But now, using social media, Jianguo has accomplished something
that his old comrades never could. He has reached the much
larger camp of Chinese liberals—educated urbanites who generally embrace Western ideas of democracy, want the rule of law,
and are critical of the party-state. Although they have flourished
in China's "reform era"—decades of fast growth that have brought
them apartments, cars, holiday travels, study abroad for their children—they are mostly convinced of the superior vitality of the
multiparty system. In a joke they liked about the 2016 US election, a bunch of eunuchs are so appalled by the bawdy quarrels
among the married folk that they congratulate themselves: "How
fortunate we are to be castrated!" Yet many Chinese liberals doubt
that the Western system is feasible in their country. They fret about
the burden of history, about the prospect of chaos and mob rule.
In their own lives, they avoid radicals and former political prisoners, for fear that such association might jeopardize their personal
freedom. They shun the sort of political action that could put their
comfortable lifestyle at risk.

These are the people I'm friends with in Beijing; they know me
as a writer and as someone who, for years, was a regular presence
on a moderate-liberal TV talk show that they all watched. (Which
is to say, I'm mindful of what lines can't be crossed when address-
ing the Chinese public on Chinese airwaves.) So why are so many
of these liberals now reading the views of a radical like my brother
Jianguo? One factor is the darkening of China's political landscape. Xi Jinping's initial speeches as president about "putting
power into a cage" had given hope to many liberal pragmatists,
but what he really meant quickly became clear: he intended to
cage any threats to his own authority. And he has managed to do
so through a ruthlessly extralegal anticorruption campaign, all in
the name of "strengthening the rule of law under the Party leadership." Amid ever harsher crackdowns on civil society, many previously tolerated liberals are feeling a chill: every day, there's more

news about arrests, detention, censorship, and blackmail. Investigative journalists, public intellectuals, media critics, college professors, editors and publishers, human rights lawyers, and environmental activists—nobody feels safe anymore.

One evening in June 2017, as I was leaving my Beijing apartment to meet some cousins of mine for dinner, I got a text message from a friend, a law professor, saying that the police had taken my brother away. Jianguo had planned to join us for dinner that evening but called the day before to cancel, because police were already stationed outside his building, in anticipation of the 28th anniversary of the Tiananmen Square massacre.

What I didn't realize was that, the day before his arrest, Jianguo had posted a short piece in which he pointed out the political instability of the moment and the possibility of an accidental eruption. He then sketched out a potential cascade of protests and crackdowns, which could culminate in a military coup. The next day, while the piece circulated among his WeChat groups, Jianguo went to a neighborhood massage parlor. Herbal pads were being laid on his face when the manager rushed in. "Some men at the door want to see you," she told him breathlessly. Jianguo assumed it was his usual tails. "Tell them to wait outside," he told the manager. But a moment later she returned, looking terrified. The men had shown her their police IDs, and insisted that her client come out right away. Jianguo knew then that it was serious. "Oh, well," he said, apologizing. "Looks like I can't finish the facial today."

When I got the news of Jianguo's arrest, I called his cell phone, to no avail. After alerting his daughter, Huiyi, who lives in Orlando, I set off for the restaurant. My cousins were concerned, but not greatly; maybe we had all grown a little blasé after witnessing Jianguo's skillful dealings with the police for so many years. As we were leaving the restaurant, I got a message from a family friend who had stopped by Jianguo's apartment. I clicked open an image of my brother, seated in his living room, in handcuffs and an olive-green prison uniform. The police had brought him home to conduct a search but were about to take him away again.

I called various activists and lawyers, and made plans to meet at Jianguo's apartment the following morning. My friends persuaded me that we should keep the news of his detention to ourselves, and make private, direct contact with the police. The next morning, to my surprise, I reached the district police officer in charge of the case, Officer Liu, on the first try. "I'm Jianguo's—" I began, and Liu replied, simply, "I know who you are." He assured me that he would meet me straightaway. I waited at Jianguo's apartment for hours. Just as I was giving up hope, the door opened, revealing several uniformed police officers and Jianguo's smiling face. Officer Liu, a genial-looking man who appeared to be in his late 30s, greeted me politely but clearly wasn't eager to engage in a conversation. "We don't want to interrupt the family reunion," he said quietly, before leaving.

The Chinese police state can be at once harsh and accommodating, insidious and absurd. I got a sense of these peculiarities in 2008, when Jianguo was released after almost a decade behind bars, and a team of policemen was assigned to monitor him daily for three months. They were unfailingly polite, even solicitous, bargaining on his behalf at shops and carrying heavy bags for him. One hot afternoon, they helped install an air conditioner in his apartment. Since they followed him everywhere, I jokingly suggested that Jianguo might as well ride in the police vehicle, to help reduce expenses and pollution. The officers happily obliged. Once, I went along, riding beside the police driver and holding my young daughter on my lap. When Jianguo went out to eat with friends, the policemen, usually two per shift, would take a table at the other side of the room, eating their meals while keeping an eye on him. They began calling him Big Brother (*dage*), with a note of affection. Jianguo laughed when he told me; his guards were oblivious of any Orwellian connotations. "But, of course, they are just doing their job," he added. They were ready to haul him off to jail, he knew, whenever they were ordered to.

  With the practice of *bei lüyou*, things grew stranger still. On the road, the three policemen assigned to Jianguo would look after him as though they were his assistants: they bought sightseeing tickets, checked in and out of hotels, helped with his luggage, took snapshots of him at scenic spots. They fussed over him at meals, heaping meats and vegetables onto his plate, ladling up additional bowls of soup for him. Sometimes they booked a trip through an agency and ended up traveling for days with a group of real tourists. The all-male quartet aroused curiosity and inspired innocent guesses about their relationships. "So, are you father and sons? Colleagues?" And, pointing at Jianguo: "Is he your boss?"

Of course, their real boss was ultimately Xi, who chairs the National Security Commission. Since Xi became China's paramount leader, it has been possible to detect a Maoist revival in state politics and stealthy moves to resurrect the chairman's cult of personality, particularly after Xi got the constitution changed to eliminate presidential term limits. But the two leaders have strikingly different styles. As Andrew J. Nathan, a China expert at Columbia University, put it to me, in a succinct formulation, "Mao was a chaos guy, whereas Xi is a control guy." Indeed, Mao sometimes called to mind the Monkey King in the classical Chinese novel, who flipped dizzying somersaults in high clouds and created constant tumult with his magic wand. "The Golden Monkey wrathfully swung his massive cudgel," Mao wrote, in a famous couplet. "And the jade-like firmament was cleared of dust." Yet, when it came to the human soul, Mao was a consummate master of control. You could see this in social attitudes he encouraged toward "political criminals." In Mao's time, hatred of the "counter-revolutionaries" was widespread and intense. They were viewed as scarcely human "enemies of the people."

Xi plainly intends to emulate Mao in all sorts of ways, but he is ruling over a different China. Attitudes have long since mellowed and grown more than occasionally irreverent, even toward the Core Leader himself. To encourage worshipful affection, state media tried to popularize the honorific Xi Dada (Bigbig Xi), which is how one addresses a father or an uncle in various dialects. But other nicknames for the potbellied leader—such as Baozi (stuffed bun) or Winnie-the-Pooh—have gone viral. Defying official bans, stinging satires about a fatuous new emperor have percolated through social media. In Mao's era, people got shot for such disrespect.

The ranks of the Communist Party are swelling—they're now pushing past 89 million members—and so are the ranks of corrupt Party cadres. Although online tribes of Little Pinks (as youthful nationalists are called) can turn hysterical and aggressive, most young people join the Party for career opportunities and material gain. Xi has urged a renewal of ideological indoctrination at all levels, but it's hard to say how effective these efforts really are.

The average person hardly notices the robotic Party-speak that has returned to television, or the kitschy propaganda billboards that have become ubiquitous in the streets. Xi's anticorruption campaigns and nationalist-strongman politics may have won popular support, but true believers are an endangered species in what has become a brazenly pragmatic society.

Sun Liping, a sociologist at Tsinghua University, once argued, in a widely circulated blog post, that the biggest danger China faced was not mass unrest or sudden collapse, as many feared, but inner rot. He referred to several concurrent phenomena: unchecked power overseeing a "warped reform," entrenched interest groups and fat cats bent on preserving the status quo, and a general unraveling of social trust. If Sun's thesis is right, the most urgent task for Chinese leaders today is not perfecting "stability maintenance" but taking on the greed and cynicism that have become a national disease. Sun was, however, not optimistic about the prospects for treatment; he thought that the decay had spread through the entire body politic.

Bei lüyou is a symptom of this disease. The scheme would seem to be the brainchild of someone who, alert to how lavishly the state will spend on all security-related affairs, figured out a way to creep through the back entrance of the great government banquet hall to join the feeding frenzy in the kitchen. The aim of *bei lüyou* was plainly to pamper die-hard dissidents enough to soften their defiant spirit, but it could also serve as a morale-booster among the rank and file of the security forces. For them, it's essentially a free vacation that counts as work. In Mandarin, this is called a *meichai,* a "beautiful duty." Jianguo was taken on four such trips between October of 2017 and September of 2018, providing almost a dozen *meichai* slots for the police. The officers varied as much as the itineraries, and I imagined them haggling over the rotation of these coveted slots. Perks must be shared. Once, Jianguo told me why an elderly policeman was assigned to his team for a trip south: the man was about to retire, and he'd never been to any tropical beaches.

It's hard to say exactly when *bei lüyou* started, but an early instance reportedly occurred in 2012, and involved a prominent environmental activist named Wu Lihong. A peasant turned crusader, Wu had exposed hundreds of companies that were illegally polluting the water in his home province, Jiangsu. His tenacious campaign to protect the beautiful Lake Tai had earned him the moniker "Lake Tai Warrior." In 2007, just as an outbreak of blue-green algae in the lake affected the drinking water of more than 2 million people, Wu was sentenced to three years in prison. Five years later, during the Communist Party's 18th National Congress, when Xi assumed power, policemen took Wu from his home to visit Xi'an and its celebrated Terracotta Army. Then, in 2014, during another "sensitive period," the Jiangsu police took him off for "sightseeing and relaxation" at a plush mountain-resort hotel usually reserved for senior state leaders—at, of all places, Lake Tai.

According to Huang Qi, a human rights advocate in Chengdu, Sichuan Province, *bei lüyou* in Sichuan typically involves ordinary petitioners. The Sichuan police, Huang told a journalist, have sometimes covered the expenses for officers' friends and relatives as well. The police even paid a "lost-work fee" to those petitioners who negotiated for a compensation of income they were forgoing during the trip. Those who refused to go on the trip, though, were handled roughly.

In Beijing, Jianguo has been treated with more delicacy. On all but one of his trips, he was the lone "guest," accompanied by three guards. Then, this spring, he refused to go on a scheduled trip. His leg was hurting; he was fed up with the forced excursions. "I'll stay home—you can monitor me right here all day," he told the police. They panicked. A charm offensive ensued, as officers kept visiting him with different proposals. Too warm in the south? How about the wooded regions in the northeast? Can't sleep well with another person in the same room? From now on, you can have a hotel room to yourself. After three rounds of patient coaxing, Jianguo gave in.

In a photograph from his northeastern tour—it was taken by one of his police handlers—he is standing on an observation deck in Hunchun, Jilin Province, which overlooks both a river bordering North Korea to the south and a range of wooded Russian mountains to the north. "The spot is called Three Countries at One Glance," Jianguo told me. "For the first time in my life, I actually set eyes on two foreign territories." Later, when we met up for lunch, Jianguo brought a present for my daughter: a pocket mirror with gilded carvings of an old Eastern Orthodox cathedral, packed in a gaudy gift box. He had bought it at a souvenir shop in Harbin, an old Russified Manchurian city in Heilongjiang Province. I gazed into the mirror and caught an odd expression gazing back at me: Was it a grimace or a smile?

The truth is, I've wondered about the possibly corrupting influence of Jianguo's tangled dealings with the police. That formula of Nietzsche's comes to mind: If you gaze long enough into an abyss, the abyss will gaze into you. Had Jianguo's experiences with *bei lüyou* instilled in him a measure of sympathy toward the officers entrusted with his fate? Was it having—in some small part—its intended effect?

It's plain that Jianguo's years of arrests and imprisonment haven't bent his will. In matters of principle, he has never backed down. He openly condemns the despotic rule of the party-state, and he refuses to stop writing or posting his criticism. But, when he's in actual contact with the police, he responds to civility in kind. And here things get more complicated, because some police officers have gone further than civility. One officer told him, "I've read your book and my admiration for you is total." The phrase he used, *wuti-toudi*, literally means "with four limbs and a head touching the floor"—admiration to the point of prostration.

Even when Jianguo was arrested a year and a half ago, his police guards stopped by a restaurant to let him "have a good meal" before taking him to a secret detention site. The next day, picking him up to go home, they brought him yogurt and a meat pie. During initial questioning about his online post, the police appeared to want to get him off the hook.

"Maybe you didn't write this piece yourself," an officer suggested. "Maybe you copied it from some website?"

"No," Jianguo replied. "I wrote it, and I'm one hundred percent responsible for it."

"Okay, but maybe you haven't sent it to too many other people besides this one small WeChat group?" The group has about 70 people, closely watched by the police because several members are well-known intellectuals.

"I've sent it to a lot of other groups and people," Jianguo said. "But I can't recall the list or give you the names."

The officers scratched their heads and sighed. They told him they were trying to make it easy for him. Using a term for revered elders, they addressed him as Zha *lao*.

It would be wrong to assume that these policemen were moved

to help Jianguo out of human kindness. If a "stability-disrupting" case happens on their watch, the officer in charge may take some blame. "We've been scolded by the higher-ups for being too soft on you," an officer complained to Jianguo, "and now you post this call for a military coup! You're putting us in a very difficult position, Zha *lao*!"

Once, Jianguo told me about an insight he had gained from years of prison life. There's an old Chinese saying: *Jingfei-yijia*, "Cops and gangsters belong to the same family." The phrase usually suggests a corrupt equivalence between the two, but Jianguo discovered something else: they share a similar code of honor. Honor, though, takes a variety of forms, being associated with character, with money, or with knowledge. According to Jianguo, an implicit hierarchy exists behind Chinese prison walls, with the political prisoners at the top, thieves and other common criminals in the middle, and sex offenders at the bottom. Wealthy convicts bribe jailers for favors. A well-educated inmate enjoys esteem and privileges because the warden can ask him to write papers for an online diploma the warden might be pursuing or to tutor his son for a college exam. Political prisoners enjoy the highest prestige because of the power of their personal courage. Violence—brawls, bullying, beatings—is a daily reality in Chinese prisons. A prisoner of conscience, however, is usually left alone by his fellow inmates; a tacit distinction is made.

I once heard a similar account from the late Nobel Peace Prize laureate Liu Xiaobo. At the same time, there have been plenty of reports about officers abusing, even torturing, political prisoners. Two activists I know have told me in detail about their horrendous treatment during detention: one, in Beijing, was savagely beaten and shocked with electric prods; the other, based in Guangzhou, was interrogated continuously for four days and nights, until he suffered a physical breakdown and lost consciousness. Huang Qi, the Sichuan activist, was reportedly beaten and abused in jail, and denied proper medical attention for his ailments. Several detained human rights lawyers said they were forced to take drugs that made them feel dizzy and enervated. One of them, Xie Yang, told his attorney about his treatment (which also included beatings and sleep deprivation). The attorney made it public; subsequently, on state and social media, Xie renounced his own account as a fabrication. For many observers, it was an updated version of the public self-denunciations of the Cultural Revolution.

When I discussed the reports about drugs with Jianguo, he seemed less than persuaded, and told me that police officers he knows scoffed at the suggestion. It was as if, having spent so much time among security personnel, he could now easily inhabit their perspective. He told me a story of milder abuse, an officer deliberately shining a very bright light on a political prisoner's face during interrogation, making the inmate sweat profusely. "I know both the officer and the prisoner," my brother said. "The officer has a low opinion of the man, because he considers him a wimp. As a rule, the police are soft on the tough, and tough on the soft. So, if they sense a weakness in you, it will bring out the bully in them."

His words reminded me of a sad story about one of his fellow political prisoners. Wen (as I'll call him) was sentenced to 20 years on charges of "organizing and leading a counter-revolutionary group." During his first 11 years behind bars, his mother died and his wife divorced him, and he was allowed to see his only child, a girl, just once. In a moment of despair, Wen signed an admission of guilt, in the hopes of having his sentence reduced. After the news of what he'd done spread, a dramatic change in attitudes occurred: inmates made snide remarks, while jailers gave Wen spoiled food and picked on him. He eventually received a reduction of four years, but he was no longer considered a man of honor. His hair swiftly turned white.

In order to persuade Jianguo to stop writing "dangerous articles," Officer Liu had talked about the prospect of another long sentence. "Look, it's been exactly nine years since you finished your nine years in prison," Liu had told him. "If you get another nine years, it wouldn't be a nice way to live out your old age, would it? Think about your daughter, your grandchildren." With a small flexing of the wrist, the line suddenly drew taut.

Jianguo has been divorced twice, and Huiyi, his only child, moved to America many years ago. In Orlando, she got her first job, at Disney World, and eventually, with her husband, started two small companies, in real estate and rental management. The companies now have dozens of employees. Huiyi and her husband have a daughter and a son. Jianguo speaks about the family's immigrant success with parental pride, impressed by their entrepreneurial pluck. He cherishes the annual reunion when his daughter and son-in-law arrive from Florida with their two healthy, bounding children. But, despite Huiyi's repeated invitations, Jianguo won't leave China; he fears that he would be forbidden to return.

Others have made a different choice: there has been a growing exodus of dissidents and activists from China, including some of Jianguo's old Democracy Party comrades, spurred in large part by constant harassment. Economic uncertainties, heightened now by the US-China trade war, are making many affluent Chinese jittery. Some have already decamped or hedged their bets by transferring capital and setting up a second base abroad. In liberal WeChat groups, the mood swings between bravado, defeatist humor, and gloom; rumors about collapsed trade talks are often accompanied by whispered warnings of a coming storm.

Recently, stirred by news of more departures, Jianguo posted an unusually emotional piece, expounding on the nature of patriotism. In his view, it arises from a deep love of the land and the people, not necessarily of the state or the ruling regime. He understands those friends who have decided to leave and wishes them the best for a new life in a freer country. He even appreciates a motto widely quoted in his circles: "Wherever there's freedom, there is my homeland." But that's not *his* motto. "I'll never leave," he wrote. He'll never leave, and he'll never quit.

That's what he concluded after a careful consideration of Officer Liu's warning. "In the end, my mind is clear and at rest, as always," Jianguo said. He has told me repeatedly that he is prepared to return to prison at any time, for any number of years. My own mind is not at rest; at the moment, I'm all too conscious of the Chinese government's habit of jailing activists around Christmas, a down period for the media and the diplomatic services. Since Xi came to power, a number of Jianguo's Democracy Party comrades have been sent back to prison, and their sentences are heavy. At 65, Qin Yongmin, a widely admired activist and the founder of the party's Hubei branch, is serving a sentence of 13 years. It is his fourth; he has already spent 26 years behind bars. In July 2017, Liu Xiaobo, the long-imprisoned Nobel laureate, died of liver cancer during his fourth prison term, set for 11 years. The dissident community, mourning Liu's death, took note of the cool responses of many Western governments.

Jianguo views these developments soberly. He has long since

shed any illusions of fast social change or enduring media attention. "If I'm sentenced for another nine years, or twelve or thirteen years," he told me calmly, "I'll just forget about the outside world and focus on my life inside prison. Family and loved ones —well, those thoughts will be there for a while. It will take time. I'll read some books, play some Go, get on with my cellmates. I'll try to make the best out of each day. I'll think about nothing else, nobody else." I was at once chilled and comforted by his resolve. The words floated back to me: *Your brother looks like a Buddha now.*

On November 6, when I was in New York, Jianguo texted me about the midterm elections and made me promise to inform him of the results as soon as I heard. He was going to a dinner the following evening with some Beijing intellectuals, and everyone was keen to hear the latest news. Twelve hours later, when I forwarded the first posted results to his WeChat account, a message flashed on my phone's screen, informing me that the account I'd directed the message to had been blocked, and that "no information can reach the destination." For the fifth time, the censors had shut Jianguo's account down.

A day later, he opened a new account, with the name "Beijing-ZhaJianguo6," but a line had been crossed. After five shutdowns, as the police had warned him, he was blocked from large online groups. This is how all Chinese companies, including giants like Alibaba and WeChat's owner, Tencent, defer to the police state. Savvy Chinese internet users, with or without the aid of a VPN, employ all sorts of techniques to break through the Great Firewall, and Jianguo has definitely learned a few tricks to evade the censors. But lately the situation has deteriorated. On certain days, even after all the camouflaging maneuvers, a fresh opinion piece of his would vanish mysteriously, with no error message. Neither the sender nor the recipients would even know that something had gone amiss unless they checked with one another.

This is *bei hexie,* "to be harmonized," a form of virtual erasure. Bent on transforming the global internet into a Chinese intranet, official censors have made deft and extensive use of the method. You may know about Vice President Mike Pence's recent speech on the Trump administration's China policy, viewed by many as a declaration of a new cold war. But in China very few saw the actual text; it was met with swift *bei hexie.* The current arms race between the censors and the censored in China can be summed up in an old proverb: The monk grows taller by an inch, but the monster grows taller by a foot.

Now Jianguo has been shut out of all large online groups. "I'm forced to post my articles less often," he announced in a recent post. He's decided to write longer pieces and send them to smaller groups, in the hope that members will repost them in larger groups. "But I trust that all free voices cannot be blocked. Even if all the roosters are silenced, the dawn shall still come."

Contributors' Notes
Notable Travel Writing of 2018

Contributors' Notes

Stephen Benz has published two books of travel essays, *Guatemalan Journey* and *Green Dreams: Travels in Central America,* as well as work in *Creative Nonfiction, River Teeth, TriQuarterly, New England Review,* and other journals. *Topographies,* a collection of essays and journalism, is forthcoming in 2019. For more, visit stephenconnelybenz.com.

Maddy Crowell is a freelance writer based in New York City. She has previously lived in and written from India, Cambodia, Morocco, and Ghana. She holds an MA in politics from Columbia Journalism School.

David Fettling's writing focuses on the places where people of different countries and cultures meet. He has spent the past three years living in Indonesia, Singapore, and Malaysia. His first book is *Encounters with Asian Decolonisation.*

Alice Gregory is a correspondent for *GQ* and a contributing editor at *T.* She writes regularly for publications including *The New Yorker* and the *New York Times* and is at work on her first book.

A veteran food and travel writer, **Matt Gross** has had stories published in the *New York Times* (where he formerly wrote the Frugal Traveler column, 2006–2010), *Bon Appétit, Saveur, Food & Wine, Airbnb Magazine, Afar, Bloomberg Businessweek,* and many other outlets. His latest project, *Hot Pursuit,* is a documentary video series that traces how chile peppers spread around the world over the past 500 years. He lives in Brooklyn with his wife and two daughters.

Rahawa Haile is an Eritrean American writer. Her work has appeared in the *New York Times Magazine, The Atlantic, The New Yorker, Outside Magazine,* and *Pacific Standard. In Open Country,* her forthcoming memoir about thru-hiking the Appalachian Trail, explores what it means to move through America and the world as a black woman.

Peter Hessler was sent to China as a Peace Corps volunteer in 1996, and after completing his service, he stayed in the country as a writer. He eventually became the Beijing correspondent for *The New Yorker,* as well as a contributing writer for *National Geographic.* In 2011, he moved with his family to Cairo, where he studied Arabic and covered the Egyptian Arab Spring. His book about this experience, *The Buried,* was published in May 2019. He currently lives with his family in Chengdu, China.

Cameron Hewitt was born in Denver, grew up in central Ohio, and settled in Seattle in 2000. Since then, he has spent three months each year in Europe, contributing to guidebooks, tours, radio and television shows, and other media for Rick Steves' Europe, where he serves as content manager. Cameron married his high school sweetheart (and favorite travel partner), Shawna, and enjoys taking pictures, trying new restaurants, and planning his next trip. He blogs about his travels at https://blog.ricksteves.com/cameron.

Brooke Jarvis is a contributing writer for the *New York Times Magazine* and the *California Sunday Magazine.* She won the Livingston Award for national reporting and the NYU Reporting Award, and has been a finalist for a PEN America Literary Award and the Livingston Award for international reporting. Her work has been anthologized in *The Best American Science and Nature Writing* (2015 and 2019), *Love and Ruin: Tales of Obsession, Danger and Heartbreak from the Atavist Magazine,* and *New Stories We Tell: True Tales by America's Next Generation of Great Women Journalists.* She lives in Seattle.

Saki Knafo is the host of *Conviction,* a podcast from Gimlet Media about a crusading private detective in the South Bronx. His travel pieces about the Arctic, Johannesburg, and Iraq have appeared in *Men's Journal, Travel + Leisure,* and *GQ.*

Lucas Loredo was born and raised in Austin, Texas. His work has been published in the *Oxford American,* the *Masters Review, The Rumpus,* and the *Washington Square Review,* among others, and profiled by *Time Out New York, Juxtapoz,* and the *Wall Street Journal.* He has been twice named a finalist for

The Best American Short Stories. He recently earned his MFA at the Michener Center for Writers in his hometown.

Alex MacGregor is an Atlanta-based port and railroad consultant, an avid traveler, and an amateur geographer. He focuses on the intersection between the natural, social, and political landscapes, and scours the world for overlooked places. His favorite countries are Haiti and Mexico.

Jeff MacGregor is writer-at-large for *Smithsonian.* He is the author of the critically acclaimed *Sunday Money* and has written for the *New York Times* and *Sports Illustrated.* This is his first appearance in *The Best American Travel Writing.*

Lauren Markham is the author of *The Far Away Brothers: Two Young Migrants and the Making of an American Life,* which won a Northern California Book Award, a California Book Award Silver Medal, and a Ridenhour Prize. Her fiction and essays have appeared in outlets such as *Guernica, Freeman's, Orion, Harper's Magazine, Longreads,* the *New Republic,* and *VQR,* where she is a contributing editor. In addition to writing, she has spent nearly 15 years working with immigrant and refugee youth in her home state of California.

Ben Mauk is a writer based in Berlin. His work has appeared in the *New York Times Magazine, Harper's Magazine,* the *London Review of Books, The New Yorker,* and *Virginia Quarterly Review,* among other publications. He was a finalist for the 2018 National Magazine Award for feature writing. In 2019, he received the inaugural Jamal Khashoggi Award for Courageous Journalism. He cofounded and directs the Berlin Writers' Workshop.

Outside Magazine correspondent **Devon O'Neil** grew up on St. John in the US Virgin Islands before trading the sea for snow and settling in Breckenridge, Colorado, after college. A former newspaperman and staff writer at ESPN.com, O'Neil's work also appears often in *Men's Journal, Bike,* and *Ski* and has been a notable selection in The Best American Sports Writing. He moonlights as a hutmaster for a system of backcountry cabins above 11,000 feet.

Nick Paumgarten has been a staff writer at *The New Yorker* since 2005. From 2000 to 2005, he was the deputy editor of The Talk of the Town, to which he regularly contributes. He has also written features on subjects ranging from sports talk radio to internet dating to the World Economic Forum in Davos to a mountain climber attacked by Sherpas on Mount Everest.

Before coming to the magazine, he was a reporter and senior editor at the *New York Observer*.

Anne Helen Petersen is a senior culture writer for *BuzzFeed News*. She lives in Missoula, Montana.

Shannon Sims is a quadrilingual lawyer turned journalist. Originally from the Gulf Coast, she has reported independently from Brazil for nearly a decade for publications including the *New York Times, Bloomberg Businessweek*, the *Washington Post*, and *Pacific Standard*. When not writing about Brazil, she likes to write on two other beats: women breaking boundaries and the legal implications of climate change. She is a former fellow of the Institute of Current World Affairs, through which she reported for two years on stakeholder management of Brazil's forests, and of the International Women's Media Foundation, which supported her 2018 reporting on everything from farmworkers' legal rights along the Texas-Mexico border to Rwandan fisherwomen and Zanzibar's women's soccer team. She splits her time between New Orleans and Rio de Janeiro, or anywhere there's Carnival.

Noah Sneider is a California-born, Moscow-based writer and documentarist. He is the Moscow correspondent for *The Economist*. His work has also appeared in the *New York Times, Harper's Magazine, The Atlantic*, the *New Republic, 1843 Magazine, Slate, The Believer*, and elsewhere.

William T. Vollmann is an American novelist, journalist, war correspondent, short story writer, and essayist. He won the 2005 National Book Award for Fiction for the novel *Europe Central* and has won the PEN Center USA West Award for Fiction, a Whiting Award, and a Strauss Living award from the American Academy of Arts and Letters. He lives in Sacramento, California, with his wife and daughter.

Jason Wilson is the author of *Godforsaken Grapes, Boozehound*, and, most recently, *The Cider Revival*. He has been the series editor of The Best American Travel Writing since 2000.

Jessica Yen is a Chinese American author whose work explores the intersection of memory, family, culture, language, identity, and history. Her work has appeared in *Fourth Genre, Oregon Humanities, Blue Mesa Review*, and elsewhere. She is currently working on a book of creative nonfiction. By day, she writes grants for safety-net clinics and edits manuscripts for academics seeking to address health inequities.

Jianying Zha is a Chinese American writer, journalist, and cultural commentator in both English and Chinese. She is the author of *Tide Players, China Pop,* and several books of nonfiction and fiction in Chinese, including *The Eighties,* an award-winning cultural retrospective of the 1980s in China. Her work has appeared widely in publications such as *The New Yorker,* the *New York Times, Dushu,* and *Wanxiang.* A recipient of a Guggenheim Fellowship in nonfiction, she has been a regular commentator on current events on Chinese television and worked for many years at the India China Institute in New York City. Born and raised in Beijing, educated in China and the US, she lives in Beijing and New York.

Notable Travel Writing of 2018

SELECTED BY JASON WILSON

STEPHANIE ELIZONDO GRIEST
  The Saga Continues. *Airbnb Magazine,* Winter.
PETER GWIN
  From Sea to Sand. *Far & Away,* Spring.

ANNELISE JOLLEY
  Trick of the Light. *Hidden Compass,* November 8.

LAINE KAPLAN-LEVENSON
  The Same Mountaintop. *Oxford American,* Spring.

WILLIAM LYCHACK
  The Lady and the Monk. *American Scholar,* Autumn.

CLAYTON MAXWELL
  In the Valley. *Texas Highways,* November.
ANDREW MCCARTHY
  The Arans, Hiding in Plain Sight. *New York Times,* September 16.
REBECCA MEAD
  Meal Ticket. *The New Yorker,* June 18.
NATASHA MEKHAIL
  Peak Christmas. *Hemispheres,* December.

PEGGY ORENSTEIN
  Why I Took My Daughter to Auschwitz. *Condé Nast Traveler,* November.
SUSAN ORLEAN
  Zooming In on Petra. *Smithsonian,* October.

ADRIANA PÁRAMO
  Love on the Iditarod Trail. *Southern Indiana Review,* Spring.
JAMES PATRICK
  The Bootleggers of Madagascar. *Roads & Kingdoms,* March 5.
STEPHANIE PEARSON
  In the Land of Giants. *Outside Magazine,* September.
TONY PERROTTET
  High Spirits. *Travel + Leisure,* February.
EMILY POLK
  The Littlest Wren. *Creative Nonfiction,* Summer.

DAVE SEMINARA
  Trespassing at Ernest Hemingway's House. *Literary Hub,* July 2.
RONNIE SHUKER
  The Miracle at 14,000 Feet. *Roads & Kingdoms,* February 26.
JOHN JEREMIAH SULLIVAN
  American Beauty. *Travel + Leisure,* April.

JODIE NOEL VINSON
    Mother Russia. *December,* vol. 29, no. 1.

ALISON WILLMORE
    The Myth of Traveling Light. *Buzzfeed,* March 25.
ERIC WILSON
    Nix Hotel Savoy. *New England Review,* vol. 39, no. 3.

THE BEST AMERICAN SERIES®

FIRST, BEST, AND BEST-SELLING

The Best American Comics

The Best American Essays

The Best American Food Writing

The Best American Mystery Stories

The Best American Nonrequired Reading

The Best American Science and Nature Writing

The Best American Science Fiction and Fantasy

The Best American Short Stories

The Best American Sports Writing

The Best American Travel Writing

Available in print and e-book wherever books are sold.
Visit our website: hmhbooks.com/series/best-american